The Modern DUTCH POSTER

The First Fifty Years

1890-1940

Text by
Marcel Franciscono

Edited by
Stephen S. Prokopoff

Krannert Art Museum
University of Illinois at
Urbana-Champaign

The MIT Press
Cambridge, Massachusetts
London, England

© 1987 Krannert Art Museum
and Massachusetts Institute of Technology

Partial funding for this publication was
provided by the Print and Publicity Foundation,
Amsterdam, The Netherlands

**Library of Congress Cataloging
in Publication Data**

Franciscono, Marcel.
The Modern Dutch Poster /
The First Fifty Years / 1890-1940

"Published under the auspices of the
Krannert Art Museum, University of Illinois at
Urbana-Champaign."
Bibliography: p.
1. Posters, Dutch. 2. Posters – 19th century –
Netherlands. 3. Posters - 20th century –
Netherlands. I. Prokopoff, Stephen S. II.
Krannert Art Museum. III. Title. IV. Title: The
Modern Dutch Poster / The First Fifty Years /
1890-1940. NC1807.N4F7 1987
741.67'4'09492 86-21020
ISBN 0-262-66061-X (pbk.)

Contents

Foreword

One of the more unusual aspects of the history of the modern Dutch poster during its first half century was surely its near invisibility in the general awareness of modern graphic art. This publication and the exhibition it accompanies form the first survey ever undertaken of this diverse and exceptionally beautiful work. In the presence of the splendid images to be found in the following pages, the unfamiliarity of Dutch posters is difficult to understand. A parallel may be drawn, however, with the obscurity that has surrounded the rich artistic production found in all of the visual arts in Holland during this period, always excepting Piet Mondrian and de Stijl. A number of reasons for this neglect come to mind. Among them: that posters in Holland were commonly printed in small editions, shared the rather austere sensibility characteristic of art in the Low Countries and, in the earlier years of their production, were eclipsed in public esteem by the brilliance and verve of the poster in France. In addition, few designers in Holland devoted themselves exclusively to the poster. Commonly, these works were a part, often small, of a range of activity that embraced painterly, architectural, and design concerns, singly or in combination. Because of this unusual breadth in their creators' artistic interests, Dutch posters are often rich with a measure of allusion, aesthetic emphasis, and creative experience that is rare in the practice of the genre elsewhere. As a consequence, the Dutch poster serves as a mirror of the major stylistic developments that succeeded each other in Holland during this period.

Like many visitors to this exhibition, my awareness of a Dutch poster art developed only recently. A chance meeting a few years ago with Bernice Jackson, a dealer in posters with an especial interest in Dutch production, was fortunate in providing me an introduction to the posters of R. N. Roland Holst. Captivated, I quickly became familiar with work of other designers. Later Mrs. Jackson introduced me to Werner Löwenhardt and Martijn Le Coultre, passionate collectors, historians, and champions of these works. It is largely from the comprehensive collections of these gentlemen that the images in this publication are drawn. Several years ago they formed the Print and Publicity Foundation in Amsterdam whose efforts have been directed to the diffusion

of knowledge about the poster in The Netherlands. Without the encouragement and active support of these friends, the exhibition and this publication would not have been possible. Additional assistance came from The Directorate of International Relations, Ministry of Welfare, Health, and Cultural Affairs of The Netherlands; The Royal Netherlands Embassy in Washington, D.C.; the Office of the Consulate General of The Netherlands in New York; and KLM Royal Dutch Airlines.

The realization of this exhibition was a complex endeavor, the product of many hands, regretfully too many to thank here individually. Yet the efforts of several people were exceptional and require special mention. My colleague in the preparation of this exhibition, Marcel Franciscono, was a source of insight and valuable historial information as well as the author of the informative essay in this publication. Additional helpful suggestions came from Alston W. Purvis. Cornelia J. Perrone graciously assisted in the translation of Dutch texts. Research assistance was provided by W. H. Benier, Max Pieter Fränkel, Caroline Glazenburg, Peter Karstkarel, Pim Reynders, Henricus Rol, Jan Snoek, and Ada Stroeve. Ann Tyler designed this handsome publication. My thanks to the MIT Press and to Roger Conover, its acquisitions editor, for their encouragement and assistance in preparing this book. And thanks also to the Krannert Art Museum staff members who labored far beyond the call of duty in making the entire project a reality: Bruce Bowman, Susan Calza, George Dimock, Kathleen Jones, Joe Scott, and David Shutt.

Stephen S. Prokopoff

The Modern Dutch Poster

The First Fifty Years

In 1923 the Dutch designer Jacob (Jac.) Jongert published in English the following extraordinary tribute to advertising.

Advertising is all-powerful; it adorns the world with fresh raiment. It is advertisement and the commercial traveler that spread our civilization over the whole world, even unto the remotest corners. The fashionable ephemeral dress of today so entirely triumphs over the stolid apparel of our forbears only on account of well organized advertisement and eloquent commercial travellers. It is they who have revolutionized the trend of thought among the Middle Classes. . . . They are wonderful people these commercial travellers, astute diplomatists. It is their task to sweep away old-fashioned conceptions in our dress, nourishment and recreation and to prepare the way for their specific article that is of today and, therefore, attractive. . . .

Advertisement is the desire for growth that is in us all, the desire for continually different development and ever more perfect form in society. And because it is so at one with the supreme will to life, it surges up in ever new places and in continually different forms. . . .

Everyone . . . who has anything to say makes use at some time or other of the revealing power of advertisement. The officials' organisation for the increase of wages, teetotalers to combat immoderate drinking, the statesman who wishes to extend his party, women who are desirous of sharing power with man, all the thousand and one sort of human desires grasp, the moment they are in earnest, at advertisement.[1]

We can hardly imagine this being written today. It is tempting to dismiss it as a mere symptom, now rather quaint, of the twenties' faith in material progress. It is certainly that; but if Jongert's sublime optimism is no longer ours, he nevertheless put his finger on one of the reasons why art posters have exerted their great attraction. They can satisfy our simple delight in visual images, but they also afford teasing glimpses into the daily life, desires, and ideals of an epoch. At their best they have the complexity of paintings, and they can communicate an infectious sense of the artist's pleasure in his task as it was expressed by Jongert in his paean to advertising.

Interest in posters by collectors, critics, and historians was already active by 1884, when the first historical study of the poster was published in France.[2] Robert Koch has discovered that by 1891 poster collecting was already well-established in Paris and had begun in Brussels, London and New York.[3] The first book on posters appeared in 1886, and by 1897 the number of works – including two journals – dedicated exclusively to that once modest branch of art had become substantial.[4]

Dutch posters have not figured in the history of publication and exhibition in numbers commensurate with their quality.[5] Dutch advertisers presumably shared Jongert's belief in the virtues of publicity; but from all accounts their most visible product, the poster, was not highly regarded until the second World War, at least in comparison with the posters of other nations. Some persistent complaints run through early commentary on the Dutch poster, both within and outside of Holland: it was too reserved, too difficult to read at a glance, and too behind times in delivering its message with maximum speed and efficiency. This criticism need hardly concern us today. The posters are old enough to

have gained the charm of distance and to permit us to admire and study them for what they express and can tell us of the circumstances in which they were made. Indeed, the idealism inspiring Jongert's tribute to advertising may well be one of the reasons why Dutch posters, up to the time of the second World War, often seemed – at least to contemporary eyes – to withhold the thrust of which they were capable. The Netherlands produced relatively few posters as instantly engaging as those of Toulouse-Lautrec, Pierre Bonnard, Alphonse Mucha, or Jules Chéret in France.

Several reasons have been proposed for this: the paucity of grand commercial thoroughfares such as were characteristic of Paris, with their need for large, bold, and quickly grasped images; the hesitancy of Dutch businessmen to take full advantage of the poster's capabilities; even Calvinism's effect on the national character, with its taste for cleanliness, purity, and sober contemplation (though in their nature such sweeping generalizations as the last are hard to prove).[6]

1

Jac. Jongert, "Posters Designed by Dutch Artists," *Wendingen*, vol. 5, no. 2 (1923), p. 3.

2

Ernest Maindron, "Les affiches illustrées," *Gazette des Beaux-Arts*, vol. 30, 1884.

3

Robert Koch, "The Poster Movement and 'Art Nouveau,'" *Gazette des Beaux-Arts*, series 6, vol. 50 (November 1957), p. 287.

4

Ernest Maindron, *Les affiches illustrées*, Paris, 1886. See Robert Goldwater, "'L'affiche moderne,'" *Gazette des Beaux-Arts*, series 6, vol. 22 (December 1942), pp. 173-174.

5

The first exhibition to include Dutch posters was the Exposition d'affiches artistiques françaises et étrangères, held in Reims November 7-17, 1896. The next was the Exposition internationale d'affiches illustrées, held in St. Petersburg by the Société Impériale d'Encouragement des Arts.

6

Dick Dooijes and Pieter Brattinga, *A History of the Dutch Poster 1890-1960*, intro. by H. L. C. Jaffé, Amsterdam, 1968, pp. 9-11.

Editions of Dutch posters were small, and they were generally displayed in shops rather than out-of-doors on hoardings. But Jongert's fervor, though it seems to embrace advertising wholeheartedly, is surely pertinent as well. It was part of a continuing belief – in its origins largely inspired by the English Arts and Crafts Movement and wide-spread among early Dutch poster designers – that art, even commercial art, had a social mission to perform. Like many modern artists on the Continent, Dutch poster-makers frequently joined this belief to the hope of a new society, one based on socialist ideals or, by some at the beginning, anarchism. This as much as anything else seems to have made them loath to turn the poster into the brilliant and often frivolous spectacle it was in France or Belgium.

The over-all impression made by Dutch posters in the first half-century of their existence, for all their variety, is one of restraint. Certainly posters of the greatest brilliance and immediacy were produced in Holland during that time, but the general effect – as was observed early on – is of designs meant more to be perused than to capture the eye at a glance.[7] In 1917, as we shall see, this trait was to become the subject of public debate.

Dutch Posters of the 1890s

Before the 1890s, posters had mainly been the work of hacks with no great artistic pretensions. The anonymous assemblage of words, pictures, and decoration with which W. P. Werker displayed the amenities and doubtful elegance of his hotel and "grand café" is well above the general run of design in the posters of its day, but it will still serve as contrast to the work that was to follow (1). France was an exception. Thanks to Jules Chéret, the first specialized poster designer of stature in Europe, French boulevards were decorated with an art of eye-catching vivacity as early as the 1860s. But it was not until the end of the eighties or the beginning of the nineties that the golden age of the poster began, when Bonnard and Toulouse-Lautrec created the first posters we may call high art.

Holland, like the rest of Europe, was not long behind France in exploiting the artistic possibilities of the poster. The Dutch economy had grown slowly in the third quarter of the nineteenth century, despite a population increase during that time of almost 17 percent. The years 1882-1886 in particular were a time of economic stagnation, a consequence of the international depression that had begun in 1873, but in the 1890s the Dutch economy grew rapidly.[8] In the applied arts, the English Arts and Crafts Movement, with its powerful ethos of a morally renewed art in the direct service of society, soon made itself felt.

Joining this, as far as the poster is concerned, was a new way of conceiving art. Post-impressionism and above all the Japanese print gave unprecedented expressive and symbolic value to surface pattern. Illustrated posters, as conjunctions of word and image, had always in one way or another called attention to their surfaces, but with the new importance placed on pattern by artists in the nineties, posters could become a major vehicle of expression, becoming at once decorative, expressive, and coherent in their visual effects. In 1885 René Martin in *Le Figaro* was already observing, probably in reference to Chéret, that "there is far more talent shown in a poster than in many of the most discussed paintings in the Salon."[9] Toulouse-Lautrec's posters are not different in kind – or inferior – to his paintings. They are rather a distillation: simpler perhaps in their psychology but comparably heightened renderings of the world of the cabaret and the *amateur.*

7

See, e.g., Jean Louis Sponsel, *Das moderne Plakat*, Dresden, 1897, p.297, who refers to the "auffallend spröde verhalten" of Dutch posters.

8

E. H. Kossmann, *The Low Countries, 1780-1940*, Oxford, 1978, pp.265-266, 315, 412-413.

9

Quoted in Jane Abdy, *The French Poster: Chéret to Cappiello*, New York, 1969, p.9.

Dutch posters of the 1890s by and large lack the verve of their French counterparts. Indeed, at the beginning of the nineties a Dutch newspaper drew an explicit comparison between Dutch posters and one of Chéret's posters of 1890 for La Diaphane rice powder, which was to be seen on Dutch hoardings: ". . . to see that refined painting on paper celebrating among our dull advertising bills, joyously sounding its loud fanfares of movement and color even more prettily than elsewhere under our heavy gray skies." (fig. 1)[10] The complaint is justified if Chéret and the French poster are taken as the norm. Clearly, however, Dutch poster designers of the nineties did not do so. While their work shared in the artistic tendencies of the period, it took a different direction from that of the French, with results having considerable force and appeal in themselves.

One of the first examples of the new Dutch poster art is the announcement and timetable for the North-Holland Tramline Company of Amsterdam by the great Dutch architect and architectural theorist H. P. Berlage (2). Like Berlage's architecture, whose artistic principles were elaborated in his writings, the placard emphasizes precisely defined geometric planes. It is anything but ingratiating, and its rather tame symmetry is strikingly at variance with the boldly asymmetrical style of

**Figure 1
Jules Chéret
La Diaphane
Lithograph, 1890**

10

From an unidentified newspaper item of April 15, 1891, affixed to the rear of the Chéret poster. I am indebted to Martijn Le Coultre for the citation.

decorative arts then common in France. Its interest lies, rather, in its severe style and its clear authorial stamp, symptomatic of the aspiration of artists in the nineties to turn their artistic talents to the more modest everyday tasks of design; though in the case of Holland it would perhaps be more accurate to say that they thought to bestow on design something of the dignity and value of the fine arts.

This aspiration can be no better illustrated than by a poster of 1896 for the arts and crafts journal *Revue bimestrielle pour l'art appliqué* by the noted symbolist painter John Thorn Prikker (6). In 1892 Thorn Prikker joined the Rose + Cross, the mystical artistic order founded in 1888 in Paris by Joséphin Péladin, and until the mid-nineties he was almost exclusively a painter of religious subjects.[11] His poster is an extraordinary attempt to lend his vision of a monumental and deeply serious art to the promotion of a specific product. The results are still something of a puzzle; for while we can easily see how his profusely elaborated scrollwork means to illustrate, or symbolize, the role of decoration in art, his bleak religious subject – one of the harshest images of the crucifixion among the many conceived in the period – almost bursts the bonds of its ostensible context, the decorative arts. We can only wonder – incorrectly, as it happens – whether the journal might

not have been theological, or perhaps devoted exclusively to religious art.

The extreme severity – not to say grimness in the one case – of such posters as Berlage's or Thorn Prikker's is not characteristic of Dutch design of the nineties; the decorative curves of the Belgian and French art nouveau may be seen abundantly in Dutch posters. Yet with a few notable exceptions they are rarely more than embellishments to more austere designs, or in the case of Willem van Konijnenburg's timetable for an excursion boat line, stylized evocations of nature such as were common in the German Jugendstil (19). The poster designed by Johannes Aarts in 1897 for a Dordrecht exhibition of arts and crafts, with its loose drawing and irregular silhouettes reminiscent of Bonnard, Georges de Feure, or Georges Meunier, is one of those exceptions, as is Tiete van der Laars' ornate 1898 poster, inspired by Mucha, for an exhibition of Dutch national costumes (20). But by and large, Dutch designers of the nineties have more in common with English illustrators – Walter Crane, or the expatriate Englishman Louis Rhead – than with French or Belgian designers.

The avoidance by Dutch poster artists of the extravagances of the

latter may be seen in another striking example of Dutch poster restraint, the placard designed in 1897 by Th. H. A. A. Molkenboer in competition for the bookbindery of Elias van Bommel (16). It is likely that its stark, unmodulated rendering was influenced by Felix Vallotton, whose woodcuts were widely known, but it has little parallel among French and Belgian posters. The stiffness of its forms and its schematic composition bring to mind instead the crude popular woodcuts of the type traditionally known in France as the *images d'Epinal,* so called after one of the principal centers in which they were produced. In fact, Molkenboer's poster is a woodcut, a medium presumably chosen by him, since he made other woodcut posters as well. Its very use, rather than the more easily handled lithograph, would seem to indicate his intention, like other artistic reformers of the time, to restore the handicrafts to their pre-industrial purity.

We should expect to find a difference in treatment between posters for a commercial product, meant to turn a profit for its company, and cultural, institutional, and political posters (among which may be included those for serious art and literary journals), the latter usually permitting a greater freedom of expression. But in the 1890s this distinction tended to blur, and no more so than in two posters designed in 1893 and in

11

On Thorn Prikker see Bettina Polak, *Het fin-de-siècle in de Nederlandse schilderkunst: De symbolistische beweging 1890-1900.* The Hague, 1955, pp.152-186; esp. 171.

1894 or 1895 for the Dutch Oil Works (Nederlandsche Oliefabriek) in Delft, manufacturers of *Delftsche Slaolie*, or Delft Salad Oil (*3* and *5*).

The earlier of the two is by Theodorus (Theo) Nieuwenhuis, one of that first generation of young artists on the Continent who were inspired to devote themselves to the applied arts. The poster displays its product clearly enough: two large bottles of salad oil stand to either side, and the names of the company and product are emblazoned above and below. But these are subordinated to the great swaths of black lithographic ink next to the bottles and to the reserved yellow streaks and border decorations. It is with some difficulty that we recognize the yellow center stripes as streams of oil and the three objects above them – surrounded as they are by an overpowering black ground and the equally salient patterns of lettuce leaves and peanuts – as oil bottles spilling their contents down the middle of the poster. Everything is brought into the picture plane, and the result is as richly textured and "painterly" as any painting. A certain wit is involved in all this. The bottles, with their prosaic forms and printed labels, strike rather humorously with the accoutrements of art. On the other hand, the painterly streams of oil and their black surroundings can be seen as punning allusions to the "oil" of high art. Commerce is thrust into the context of art with an altogether satisfying literalness. In no allegory do the river gods spill out their amphoras with greater solemnity. We do not know how successful the poster was as an advertisement, but, as we shall see, there is some indication that the Nederlandsche Oliefabriek was not altogether displeased with it.

The second of the slaolie posters is perhaps the best known of all Dutch posters. Its designer was the painter Jan Toorop, whose large drawing *The Three Brides* of 1893 had been published the same year in the London *Studio* and had at once made his work known beyond the borders of the Netherlands. His poster, designed about a year or two later, was an attempt to apply the same symbolist style to advertising. The result was greeted with some astonishment. J. M. Sponsel, in his *Das moderne Plakat* of 1897 referred to him as "one of the oddest [*wunderlichste*] and most controversial of modern artists." His few posters, Sponsel continued, "are not likely, with their mystical conception and puzzling manner of expression, to attract a wider circle to the new art. Still, his poster for a salad oil, Delftsche Slaolie, is one of the most easily understood of them and despite its curlicues and its curiously stylized women, has a true poster style."[12]

Like Nieuwenhuis' poster, it immediately lets us know what is being sold, but if the latter requires something more than a glance to understand its illustration, Toorop's takes even longer. Its two wan and attenuated women in vaguely medieval gowns, like figures from a symbolist play by Maeterlinck, seem to participate in a mysterious ritual. The figure on the right raises her hands as if in benediction, or perhaps to ward off some invisible and vaguely disquieting power. Her stylized profile and pose, like those of many of Toorop's women of 1893-94, including *The Three Brides*, only increase her air of devotion to her solemn mystery. They show the unmistakable influence of the Javanese shadow puppets – the wayang puppets – and recall that Toorop was born in Java. Surrounding the figures is their extraordinary hair, that ubiquitous 1890s symbol of woman's spiritual or sexual power (sometimes both together), which flows from them to create a dense background of waving lines. It is this remarkable decoration that gave the art nouveau in Holland the sometime name "Slaolie Style."

12

Sponsel, *Das moderne Plakat*, p. 297.

Figure 2
G. H. Breitner
Delft Salad Oil
Photolithograph, 1905

After all of this, it is close to astonishing to realize that the seated maiden is doing nothing more mysterious than pouring oil – straight from the bottle – into a salad.

It is almost a century since Toorop designed his poster, and preparing a salad still seems a curious activity for the rarefied creatures it depicts. But it is surely no more curious than the ecstasy in washing, buying, and drinking seen in advertisements of supposedly more realistic stamp. What remains of interest in it is not the success or lack of success of its message but the charm of its patterns, its irreconcilable elements, and the purely historical question, yet to be answered, of how such a discrepancy between the requirements of the commission and the results could have arisen.

The answer may lie in part with the official of the Nederlandsche Oliefabriek (which in 1898 merged with the Calvé oil factory of Bordeaux) who commissioned these early posters. Credit has been given to one of its directors, the socially enlightened J. C. van Marken.[13] Some years later – in 1905 – the company commissioned a reproduction, with its name and product on it, of a painting of two cart horses by the then popular Dutch landscape painter G. H. Breitner (fig. 2). Breitner's painting

13

See Hedwig Saam, "Calvé," in *Industry and Design in the Netherlands 1850-1950* (cat.), Stedelijk Museum, Amsterdam, December 21, 1985-February 9, 1986, p.146.

was not meant as a poster but rather as a promotional gift to storekeepers.[14] Clearly, van Marken's inclination ran to the elevation of commerce through art. Nieuwenhuis' and Toorop's posters were not the only ones with a self-consciously artistic or "cultured" look to be commissioned by the *oliefabriek*. Jacques Zon's slaolie poster, designed about 1897, makes the salad oil the center of a parodic bluebeard drama. A pre-raphaelite damsel in her castle, having broken a bottle of slaolie, looks despairingly to her sister in the battlements (or is it a representation of herself later in time?), who waves frantically to two knights galloping to the rescue with another bottle of oil (*13*).

Like many designers of the nineties, Zon could suit his style to the requirements of his product and its potential buyers. His poster of about 1898 for lamp methanol, manufactured by the Nederlandsche Gist & Spiritus-Fabriek, of which J. C. Marken was also director,[15] is drawn in a more decorative and allegorical manner, suitable to the elevated matters traditionally associated with the giving of light (*14*). Similarly, C. A. Lion Cachet's poster of 1897 for the W. G. Boele cigar company, which sponsored a competition for it, is in a style quite unlike his usual one (*8*).

Lion Cachet is usually grouped with his early collaborators, Nieuwenhuis and G. W. Dijsselhof, as one of a trio of fantasists among Dutch designers of the period. He had studied collections of batik and the art of the Near East – including Turkish, Moorish, Persian, Byzantine, Coptic, and Japanese decoration – and these artistic experiences permanently shaped his work.[16] They gave rise to a style of intricate, small-scale decoration only rarely employing the freer-swinging "Belgian" line of the art nouveau. Lion Cachet's teeming forms are usually held in check by a structure of rectangles,[17] and his cigar poster has only that in common with his other designs. We may assume that he recognized a certain propriety in making the advertisement for a man's product direct and "manly"; the only concession to his usual inventive patterns is in the cigar smoke, which, in keeping with the humor of the piece, rises upward in palpable curls from cigars on either side.

Adaptability seems also to have been a trait of one of the boldest and most influential Dutch poster designers of the period, Johan van Caspel.

Van Caspel's first poster, designed in 1896, was for the Hinde bicycle factory (*9*). It concedes almost nothing to the fashion for decorative curves. A young woman, her eyes fixed ahead of her and the hint of a smile on her face, pedals along a country road while two admiring children watch with comparable expressions of quiet pleasure. The poster's flat unadorned patterns and bright simplicity echo the solitary enjoyment presented in it by the then fashionable sport of bicycling. The precise geometry and parallel edges of the road, hedgerow, horizon, and fields in the distance give the work the appearance of a reduced neo-impressionist composition (by the mid-nineties neo-impressionism, with its simplified geometric rendering of forms, was a widespread style in France and Belgium); but if anything, its unadorned contour style of drawing recalls such English illustrators as Walter Crane, especially in his drawings for children's books. Its evocation of the tranquil satisfaction to be had from bicycling is quite unlike what we usually find at the time in bicycle posters, where the pastime is treated either with conspicuous humor, as an athletic contest, or as a social occasion.[18]

Van Caspel's poster style changed after his Hinde advertisement, but it

14

W. H. Benier, "Langs reclamewegen," *Revue der Reclame*, vol.8, no.6-7 (1948), p.158, from an interview with one of its early directors (1884-1920), J. R. Tutein Nolthenius.

15

Saam, p.146.

16

A. van der Boom, *C. A. Lion Cachet 1864-1945*, Bussum, 1952, pp.14, 17, 26.

17

Boom, p.26.

18

See the examples in Charles Hiatt, *Picture Posters: A Short History of the Illustrated Placard, with Many Reproductions of the Most Artistic Examples in All Countries*, London, 1895, pp.93, 139; Abdy, *French Poster*, p.106; *La Belle Epoque: Belgian Posters, Watercolors, and Drawings from the Collection of L. Wittamer-DeCamps* (cat.), with an introduction by Yolande Oostens-Wittamer, Library of Congress, Washington, D.C., 1970, nos.10, 104, 105; or the copiously illustrated catalogue of the recent poster exhibition held in Japan, *The Poster*, Takashimaya Art Gallery, Nihon-bashi, April 18-May 7, 1985, nos.26, 51. Georg

is uncertain whether this was because of a general change in his way of working or the specific requirements of his commissions. A poster for Karstel cocoa from about the same year is most probably by him (12). Its forms are more stylized and perfunctory, and their effect is to move us out of the world of activity into a more frozen, iconic realm. Is this because the sedentary pleasures of taking Sunday cocoa in a park seemed to call for a less physical rendering? A similar question is raised by another van Caspel, a poster of about two years later for Ivens & Company's photographic equipment (11). Here, the art nouveau curls in the woman's hair serve to give her greater elegance. She is not merely riding a bicycle or taking cocoa in the park, like ordinary well-off people, we might say. Her wares – a large view camera and a tripod – were items both of luxury (when not professionally intended) and of art, and both aspects are heightened by the stylization.

When it comes to an item of popular culture, however – something intended for a wide public (*Boon's Illustrated Magazine*) – van Caspel again designs a more realistic work (10). What counts here is not abstract elegance but our identification with the girl's rapt absorption – with her pleasure in the act of reading – while we are reminded by the emblem and motto that time flies.

Cocoa, too – like all enticements of the senses – could be made inviting through stylization or decorative detail. Jan Ros' vivid poster of 1895 for Blooker's cocoa not only flanks its figures with an elaborate border of cacao tree, beans, and an escutcheon but puts them in the elegant setting of good society, where fashionable visits are paid amid the appointments of amphoras and neo-classical tables (4). Asia Tea, by Georg Rueter, dated 1896, is given a more modest domestic setting, though it, too, is made into an icon of enjoyment by Rueter's simplification and his decorative border of leaves, blossoms, and fruit (18). Wilhelm Pothast's poster for a cocoa drink ("It's drunk cold"), from about 1900, returns us to Ros' elegance, without being quite so illustrative (17). Here the good taste of drinking Korff's cocoa is implied by its decorative forms: by its background ornament, whose intricacy, like that of much Dutch design before 1920, suggests the influence of Indonesian patterns, and by the flowing art nouveau lines of the figures as they serve themselves – two friends evidently preparing for a tête-à-tête.

The New Century

After 1900, the most distinctive posters in Holland from an artistic point of view tend to be either noncommercial or designed for cultural products. This should be no surprise, given the greater limitations on artistic ingenuity imposed by the need to sell a product. On the contrary, what is surprising is that during the nineties there should have been so little distinction in style and approach between the best of commercial and non-commercial work; as we have seen, Toorop's slaolie poster is one of the most esoteric of the period. In the new century the number of impressive, well-designed commercial posters increased steadily in Holland, though remaining in the distinct minority. But at the same time they tended to diverge in character from the others, becoming less symbolic or allegorical and more illustrative. Another way of putting it is that after the turn of the century they became more specialized – perhaps because commercial advertisers became surer of their need for rapid comprehension – and left the field of the "artistic" poster largely to the noncommercial client.

One of the liveliest designers of commercial posters in the new

Rueter's poster for Hinde, Will Bradley's for Victor bicycles, and Steinlen's for Comiot motorcycles are among the exceptions. (The first is illustrated in Dooijes and Brattinga, fig. 92, the others in Hayward and Blanche Cirker, *The Golden Age of the Poster*, New York, 1971, pp. 14, 61.)

century was Willy Sluiter. Though scarcely younger than some of the poster artists of the 1890s (having been born in 1873), he took his work in a distinctly different direction. A notable political cartoonist, Sluiter, who did not draw on the stone himself,[19] took his style of bold angular contours from the satirical German magazine *Simplicissimus*, especially from the caricatures of Bruno Paul and Olaf Gulbransson, who about the turn of the century were perhaps the most highly regarded political and social caricaturists on the Continent. Sluiter's poster for oriental carpets carries their style to burlesque – while perfectly obvious in what it is trying to sell, it hardly seems calculated to convey the elegance or luxury of its wares (*42*). His poster of 1915 for festivities connected with an exhibition in the city of Laren is somewhat more restrained, advertising as it does a cultural event; but it, too, is rather broad in its humor, stressing the gaiety of the entertainment rather than the cultural significance of the occasion (*33*).

Piet van der Hem also used caricature in his poster designs, which are strongly anecdotal. His style is less terse than Sluiter's, but he compensates for it by a greater subtlety in his humor and a more refined manner of drawing. Although he, too, drew political cartoons, he was known –

notorious might be the better word – early in his career primarily for his worldly portraits, which were attacked at times for being coarse and at times for being decadent. Van der Hem, whose first posters date from 1907, was some twelve years younger than Sluiter – of the same generation as the pioneer modernists of the new century – but his work ignores the intervening symbolist movement, taking up instead the thread of nineteenth-century realism, as a recent study of the artist has observed, and especially the vein of scurrility associated with Toulouse-Lautrec and Félicien Rops.[20] The greatest number of his posters was made for the theater, and they have been called a piece of theater history, for in them he depicted many of the important Dutch actors and acting companies of his time.[21] Those he designed for exhibitions of his work show a tarter, more personal side of his art. His posters of 1912 for the Frascati acting ensemble and for the luxurious Spyker automobiles – one of two he made for them before 1914 when production on the vehicle ceased – are among his more reserved and less personal, but few illustrators, whatever their styles,

were able to present their products with so much charm and fluency of line (*29 and 30*).

Institutional and cultural posters, too, sometimes show a more descriptive realism after the turn of the century, especially in the political poster, as we shall see later. The tourist poster by Albert Hemelman attempts to convey the charms of the Dutch countryside, as represented in the ubiquitous symbol of picturesque Holland, the windmill (which, the poster shows us, may be visited by train or by roadster). Hemelman retains the flat bold planes of posters from the turn of the century but renders them with a high degree of descriptive realism (*44*). More impressive is the woodcut poster of 1914 by Huib Luns for the Dutch health organization the Green Cross, which gave him full control over his design.[22] Its grim warning against flies and the diseases they carry is made all the more sobering by its rigid organization and by its splendidly detailed rendering of the insect and of potential places of contamination (*39*).

It is appropriate to include Jan Toorop's strikingly bold poster of about 1900 for the tourist association of Katwijk aan Zee in this list of more realistic works (*21*). It is one of the distinct exceptions among his posters of the period, which on the whole remained strongly symbolist. The

19

Otto van Tussenbroek, "Willy Sluiter en zijn werk," *De bedrijfsreklame*, vol.2, no.3 (April 1917), p.79.

20

On van der Hem see Peter Karstkarel, "De reclame door Jan Rotgans, Piet van der Hem en Jan Wijga," *Alternatijf* (1976), pp.20-29; also Hans Martin, "Iets over Piet van der Hem," *De bedrijfsreklame*, vol.2, no.4 (May 1917), pp.110-113.

21

Ibid., p.26.

22

Huib Luns, "Umberto farà da sé . . . ," *De bedrijfsreklame*, vol.6, no.6 (August 1919), p.96.

placard retains a considerable degree of stylization, but its figure is less mannered and distorted than most of his others and more immediately grasped as an image. Toorop no doubt understood the practical value of keeping his mystical inclinations out of a poster intended to attract the tourist trade, yet his advertisement makes no concession to the picturesque. It shows nothing that could appeal to a casual visitor – neither the beauties of the village nor its comforts. Like many artists of his generation who saw in radical political movements solutions to the social and cultural ills of their day, Toorop had anarchist leanings, despite his taste for the occult.[23] His representations of common men are invariably more naturalistic and down-to-earth than the rest of his work, as his poster of 1901 for Herman Heyermans' play *Het Pantser* shows, with its simple rendering of a soldier pinned under a great block. Toorop lived in Katwijk from 1890 to 1892 and again from 1899 to 1904,[24] and his fellow feeling for the fishermen of the town – the concomitant of his political sympathies – was surely one of the reasons why he gave exclusive place in his poster, and a simple human expression, to the figure of a simple toiler.

These few examples of relatively descriptive noncommercial posters are among the exceptions in the first two decades of the century. In comparison to the commercial poster, with its lively new style of anecdote, most of the cultural posters designed in the Netherlands after the turn of the century seem decidedly conservative in spirit. The desire of artists to demonstrate an ethical purpose in their work often led to compositions of rigid symmetry, to the elaboration of allegorical and symbolic detail, and even to traditional forms. If Dutch posters of the 1890s, taken all in all, gave primary place to the charms of decoration, the cultural posters of the first two decades of the new century seem to aim for high seriousness before anything else.

This tendency toward greater formalism – one might say toward a more impersonal art – was not confined to posters alone, or even to Holland; it appears in all of the applied arts everywhere in the first two decades of the century. But Dutch posters show it to a striking degree. The results are often impressive, even when they offer no particular novelties or innovations.

Georg Rueter's poster of 1918 for an exhibition in Rotterdam of crafts and folk art continues to rely at this late date on the image of the standard bearer – a nude youth humbly kneeling with his banner before the teeming field of art, or rather, since the background is filled with stylized plants, of nature in art (*40*). But Rueter's bold contrasts and sure rhythms still bring eloquence to the theme. Cornelis Rol's prize-winning poster for the First Dutch Maritime Exhibition, held in Amsterdam in 1913, is filled with decoration based on waves, fish, and sea foam (*31*). These were common motifs in the art nouveau period, but Rol gives them no rhythmical impetus of the sort they received then. He invokes not so much the activity of ocean voyaging as the material culture of which it was a part. His pattern of prickly details seems to take up and amplify the carving on the square rigger and by extension becomes a restless evocation of the adornment that marked Holland's golden age as a seafaring nation.

Wilhelmina Drupsteen's early studies (1898-1900) with the "rationalists" among Dutch designers of the nineties, J. L. M. Lauweriks and K. C. P. de Bazel, are reflected in her symmetrically designed poster of 1913 for an exhibition on women, with its emblematic representation of woman as mother, homemaker, and protectress of civilization (a radiant steeple-crowned skyline extends behind her outstretched

---

23

On Toorop's political views see Polak, *Het fin-de-siècle*, pp.4, 82, 89-90.

24

Polak, pp.94, 115.

arms within a surrounding glory) (32). Chris Lebeau also studied briefly with Lauweriks and de Bazel in 1898, and as with Drupsteen's exhibition poster, their taste for geometric clarity is seen again in his rather similar posters of about 1914 for productions of *Hamlet* and G. K. Chesterton's *Magic*, for which he also designed the settings (38 and 37).[25] In both, the loftiness of the dramas is evoked by the posters' symmetry and by the hieratic placement of the principal figures within mandorlas.

Antoon Molkenboer's grave poster for a Beethoven series of 1911 in The Hague celebrates music with an emblematic composition of the strictest symmetry (28). Below the main text and a garlanded head of Beethoven is set a roundel containing Berlage's (unbuilt) 1908 project for a concert hall, the Beethovenhuis. Below that, an allegorical winged figure personifies the promise made by the scroll over her head, in which are written words from Schiller's "Ode to Joy," the text used by Beethoven for the final movement of his ninth symphony: "All men shall be brothers." The whole is framed in an elaborate architectural setting of medieval arcades.

Lion Cachet's later designs – book and wall decorations as well as posters – also tend toward symmetry, and his 1917 poster for the first annual industrial fair in Utrecht is no exception. Intended, like his poster for Boele cigars, to advertise a relatively practical affair, it has less of his usual elaborate and often rather indistinct type of overall pattern (47). Its most curious feature is the treatment of the bust in the lower center. Set as it is within an interacting pattern of blue and red, its surrounds appear to lend it waving tentacles instead of arms. For the rest, once we have separated figure from ground, its heraldic lions offer no perplexity.

The spokesman for those designers who saw their duty in the furthering of social and ethical values through art was Richard Nicolaus Roland Holst. In 1917, on the occasion of an exhibition of Art in Advertising held in Amsterdam, Roland Holst delivered a lecture in which he drew a sharp line between his own conception of the poster and what he saw as a dangerous opposite tendency. "On one side is a group which is interested in the art of the poster and which demands from this means of expression that before anything else it should be an advertisement and concern itself with the requirements of advertising; in other words, that it should place itself entirely in the service of advertising. But there is another group that says yes, but before we do that we have to see what advertising really means. I don't mean in a particular case, but what kind of value advertising has as a general phenomenon, what significance and what ethical value it possesses which will give it the right to influence or determine the artist's conception. The two parties stand opposed in the matter of the poster: as art and as an object of use."[26]

What this meant to Holst was made clear by his inclusion of the poster within the broader issue of art and society: "We [applied or commercial artists] are dependent on society, we also want to join society, we demand in a way that society give us the material means necessary for our work, but we also expect to find in society those living ideals which our work is able to stimulate, and which can be made wider, more general, and deeper by our art. In that respect we stand in relation to society – even though the relationship is very much weaker – as art stood from antiquity to the Renaissance. . . . But when we say that we are social artists, that we desire strong ties with society, that does not mean yielding ourselves to society and its demands without

25

See *Chris Lebeau (1878-1945)* (cat.), Drents Museum, Assen, October 12, 1985-January 5, 1986, p.27.

26

The lecture was published in R. N. Roland Holst, "Moderne eischen en artistieke bedenkingen," *Wendingen*, vol.2, no.5 (May 1919); see p.3.

criticism, without insight, and without reservation."[27] Holst offered a choice: one could either challenge society or accept it as it is.

What was involved, Holst explained, was the opposing attitudes of the English Arts and Crafts Movement (by which he had been profoundly influenced) and of artists in Germany: the former held up the ideal to society, the latter accepted their society without question. Indeed, unlike the English, German artists celebrated naked material power. Of course, Holst was delivering his lecture during the first World War. Even though the Netherlands remained at peace, the possibility of a German invasion could not be overlooked, and this did not predispose him to any great good will toward Germany. Nevertheless, the German work he cited seemed proof enough of his claim, for it was of a kind hardly found among English artists, or for that matter among the Dutch. Three years before, he recalled, he had visited the Deutsche Werkbund exhibition in Cologne and had wondered why "all those figures there of horses, women, and men [were] so uncommonly brawny." "I can assure you," he concluded, "that we have the right to hold German artists responsible, too, for what is now happening, inasmuch as they have spent the last twenty years making idols to the cult of power."[28]

Roland Holst saw the true end of art instead as the creation of what he called "the dream of art, that specialness which surrounds the work of art with an atmosphere we cannot enter with our bodies but where our spirits may linger from time to time and whence they return full of nostalgia. . . . This dream can be achieved even by the simplest objects we make." Roland Holst showed his enduring allegiance to the faith of the Arts and Crafts Movement by naming the artist he believed had done more than any other to reshape society through the ideal of art, William Morris.[29]

The poster artist could help reform society by a more or less temperate approach, and in his lecture Roland Holst presented the choice in a memorable phrase: "You see, ladies and gentlemen, the poster can satisfy two requirements. It can be a simple communication or it can be a shout."[30] Given his lingering fin-de-siècle belief in art as a "dream," it goes without saying that Holst saw little value in the shout. He had been one of the first Dutch artists to work in the style of the art nouveau. About 1900 he sought to give his work a more monumental, architectural character, realizing his ambitions in designs for stained glass windows and in his murals for Berlage's Amsterdam Stock Exchange. His posters from the first two decades of the new century present their subjects in a compressed, brooding style that aims to be both monumental and impassioned. In his 1910 placard for *Lucifer*, a tragedy by the great seventeenth-century Dutch poet Joost van den Vondel, staged by Willem Royaards with costumes and sets by Roland Holst himself, the columnar form of the fallen angel is set between romanesque columns and banks of swirling flame (*25*). A similar architectural treatment is given to two later posters. The first, for the 1918 premier of a Royaards production of *Faust*, shows an equally compressed image of Faust and Mephistopheles standing upon the ledge of the inscription (*26*). The second, a 1920 poster by the government labor board advertising its various workers' benefits, again places its figures on a ledge in order to monumentalize its image of the archer-champion (*49*). The figure forms part of an emblem with an elaborate stepped frame. The insistent geometry of the design, with its

27
Ibid., pp. 3-4.

28
Ibid., pp. 6, 14.

29
Ibid., p. 6.

30
Ibid., p. 7.

maze-like inner border, is shared by much Dutch design of the early twenties, especially in the Amsterdam school, but Holst's basic conception does not differ appreciably from that of his earlier posters.

This poster was to be Roland Holst's last for over a decade. It came in for severe criticism because of its obscure wording and seemed to give point to the objection that had been made to his conception of poster designing.[31]

Roland Holst's slogan, communication or shout, had at once been taken up as a challenge by Albert Hahn, Sr., a noted political caricaturist. In so many words Hahn argued that by its nature an advertisement was precisely a shout: "[Advertising] is a street art pure and simple, and as such an out and out popular art. . . . We live, unfortunately, in capitalist circumstances still, our world is still one of competition. Under the social conditions in which we live things are not produced in order to satisfy human needs but, on the contrary, in a manner that is utterly anarchistic."[32] In the circumstances, "the artist working in advertising has to be universal; he has to judge and conscientiously try to understand each commission individually, so as to arrive at the necessary method of expression. In accordance with his task, then, the artist will produce a 'shout.' . . ."[33]

The notion of a designer cutting his style to the shape of his client, while no different from what any advertising artist would argue today, may nonetheless sound a little cynical, coming from an artist with no great sympathy for the capitalist system. Still, Hahn's work is as consistent – and one might say as conscientious – as that of any poster artist of the time. Like Willy Sluiter, he took his more serious style of boldly drawn figures from *Simplicissimus* and applied it to posters with a wide variety of subjects: a Verkade production of *Hamlet*, illustrated by a contemplative prince between columns; accident insurance, for which, in 1909, he drew the despairing image of a woman stricken by symbolic lightning; the election campaigns of the Social Democratic Workers' Party (SDAP), dramatized by the broad figures of red-shirted workers gazing into an industrial future or hacking at the octopus of anarchy, capitalism, hunger, the sufferings of war, and price-gouging on scarce foods (*22*, *34*, and *48*).

Hahn had a gift for dramatic expression, and while his posters have something of the oversimplification of political cartoons, they are surprisingly restrained, rarely descending to the bathos frequently present in other political posters of the time. It is worth noting that his Fatum accident insurance poster is considerably more subdued than his rather melodramatic preliminary study for it (fig. 3).

It goes without saying that the pictorial movements of the new century made themselves felt in Dutch posters of the period. Even older masters were not immune to their influence. One of the most memorable images in Dutch posters was created by Toorop in 1919 for the play *Pandorra* by Arthur van Schendel (*45*). The decorative swirls about the central figure are carry-overs of his patterns of the eighteen nineties, as is its angular theatrical pose; but these are now given energy by clashing diagonal planes unmistakably derived from cubism and futurism, even if very late in the decade. The effect is of tensions barely held in check by the rigid borders of praying figures.

Other posters before 1920 also show the influence of futurism, like Pieter Hofman's 1919 advertisement for an aviation show held near The

31

For what was apparently a widespread criticism, see J. C. van den Berg, "Een ondoelmatige affiche," *De bedrijfsreklame*, vol.9, no.2 (February 1921), p.28.

32

Quoted from Dooijes and Brattinga, *Dutch Poster*, p.28.

33

Quoted from *60 Plakate neun holländische Graphiker 1956-1970* (cat.), Hilversum, 1972, unpaged.

Figure 3
Albert Hahn, Sr
*Fatum Accident
Insurance*
Drawing, 1909
Coll. Nationale
Nederlanden Insurance
Company, The Hague

Hague, its stylized curves representing flight paths; or the somewhat crude but vigorous poster for the Kotting Press by an otherwise unknown designer named Verschuuren, whose broad stylization includes sweeping curves and intersecting planes (*43* and *53*). Sometimes in Dutch posters modern abstraction comes so close to conventional stylization that it is hard to decide whether it is present at all. The background of Willem Arondéus' 1922 poster for a Dutch exhibition in Copenhagen is composed of restless intersecting background planes vaguely suggestive of futurism, but they do not involve his figures at any point. Arondéus was noted primarily for his wall paintings, and his design has the decorative effect of a stained glass window (*50*).

Among the new generation of twentieth-century poster artists, Jan Sluyters was one of the most vigorous and attractive. Sluyters' posters are closer to paintings than most, for he brought to the lithographic stone a style of broad strokes and loose drawing more characteristic of oils. They have been rightly compared in their fluency and charm, in their quality of being "intense and volatile at the same time," in their "play of swift line and color," to the work of the great French poster artists.[34]

34

W. F. Gouwe, *De grafische kunst in het praktische leven*, Rotterdam, 1926, p.24; quoted in Kurt Löb, *De onbekende Jan Sluijters*, The Hague, 1968, p.39.

His early (1904) poster for Israel Querido's novel *Zegepraal (Victory)* still has a symbolist flavor, with its symmetrical design and its iconic figure of victory stretching out its arms within great butterfly wings (*23*). But the result is very different from the flat, stylized patterns of most Dutch posters of the period. There is no attempt to give strong expression to the figure. Instead the poster's expressive effect is largely conveyed by its lively brush work and its strong red-blue contrasts, which suggest that Sluyters may already have been familiar with the similar contrasts in French fauvism.

As a painter Sluyters went through a number of styles in his early career, including impressionism, neo-impressionism, and for a brief time futurism. But the style that most strongly affected his work was fauvism. If there is some question about fauve influence in his *Zege-praal* poster, there is none about its presence in his "evening party" poster of 1915 for the League of Dutch Artists' Unions, and his even more brilliant announcement of 1919 for an artists' winter festival in The Hague (*24 and 41*). Printed in intense colors, they are drawn with the rapid,

simplified contour lines of Matisse, Dufy, or van Dongen. Indeed, Sluyters' are among the few fauve posters anywhere, closer to paintings in their variety and freedom of tone and line than to the linear patterns more usually favored by poster makers. They lack a degree of clarity, but this is not a significant drawback in posters announcing merriment; rarely has a poster style been joined so felicitously with its subject.

Sluyters' fauve style was no doubt unsuitable for posters with more elevated subjects. For displays of culture, a more "serious" modernism was wanted. In practice this meant some form of expressionism, in effect using strong color or value contrasts, sharply angled forms, and a more or less bold manner of drawing. It could be applied even to so light-hearted a classic comedy as *La Locandiera* by the eighteenth-century Venetian playwright Carlo Goldoni, as it was by Raoul Hynckes (*55*).

One of the most dramatically expressionistic of all Dutch posters is H. Th. Wijdeveld's black and white placard of 1922 for an international theater exhibition at the Stedelijk Museum in Amsterdam (*58*). Its composition – almost a parody of the popular concept of expressionism – centers upon a tiny figure in black silhouette with outstretched arms, the actor,

whose art sets off a great explosion of light culminating in the outline forms of a bird and partial head with veiled eyes.

Expressionism of one sort or another continued in Dutch posters into the 1930s, as it did in posters elsewhere in Europe. But as in Germany, where the Nazis (in spite of their official opposition to modernism) retained the harsh forms of expressionism in anti-Semitic or war posters in order to stir hatred,[35] its use in the Netherlands after the early twenties lingered on for subjects lending themselves to a certain urgency of expression.

Leo Gestel's poster of about 1922 for Philips' Arga light bulbs makes them the product of an expressionistic volcano of energy (*59*). Posters for the SDAP characteristically stress the hardships of workers. In her poster of 1930 for the socialist Dutch Federation of Trade Unions (NVV), Fré Cohen, who was born into a family of diamond workers and had strong socialist sympathies,[36] presents a grimly determined family of laborers holding the red banner, their images

---

35

On this use of expressionism in the period of World War I see Philipp Fehl, "Propaganda and the Integrity of Art: Notes on an Exhibition of War Posters 1914-1918," in *World War I Propaganda Posters: A Selection from the Bowman Gray Collection of Materials Related to World War I and World War II* (cat.), Ackland Art center, University of North Carolina, Chapel Hill, January 12-February 23, 1969. For the Nazi use of expressionist techniques, see Hildegard Brenner, *Die Kunstpolitik des Nationalsozialismus*, Hamburg, 1963, fig.1, and the anti-Semitic posters in *Kunst im 3. Reich. Dokumente der Unterwerfung* (cat.), Frankfurter Kunstverein, Frankfurt am Main, October 15-December 8, 1974, pp.203, 205, 209.

36

"Willem Arondéus, Else Berg, Fré Cohen, Henk Henriët: Vier vergeten kunstenaars," *NRC Handelsblad; cultureel supplement* 338 (April 15, 1977). See also Frank Gribling, "Meijer Bleekrode en de socialistische kunst tussen de twee wereldoorlogen," in *Meijer Bleekrode: schilder, ontwerper, socialist 1896-1943* (cat.), ed. Carry van Lakerveld, Amsterdams Historisch Museum, 1983, p.33.

made still grimmer by the squarish rendering of their forms (72). Meijer Bleekrode's poster of the same year for a conference of the NVV issues its appeal against war and for state pensions with a dramatically angled arrangement of white old age in the foreground, a dark figure of death with helmet and bayonet in the rear, and in between, its stern visage interceding, a heroic worker in red (85). Like Cohen, Bleekrode came from a family of diamond workers and was socialist in his sympathies. This poster is one of many works – posters and illustrations – he designed for the Dutch socialist movement in the twenties and early thirties.[37]

Funke Küpper's 1927 poster for the socialist journal *Voorwaarts* is not expressionist in the same way as these (74). Its clean-edged forms seem at first to share the impersonal geometric aesthetic of the 1920s. But in fact its planes of light cutting through the sharply defined form of a lighthouse have less in common with the geometric elementarism practiced in Holland at the time by de Stijl than with the visionary paintings of Lyonel Feininger, whose de-materialized images of architecture caught in planes of light even include lighthouses. Feininger's fusions of architecture and space, with their aim of sublimity, seem fitting models to represent the poster's motto: "*Voorwaarts*, your beacon."

Russian subjects seem almost inevitably to have called for expressionist treatment. Dolly Rüdeman's widely disseminated poster for Sergei Eisenstein's 1925 film of the revolution, *Potemkin* – her first for the films – is reminiscent of German expressionism before the first World War, with its jagged lines and clashing diagonals (71). It received considerable attention in the press, partly because it seemed to capture the spirit of the film. While it conveys nothing of Eisenstein's montage technique with its complex patterns of men and machinery in action, it succeeds in a general way in evoking the violence of social upheaval, and its distinctive style launched Rüdeman on her career as a designer of film posters.[38]

Samuel Schwarz's poster of 1930 for Trotsky's autobiography has a similar style of angular, clashing forms (84). Its superimposed layers – a brandished fist, a wall, a trestle, the toppling towers of the Kremlin, and a steaming train[39] – lack Rüdeman's spontaneity, but they show a greater sophistication than does her design.

The third of our "Russian" posters, from 1931, returns us to theater: Mussorgsky's *Boris Godounov*, with the great Russian bass Chaliapin (97). Its political drama is of the distant past rather than of the present, and it is surely one of the reasons – nineteeth-century grand opera now tending to work on disinterested emotion rather than firing up our political sentiments – that Joop Sjollema softened his dramatic imagery with decorative rectangles and the scrolled neck of a double bass at the left.[40]

37

After ca. 1935 he devoted himself largely to painting, without political themes. See the illustrations in *Meijer Bleekrode: schilder, ontwerper, socialist* and Bleekrode's biography, id., by his nephew Steef Davidson, "De onvoltooid tegenwoordige tijd," pp. 9-25.

38

The poster was printed in 7500 copies. On Rüdeman's early career, see Rob Geraerds, "Film-affiches Dolly Rüdeman," *Op de Hoogte*, May 21, 1931, pp. 146-148, and the article on her in *Het Vaderland* (The Hague), March 2, 1929.

39

The train and trestle were described at the time as "the symbol of transition to a better future." See Otto van Tussenbroek, "Twee affiches," in *Balans: Algemeen jaarboek der Nederlandsche kunsten 1930-31*, Maastricht, 1930, pp. 72-73.

40

Sjollema recalls having received 200 guilders for his poster, a figure on the high side, since designers generally received between 100 and 250 guilders a poster, depending on whether they themselves drew the design on the stone. Sjollema ordinarily did so. His request for a more vivid red in the background of the Boris Godounov poster was turned down because the additional color required would have made the work more expensive.

New Tendencies in the 20s and 30s

The more objective artistic tendencies of the mid-twenties – geometric abstraction on the one hand and a greater descriptive realism on the other (what in Germany was labeled the New Objectivity) – affected poster design as well. What most Dutch posters from the mid-nineteen-twenties to the beginning of the second World War have in common is a greater impersonality of style. Expressive drawing, whether of the monumental and decorative types represented by Roland Holst and Jan Sluyters respectively or the harsher style developed under expressionist influence, tended to yield to geometry, to smoothly stylized and simplified forms, or to a detailed rendering conveying meaning through illustration rather than through distortion of form.

This last may be seen in Chris Lebeau's linocut poster of 1925 for the art dealer Willem Brok in Hilversum. It marks a radical departure from his work of the previous decade (56). In place of his hieratic figures, with their solemn evocations of high art, we now see the carefully modeled figure of a connoisseur peering at some troublesome detail of a work of art through cupped hands. Its naturalistic form and its even, closely spaced hatchings might almost be out of the pages of a commercially engraved volume of the nineteenth century. The naturalism of Aart van Dobbenburgh's poignant 1935 image of a poor drunk is perhaps more justified. Dobbenburgh, who worked in the realist tradition, could not have created a more eloquent and immediately grasped appeal against alcoholism – the object of his poster – than this finely detailed *cri de coeur*, as it was described in the press (98).

The work of Jac. Jongert was to undergo an equally striking change. In fact, he was able to make the transition from a disciple of Roland Holst to a thoroughgoing modern designer for industry.

Jongert began his career in 1904-1907 as Roland Holst's assistant on the mural decorations of Berlage's building for the Dutch Diamond Workers' Union in Amsterdam (Algemeene Nederlandsche Diamantbewerkers Bond), and as late as 1923, in his article of that year quoted at the beginning of this survey, he was still expressing Roland Holst's idealistic view of design: "Advertisement never leaves the earth but the atmosphere it conjures around things earthly is often reminiscent of the all-highest.

. . . A poster should be sufficiently important to continue to interest for a long time. Importance is the great gift the artist gives to advertisement. Its profit goes to the society or Company which gives its order to the advertising artist. Good posters are long attractive because the inspiring power of art is eternal and they are therefore taken up and protected by art patrons and art lovers." [41]

This conviction no doubt helps to explain why Jongert's early designs tend to be richly decorative. His first poster, the prize-winning entry for an international exhibition of the gas industry held in Amsterdam in 1912, has the elaborate borders and allegorical forms of much Dutch poster art of the period, his tour of the gas plant in Purmerend evidently having provided him with little direct inspiration (27).[42] The heroic form of the sun god Apollo (or Helios, as the figure seems to have been called at the time), symbol of energy and light, steps from his golden winged chariot to the accompaniment of the red roses of dawn. He frames the orb of the sun with his hand and – appropriately for the poster's subject – carries in his arms the infant Hermes, god of wealth and commerce, to whom Apollo gave the caduceus and who taught the gods how to make fire.

41

Jongert, "Posters," pp.5, 10.

42

Jongert was paid 500 guilders for the poster, with another 200 guilders allotted for its transfer to the stone and printing. See Emy Hoogenboezem, "Een onderzoek naar Jac. Jongert 1883-1942, toegespitst op zijn gebruiksgrafiek," Ph.D. diss., Kunsthistorisch Instituut, Utrecht, 1979, pp.39-41. On Jongert's career in general, id., *Jac. Jongert 1883-1942: Graficus tussen kunst en reclame* (cat.), Gemeentemuseum, The Hague, 1982.

Despite its victory in the competition – in part due to the number of important designers who stayed away – Jongert's design did not find general approval, not even with the jury (which included Roland Holst). Critics complained of its dependency on Roland Holst's murals for the diamond workers' building, of its weakness as a design, and of its abstruse imagery. The last objection was certainly justified, for it depends for its understanding on a knowledge of mythology which, though elementary, was obviously not shared by everyone who might have been attracted to the exhibition.

Jongert's conversion to a more industrial aesthetic was begun, according to him, by a visit to the Deutsche Werkbund exhibition held in Cologne in 1914. It was there that he discovered the new possibilities for design offered by machine production.[43] That visit, however, seems to have had little immediate effect on his poster work. Although he ceased working in the monumental style of his first poster, as late as the early twenties he was still designing posters in an "artistic" and highly personal manner.

One of them, made in 1920 for the Volksuniversiteit in Rotterdam, a new university founded in 1917, makes use of the angular, schematic forms associated with expressionism. Its motif was at once adopted by the institution as its logo: a geometrically stylized sower, accompanied by birds, who with energetic stride scatters the seeds of knowledge (46).

At about the same time Jongert also made a poster for the wine and spirits firm of Oud in Purmerend, for which he had earlier designed bottles and bottle labels (52). Like most of his graphic design from the midteens to the beginning of the twenties (his university poster being an exception), it is strongly symmetrical, and its decoration, like that of Roland Holst and many other Dutch poster designers of the time, is based on rectangular forms. Unlike most such poster design, however, Jongert's is enlivened by a freely brushed surface, which gives the work a strongly individualistic stamp.

About a year before these posters were made, in 1919, Jongert received the first of his advertising commissions from the van Nelle company in Rotterdam, a complex founded in the late eighteenth century as a tobacco, coffee, and tea shop. Jongert's initial poster for van Nelle, designed in the same year as his Volksuniversiteit poster, scarcely conforms to a modern conception of machine design, any more than does the latter (51). It is an elegant, personal affair like his brandy poster for Oud: a loosely brushed, symmetrical design dominated by a vivid red and green, with smoke rising in almost art-nouveau curves from a mass of stylized tobacco blossoms. Its lettering, closely spaced and exaggerated in proportion, forms an integral part of the design; readable, but almost joined to the surrounding smoke.

In 1923 Jongert was made advertising director of van Nelle, a position he was to hold until 1940.[44] Now, charged as he was with giving artistic unity to all of van Nelle's advertising displays, he was to drop the obvious personal touches – the freely brushed surfaces and elaborate ornamentations. Now he would make extensive use of typography, simple geometric forms, and – in the mid-thirties – photography.

Did C. H. van der Leeuw, the director of van Nelle, who hired Jongert have anything to do with steering the artist towards a simpler and less personal style? If so, Jongert was able without difficulty to incorporate the change into his ethos as a designer.

43

Hoogenboezem, "Onderzoek," pp. 41-42.

44

Ibid., pp. 48, 52.

Ultimately, Jongert's transformation in the mid-twenties was due to the same idealism that had motivated his earlier work: "Beside the wish for new forms of advertisement in commerce," he wrote in his article of 1923, "the desire grew in the artist to be allowed to share in real life and to be a member of the army of productive workers. In these days it is certainly the great wish of the artist to be once more useful and necessary in Society. . . . The desire to penetrate once more into the process of production demands of us that we should demonstrate to that productive community that our work is essential to the success of the whole."[45]

Jongert's concept of the artist as a shaper of society, at least as stated here, has no necessary connection with the collectivist sentiments of de Stijl.[46] Nevertheless, it readily justified the functional kind of design promoted by that group: for what, after all, could better express the ideal of social harmony than a style of clear, simple patterns and colors, easily read type, and a de- emphasis of drawing and ornament, those aspects of design which most surely displayed the designer's individual skills and vision?

In this Jongert followed a broad trend in European design of a purified geometric abstraction. It had developed first and most insistently in Russia with the suprematist and constructivist movements and in Holland with de Stijl, the group of artists and designers organized around Piet Mondrian and Theo van Doesburg. By 1921 the Russian movements had begun to influence western Europe, including the Netherlands, and by the mid-twenties the abstraction of the two nations had essentially merged into an international elementarist style. In graphic design this process of assimilation was facilitated by the efforts of the Russian painter and designer El Lissitzky, whose travels after the first World War did much to spread Russian modernism to the West.

A van Nelle poster of about 1930 by Jongert advertising tea and coffee, though rather late in the adoption of that tendency, is strongly elementarist in conception (73). Its geometric layout, designed primarily with typographical elements, has scarcely a trace of Jongert's former pictorialism. This has been replaced by a simple asymmetrical composition with the name of the company angled across the surface in bold sans-serif capitals set at right angles to geometric planes bearing emblems of coffee and tea. The diagonal cross-shaped design closely follows the dynamic patterns established by van Doesburg and by Lissitzky, whose designs could be seen in Holland as early as 1921.[47] Jongert's poster even has the characteristic color scheme – red, yellow, and black – of the Russian abstractionists.

The use of lettering as the primary element in graphic design was far from exclusive to elementarism (though advertising designers who chose to follow the stern discipline of pure geometry were bound to rely largely on typography). The typographical poster was in fact widespread in the twenties and thirties, particularly in the Netherlands.

In a poster for an exhibition of factory and office administration (F.E.K.A.), probably from 1923, Machiel Wilmink includes small triangles of a sort recalling those in the paintings of Bart van der Leck of de Stijl (61).[48] But here they are little more than border decorations within a conservative design of strict symmetry, whose focus is the faintly caricatural drawing of a figure behind a typewriter. In

45
Jongert, "Posters," pp.12-13.

46
On the political sentiments of de Stijl, see Ger Harmsen, "De Stijl and the Russian Revolution," in De Stijl 1917-1931: Visions of Utopia, ed. Mildred Friedman, Oxford, 1982, pp.45-49.

47
As a lithograph on the cover of Wendingen, vol.4, no.11.

48
Wilmink ran one of the three most important Dutch advertising studios in the 1930s. Begun in the mid twenties, it was located in Rotterdam. The other two were the Studio Frits van Alphen in Amsterdam and the studio of N. V. Remaco.

contrast, Sjoerd de Roos' elegant poster of a decade later for a jubilee festival of music, art, and sports makes no pretense whatever to modernity. Its appeal lies entirely in the beauty of its lettering, which was designed by de Roos himself, a graphic artist and designer of typefaces (96). A poster from 1927 for an exhibition of garden art in The Hague has the stylized sans-serif capitals used in the 1920s by Pieter Hofman, with their exaggerated contrast of thick and thin strokes (75). Hofman was active in The Hague, and the poster's compact design of overlapping rectangles, reminiscent in its density of some of H. Th. Wijdeveld's designs, seems likely to be by him.

Wijdeveld was one of the most influential of the typographic designers in Holland. His style of bold sans-serif letters, with their rectangular, meandering forms, was not invented by him; it had been used by J. L. M. Lauweriks as early as 1911-12, and a somewhat simpler though related form of square lettering had appeared on the title pages of *De Stijl* since its inception in 1917.[49] But thanks to its regular use in the more widely known art journal *Wendingen*, of which Wijdeveld was editor, it had

extensive circulation and even acquired the label of the *Wendingen* or Wijdeveld style (66 and 68).[50]

The Wijdeveld style continued to be used occasionally in typographic design into the 1940s,[51] but by the thirties it was already out of favor, and today for all its striking visual effect, it seems very much bound to a particular time. Its letter forms were conceived as decorative in themselves, making them difficult to read – an objection raised from the start – and though Wijdeveld lightened and clarified his lettering somewhat in the late twenties and early thirties, as witness his elegant poster for an exhibition of Frank Lloyd Wright of 1931 (67), his posters and those of designers influenced by him – J. J. Hellendoorn and Anton Kurvers, for instance – tend to have dense, rigid compositions (65 and 69).

The posters of de Stijl and of other artists influenced by the new elementarism have not dated nearly as much. Their open, dynamic patterns and their simple, readily legible sans-serif lettering continue to attract graphic designers even today.

Bart van der Leck's poster for the Batavier steamship line, from 1914-15, precedes his entrance into de Stijl by some two years, but it already displays many of the later characteristics of graphic design by the

group as a whole: a simple layout with rectangular compartments, an absence of decorative embellishment, a generous use of empty space, and above all a pervasive geometry which in this case renders the forms – ship and figures alike – as elementary signs comparable to what has since become the pictorial language of international travel, marking locations on highways and in public buildings (35).[52] Van der Leck was one of the founding members of de Stijl, the first of the group to use flat, primary colors and the first to adopt its strict geometry. This poster does not yet show the pure colors and abstraction of van der Leck's slightly later work, but it otherwise exhibits the precocity of style that was to influence Mondrian.

The artists of de Stijl did not design many posters – van der Leck himself made few, and none at all during the two years, 1917-18, he was a member of the group; their graphic design was confined mainly to the pages of avant-garde art books and journals. As we have seen in the case of Jac. Jongert, it was left largely to others to carry their artistic principles to the hoardings. Jongert himself did not

49

For Lauweriks' early typography see Hans Oldewarris, "L'arte tipografica di 'Wendingen,'" in *Wendingen 1918-1931: Documenti dell'arte olandese del Novecento* (cat.), Palazzo Medici-Riccardi, Florence, April 3-June 5, 1982, p.83.

50

Ibid., p.81.

51

Ibid.

52

According to R. W. D. Oxenaar, in *Bart van der Leck, 1876-1958* (cat.), Rijksmuseum Kröller-Müller, Otterlo, July 18-September 5, 1976, unpaged, the first studies for the poster date from December 1914. Van der Leck's original style of lettering was rejected by the company and pasted over with new panels of text. Two proofs of the poster are known in which the faces are colored yellow-brown.

fully accept the elementarist aesthetic of the 1920s; the representational forms of cups and saucers in his poster of about 1930 for van Nelle, and the curls of steam rising from them, are indication enough (73). Other designers were bolder.

Piet Zwart was not a member of de Stijl, but he had become acquainted with the ideas of the group in 1919, occasionally exhibited with it, and in 1920 and 1921 collaborated in designing furniture and interiors with two actual members, Vilmos Huszar and the architect Jan Wils. Zwart began designing typographically in 1921 under Wils' influence. The monogram "Laga," in his poster of about 1922 for rubber flooring, is based on Wils' own monogram, and the highly stylized lettering of the poster as a whole has much in common with the early typographical designs of Huszar and van Doesburg, both of whom about 1920 were still working with rectangular letters in the spirit of Wijdeveld (63).[53] A later work by Zwart, a poster of 1928 for an international film exhibition at The Hague, is more open in composition, with simple, easy-to-read block letters. Its overlapping forms, the diagonal word "film" floated across the blue square,

and its collage-like elements probably reflect the work of Lissitzky, who by then had had a pervasive influence on de Stijl (70).[54]

Lissitzky's influence is thoroughly apparent in a poster of about 1927 for an exhibition of home industry by the architect S. van Ravesteyn, who had met the Russian artist in Utrecht and who in 1927 visited the Bauhaus in Dessau, another, indirect fount of Russian influence (62).[55] Its diagonal streamers of type, its large expanses of empty space, and its black and red color scheme were by then, under the impact of Russian art, in international use among modern designers. Indeed, in design and color his poster is remarkably like a slightly later one from Germany announcing a handicraft exhibition in Oldenburg.[56]

Perhaps even more impressive than the posters of Zwart and van Ravesteyn are those of Hendrik Nicolaas Werkman. Like theirs, Werkman's posters, with their grid patterns and play of rectangles, were strongly influenced by de Stijl; but unlike theirs, his also come under the influence of the dada movement; not, it should be said at once, of its nihilism but of its formal design. The chief dada spirit among Dutch artists was, of all people, Theo van Doesburg, whose dadaist pseudonyms were I. K. Bonset and Aldo Camini. (Not even Theo van Doesburg was

his real name.) Doesburg, like Werkman after him, drew upon the typographical experiments of the dadaists, in which stock elements were arranged in relatively free compositions based on cubism. Among the dadaists, Marius de Zayas had begun making such typographical designs as early as 1915 in the pages of the journal 291, and by the early twenties they could be seen everywhere dadaism flourished, which in practice meant everywhere modern art had taken hold.

Werkman, a professional printer, commonly made use of existing type material. Most of his posters were designed for exhibitions of the artists' group de Ploeg (The Plough) in Groningen, of which he was a member, and usually published in small editions.[57] His de Ploeg poster of 1925 is characteristic (64). Printed by him in letterpress, a portion at a time so as to control its effects more closely, its composition of horizontal bars cantilevered off verticals is of a kind familiar from the paintings of van Doesburg. But unlike van Doesburg, who tends to be more formal, Werkman loosens his design by the

53

On Zwart, see Kees Broos, *Piet Zwart 1885-1977*, Amsterdam, 1982, p.36; id., "From De Stijl to a New Typography," in *De Stijl 1917-1931: Visions of Utopia*, ed. Mildred Friedman, Oxford, 1982, pp.152-153.

54

Broos, "From De Stijl," p.163.

55

S. van Ravesteyn (cat.), Nationaal Architectuur Museum, Amsterdam, 1977, p.9. Information on the date of the poster is from the artist.

56

Illustrated in *The Poster* (see note 18 above), no.171, and dated there as ca. 1930. The name of the designer is not given.

57

On Werkman's career, see Dick Dooijes, *Hendrik Werkman*, Amsterdam, 1970, and *Hendrik Nicolaas Werkman 1882-1945: "Druksel" Prints and General Printed Matter* (cat.), Stedelijk Museum, Amsterdam, 1977.

relatively casual alignment of his bars, by the short diagonal at the upper left, and by irregular inking.

Werkman was to have considerable influence on Dutch poster design, particularly on the work of W. J. H. B. Sandberg, one of the most important designers of noncommercial posters in the thirties and post-war years. Sandberg's poster of 1935 for an exhibition in the Stedelijk of monumental art is not as obviously influenced by Werkman as some of his others; its floating diagonal lines and blocks of type are closer to elementarism (86). But its varied typefaces and its free spots of shading have something of Werkman's richness and informality of approach.

As the posters of Werkman and Sandberg indicate, by the late twenties modern typographical design in the Netherlands had spread beyond the austere limits of elementarism – especially as it was practiced by de Stijl. One of the most important figures in this development was Paul Schuitema, who among avant-garde designers exerted, with Zwart, a major influence on European poster design of the thirties, especially, in his case, in the use of photomontage. The advantage of illustration in posters was difficult to ignore, and geometric design of the modern

abstract variety was frequently joined in an effective union with photography. This union was particularly suited to posters with political and social import, for it offered the dynamism of modernist design, already long associated symbolically with radical politics, and the actuality of the photograph.

Meijer Bleekrode's 1932 poster announcing evening classes for workers uses photomontage to place the figure of a worker against a slanting background of words repeating over and over again the name of the school, its character, and what it has to offer (78). Shown from the rear in the act of writing, the figure casts long double shadows over the print and so demonstrates his conquest of the written word.

Bleekrode's emphasis is primarily on typography and on the dramatic oppositions of large lettering against small, figure against abstract space. In contrast, Louis Frank's poster of the previous year for the journal *Volksblad* ("workers, your own newspaper"), whose similar composition shows a man from the back

reading a newspaper, shifts the burden of its image to the photomontage (79).[58] The figure is given a partial ambience by the photograph of a factory building, and the message – in Bleekrode's poster emblazoned in diagonals across its face – is with one exception confined, in bold letters but soberly, to a conventional horizontal position at top and bottom.

Wim Brusse's poster of about 1932, calling for increased employment, puts even greater weight on photographic imagery. The lettering, prominent as it is, is markedly subordinate to the powerful colored image in the center (80).

Designers of commercial posters were less ready to adopt the modern photomontage, with its disjunctions and abstract planes. A poster of 1928 by the architect and industrial designer Willem Gispen, advertising his own lamps, is exceptional in Holland (77). In this early use of photography in posters, Gispen turned the pure forms of his Bauhaus-influenced lamps (in photographs by J. Kamman) together with his rounded lettering into the geometric elements of a constructivist composition. We see at a glance not only the kind of

58

Frank's poster was illustrated in the November 1931 issue of *De Reclame*. Frank, who used a photograph of himself as the man reading, dates it to 1931.

product being sold and its character but – like many later advertisements for modern industrial design – the modern cachet bestowed by its use. Gispen's design is at once an illustration of a product and a symbol of its modernity and distinction.

By and large, in posters for products not themselves created by modern designers, like Gispen's lamps, photography served in the Netherlands less as a medium of experimentation than as the basis or inspiration for illustration. A first look at Jan Wijga's 1930s poster for Oranjeboom beer suggests that its still life is nothing more than a retouched photograph. But the cigarette, match box, and ashtray are rather freely worked, and more careful inspection reveals that the still life is not drawn in accurate perspective and that even the letters of the open book have been painstakingly rendered by hand (93). Whether or not Wijga was helped by photography in this poster, the illustration was painted by hand from the model, in accordance with Wijga's usual way of working.[59]

Wijga's reputation was made with his many beer posters. Peter Karstkarel has proposed that in using the still life as a motif in them Wijga was deliberately appealing to the rich tradition of Dutch art. Beer, he observes further, was at that time scarcely drunk at home, and the poster's up-to-date style seems to suggest that home was in fact a place where modern people were beginning to drink it.[60] Wijga's first beer poster, from 1929, was so popular that it was hung on the walls of cafés and restaurants like a painting, and it could still be found in a few such places after World War II.[61]

Most of Wijga's work is more stylized than his Oranjeboom poster. Like many Dutch designers in the 1930s – particularly when they worked on commercial posters – he was influenced by French developments, specifically by the sleek geometric stylization in the decorative arts that has come to be known as art deco. That tendency differed from the more abstract use of geometry by the elementarists in being representational and unequivocally decorative. Geometric stylization took a variety of forms in commercial posters of the 1930s. What they have in common is a concentration on the image of the product itself, which was to be presented with as flawless an appearance as possible.

The image may be as direct and close to unstylized as Kees Dekker's highly regarded display of biscuits of 1933 (whose prominence in the composition would have been greater if he had not been required against his wishes to put a face on the cook),[62] or as smoothly refined as the etiolated face of Marlene Dietrich, coolly staring us down in a poster of 1937 for Ernst Lubitsch's *Angel* by Frans Mettes, who became an important designer of commercial posters after World War II (94 and 100).

In two beer posters by N. P. de Koo from about 1930, realistically rendered bottles are placed against schematic images of a table and a goat respectively (87 and 88). In both the design is so arranged as to bring attention instantly to the product; in the one by the overwhelmingly obvious but effective means of centering the bottle within a bullseye, in the other by pointing to the beer with an orange stripe that runs in a tapered curl down the goat's body.

The products of technology lent themselves particularly well to stylization, in part because of their own geometry, in part because stylized treatment suited them as icons of the modern age. Louis Kalff's poster for Philips radio of about 1931 features two vacuum

59

On Wijga see Karstkarel (note 20 above), pp. 30-40.

60

Ibid., p. 30.

61

Ibid., pp. 30-36.

62

Information from the artist.

tubes set in front of the globe (91). Their streamlined patterns, simplified to a few bands of reflection and shade, are almost enough by themselves to suggest the enigmatic power of modern communications.

The promises of modern technology to construct a better society could be communicated even more effectively by idealizing its largest and most visible products, the images of buildings – by emphasizing the clean geometry of their lines and the smoothly functioning harmony of their parts, as Henri Pieck does in his poster of about 1933 for the annual industrial fair in Utrecht, or the unknown designer of a curious poster from the same year for an architectural exhibition in Haarlem, which bears the initials Z. W. (82 and 81). This work, with its thin decorative lettering and borders and its beam of light shining down on the building from heaven, reminds us that modernism in the design of the twenties and thirties could go well beyond the functionalist styles of its principal figures to include much that was decorative and even popular. It

glamorizes architecture in a way not so very dissimilar to the way Hollywood, and Mettes in his poster, glamorized Marlene Dietrich and the movies.

Cultural posters of the twenties and thirties, because of their greater tolerance for artistic complication, often come closer than their commercial counterparts to the style of art deco as we know it from the decorative arts. Harmen Meurs' poster of about 1923 or 24 for an exhibition at the Stedelijk turns a landscape of Holland into an unapologetic decoration (60). Fré Cohen's poster for the 1933 premier of Willem Pijper's opera Halewijn, commissioned by the Wagner Society, bears little resemblance to her trade union work of two years earlier (99). Gone is her expressionist brusqueness. The opera announcement plainly required a more graceful approach. The profile mask with its parallel waves of flying hair resembles innumerable pieces of decorative sculpture designed in the 1930s. This is also true of Pieter Hofman's 1930 poster for the Utrecht industrial fair. Hofman designed murals and stained glass, and the poster's elongated figure of Mercury bounding across a restless pattern of angles, waves, and zigzags would be at home on the facade or in the lobby

of almost any commercial and public building of the 1930s, whether in Europe or America (83). A more restrained decorativism appears in Raoul Hynckes' 1932 poster for a summer art exhibition at the Stedelijk (95). Its still life pattern recalls the decorative cubism of Juan Gris and Fernand Léger of a decade before.

The reductive geometry of Jacq. Bodaan's announcement of 1933 for an exhibition of The Hague Sketch Club instead brings its figure closer to caricature (76). It has something of the comic simplification of A. M. Cassandre's famous Dubonnet man of 1932, the little bowler-hatted boulevardier taking his apéritif at a café (fig. 4).

The immensely popular French designer Cassandre, whose real name was Adolphe Jean-Marie Mouron, was one of the most influential figures in Dutch poster design of the thirties. Among the numerous Dutch companies for which Cassandre worked were the Holland-America Line, Philips, van Nelle, and Droste. So much in demand was he in Holland that he was able to command a fee of 1000 guilders for his

Statendam poster, a figure roughly five to ten times what was normally paid Dutch poster artists.[63]

Cassandre brought to the poster a simplified style of representation that contracted its subject to a single forceful image instantly identifiable and at the same time enhanced by an immaculate rendering of outline and surface. He was at his best in images of transportation – in a 1930 poster for an Amsterdam exhibition of automobiles and motorcycles, for example, and in travel posters – in images themselves (like his style) with a clean-edged, mechanical look: trains, railway tracks, and above all the great ocean liners with their surging forms (fig. 5).

Cassandre and the designers he influenced, like J. A. W. von Stein and Wim ten Broek, helped give the memory of the once mighty ocean liner a glamour it has retained to this day. Who, remembering those marvels of luxury and power, does not immediately conjure up a sleek looming prow or giant sloping smokestacks, more decorative than functional but instantly expressive of

Figure 4
A. M. Cassandre
Dubonnet
Lithograph, 1932

Figure 5
A. M. Cassandre
Holland-America Line
Lithograph, 1928

63

According to W. H. Benier, in conversation with Martijn Le Coultre.

those great mobile hotels (92 and 101). Travel posters of the late twenties and thirties did almost as much as the movies to make ocean travel seem not a matter of emigrants in steerage but of vacationers enjoying the luxury of first class.

Other 1930s images of transportation are almost as affecting, as in Agnes Canta's poster for Utrecht's annual industrial fair of about 1937 (102). Instead of the usual image or symbol of industry, hers illustrates a boat in full sail, the simple forms of bow and swelling sails making a vivid pattern against the blue sky.

Contemporary representations of airplanes no longer have quite the same appeal, doubtless because unlike sailing vessels and the great ships, which had already attained their more or less definitive form, the airplane was an ungainly fledgling destined to change in the years ahead. Still, it is easy to imagine the impression of novelty and speed commercial flight must have made in the twenties and thirties. This impression was exploited by the ad campaign of KLM, Royal Dutch Airlines. In a series of evocative and witty posters, KLM punned with the theme of the Flying Dutchman, contrasting the legendary ghost ship, doomed to sail forever, with its modern replacement in the air.

The earliest of the KLM posters represented here, a 1924 design by A. M. Guthschmidt, is the most explicit in its use of the legend. A perhaps overly complacent aviator aboard the ship – left white to indicate its ghostliness and its obsolescence – points out the soaring airplane that has superseded it to the dismayed captain of the ship, himself equally white. The text reads, "No legend, but reality." Its anecdotal flavor and its detailed, curvilinear forms give the poster a somewhat old-fashioned appearance, but one that is in character with the implications of the revolutionary new means of transportation. All of the poster's drama takes place on its extravagantly stormy, cloud-covered sea; the boxy single-engine aircraft, in fairy-tale contrast, hovers effortlessly in a bright blue sky (54).

Later KLM posters would not be quite so explicit. In them the smooth, simplified forms of the thirties would be joined to a more understated treatment of the Flying Dutchman motif: a simple juxtaposition of the vividly rendered plane in the foreground and the pale ghost ship behind. The result, as in the images

of ocean liners, is to put emphasis on the streamlined form of the Dutchman's modern counterpart (89 and 90). Jan Wijga's version from 1933 is particularly handsome with its limpid tonalities of blue, green, and purple.

It seems fitting to conclude this survey of Dutch posters with these images of ships and airplanes. The postwar world would see the virtual end of the former and the radical transformation of the latter: the great ocean liners reduced to pleasure craft and the airplane into a commonplace as familiar as the train (far more familiar in the United States), and in some ways less impressive. In other respects, too, they mark the end of an era: in their insistent elegance and in the promise they held out – partly on the basis of that elegance – of a good life made possible by technology. The good life in these posters, of course, is one of material advantage, but they promised nothing not promised by more "serious" advertising as well. As Jac. Jongert reminds us, it was still possible for designers to believe that advertising had something like a noble mission to perform, even when its purpose was commercial. Cultural and political posters necessarily aimed at something higher, but not as a substitute for the other. In both commercial and noncommercial

advertising, hope for a new society was predicated on material progress. Our travel posters can hardly be said to advocate a new society (whatever personal convictions their designers may have held). But in their less elevated way they, too, evoke hopes difficult to regain in the world today. Their primary intention, the selling of a particular experience of travel, has now only historical interest; but like all works of art, they can still reach us, if only by creating a deceptive nostalgia for better times.

Needless to say, fifty years of posters cannot sum up an age or nation, and except for observing a certain tendency toward restraint in design, form, and message, no attempt has been made in this survey to give the history of the Dutch poster a coherence beyond what affinity and common goals can bring to it. One of these goals pervades the entire period under consideration; indeed, was largely responsible for the creation of a poster art in the first place: the desire to infuse everyday life with the dignity of art and conversely to reinvigorate art by closer contact with life.

It was undoubtedly this desire that led most of the lithographers discussed here to draw their designs on the stones themselves instead of leaving the transfer of work to commercial printers. Whether in fact such desire was greater in Holland than in other countries would be difficult to argue, but it is nevertheless true that the care Dutch poster artists took to execute their work marks them off from the run of poster artists elsewhere. Most of the posters illustrated in this book have the power to affect us by their artistic character: some by the distinctiveness of their drawing and the aptness of their formal solutions, others by their wit and humor or their highmindedness. Still others succeed by their vigor in reanimating the political and social struggles of which they were a part. All of them are social documents of commanding interest.

Marcel Franciscono

I am indebted to Martijn Le Coultre for sharing his wide knowledge of Dutch posters with me. Much of his information was derived from interviews with the designers themselves, and these have been duly noted where they seemed pertinent.

Plates

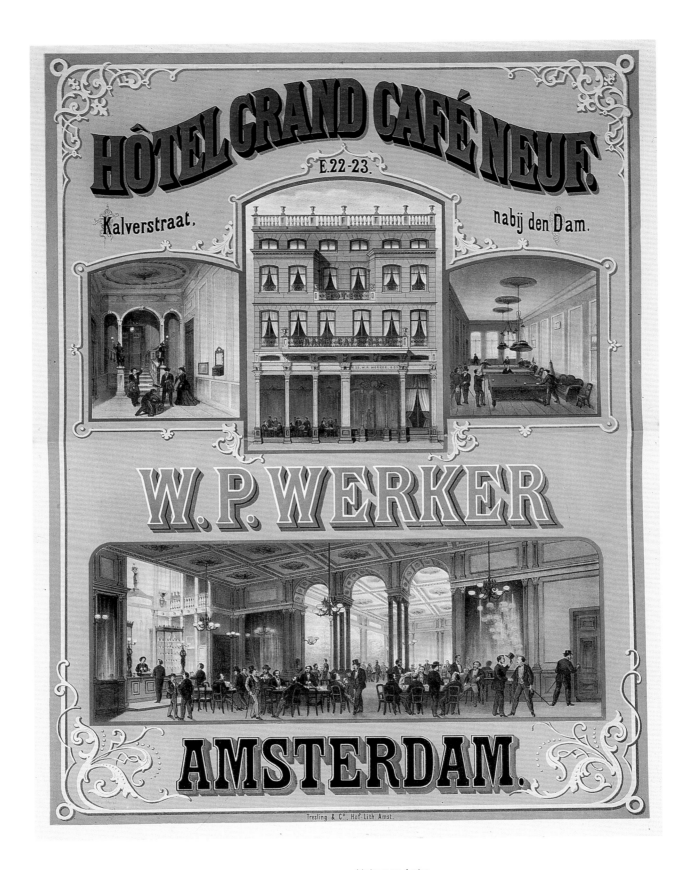

Unknown Artist

Hotel Grand Café Neuf
1870-76

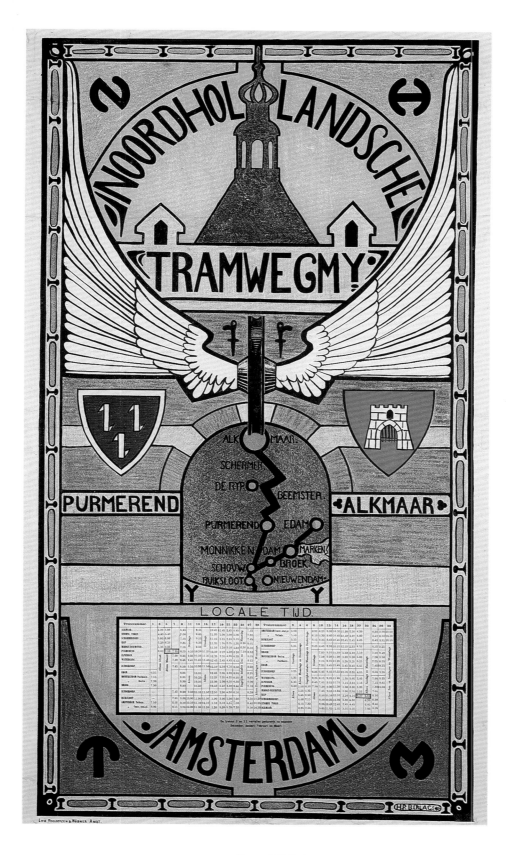

2   H. P. Berlage

North Holland Tramline
ca. 1893

3   Th. Nieuwenhuis

Delft Salad Oil
1893

DRUK VAN DE ERVEN J.J. TIJL, ZWOLLE.

4   Jan Ros

Blooker's Cocoa
1895

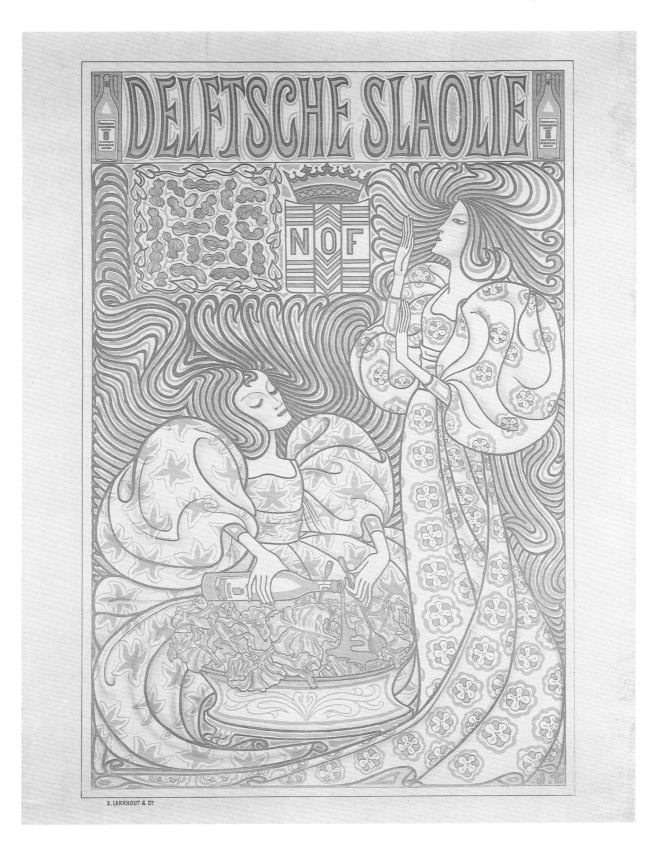

5   Jan Toorop

Delft Salad Oil
ca. 1895

6   Johan Thorn Prikker

"Bimonthly Review of the Applied Arts"
1896

7   Johannes Aarts

National Exhibition of Industry and Art
1897

8   C. A. Lion Cachet

Boele Cigars
1897

9   J. G. van Caspel

Hinde Bicycles
1896

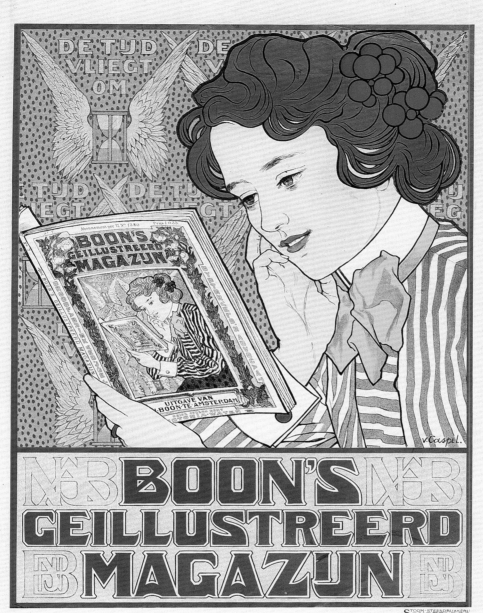

Bij <u>dezen</u> boekhandelaar ontvangt ieder, die hier <u>DRIE</u> abonné's op dit blad aanbrengt, eene premie.

MAX R. NUNES.

10   J. G. van Caspel

"Boon's Illustrated Magazine"
ca.1898-1900

11   J. G. van Caspel

Ivens and Co. Photographic Equipment
ca. 1899

12   J. G. van Caspel (attr.)

Karstel Cocoa
ca. 1897

13   Jacques Zon

Delft Salad Oil
ca. 1897

14   Jacques Zon

Spirit Incandescent Light
ca. 1898

15   Jacobus Veldheer

Aurora Press
ca. 1899

16   Th. H. Molkenboer

Elias van Bommel Bookbinder
1897

17   Wilm. Pothast

Fosco Cocoa
ca. 1900

18   Georg Rueter

Asia Tea Enterprise
1896

19   Willem van Konijnenburg

Fopsmit Water Excursions
1900

20   Tiete van der Laars

National Costume Exhibition
1898

21   Jan Toorop

Association for the Promotion of Tourism, Katwijk aan Zee
ca. 1900

22   Albert Hahn, Sr.

Fatum Accident Insurance
1909

23   Jan Sluyters

Israel Querido's "Victory"
ca. 1904

24   Jan Sluyters

Artists' Evening Party
1915

25   R. N. Roland Holst

Vondel's tragedy "Lucifer"
1910

26   R. N. Roland Holst

Goethe's "Faust"
1918

27   Jac. Jongert

International Gas Exhibition
1912

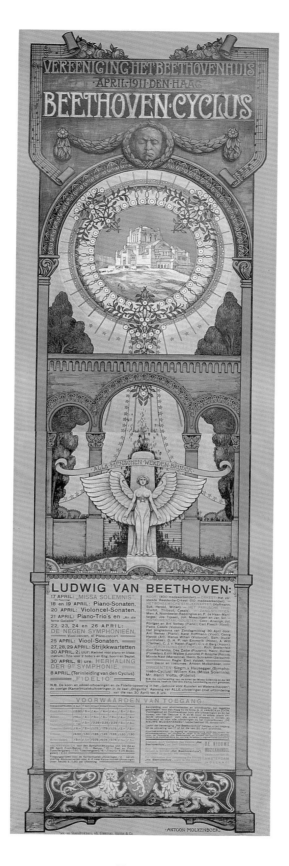

28   Antoon Molkenboer

Beethoven Cycle
1911

29   Piet van der Hem

Frascati Ensemble
1912

30   Piet van der Hem

Spyker Autos
before 1914

31   Cornelis Rol

First Dutch Maritime Exhibition
1913

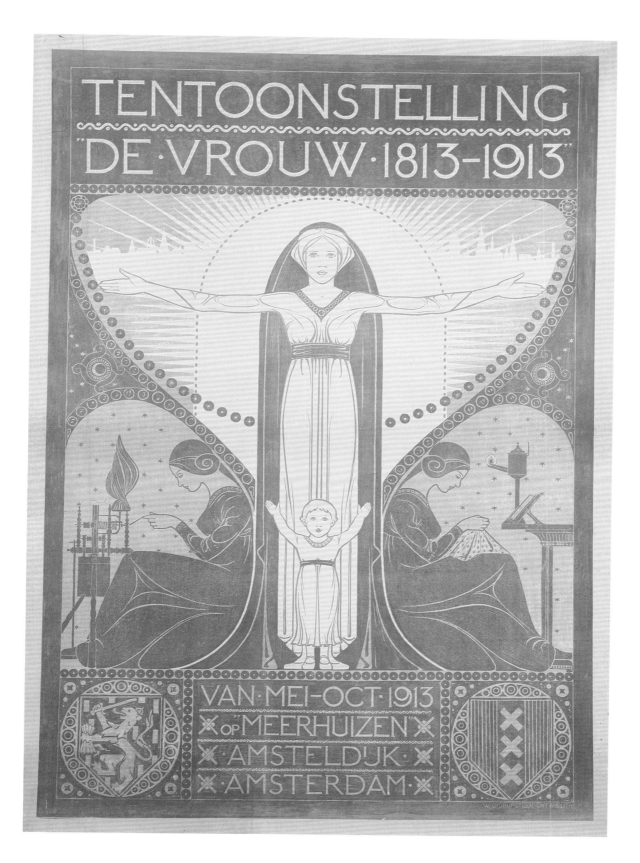

32   Wilhelmina Drupsteen

The Woman 1813-1913
1913

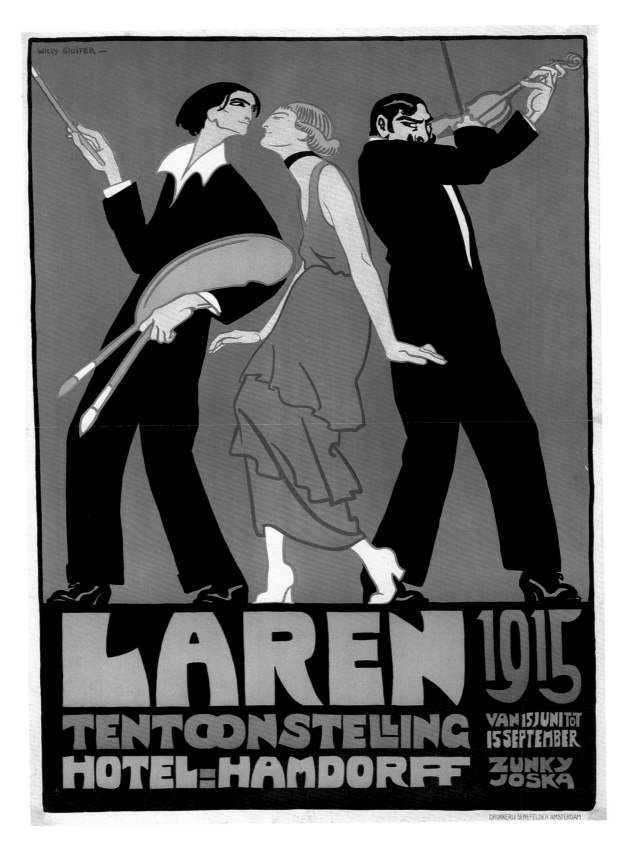

33   Willy Sluiter

Laren Exhibition
1915

34   Albert Hahn, Sr.

Vote Red!
ca. 1912

35   Bart van der Leck

Batavier Line
1914

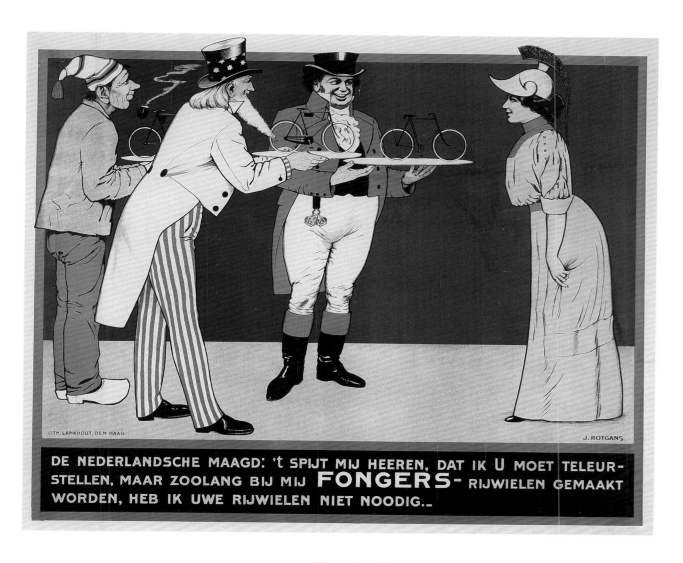

DE NEDERLANDSCHE MAAGD: 't SPIJT MIJ HEEREN, DAT IK U MOET TELEUR-STELLEN, MAAR ZOOLANG BIJ MIJ FONGERS- RIJWIELEN GEMAAKT WORDEN, HEB IK UWE RIJWIELEN NIET NOODIG..

36   Jan Rotgans

Fongers Bicycles
ca.1910-14

37   Chris Lebeau

"Hamlet"
ca. 1914

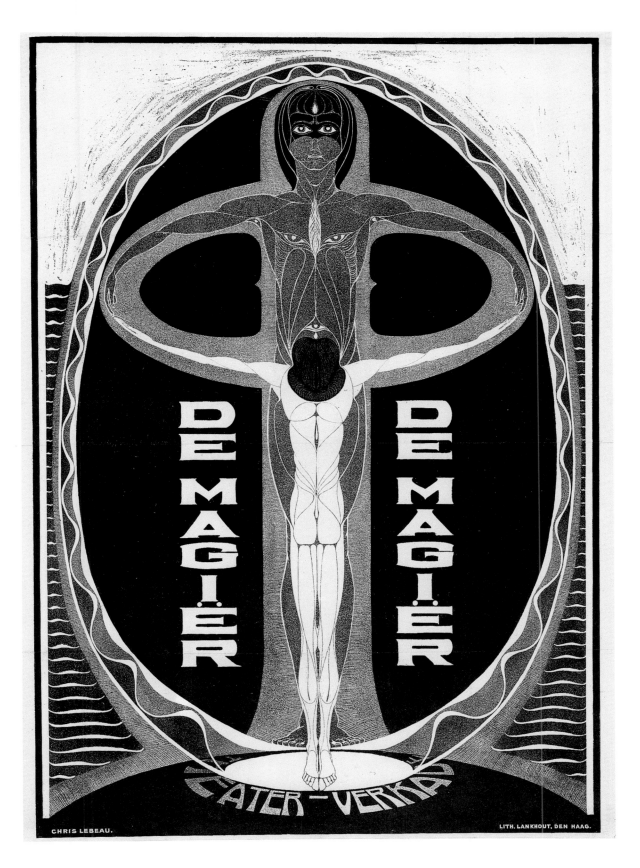

38 Chris Lebeau

"The Wizard"
ca. 1914

39   Huib Luns

The Green Cross
1915

40   Georg Rueter

South Holland Society Exhibition
1918

41   Jan Sluyters

Artists' Winter Festival
1919

42   Willy Sluiter

't Woonhuys Oriental Rugs
1916

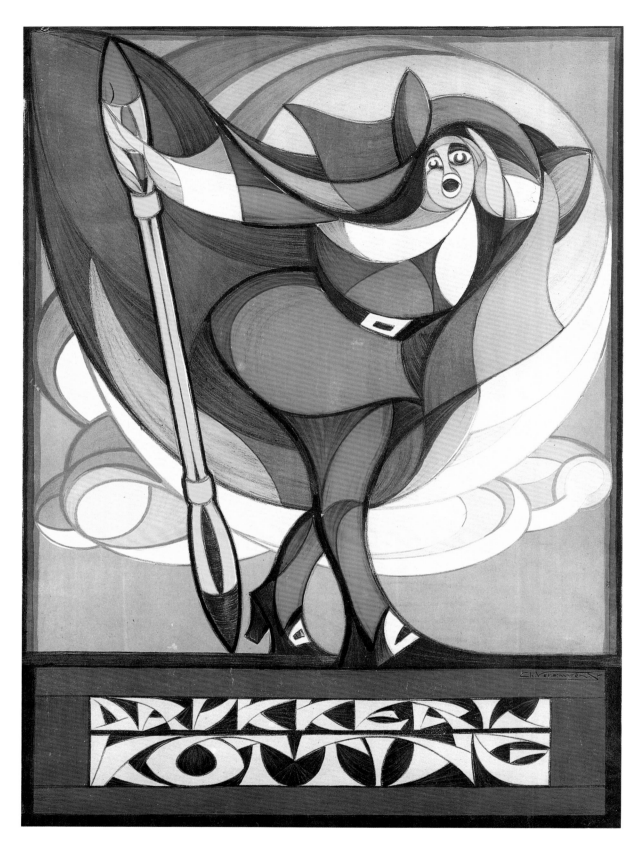

43   Ch. Verschuuren, Jr.

Kotting Press
ca. 1917

44   Albert Hemelman

Dutch Tourist Information Office
ca. 1919

45   Jan Toorop

Arthur van Schendel's "Pandorra"
1919

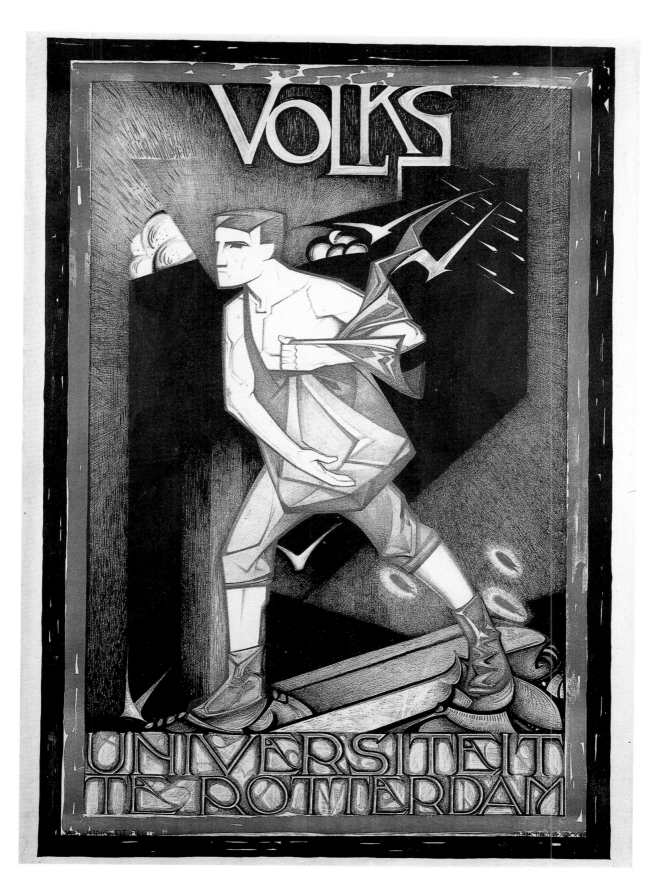

46   Jac. Jongert

University of Extramural Studies
1920

47   C. A. Lion Cachet

Annual Industries Fair, Utrecht
1917

48   Albert Hahn, Sr.

Vote Red!
1918

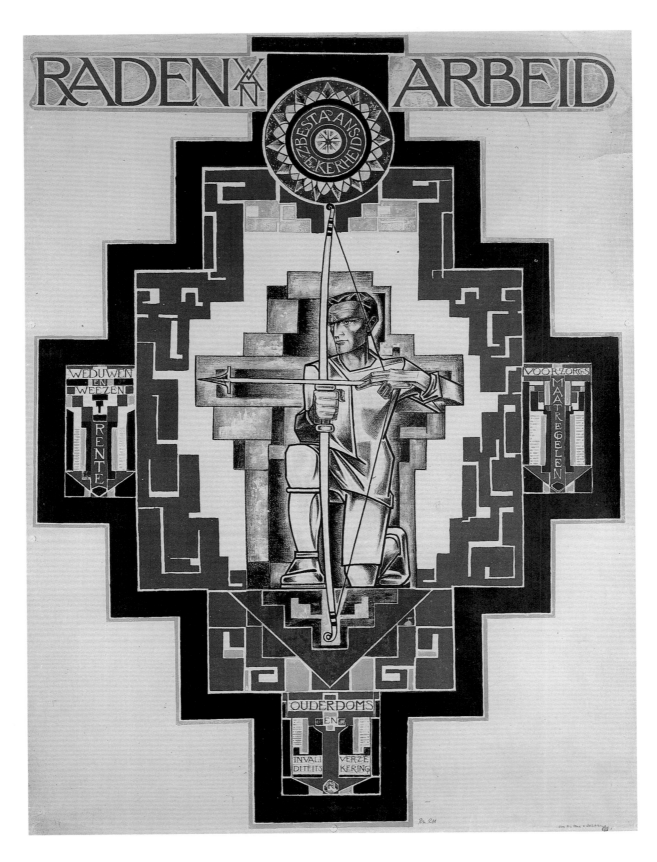

49   R. N. Roland Holst

Labor Boards
1920

50   Willem Arondéus

Dutch Exhibition, Copenhagen
1922

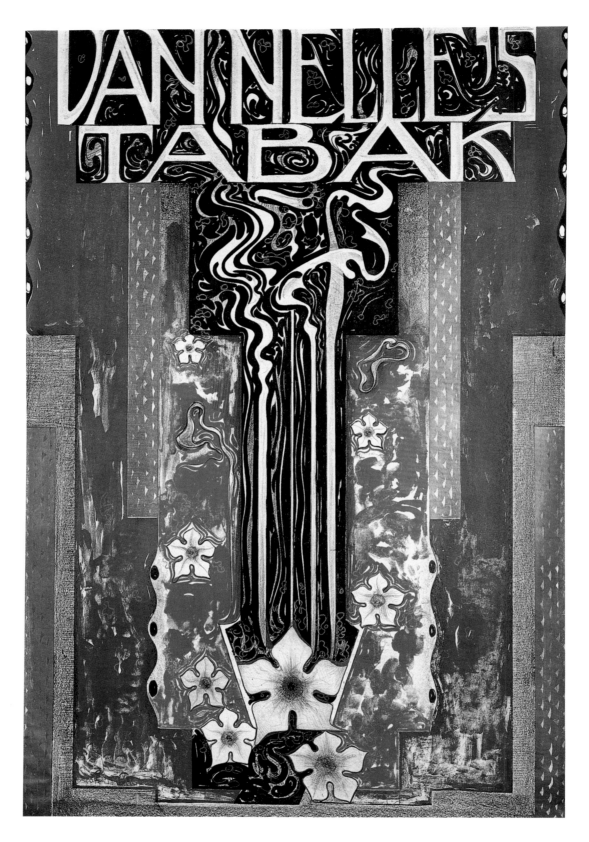

51   Jac. Jongert

Van Nelle Tobacco
1920

52   Jac. Jongert

Apricot Brandy
ca. 1920

53   Pieter Hofman

Aviation Show, The Hague
1919

54   Anthonius Guthschmidt

Royal Dutch Airlines
1924

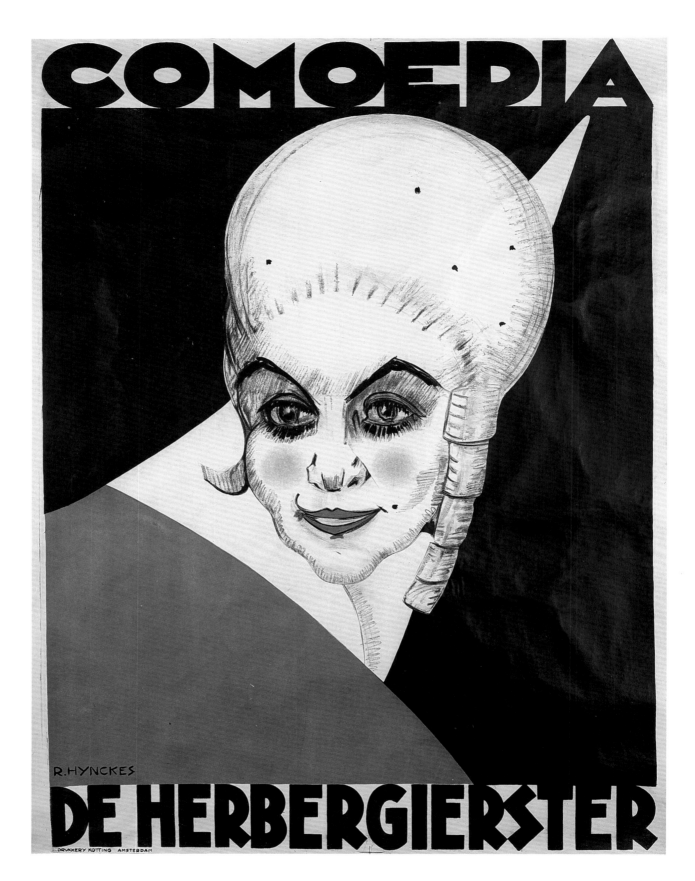

55   Raoul Hynckes

Goldoni's "La Locandiera"
1921

56   Chris Lebeau

Willem Brok Art Gallery
1925

57   Louis Raemaekers

Syphillis
ca. 1922-23

58   H. Th. Wijdeveld

International Theater Exhibition
1922

59   Leo Gestel

Arga Lamp
ca. 1922

60   Harmen Meurs

Exhibition of Independent Artists
ca. 1923-24

61   Machiel Wilmink

Exhibition of Factory and Office Administration
ca. 1923

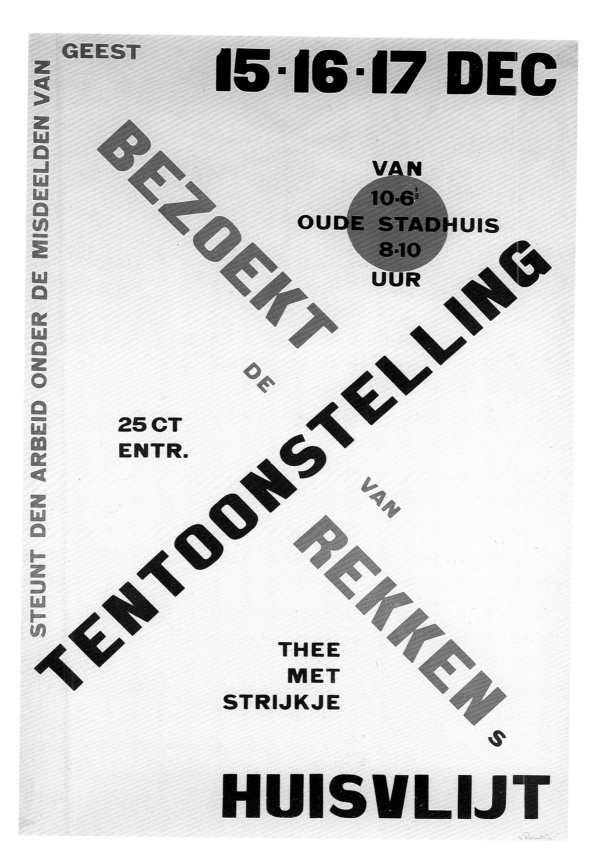

62   Sybold van Ravesteyn

Crafts Exhibition, Rekken
ca. 1927

63   Piet Zwart

Laga Rubber Floors
ca. 1922

64   Hendrik Nicolaas Werkman

Exhibition of De Ploeg
1925

65   J. J. Hellendoorn

Exhibition of Art and Industry
ca. 1923

66   H. Th. Wijdeveld

Exhibition in Honor of Th. Colenbrander
1923

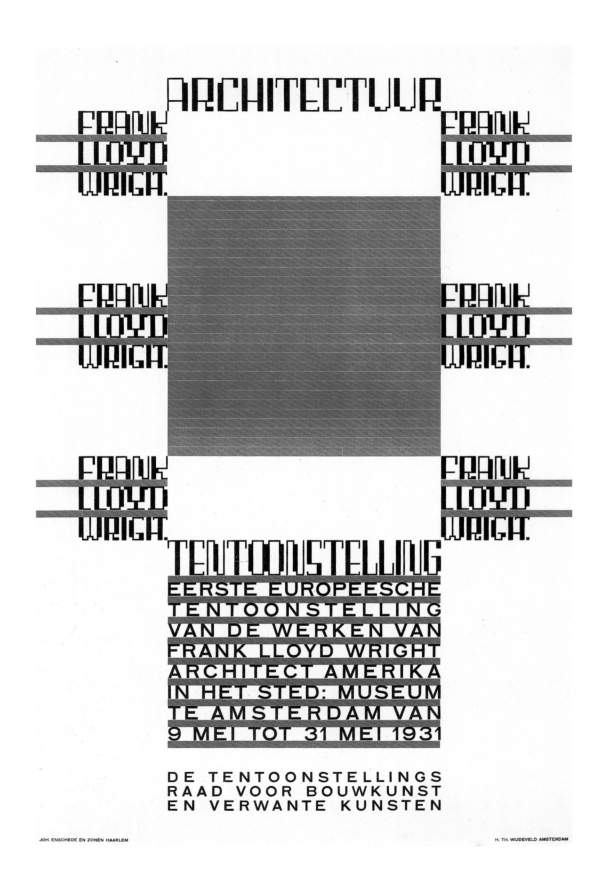

67 H. Th. Wijdeveld

Frank Lloyd Wright Exhibition
1931

68   H. Th. Wijdeveld

International Exhibition of Economics and History
1929

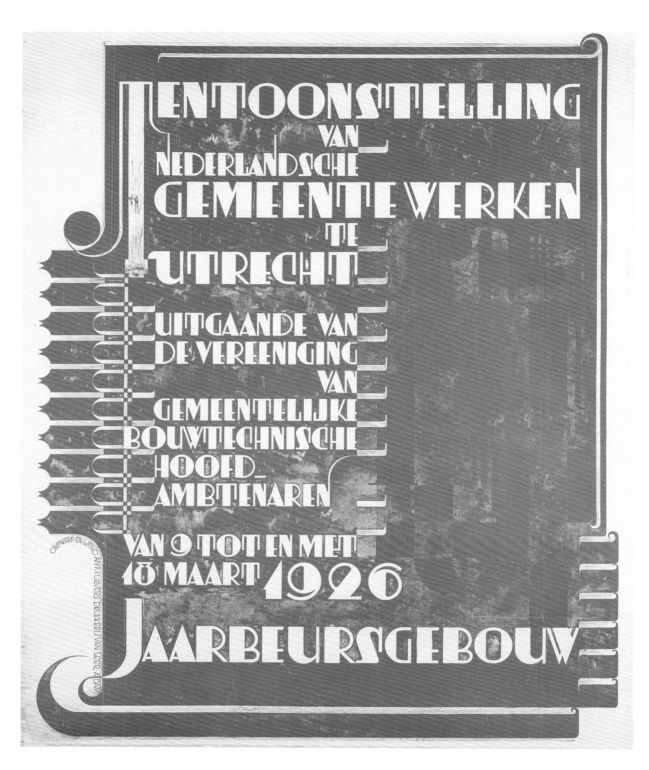

69 Antoon Kurvers

Exhibition of Dutch Municipal Works in Utrecht
1926

70   Piet Zwart

International Film Exhibition
1928

71   Dolly Rüdeman

"Potemkin"
ca. 1926

72   Fré Cohen

Dutch Federation of Trade Unions
1930

73   Jac. Jongert

Van Nelle Coffee and Tea
ca. 1930

74   A. J. Funke Küpper

"Voorwaarts"
1927

75   Pieter Hofman (attr.)

Exhibition of Garden Art
1927

76   Jacq. Bodaan

Jubilee Exhibition, The Hague Sketch Club
1933

77   Willem Gispen

Giso Lamps
1928

78   Meijer Bleekrode

Institute for Workers' Education
1932

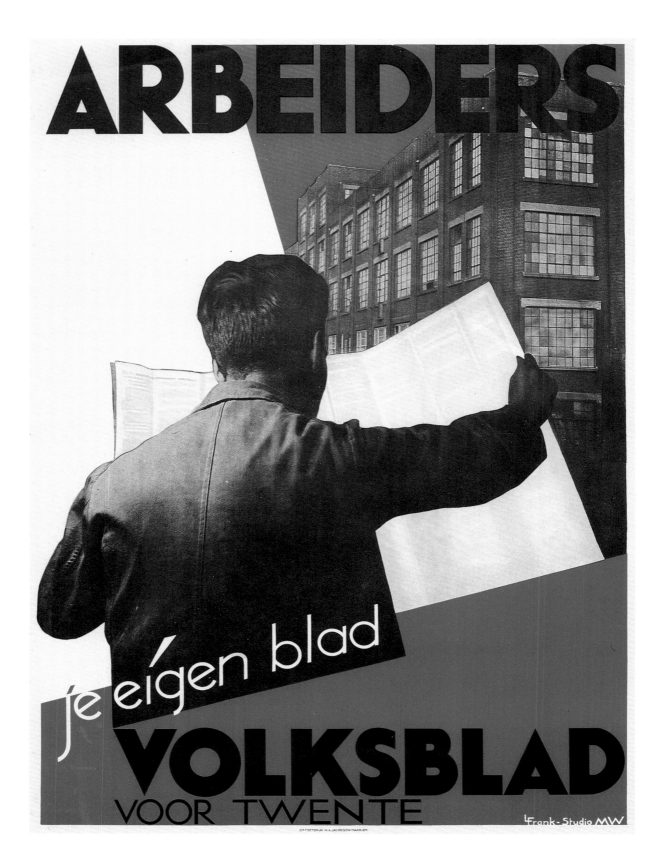

79   Louis Frank

"Volksblad," Twente
1931

80   Wim Brusse

Strong Through Work
ca. 1932

81   Z.W.

Architecture Exhibition Haarlem
1927

82   Henri Pieck

Annual Industries Fair, Utrecht
ca. 1933

83   Pieter Hofman

Annual Industries Fair, Utrecht
1930

84   Samuel Schwarz

Trotsky's "My Life"
1930

85   Meijer Bleekrode

Dutch Federation of Trade Unions Meeting
1930

86   W. J. H. B. Sandberg

Anniversary Exhibiton, The Stedelijk Museum
1935

87   Nicholaas de Koo

Castle Beer
ca. 1930

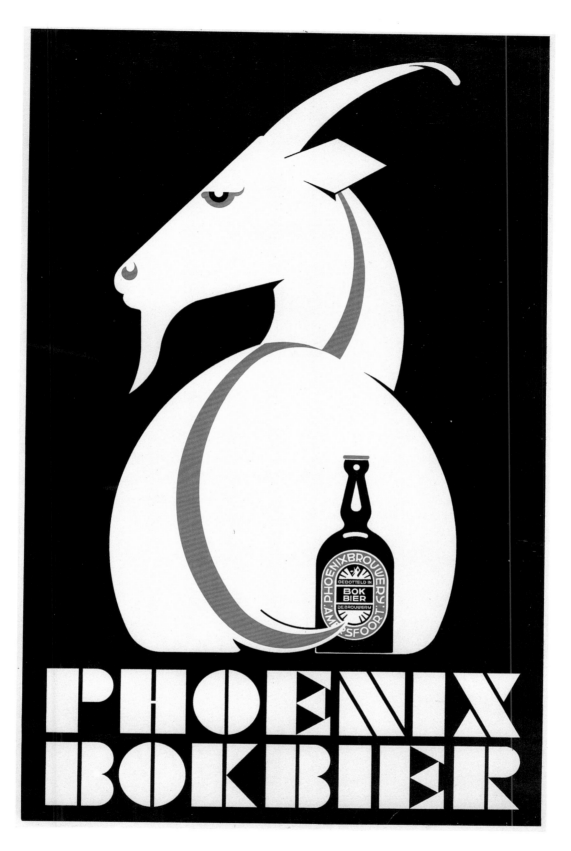

88   Nicholaas de Koo

Phoenix Beer
ca. 1930

89   Arjen Galema

Royal Dutch Airlines
ca. 1930

90   Jan Wijga

Royal Dutch Airlines
1933

91   Louis Kalff

Philips Radio
ca. 1931

92   Johann von Stein

Lloyd Lines
ca. 1930-31

93   Jan Wijga

Oranjeboom Beer
ca. 1932

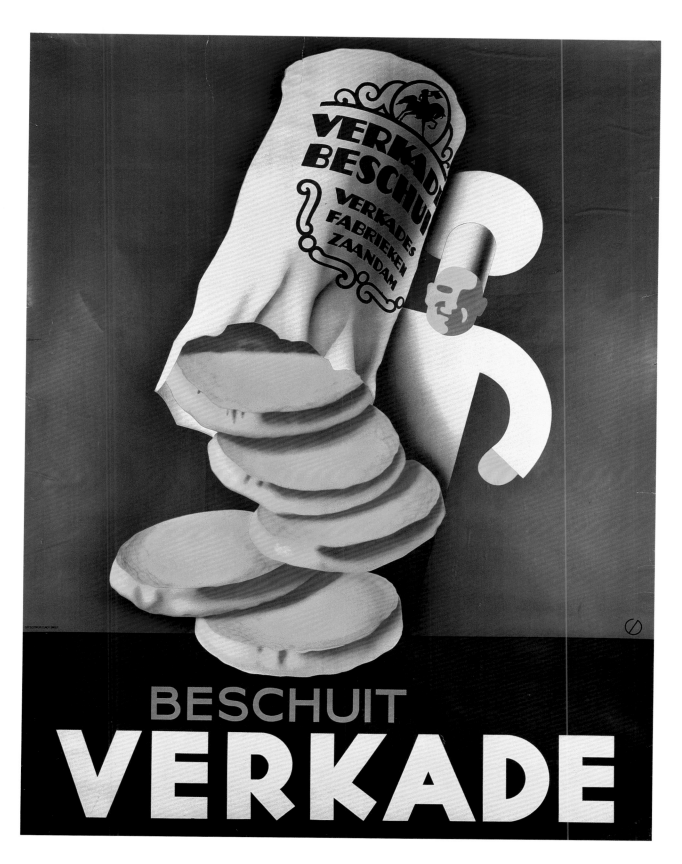

94   Kees Dekker

Verkade Biscuits
1933

Zomerfeesten Amsterdam 1932

Tentoonstelling van Kunstwerken Nederlandsche Levende Meesters Stedelijk Museum. 11 Juni-1 Sept.

95   Raoul Hynckes

Amsterdam Summer Festival
1932

96 Sjoerd de Roos

Amsterdam Music Festival
1933

97   Joop Sjollema

"Boris Godounov"
1931

98   Aart van Dobbenburgh

The Drinker
1935

99   Fré Cohen

Willem Pijper's "Halewijn"
1933

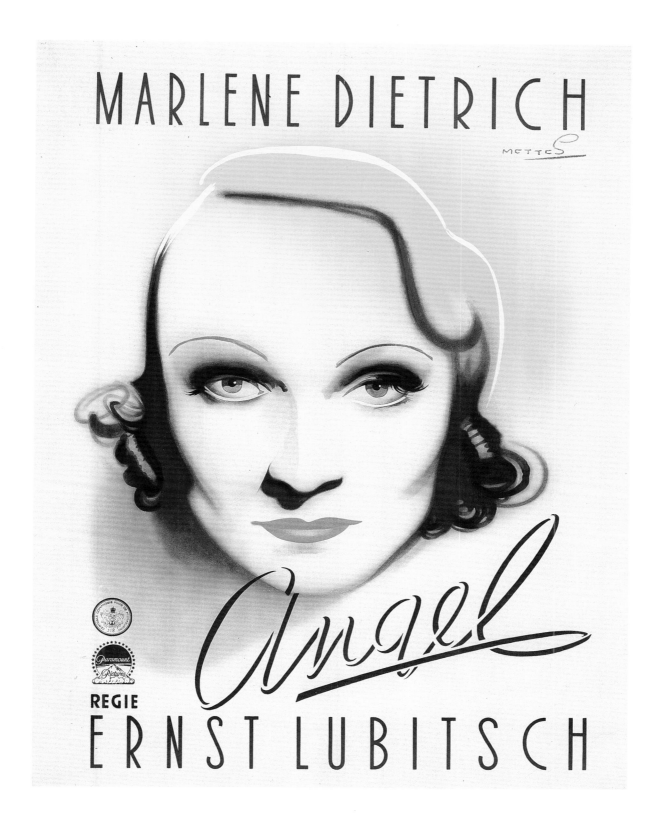

100   Frans Mettes

"Angel"
1937

101   Wim ten Broek

Holland-America Line
1936

102   Agnes Canta

Annual Industries Fair, Utrecht
ca. 1937

Catalogue

In the listing the following information is given: artist, date of work, medium, dimensions in centimeters and inches, printer, lender, and translated text. Lenders are indicated by initials.
Bernice Jackson: BJ
Jacques G. de Jong: JJ
Krannert Art Museum: KAM
Martijn Le Coultre: MLC
Werner Löwenhardt: WL
Stedelijk Museum: SM

1
Artist Unknown, 1870-76
Lithograph
86 x 62cm, 34 x 24¾in
Tresling and Co., Hof-Lith., Amsterdam
WL

Hotel Grand Café Neuf
Kalverstraat near the Dam Square
W. P. Werker
Amsterdam

2
H. P. Berlage, ca.1893
Lithograph
103 x 58cm, 40½ x 22½in
Roeloffzen and Hübner, Amsterdam
MLC

North Holland Tramline
Purmerend-Alkmaar
local time (with timetable)
Amsterdam

3
Th. Nieuwenhuis, 1893
Lithograph
68 x 57cm, 27 x 22¼in
L. Kuipers, Amsterdam
MLC

Dutch Oil Works, Delft
Delft Salad Oil

4
Jan Ros, 1895
Lithograph
86 x 63cm, 34¼ x 24¾in
De Erven J. J. Tijl, Zwolle
BJ

Blooker's Cocoa
Blooker pure cocoa
registered trademark

5
Jan Toorop, ca.1895
Lithograph
100 x 70cm, 39½ x 27½in
S. Lankhout and Co.
MLC

Delft Salad Oil
Dutch Oil Works (NOF)

6
Johan Thorn Prikker, 1896
Lithograph
135 x 99cm, 53 x 39in
Lith. S. Lankhout and Co.
MLC

Bimonthly Review of the Applied Arts
editor and publisher, H. Kleinmann and Co., 9 Kenaupark, Haarlem, Holland.
price 20 guilders a year, 15 prints in every issue.

7
Johannes Aarts, 1897
Lithograph
150 x 88cm, 59 x 34½in
Lith. Lankhout, The Hague
WL

Dordrecht June-September 1897
national exhibition of industry and art

8
C. A. Lion Cachet, 1897
Lithograph
74 x 57cm, 29 x 22½in
Lith. Lankhout, The Hague
WL

Cigars
W. G. Boele, Sr.
By appointment to the Court
Kampen, 1847-1897

9
J. G. van Caspel, 1896
Lithograph
80 x 108cm, 31½ x 42½in
Steendruk v/h Amand, Amsterdam
WL

Hinde bicycles
Amsterdam factory

10
J. G. van Caspel, ca.1898-1900
Lithograph
82 x 51cm, 32½ x 20½in
Stoom-Steendrukkerij Senefelder, Amsterdam
MLC

Boon's Illustrated Magazine
On the wall: Time flies
Whoever brings in *three* subscribers of the
magazine to this book dealer will receive a
premium.

11
J. G. van Caspel, ca.1899
Lithograph
64 x 98cm, 26 x 39¼in
Printer unknown
JJ

Ivens and Co. photographic equipment

12
J. G. van Caspel (attr.) ca.1897
Lithograph
91 x 133cm, 35 x 52½in
Lankhout, The Hague
WL

100 grams, 24 cents
Karstel Cocoa

13
Jacques Zon, ca.1897
Lithograph
182 x 70cm, 71½ x 27½in
Lith. S. Lankhout and Co., The Hague
MLC

Delft Salad Oil
Delft, Dutch Oil Works

14
Jacques Zon, ca.1898
Lithograph
97 x 63cm, 38 x 25in
Emrik and Binger, Haarlem
WL

Spirit incandescent light
Dutch Yeast and Spirit Factory

15
Jacobus Veldheer, ca.1899
Woodcut
75 x 53cm, 29½ x 21in
Aurora, Amsterdam
WL

Steam Printing Press "Aurora"
founded 1894
14 St. Luciensteeg, Amsterdam

16
Th. H. Molkenboer, 1897
Woodcut
85 x 61cm, 33½ x 24½in
Printer unknown
MLC

Elias van Bommel
bookbinder
53 Kerkstraat
Amsterdam

17
Wilm. Pothast, ca.1900
Lithograph
112 x 80cm, 44 x 31½in
Lith. J. A. Luii and Co., Amsterdam
MLC

F. Korff & Co.
cocoa manufacturers, Amsterdam
Fosco
It's drunk cold.

18
Georg Rueter, 1896
Lithograph
99 x 65cm, 39 x 25½in
Lith. Braakensiek Brothers, Amsterdam
WL

Asia Tea Enterprise
Grippeling and Co.
Amsterdam

19
Willem van Konijnenburg, 1900
Lithograph
100 x 66cm, 39½ x 26in
J. Vurtheim and Son
MLC

Fopsmit and Co.
timetable
summer timetable from 10 March to 20
October
water excursions

20
Tiete van der Laars, 1898
Lithograph
148 x 48cm, 58 x 19in
van Leer, Amsterdam
WL

Inauguration exhibition
national costumes of Her Majesty's subjects
Stedelijk Museum in Amsterdam
August to November 1898

21
Jan Toorop, ca.1900
Lithograph
99 x 70cm, 39 x 27½in
S. Lankhout and Co., The Hague
MLC

Association for the Promotion of Tourism,
Katwijk aan Zee

22
Albert Hahn, Sr., 1909
Lithograph
99 x 62cm, 38¼ x 24¼in
Drukkerij Senefelder, Amsterdam
MLC

Fatum Accident Insurance Company
The Hague-Batavia

23
Jan Sluyters, ca.1904
Lithograph
116 x 66cm, 45¾ x 26in
Drukkerij Senefelder, Amsterdam
MLC

Victory
by Israel Querido
Scheltens & Giltay, Amsterdam

24
Jan Sluyters, 1915
Lithograph
115 x 72cm, 45 x 28¼in
Drukkerij Senefelder, Amsterdam
WL

Evening party
29 May 1915
Concertgebouw, Amsterdam
Association of Dutch Artists' Societies

25
R. N. Roland Holst, 1910
Lithograph
123 x 75cm, 48½ x 29½in
Tresling and Co., Amsterdam
MLC

The Stage, Ltd.
director, Willem Royaards
Lucifer
tragedy by Vondel
music by Robert Cuypers
stage and costume designs by R. N. Roland
Holst

26
R. N. Roland Holst, 1918
Lithograph
115 x 85cm, 45¼ x 33¼in
Drukkerij Senefelder, Amsterdam
MLC

The Stage, Ltd.
director, Willem Royaards
Goethe's *Faust*

27
Jac. Jongert, 1912
Lithograph
150 x 75cm, 59 x 29½in
Printer unknown
WL

International gas exhibition, Amsterdam
14 September-6 October 1912
in the Paleis voor Volksvlijt

28
Antoon Molkenboer, 1911
Lithograph
199.5 x 62.7cm, 78½ x 24¾in
Boek- en Steendrukkerij v/h Ellerman,
Harms and Co.
KAM

Beethoven House Society
April 1911, The Hague
Beethoven cycle
All men shall be brothers
Ludwig van Beethoven
(program and terms of admission)

29
Piet van der Hem, 1912
Lithograph
150 x 84cm, 59 x 33¼in
L. van Leer and Co., Amsterdam
MLC

Frascati Ensemble
Directors: L. Chrispijn, Jr., and Jacq. van Biene
The Little Café

30
Piet van der Hem, before 1914
Lithograph
112 x 84cm, 44¼ x 32¾in
Drukkerij Senefelder, Amsterdam
MLC

Spyker autos
Industrial Company Trompenburg, Amsterdam

31
Cornelis Rol, 1913
Lithograph
104 x 63cm, 41¼ x 25¼in
Ellerman, Harms and Co.
MLC

ENTOS
first Dutch maritime exhibition
1913
from June to October
Amsterdam

32
Wilhelmina Drupsteen, 1913
Lithograph
117 x 81cm, 46 x 32in
Printer unknown
WL

Exhibition
The Woman, 1813-1913
from May to October 1913, in Meerhuizen,
Amsteldijk, Amsterdam

33
Willy Sluiter, 1915
Lithograph
109 x 76cm, 42¾ x 29¾in
Drukkerij Senefelder, Amsterdam
MLC

Laren exhibition
Hotel Hamdorff
1915, from 15 June to 15 September
Zunky Joska (violinist)

34
Albert Hahn, Sr., ca.1912
Lithograph
110 x 79cm, 43½ x 31½in
Printer unknown
MLC

Vote Red!

35
Bart van der Leck, 1914
Lithograph
74 x 110cm, 29¼ x 43¼in
Geuze, Dordrecht
MLC

Batavier Line
the cheapest and most convenient way
regular service for cargo and passengers
Rotterdam-London
custom house & wool quays
Lower Thames Street, London
Wm. H. Müller & Co.
Rotterdam, Willemsplein

36
Jan Rotgans, ca.1910-1914
Lithograph
97 x 117cm, 38 x 46¼in
Lankhout, The Hague
WL

The Dutch maiden: "I'm sorry, gentlemen, to
have to disappoint you, but as long as Fongers
makes bicycles here at home, I have no need
of your bicycles."

37
Chris Lebeau, ca.1914
Lithograph
124 x 88cm, 49¼ x 34¾in
Mortelmans' Drukkerij
MLC

Hamlet
EV (Eduard Verkade)
The Hague Players

38
Chris Lebeau, ca.1914
Lithograph
124 x 89cm, 49 x 35in
Lankhout, The Hague
MLC

The Wizard (G. K. Chesterton's *Magic*)
Verkade Theater

39
Huib Luns, 1915
Linocut
85 x 50cm, 33½ x 19¾in
Printer unknown
MLC

South Holland Society
The Green Cross
Kill flies
Be tidy
and you save human lives
No dirt, no flies
Scarlet fever, typhus, cholera, tuberculosis,
diphtheria can be transmitted by flies
Fight the danger of flies
Kill flies, especially early in summer, for they
multiply very quickly.

40
Georg Rueter, 1918
Lithograph
114 x 79cm, 44¾ x 31¼in
Corns. Immig, Rotterdam
WL

South Holland Society for the Promotion of
Applied Art and Folk Art
exhibition
Academy Coolvest, Rotterdam
27 April-27 May

41
Jan Sluyters, 1919
Lithograph
115 x 80cm, 45¼ x 31¼in
Printer unknown
WL

Artists' winter festival
The Hague, 1919

42
Willy Sluiter, 1916
Lithograph
145 x 99cm, 57 x 39in
Drukkerij Senefelder, Amsterdam
MLC

Oriental rugs 't Woonhuys, Amsterdam

43
Ch. Verschuuren, Jr., ca.1917
Lithograph
110 x 80cm, 43½ x 31½in
Kotting
MLC

Kotting Press

44
Albert Hemelman, ca.1919
Lithograph
100 x 70cm, 39¼ x 27½in
Imp. van Roessel and Co., Amsterdam
WL

Official Dutch Tourist Information Office
The Hague
30 Hooge Nieuwstraat

45
Jan Toorop, 1919
Lithograph
113 x 84.5cm, 44½ x 33¼in
Lankhout, The Hague
MLC

Pandorra
(by) Arthur van Schendel
K. V. the Dutch Theater

46
Jac. Jongert, 1920
Lithograph
125 x 86cm, 49 x 34in
Immig and Son
MLC

University of extramural studies, Rotterdam

47
C. A. Lion Cachet, 1917
Lithograph
99 x 68cm, 40 x 27in
Lith. v/h Roeloffzen-Hübner, and van Santen,
Amsterdam
MLC

1917
Utrecht
annual industries fair
26 February-10 March

48
Albert Hahn, Sr., 1918
Lithograph
109 x 79cm, 43 x 31in
Drukkerij v/h Luii and Co., Amsterdam
WL

Vote Red!
capitalism, anarchy, hunger, the sufferings
of war, price-gouging
Vote for the candidates of the Social
Democratic Workers' Party

49
R. N. Roland Holst, 1920
Lithograph
110 x 80cm, 43¼ x 31½in
Printer unknown
MLC

Labor Boards
social security
widows' and orphans' funds
preventive measures
old age and disability pensions

50
Willem Arondéus, 1922
Lithograph
84 x 62cm, 33¼ x 24¼in
Drukkerij Senefelder, Amsterdam
MLC

The Dutch Exhibition
Copenhagen, July-August, 1922

51
Jac. Jongert, 1920
Lithograph
99 x 65cm, 39 x 25½in
Immig and Son
MLC

Van Nelle's tobacco

52
Jac. Jongert, ca.1920
Lithograph
100 x 77cm, 39½ x 30½in
Immig and Son
MLC

Apricot brandy
Wed. G. Oud Pz. & Co., Purmerend
sales office, Surabaya

53
Pieter Hofman, 1919
Lithograph
64 x 43cm, 25 x 17in
Lith Lankhout, The Hague
MLC

National-international 3-day aviation show
on the Ockenburgh Estate
Loosduinen, The Hague
26-27-28 September 1919

54
Anthonius Guthschmidt, 1924
Lithograph
102 x 77cm, 40 x 30in
van de Ven, The Hague
MLC

Royal Dutch Airlines
The Flying Dutchman
No myth but reality

55
Raoul Hynckes, 1921
Lithograph
110 x 80cm, 43¼ x 31½in
Drukkerij Kotting, Amsterdam
MLC

Comedy
De Herbergierster (Goldoni's La Locandiera)

56
Chris Lebeau, 1925
Linocut
125 x 86cm, 49¼ x 34in
Luctor et Emergo
WL

Art Gallery Willem Brok, Hilversum
permanent exhibition of visual arts
6 van Lenneplaan, tel. 628
opening November
admission 50 cents, Saturdays 25 cents,
closed Sundays
with the cooperation of . . .

57
Louis Raemaekers, ca.1922-23
Lithograph
119 x 77cm, 47 x 30¼in
J. E. Goossens, Brussels
MLC

The hecatomb
syphilis

58
H. Th. Wijdeveld, 1922
Lithograph
140 x 60cm, 55 x 23½in
Printer unknown
BJ

Art to the people
international theater exhibition
Stedelijk Museum, 21 January-28 February,
Amsterdam

59
Leo Gestel, ca.1922
Lithograph
103 x 78cm, 40½ x 30½in
Printer unknown
WL

Philips
Arga Lamp

60
Harmen Meurs, ca.1923-24
Lithograph
108 x 76cm, 42½ x 30in
van Roessel and Co.
MLC

The Independents
exhibition
drawings, graphic art, sculpture
Stedelijk Museum
from 23 November to 15 December
admission 25 cents, tax included
catalogue 10 cents

61
Machiel Wilmink, ca.1923
Lithograph
101 x 66cm, 40 x 26in
Drukkerij De Ijsel, Deventer
MLC

FEKA
exhibition of factory and office administration
29 September-7 October
at the Buitensociëteit in Deventer
open from 12:30 to 5 and from 7 to 10

62
Sybold van Ravesteyn, ca.1927
Lithograph
99 x 65cm, 39 x 25½in
Printer unknown
MLC

Support the work of the poor in spirit
Visit the exhibition of the home crafts of
Rekken
tea, with a string orchestra
15-16-17 December
from 10-6:30, 8-10
Old City Hall
admission 25 cents

63
Piet Zwart, ca.1922
Offset
91 x 65cm, 36 x 25½in
Printer unknown
MLC

Laga "Loco"
rubber floors
imported by Vickers House Laga
21 Prinsessegracht, The Hague

64
Hendrik Nicolaas Werkman, 1925
Letterpress
92.3 x 40.6cm, 36¼ x 16 in
Printed by Werkman
SM

2-17 May
de Ploeg in pictures (art
exhibition poster)

65
J. J. Hellendoorn, ca.1923
Letterpress
89 x 59cm, 35¼ x 23½in
Printer unknown
MLC

Dutch Society for the Preservation of the
Applied Arts
arti et industriae
exhibition
modern interior art
16-24 April
Doornstraat, near Statenlaan
admission 25 cents
illustrated catalogue included

66
H. Th. Wijdeveld, 1923
Letterpress
100 x 58cm, 39½ x 23in
Printer unknown
MLC

Exhibition in honor of Th. Colenbrander
earthenware and rugs
Stedelijk Museum, Amsterdam, 1923
31 October-30 November
10-4, admission 25 cents

67
H. Th. Wijdeveld, 1931
Letterpress
78 x 50cm, 30½ x 19½in
Joh. Enschedé and Sons, Haarlem
MLC

Architecture
Frank Lloyd Wright
exhibition
first European exhibition of the work of Frank
Lloyd Wright, architect, America, in the
Stedelijk Museum in Amsterdam, from 9 May
to 31 May 1931
The Exhibition Council for Architecture and
Related Arts

68
H. Th. Wijdeveld, 1929
Letterpress
65 x 60cm, 25½ x 20in
De Bussy, Amsterdam
WL

International exhibition of economics and
history
4 July-15 September 1929
paintings, miniatures, tapestries, documents,
models, prints, etc.
Stedelijk Museum, Amsterdam

69
Antoon Kurvers, 1926
Lithograph
99 x 79cm, 39½ x 31½in
Drukkerij van Leer, Amsterdam
MLC

Exhibition of Dutch municipal works in Utrecht
organized by the Society of Senior Municipal
Building Officials
9-10 March 1926
Industries Fair Building

70
Piet Zwart, 1928
Photolithograph
109 x 78cm, 43 x 30½in
J. Strang and Co., The Hague
MLC

International exhibition of film
IFT
film
14 April-15 May 1928
Grote Koninklijke Bazar, 82 Zeestraat,
The Hague

71
Dolly Rüdeman, ca.1926
Lithograph
105 x 63cm, 41½ x 24½in
Printer unknown
WL

Potemkin

72
Fré Cohen, 1930
Lithograph
90 x 59cm, 35½ x 23¼in
Printer unknown
WL

Dutch Federation of Trade Unions (NVV)-Social
Democratic Workers' Party (SDAP)
It's the future of your child that counts – the
child born for happiness
14 September, Rotterdam

73
Jac. Jongert, ca.1930
Photolithograph
78 x 63cm, 30¾ x 24¾in
Printer unknown
WL

Van Nelle
coffee
tea
produced with care

74
A. J. Funke Küpper, 1927
Lithograph
117 x 84cm, 46 x 33in
M. A. Jacobson, Haarlem
MLC

Voorwaarts
Your beacon

75
Pieter Hofman (attr.), 1927
Photolithograph
83 x 62cm, 32¾ x 24¼in
Lith. Lankhout, The Hague
MLC

17-29 September 1927
exhibition of garden art
8 Binnenhof, The Hague
Union of Dutch Market Gardeners (BNT)
The Hague Art Society (HK)
open from 11-5
admission 25 cents

76
Jacq. Bodaan, 1933
Lithograph
88 x 72cm, 34¾ x 28¾in
Printer unknown
MLC

Jubilee
1903-1933
exhibition
The Hague Sketch Club
open from 4-27 November 1933, 10-5,
Sundays 2-5, in the Koninklijke Kunstzaal,
Kleykamp

77
Willem Gispen, 1928
Photolithograph
100 x 71cm, 39¼ x 27½in
Kühn and Son, Rotterdam
MLC

Giso lamps
Gispen, 101 Voorhaven, Rotterdam
Showroom: 299 Singel, Amsterdam

78
Meijer Bleekrode, 1932
Photolithograph
60 x 41cm, 23½ x 16in
Offset De Jong and Co., Hilversum
MLC

Institute for Workers' Education
workers' evening schools
our work
Become a student!
clubs and lectures, workers' evening schools
and leadership training
IVAO

79
Louis Frank, 1931
Photolithograph
76 x 55cm, 29¾ x 21½in
Offsetdruk M. A. Jacobson, Haarlem
MLC

Workers
your own newspaper
Volksblad for Twente

80
Wim Brusse, ca.1932
Photolithograph
99 x 58cm, 39 x 23in
Kunstrdruk Luii and Co., Amsterdam
MLC

Strong through work
Do not wait
Now
Place orders!

81
Z. W., 1927
Lithograph
109 x 59cm, 43 x 23in
Neodruk N. V. Wed. J. Ahrend and Son, Amsterdam
MLC

Architecture exhibition
1927
Haarlem, 22-30 October
regional branch of the Union of Dutch Ar-
chitects
Statenzaal, entrance Pandpoort
open 10-5 and 8-10, Sundays 2-5
admission 50 cents

82
Henri Pieck, ca.1933
Lithograph
101 x 75cm, 40 x 29½in
Steendrukkerij DeMaas, Rotterdam
WL

Dutch international industries fair, Utrecht
9 to 18 March

83
Pieter Hofman, 1930
Photolithograph
62 x 79cm, 24¼ x 31½in
Printer unknown
JJ

Annual Dutch international industries fair,
Utrecht

84
Samuel Schwarz, 1930
Lithograph
87 x 53cm, 34¼ x 20¾in
Printer unknown
MLC

Trotsky
My Life

85
Meijer Bleekrode, 1930
Photolithograph
80 x 55cm, 31½ x 21¾in
Printer unknown
MLC

14 September (meeting) in Amsterdam
Dutch Federation of Trade Unions (NVV)
Social Democratic Workers' Party (SDAP)
against war
for state pensions

86
W. J. H. B. Sandberg, 1935
Photolithograph
98 x 69cm, 39¼ x 27in
Printer unknown
WL

Exhibition on the occasion of the 40th
anniversary of the Stedelijk Museum in
Amsterdam
monumental art
14 September-13 October 1935

87
Nicolaas de Koo, ca.1930
Photolithograph
105 x 53cm, 41½ x 21 in
Printer unknown
MLC

anno 1436
Castle Beer

88
Nicolaas de Koo, ca.1930
Photolithograph
88 x 56cm, 34½ x 22¼in
Printer unknown
WL

Phoenix Beer

89
Arjen Galema, ca.1930
Photolithograph
100 x 66cm, 39½ x 25¾in
Kunstdruk Luii and Co., Amsterdam
WL

KLM
The Flying Dutchman

90
Jan Wijga, 1933
4-color photolithograph
99 x 63cm, 39 x 24¾in
Kunstdruk Luii and Co., Amsterdam
MLC

Royal Dutch Airlines
The Flying Dutchman
Fiction becomes fact

91
Louis Kalff, ca.1931
Photolithograph
111 x 77.5cm, 44 x 30½in
Smeets, Weert
JJ

Philips Radio

92
Johann von Stein, ca.1930-31
Gravure
72 x 45cm, 28½ x 18in
Nederlandse Rotogravure My N. V., Leiden
MLC

Sumatra-Java
Rotterdam Lloyd

93
Jan Wijga, ca.1932
4-color photolithograph
79 x 56cm, 31 x 22in
Luii and Co., Amsterdam
MLC

Oranjeboom Beer

94
Kees Dekker, 1933
4-color photolithograph
120 x 88cm, 47 x 34¾in
Offsetdrukkerij Flach, Sneek
WL

Verkade Biscuits

95
Raoul Hynckes, 1932
Photolithograph
89 x 63cm, 34½ x 25in
Printer unknown
MLC

Summer fesitval, Amsterdam, 1932
exhibition of works of art by living Dutch
masters
Stedelijk Museum, 11 June-1 September

96
Sjoerd de Roos, 1933
Photolithograph
100 x 62cm, 39¾ x 24½in
L. van Leer and Co., N. V., Amsterdam
MLC

Amsterdam music festival
International Society for Contemporary Music
art exhibitions
sports demonstrations
jubilee, Dutch Automobile Association
summer 1933
Dutch Railways

97
Joop Sjollema, 1931
Lithograph
92 x 123cm, 36 x 48in
L. van Leer and Co., Amsterdam
MLC

Chaliapin
Boris Godounov

98
Aart van Dobbenburgh, 1935
Lithograph
106 x 75cm, 42½ x 29¼in
Printer unknown
MLC

The drinker
The Blue Week Committee

99
Fré Cohen, 1933
Offset
74 x 120cm, 29 x 47in
van Leer and Co., Amsterdam
BJ

Wagner Society
City Theater
14 June 1933
Willem Pijper
Halewijn

100
Frans Mettes, 1937
Photolithograph
80 x 62cm, 31¾ x 24¼in
Printer unknown
MLC

Marlene Dietrich
Angel
directed by Ernst Lubitsch

101
Wim ten Broek, 1936
4-color photolithograph
99 x 64cm, 38¼ x 25¼in
Joh. Enschedé and Sons, Haarlem
WL

Holland-America Line

102
Agnes Canta, ca.1937
Photolithograph
100 x 73cm, 39 x 29¼in
Printer unknown
WL

6-15 September
Utrecht
annual international industries fair

Biographies

Aarts, Johannes Josephus
(The Hague, August 18, 1871-Amsterdam, October 19, 1934) Landscape painter and art critic but known primarily as a graphic artist. Studied at The Hague Academy of Fine Arts, where he later taught. Afterward appointed professor at the Rijksakademie in Amsterdam. Active in The Hague until 1911, then in Amsterdam.
Plate 7

Arondéus, Willem John Cornelis
(Naarden, August 22, 1894-Haarlem, July 1, 1943) Figure painter, decorator, art critic, and novelist; known mainly for his wall paintings in a symbolist vein, among them decorations for the Rotterdam city hall. Studied at the Quellinusschool, Amsterdam. Active in Amsterdam, Rotterdam, Apeldoorn.
Plate 50

Berlage, Hendrik Petrus
(Amsterdam, February 21, 1856-The Hague, August 12, 1934) Architect and designer, the leading Dutch architect of his generation. Early in his career he also painted. Best known for his design of the Amsterdam Stock Exchange (1898-1903). 1875-78 studied at the Polytechnikum in Zurich. 1889 began independent practice in Amsterdam, where he exerted a major influence on 20th-century Dutch architecture. His conception of building, according to which decoration must always be subordinated to structure and the definition of space, was published in his *Gedanken über Stil in der Baukunst*, Leipzig, 1905.
Plate 2

Bleekrode, Meijer
(Amsterdam, February 13, 1896-Sobibor [Poland], April 23, 1943) Best known for his political prints and drawings. Trained in the family business as a diamond worker. 1922-23 studied at the Quellinusschool in Amsterdam and from 1923 at the Rijksnormaalschool, Amsterdam. Ca.1935 he abandoned his political work to devote himself to painting, chiefly portraits and still lifes. Active in Amsterdam.
Plates 78, 85

Bodaan, Johan Jacob
(The Hague, February 1, 1881-The Hague, September 2, 1954) Figure and still life painter. Studied at the Ambachtsschool, the Kunstnij-verheidsschool, and the Academy of Fine Arts in The Hague. 1908-33 taught drawing in secondary school. Founding member and chairman of the Haagsche Schetsclub. Lived in Rijnsaterswoude 1936-45, then in The Hague; also in Brussels, Antwerp, Paris.
Plate 76

Broek, Willem ten (Wim)
(Amsterdam, January 2, 1905-still living in 1986) Primarily a painter. Also painted murals and designed stained glass and sgraffiti. Studied at the School voor Kunstambachten and the Rijksakademie in Amsterdam. Student of H. A. van der Wal. Lived in Amsterdam, Goor, and from 1967 on in Ommen.
Plate 101

Brusse, Willem Lucas
(Rotterdam, October 30, 1910-Amsterdam, February 20, 1978) Draftsman. Lived in Amsterdam from 1936 on.
Plate 80

Canta, Agnes Catharina
(Rotterdam, November 14, 1888-Rotterdam, August 8, 1964) Poster artist and printmaker, painter of still lifes and landscapes. Studied at the Academy of Fine Arts in Rotterdam with F. G. W. Oldewelt, A. H. R. van Maasdijk, and J. H. F. C. Nachtweh. Active in Rotterdam.
Plate 102

Caspel, Johann Georg van
(Amsterdam, March 24, 1870-Laren, July 14, 1928) Graphic and poster artist and furniture designer; later also painted portraits, figures, and genre. 1889-1890 studied at the Rijksakademie, Amsterdam; afterwards took lessons in a private school whose faculty included G. W. Dijsselhof, G. H. Breitner, Jacob van Lory, and M. W. van der Valk. He worked from the model and drew his own designs on the stone. Lived in Amsterdam, Amstelveen, and Laren.
Plates 9-12

Cohen, Frederika Sophia (Fré)

(Amsterdam, August 11, 1903-Hengelo, June 14, 1943) Graphic designer, printmaker, and illustrator. Studied briefly at the Grafische School in Amsterdam, 1927-29 at the Kunstnij-verheidsschool in Amsterdam and life drawing with Wim Schuhmacher. 1929 began work at the Amsterdam Stadsdrukkerij as a graphic designer. Active in Amsterdam.

Plates 72, 99

Dekker, Cornelis (Kees)

(Zaandam, January 23, 1900-still living in 1986) Draftsman and graphic designer. Except for evening courses in drawing he was self-taught. Advertising and package designer for Verkade for 38 years. Little contact with other artists.

Plate 94

Dobbenburgh, Aart van

(Amsterdam, September 30, 1899-still living 1985) Graphic artist, painter, and prize-winning illustrator. 1914-1918 studied at the Quel-linusschool in Amsterdam. Lecturer at the Academy of Fine Arts, The Hague.

Plate 98

Drupsteen, Wilhelmina Cornelia

(Amsterdam, October 10, 1880-Oosterbeek, April 2, 1966) Painter and graphic artist. Studied at the Rijksnormaalschool, 1897-1900; Rijksschool voor Kunstnijverheid, 1898-1900, with J. L. M. Lauweriks and K. P. C. de Bazel; and the Rijksakademie, 1902-06, all in Amsterdam. Active in Amsterdam until 1939.

Plate 32

Frank, Louis

(Amsterdam, May 5, 1907-still living in 1986) 1929-39 worked in the advertising studio of M. Wilmink; 1939-40 in the studio of Frits van Alphen; 1946 on, as an independent designer. Contributed to the journal *Verpakking en Vormgeving*.

Plate 79

Galema, Arjen

(Amsterdam, July 8, 1886-Amsterdam, May 11, 1974) Painter. Worked in Paris and, from 1925 on, in Amsterdam.

Plate 89

Gestel, Leendert (Leo)

(Woerden, November 22, 1881-Hilversum, November 26, 1941) Painter. Began as an impressionist, turned to pointillism and cubism, and finally to abstraction. Visits to Germany, France, Mallorca, Vienna. Also worked in Belgium and Paris in the 1920s.

Plate 59

Gispen, Willem Hendrik

(Amsterdam, December 7, 1890-The Hague, May 10, 1981) Industrial designer, especially of lamps and furniture. Studied architecture at the Academy of Fine Arts in Rotterdam, afterwards at the Academy in The Hague. 1916, under the influence of Ruskin, Morris, and the English Arts and Crafts Movement, established the metalworking firm of W. H. Gispen in Rotterdam where, in the same year, he also opened an arts and crafts store, Het Gulden Vlies, to sell his work and that of other designers. 1919 founded Gispen's Industrieele Ondernemingen NV in Rotterdam. 1926 began production of lamps under the tradename Giso.

Plate 77

Guthschmidt, Anthonius Mathieu

(Haarlem, August 26, 1887-Leiden, December 4, 1958) Fine and commercial artist. Studied at the Academies of Fine Art in Antwerp and The Hague.

Plate 54

Hahn, Albert Pieter

(Groningen, March 17, 1877-Amsterdam, August 3, 1918) Graphic artist, known mainly for his political drawings. Studied at the Akademie Minerva in Groningen, 1890-96; Rijksschool voor Kunstnijverheid, Amsterdam, 1896-1900; Rijksakademie Amsterdam, 1898-1901. Worked for *Het Volk*, 1920ff; also contributed to *De Notenkraker*, *Ware Jacob*, and *Hollandsche Revue*.

Plates 22, 34, 48

Hellendoorn, Jacobus Johan

(Hengelo, November 1, 1878-The Hague, September 19, 1959) Architect and interior designer. Studied at the Middelbare Tech-nische School in Zwolle. Most important work: the rebuilding of the town of Vriezen-veen, housing estates in Lochem, Heemstede, The Hague. Co-editor of *Architectura* and an editor of *Bouwfragmenten*.

Plate 65

Hem, Pieter van der (Piet)

(Wirdum, September 9, 1885-The Hague, April 24, 1961) Graphic artist, political cartoonist, and painter. Studied at the Rijksschool voor Kunstnijverheid and the Rijksakademie, Amsterdam, 1904-07. Active in Amsterdam, 1902-07; Paris, September 1907-summer 1908; Amsterdam, 1908-1910; Rome, 1910; Paris, 1910-1911; Moscow and St. Petersburg, 1912; Spain, 1912-1914.

Plates 29, 30

Hemelman, Albert

(Neede, January 7, 1883-Amsterdam, January 25, 1951) Painter and printmaker. Worked in Amsterdam and Norway (Spitzbergen). Studied at the Rijksschool voor Kunstnij-verheid and the Rijksakademie, Amsterdam, 1905, 1908-09.

Plate 44

Hofman, Pieter Adrianus Hendrik

(Teteringen, May 4, 1885-The Hague, July 10, 1965) Painter, printmaker, craftsman; among his works are wallpaintings, stained glass windows, and book covers. Studied at the Academy of Fine Arts, The Hague. Active in Amsterdam until 1906, then in The Hague.

Plates 53, 75, 83

Hynckes, Raoul

(Brussels, May 11, 1893-Blaricum, January 19, 1973) Magic realist painter of still lifes and landscapes. Studied at the Royal Academy of Fine Arts, Brussels. Active in Brussels and Amsterdam.

Plates 55, 95

Jongert, Jacob (Jac.)
(Wormer, June 22, 1883-Reeuwijk, November 9, 1942) Graphic designer and painter. Studied at the Quellinusschool, Amsterdam, 1899-1902; the Rijksschool voor Kunstnijverheid, Amsterdam, 1902-03; and with Roland Holst at the Rijksakademie, Amsterdam, 1903-04. 1904-07 assistant to Roland Holst as a wall painter. Taught in Purmerend (drawing), 1905-1918; at the Industrieschool voor Meisjes in Amsterdam, 1908-11; and at the Dagteeken- en Kunstambachtsschool voor Meisjes in Amsterdam, 1911-18. 1923-1940 director of advertising for De Erven De Wed. J. Van Nelle, Rotterdam.

Plates 27, 46, 51, 52, 73

Kalff, Louis Christiaan
(Amsterdam, November 14, 1897-Waalre, September 16, 1976) Industrial and graphic designer, architect, interior designer, and pioneer in light-effects. Studied at the Technische Hoogeschool, Delft, 1916-1923, and designed his first poster while still a student. 1925 began working for Philips as an industrial and advertising designer, soon becoming general art director of the Philips company. 1928 made head of a new Philips department of "artistic propaganda." 1962 retired from Philips after his design and construction of the Philips museum in Eindhoven, the 'Evoluon.'

Plate 91

Konijnenburg, Willem Adriaan van
(The Hague, February 11, 1868-The Hague, February 28, 1943) Painter, decorative artist, and sculptor; among his works are designs for postage stamps. Studied at the Academy of Fine Arts, The Hague, 1884-86. Study trips to Paris, 1901 and 1906. Between 1908 and 1916 published a number of works on art and aesthetics.

Plate 19

Koo, Nicolaas, Petrus de
(Amsterdam, August 4, 1881-Laren, December 1, 1960) Decorative artist, graphic designer, and architect

Plates 87-88

Küpper, Albert Johann Funke
(Duisburg [Germany], March, 24, 1894-Vierhouten, November 23, 1934) Artist and caricaturist. Studied at the Academy of Fine Arts, Rotterdam.

Plate 74

Kurvers, Antonius (Antoon)
(The Hague, July 23, 1889-Amsterdam, January 1, 1940) Lithographer and decorative painter. Active in The Hague until 1908, Haarlem until 1918, Amsterdam after 1918.

Plate 69

Laars, Tiete van der
(Leeuwarden, August 6, 1861-Hilversum, April 27, 1939) Decorator and designer of heraldic emblems. Studied at the Rijksschool voor Kunstnijverheid, Amsterdam, under W. B. G. Molkenboer, and at the Rijksakademie, Amsterdam. Taught at the former. Active in Amsterdam until 1921.

Plate 20

Lebeau, Joris Johannes Christiaan (Chris)
(Amsterdam, May 26, 1878-Dachau, April 2, 1945) Graphic designer and decorative artist; designer of textiles (including batik), glass, and ceramics; printmaker. Studied at the Quellinusschool, Amsterdam, 1892-1895, with the influential design theorist J. H. de Groot; Rijksschool voor Kunstnijverheid, Amsterdam, 1895-99; evening courses at the Rijksakademie, Amsterdam, 1895-99; drawing lessons with K. P. C. de Bazel and J. Lauweriks, ca.1898; Academy of Fine Arts, Antwerp, 1905-08. Taught at the Kunstnijverheidsschool, Haarlem, 1903-12. Active in Haarlem, 1900-13; Czechoslovakia, 1926-27, 1928-29; Berlin, 1931.

Plates 37, 38, 56

Leck, Bart Anthony van der
(Utrecht, November 26, 1876-Blaricum, November 13, 1958) Painter and designer. 1891-1899 worked in various glass studios in Utrecht and in 1896-1900 took evening classes there in life drawing. Studied at the Rijksschool voor Kunstnijverheid, Amsterdam, 1900-04, and evening drawing classes at the Rijksakademie, Amsterdam, 1901-04. 1917, founding member of de Stijl.

Plate 35

Lion Cachet, Carel Adolph
(Amsterdam, November 28, 1864-Vreeland, May 20, 1945) Designer, decorator, and interior architect. 1881-1885 studied at the Gemeente Kweekschool voor Onderwijzers in Amsterdam, then three more years as an apprentice. Took drawing classes with B. W. Wierink, but regarded G. W. Dijsselhof, with whom he was friends, as his true teacher. Active in Amsterdam until 1897, then in Vreeland.

Plates 8, 47

Luns, Hubert Marie (Huib)
(Paris, June 6, 1881-Amsterdam, February 24, 1942) Painter and graphic artist, art historian. Studied at the Rijksnormaalschool voor Tekenonderwijs, Amsterdam, 1898-1901; Rijksakademie, Amsterdam, 1901-02; in Brussels and Paris, 1902-08. Professor at the Tekenakademie, Rotterdam, 1908-18; director of the Koninglijke School, The Hagues, 1918-23; director of the Rijksinstituut tot opleiding van tekenleraren, Amsterdam; professor of drawing and art history at the Technische Hoogeschool, Delft, 1931 on. Teacher of M. Wilmink. Active in Amsterdam until 1902; Brussels, 1902-08, Rotterdam, 1908-18; The Hague, 1918-23; afterward in Amsterdam.

Plate 39

Mettes, Franciscus Joseph Engbertus (Frans)
(Amsterdam, March 18, 1909-Amsterdam, November 30, 1984) Designed numerous film posters before the war; attained his highest reputation for his work later.

Plate 100

Meurs, Harmen Hermanus
(Wageningen, January 17, 1891-Ermelo, November 16, 1964) Painter and printmaker. Studied at the Rijksschool voor Kunstnijverheid, Amsterdam, ca. 1909-11; evening courses at the Rijksakademie, Amsterdam, 1911-1912. Influenced by expressionism and cubism. Active in Wageningen and Amsterdam. Numerous trips to France. Member of the Haagse Kunstring.

Plate 60

Molkenboer, Antonius Henricus Johannes

(Leewarden, April 8, 1872-Haarlem, March 10, 1960) Painter, graphic artist, muralist, and designer of mosaics. Studied at the Rijksnormaalschool, Amsterdam, 1889-1892; Rijksakademie, Amsterdam, 1890-95; Académie Julian, Paris, 1903; Art Students' League, N.Y., 1906. Active in Amsterdam until 1906; U.S., 1906-11; later in Amsterdam, The Hague, Haarlem.

Plate 28

Molkenboer, Theodorus Henricus Antonius Adolf

(Leewarden, February 23, 1871-Lugano, December 1, 1920) Architect, designer, and painter. Studied at the Rijksnormaalschool voor Tekenonderwijs, Amsterdam, 1889-91; in the office of the architect P. J. H. Cuypers until 1891; at the Rijksakademie, Amsterdam, 1891-92; and with the designers G. W. Dijsselhof and A. J. Derkinderen. Director of the Hendrick de Keyser drawing school in Amsterdam.

Plate 16

Nieuwenhuis, Theodorus Wilhelmus (Theo)

(Noordscharwoude, April 26, 1866-Hilversum, December 5, 1951) Graphic designer, furniture designer, and interior decorator. Studied at the Rijksschool voor Kunstnijverheid, Amsterdam, 1883-88. Travels to Germany, Prague, Vienna, and Paris, 1889-90. Active in Amsterdam ca. 1883-1888.

Plate 3

Pieck, Henri Christiaan

(Den Helder, April 19, 1895-The Hague, January 12, 1972) Artist and architect. Studied at the Tekeninstituut Bik en Vaandrager, The Hague; Rijksakademie, Amsterdam, 1912-13. Lived in The Hague, 1906-16, 1918-22; Amsterdam, 1916-18; London, 1922-35; The Hague from 1935 on.

Plate 82

Pothast, Wilhelm Frederik Anton

(Roermond, July 9, 1877-Haarlem, October 2, 1916)

Plate 17

Raemaekers, Louis

(Roermond, April 6, 1869-Scheveningen, July 25, 1956) Graphic artist and painter, known for his political drawings for newspapers, especially 1914-1918. Studied with Th. H. H. Molkenboer and J. R. de Kruyff at the Rijksnormaalschool, Amsterdam, 1891-93; at the Brussels Academy; and with E. Blanchard in Brussels. Taught at the Ambachtsavondschool in Tilburg, and in 1894 appointed director of the Burgeravondschool in Wageningen. Teacher of H. H. Meurs. 1924 awarded an honorary doctorate by the University of Glasgow. Lived and worked in various places, including London, Brussels, Paris, and the United States.

Plate 57

Ravesteyn, Sybold van

(Rotterdam, February 18, 1889-Laren, November 23, 1983) Architect. Studied at the Technische Hoogeschool, Delft, 1906-1912. Worked as a designer for the Dutch Railways from 1912 until his retirement in 1952. Active in Utrecht from 1918 on.

Plate 62

Rol, Cornelis

(Edam, September 2, 1877-Voorburg, January 31, 1963) Painter and graphic artist, especially known for his animal and plant studies. Studied at the Tekenschool, Edam; Rijksnormaalschool voor Tekenonderwijs, Amsterdam, 1894-98. Taught at the Quellinusschool, Amsterdam. Lived in Edam, Amsterdam, and The Hague until 1929, then in Voorburg.

Plate 31

Roland Holst, Richard Nicolaus

(Amsterdam, December 4, 1868-Bloemendaal, December 31, 1938) Wallpainter, decorator, and designer. Studied at the Rijksakademie, Amsterdam, 1885-1890. 1892 joined the Rosicrucians. 1918-1934 appointed professor and then director of the Rijksakademie, Amsterdam. Among his pupils was J. Jongert.

Plates 25, 26, 49

Roos, Sjoerd de

(Smallingerland, September 14, 1877-Haarlem, April 3, 1962) Graphic designer, craftsman, typographical designer. Studied at the Tekenschool voor Kunstambachten, Amsterdam; evenings at the Rijksakademie, Amsterdam, 1895-98.

Plate 96

Ros, Johannes Dominicus

(The Hague, June 17, 1875-The Hague January 5, 1952) Painter. Taught at the Academy of Fine Arts, The Hague. Member of the Haagse Kunstring.

Plate 4

Rotgans, Jan

(Hoorn, February 11, 1881-The Hague 1969) Graphic designer and draftsman. Studied at the Quellinusschool, the Rijksschool voor Kunstnijverheid, the Rijsnormaalschool, and the Rijksakademie, all in Amsterdam. A close friend of Albert Hahn but otherwise seems to have had little contact with other artists.

Plate 36

Rüdeman, Gustave Adolphine Wilhelmina (Dolly)

(Salatiga [Java], February 3, 1902-Amsterdam, January 26, 1980) Graphic designer, chiefly of film posters.

Plate 71

Rueter, Wilhelm Christiaan Georg (Georg)

(Haarlem, March 8, 1875-Amsterdam, August 16, 1966) Portraitist, graphic artist, commercial illustrator, designer of stained glass. Studied at the Rijksnormaalschool voor Tekenonderwijs, Amsterdam, with the painter J. D. Huibers; then at the Rijksakademie, Amsterdam. 1918-1940 reader at the Rijksakademie, Amsterdam, where he taught life classes and decorative drawing. Active in Amsterdam.

Plates 18, 40

Sandberg, Willem Jacob Henri Berend

(Amersfoort, October 24, 1897-Amsterdam, April 8, 1984) Graphic designer. Studied at the Rijksakademie, Amsterdam, 1919. Former director of the Stedelijk Museum, Amsterdam. 1964-68 coordinating director of the Israeli Museum, Jerusalem. Active in Holland, Pisa, Paris, Amsterdam, Jerusalem.

Plate 86

Schwarz, Samuel Levi (Moemie)

(Zutphen, July 28, 1876-Auschwitz, November 19, 1942) Painter and graphic artist. Studied at the Academy of Fine Arts, Antwerp. Member of the Hollandse Kunstenaarskring, Amsterdam.

Plate 84

Sjollema, Johan Sybo (Joop)

(Groningen, December 10, 1900-still living in 1986) Painter and designer. Studied at the Rijksakademie, Amsterdam, and with André Lhote, Paris.

Plate 97

Sluiter, Jan Willem (Willy)

(Amersfoort, May 24, 1873-The Hague, May 22, 1949) Painter, graphic artist, political caricaturist. Studied at the Academy of Fine Arts, Rotterdam, 1891-94; Academy of Fine Arts, The Hague.

Plates 33, 42

Sluyters, Johannes Carolus Bernardus (Jan)

(The Hague, December 17, 1881-Amsterdam, May 8, 1957) Painter. Studied at the Rijksakademie, Amsterdam, 1901-02. Prix de Rome, 1904. Designed his posters between 1913 and 1924.

Plates 23, 24, 41

Stein, Johann Anton Willebrord von (von Stein)

(Haarlem, November 21, 1896-Naarden, April 13, 1965) Painter, but chiefly a graphic artist best known for his posters. Received a teaching certificate in secondary education, then took evening courses for one year at the Rijksakademie, Amsterdam.

Plate 92

Thorn Prikker, Johan

(The Hague, June 6, 1868-March 5, 1932) Painter, designer of mosaics and stained glass. Studied at the Academy of Fine Arts, The Hague, 1883-87. Began as a neoimpressionist, but came to believe that painting should be in the service of architecture. Eventually developed a Christian-oriented art. Lived in The Hague, 1887-1904, then in Germany.

Plate 6

Toorop, Jan Theodoor

(Poerworedjo [Java], December 20, 1858—The Hague, March 3, 1928) Painter and graphic artist. Moved to The Netherlands, 1869. Studied at the Rijksakademie, Amsterdam, 1880-81, and at the Brussels Academy with A. J. Derkinderen, 1882-85. 1885 joined Les XX and visited London, where he was strongly influenced by William Morris.

Plates 5, 21, 45

Veldheer, Jacobus Gerardus

(Haarlem, June 4, 1866-Blaricum, October 18, 1954) Painter, graphic artist, art critic. Studied at the Academy of Fine Arts, The Hague, 1889-91. Active in The Netherlands; Paris, 1895; Belgium, 1895-98; Nürnberg, 1903-04.

Plate 15

Verschuuren, Jr., Ch.

No information available.

Plate 43

Werkman, Hendrik Niolaas

(Leens, April 29, 1982—Bakkeveen, April 10, 1945) Printer, painter, graphic artist. Trained at printing establishments and self-taught as a painter and graphic artist. 1903–ca.1907 worked as a journalist for the *Groninger Dagblad* and then for the *Nieuwe Groninger Courant*. Began his own printing shop, 1908. Began painting, 1917. Printing shop failed in 1923 and he began again with a smaller one. That same year he began his journal, *The Next Call*, and the first of hi distinctive graphic designs. Visits to Cologne and Paris, 1929. Member of the artists' group De Ploeg in Groningen.

Plate 64

Wijdeveld, Hendrikus Theodorus

(The Hague, October 4, 1885-still living in 1986) Architect, graphic and theatrical designer. Largely self-taught. 1898 worked as a carpenter in Amsterdam; 1899 in the architecture office of P. J. H. Cuypers, Amsterdam; 1905ff. as an architect in England, where he also studied at the Lambeth School of Art. 1910 in France. Independent architect in Amsterdam since 1912. Founder and editor of *Wendingen*.

Plates 58, 66, 67, 68

Wijga, Jan

(Jelsum, December 13, 1902-December 1978) Graphic designer. Studied at the School voor Kunstambachten, Amsterdam, 1916-20; later, evening lessons at the Piersma drawing school, Amsterdam. Private instruction with the painters Henri Kötser, 1920-22, and H. M. Krabbé and Simon Garf, 1938-42. 1923 began working for the printing firm of J. A. Luii & Co., Amsterdam, where he remained until the start of the war. First beer posters, 1929.

Plates 90, 93

Wilmink, Machiel

(Zwolle, June 25, 1894-Voorburg, June 27, 1963) Active in Voorburg and Rotterdam. Commercial and poster artist. Studied with Huib Luns at the Academy in Rotterdam. Headed one of the biggest Dutch advertising studios of the 1930s.

Plate 61

Zon, Jacob Abraham (Jacques)

(The Hague, April 21, 1872-The Hague, March 27, 1932) Painter and printmaker. Studied at the Academies of Fine Arts in The Hague and Antwerp, and with Cormon in Paris. Lived in Brussels, 1897. Travels to France, Italy, and Bavaria after World War I.

Plates 13, 14

Z. W.

(No information available.)

Plate 81

Zwart, Pieter (Piet)

(Zaandijk, May 28, 1885-Voorschoten, September 24, 1977) Architect and designer. Studied at the Rijksschool voor Kunstnijverheid, Amsterdam, 1902-06. 1919- 22 was associated with de Stijl and collaborated on de Stijl projects. 1921-27 in the office of H. P. Berlage. Designed for the Dutch postal, telegraph, and telephone system.

Plates 63, 70

Bibliography

Abdy, Jane. **The French Poster: Chéret to Cappiello**. New York, 1969.

Bart van der Leck, 1876-1958 (catalogue). Rijksmuseum Kröller-Müller, Otterlo, July 18-September 5, 1976.

La Belle Epoque: Belgian Posters, Watercolors, and Drawings from the Collection of L. Wittamer-DeCamps (catalogue). Introduction by Yolande Oostens-Wittamer. Library of Congress, Washington, D.C., 1970.

Benier, W. H. "Langs reclamewegen." **Revue der Reclame**, vol.8, no.6-7 (1948), pp.156-165.

Berg, J. C. van den. "Een ondoelmatige affiche." **De bedrijfsreklame**, vol.9, no.2 (February 1921), pp.28-29.

Boom, A. van der. **C. A. Lion Cachet 1864-1945**. Bussum, 1952.

Brenner, Hildegard. **Die Kunstpolitik des Nationalsozialismus**. Hamburg, 1963.

Broos, Kees. **Piet Zwart 1885-1977**. Amsterdam, 1982.

Calker, H. van. **In het atelier van der schilder**. Amsterdam, 1941.

Chris Lebeau (1878-1945) (catalogue). Drents Museum, Assen, October 12, 1985-January 5, 1986.

Cirker, Hayward and Blanche. **The Golden Age of the Poster**. New York, 1971.

Cohen, Philip. "Het werk van Albert Hahn." **De bedrijfsreklame**, vol.3, no.2 (August 1917), pp.3-9.

Dooijes, Dick. **Hendrik Werkman**. Amsterdam, 1970.

Dooijes, Dick, and Brattinga, Pieter. **A History of the Dutch Poster 1890-1960**. Introduction by H. L. C. Jaffé. Amsterdam, 1968.

Dokkum, J. D. C. van. "C. Rol als reklamekunstenaar." **De bedrijfsreklame**, vol.3, no.4 (December 1917), pp.71-74.

"A Dutch Affichiste: J. G. van Caspel." **The Poster**, vol.2 (May 1899), pp.209-214.

Exposition d'affiches artistiques françaises et étrangères (catalogue). Reims, November 7-17, 1896.

Exposition internationale d'affiches illustrées (catalogue). Société Impériale d'Encouragement des Arts, St. Petersburg, 1897.

Gans, L. **Nieuwe kunst. De Nederlandse bijdrage tot de Art Nouveau: Decoratieve kunst, kunstnijverheid en architectuur omstreeks 1900**. Utrecht, 1966.

Geraerds, Rob. "Film-affiches Dolly Rüdeman." **Op de Hoogte**, May 21, 1931, pp.146-148.

Goldwater, Robert. "L'affiche moderne.'" **Gazette des Beaux-Arts**, series 6, vol.22 (December 1942), pp.173-182.

Gouwe, W. F. **De grafische kunst in het praktische leven**. Rotterdam, 1926.

Gouwe, W. F. "Th. Molkenboer en zijn kunst-in-reklame." **De bedrijfsreklame**. vol.4, no.2 (April 1918), pp.144-148.

De grafiek van Jan Toorop (catalogue). Rijksmuseum, Amsterdam, February 8-April 13, 1969.

Hendrik Nicolaas Werkman 1882-1945: "Druksel" Prints and General Printed Matter (catalogue). Stedelijk Museum, Amsterdam, 1977.

Hiatt, Charles. **Picture Posters: A Short History of the Illustrated Placard, with Many Reproductions of the Most Artistic Examples in All countries.** London, 1895.

Hoogenboezem, Emy. "Een onderzoek naar Jac. Jongert 1883-1942, toegespitst op zijn gebruiksgrafiek." Doctoral dissertation, Kunsthistorisch Instituut, Utrecht, 1979.

Hoogenboezem, Emy. **Jac. Jongert 1883-1942: Graficus tussen kunst en reclame** (catalogue). Gemeentemuseum, The Hague, 1982.

Industry and Design in the Netherlands 1850-1950 (catalogue). Stedelijk Museum, Amsterdam, December 21, 1985-February 9, 1986.

Jan Toorop in Katwijk aan Zee (catalogue). Katwijks Museum, Katwijk, June 29-August 18, 1985.

Jongert, Jac. "Posters Designed by Dutch Artists." **Wendingen**, vol.5, no.2 (1923), pp.1-18.

Karstkarel, Peter. "De reclame door Jan Rotgans, Piet van der Hem en Jan Wijga." **Alternatijf**, 1976, pp.3-40.

Kluyver-Cluysenaer, M. Y., and Boutens, P. C. "Willem van Konijnenburg." **Nieuwspapier Drents Museum, Assen**, vol.4, no.11 (1980).

Koch, Robert. "The Poster Movement and 'Art Nouveau.'" **Gazette des Beaux-Arts**, series 6, vol.50 (November 1957), pp.285-296.

Kossmann, E. H. **The Low Countries 1780-1940**. Oxford, 1978.

Kunst im 3. Reich. Dokumente der Unterwerfung (catalogue). Frankfurter Kunstverein, Frankfurt am Main, October 15-December 8, 1974.

Löb, Kurt. **De onbekende Jan Sluijters**. The Hague, 1968.

Luns, Huib. "Umberto farà da sé . . . . " **De bedrijfsreklame**, vol.6, no.6 (August 1919), pp.91-96.

Maindron, Ernest. "Les affiches illustrées." **Gazette des Beaux-Arts**, series 2, vol.30 (1884), pp.419-433, 533-547.

Maindron, Ernest. **Les affiches illustrées**. Paris, 1886.

Martin, Hans. "Iets over Piet van der Hem." **De bedrijfsreklame**, vol.2, no.4 (May 1917), pp.110-113.

Meijer Bleekrode: schilder, ontwerper, socialist 1896-1943 (catalogue). Edited by Carry van Lakerveld. Amsterdams Historisch Museum, 1983.

Polak, Bettina. **Het fin-de-siècle in de Nederlandse schilderkunst: De symbolistische beweging 1890-1900**. The Hague, 1955.

The Poster (catalogue). Takashimaya Art Gallery, Nihonbashi, April 18-May 7, 1985.

Roland Holst, R. N. "Moderne eischen en artistieke bedenkingen." **Wendingen**, vol.2, no.5 (May 1919), pp.3-16.

S. van Ravesteyn (catalogue). Nationaal Architectuur Museum, Amsterdam, 1977.

Scheen, Pieter. **Lexicon Nederlandse beeldende kunstenaars 1750-1950**. 2 vols. The Hague, 1969-70.

60 Plakate neun holländische Graphiker (catalogue). Hilversum, 1972.

Sponsel, Jean Louis. **Das moderne Plakat**. Dresden, 1897.

De Stijl 1917-1931: Visions of Utopia. Edited by Mildred Friedman. Oxford, 1982.

Tussenbroek, Otto van. "Twee affiches." **Balans: Algemeen jaarboek der Nederlandsche**

        kunsten 1930-31. Maastricht, 1930, pp. 72-73.

Tussenbroek, Otto van. "Willy Sluiter en zijn werk." **De bedrijfsreklame**, vol. 2, no. 3

        (April 1917), pp. 77-81.

Wendingen 1918-1931: Documenti dell'arte olandese del Novecento (catalogue). Palazzo

        Medici-Riccardi, Florence, April 3-June 5, 1982.

"Willem Arondéus, Else Berg, Fré Cohen, Henk Henriët: Vier vergeten kunstenaars." **NRC Handels-**

        blad; cultureel supplement 338 (April 15, 1977).

World War I Propaganda Posters: A Selection from the Bowman Gray Collection of

        Materials Related to World War I and World War II (catalogue).

        Ackland Art center, University of North Carolina, Chapel Hill, January

        12-February 23, 1969.

Zur Westen, Walter von. **Reklamekunst**. Bielefeld and Leipzig, 1903.

This book was set in Univers by *IntelliText Corporation* and printed by *Andromeda Printing and Graphics.*

Ann Tyler Design,
Ann Tyler and Renate Gokl

Exhibition Schedule

Krannert Art Museum, University of
Illinois, Urbana-Champaign,
November 15 to December 21, 1986;
Spencer Museum of Art, University
of Kansas, Lawrence, January 11
to March 1, 1987; Cedar Rapids
Museum of Art, Cedar Rapids, Iowa,
March 15 to May 3; Flint Institute
of Arts, Flint, Michigan, May 15 to
June 21; The Toledo Museum of Art,
Toledo, Ohio, June 27 to August 30;
Marion Koogler McNay Art Museum,
San Antonio, Texas, September 20
to November 22; Fort Wayne
Museum of Art, Fort Wayne, Indiana,
January 16 to March 12, 1988; The
Baltimore Museum of Art, Baltimore,
Maryland, May 24 to July 17;
Cooper-Hewitt Museum, New York,
New York, October 4, 1988, to
January 8, 1989

The Wooden Fence

The Wooden Fence

Dale R. Albrecht

"I'll Meet you at The Wooden Fence"

A mile down the gravel road adjoining my grandfather's magical circus lots stood 'The Wooden Fence.' This simple wooden fence marked a gateway into the woodland paradise we called, Pine Grove. There, I explored the Minnesota landscape and scaled the tall trees to steal baby hunting birds for my brother, the Budding Falconer. There was always a risk, a danger, and an adrenaline rush of excitement! Often, the raptors turned their ire on their caretakers.

Independently published.

Cover design and photo correction/placement by Theresa Stone.

ISBN: 9781076916013

Acknowledgements

A very special thank you and heartfelt appreciation to Mary Kay Proshek for believing in this project and sticking with me throughout all these years. Her interest, advice, support, and encouragement was paramount to its completion. I considered her my ghostwriter, even though she refused to take the credit. As a classmate and a friend since kindergarten, Mary Kay is a shining example of the special group of people I grew up with. Mary Kay, you are a blessing.

This book would not have been possible without the love and support of my wife. I thank you for being gracious enough to let me share your humble beginnings. You are my first and only love...

An enormous thank you to Sister Marianne for resurfacing 40 years after her sudden departure. Reconnecting with her was one of the most delightful highlights of my life.

I also want to thank brother Mike. When I started this book years ago, you provided me with an enormous amount of information essential to the story. Thank you for making my childhood magical. The Wooden Fence is our legacy!

Thank you, Theresa, for once again riding to the rescue and making my original basic book cover into something very beautiful and professional looking. You were always there for me when we were growing up and you're still here for me today.

There are no words to express the gratitude I hold dear to my entire family for being unique and so, so special. I feel very privileged having grown up with you in our little town of Belle Plaine. To my flamboyant parents and legendary grandparents, life was a circus.

Contents

Forward

"Circus Blood"

Feeling content with the 1947 season behind him, Leo Albrecht was looking forward to a little time off in his hometown this Thanksgiving. The diverse circus legend had just finished a successful fall run with Williams and Lee which was a large booking agency based out of Minneapolis, MN. They had four units entertaining town fairs and celebrations throughout the entire Midwestern section of the United States. Young Leo Jr. traveled and showed the trained dogs and ponies in one location, while his 57-year-old father, was at another, performing his King of the Slack wire routine or balancing chairs and wagon wheels on the end of his chin. Between the two, the money was finally good, but living on the road and driving from town to town was hectic, at times an all nights drive to the next day's performances. Some leisure time back home in Belle Plaine, with his wife Angela and the two younger boys, would be a pleasant change of pace. But, two days before sitting down to a relaxing feast filled with turkey and all the trimmings an unexpected phone call from Washington, IA changed his holiday plans in a big way.

On the other end of the phone line was well known Midwestern promoter, Jay Gould still out on the road and planned to stay out there until the day after the New Year. The anxiety in Jay's voice came through the faint and distorted long-distance telephone line loud and clear to Leo. Jay needed a replacement dog and pony act and he needed it yesterday. He had Christmas shows scheduled starting the day after Thanksgiving when his regular act canceled at the last minute. Before Jay picked up the telephone receiver and placed his finger in one of the ten round holes on the dial, he was already sold on Leo's acts. Jay's star clown "YO YO," who trooped with Leo, described the dog and pony act with phrase and flair, "Best around, smart white ponies that work alongside large, white Alaskan Huskies, and look really showy and stand out in the distance. Along with his trained animals, you get a wire walker and chin balancer as well. The guy is very entertaining and uses tasteful humor throughout the act. He's headquartered out of Minnesota, as well Belle Plaine."

Leo jumped at the opportunity! Besides, he didn't have the heart to turn down the renowned and much respected Jay Gould. He also knew all about the Million Dollar Circus long before he picked up the receiver and answered the career-changing phone call. In less than 24 hours Leo was sitting in circus heaven, or the closest thing to it, Jay's luxurious trailer discussing the show schedule, routine and town locations. They discovered during that first meeting they had a lot in common, besides great ideas for future Christmas parades. Each man, well known and larger than life in the circus universe, were both at the top of their profession.

Leo's circus resume read like a novel: circus owner/operator, slack wire walker; master of 24 acts, chin balancer; ending his act by balancing a 100 pound wagon wheel on his chin, animal trainer and performer; originating many of his own horse and dog acts, circus truck and tent sidewall designer/painter and circus wagon carver. There was no one else on the road as diversified or as schooled in the

Leo handstand on the slack wire

circus world. He had traveled with many shows over the years, gaining a reputation as an extremely skilled and talented man. He was also known for his bear-like determination and unparalleled work ethic. He'd put in eighteen hours a day when he was performing on the road.

Leo always described himself as a late bloomer because he didn't get married until he was 38. His wife, the 18 years younger, very attractive Angela, set off on the road with Leo less than two years after their marriage. The starry-eyed sturdy farm girl took everything in stride just as a seasoned trooper would, even making all the stunning costumes for the performers. Although somewhat bashful, Angela eventually stepped center ring wearing one of her own versions of circus apparel, performing with the high diving goats and then in later years showing the dogs and ponies. Their three sons, Leo "Sonny," Dave and Gary traveled with the circus until they were school age, and then Angela stayed home with the boys while Leo was out on the road. Sonny performed with his dad at age five and then on his own halfway through his teen years, choosing circus life in Texas over the humdrum school routine back home in Belle Plaine.

Still performing into his late 50s, Leo's small framed, muscular body showed no signs of aging and he thanked the good Lord often for his supernatural fortune. His acts required enormous strength and quick, automatic reflexes, his body and mind responding to the demand with youth and vigor. He could still perform his original wire walking routine, excluding the difficult handstand on the slack wire. "Only a couple of people in America can do that handstand and they use thicker wire," he would tell us grandkids. And he executed his entire chin balance routine by removing one of the outer steel bands of the wagon wheel, therefore decreasing the weight from 100 pounds down to 85 pounds. He abandoned the difficult table balance routine, exchanging it for the more sought-after animal acts. Leo discovered that groups of all ages, especially the children, enjoyed the trained dogs and smart ponies, which made the act much easier to book. Throughout his illustrious career, the patient and determined animal trainer had trained over 30 horses and 300 dogs.

Jay Gould was a well-known Circus Promoter throughout the Midwestern section of the United States, home quartered in Glencoe, MN. His skills were as a businessman, not a performer. He owned and operated an entertainment traveling show, "Jay Gould's Million Dollar Circus," a carryover from his earlier show entitled "Jay Gould's Million Dollar Gems," vaudeville show. Ringling Brothers Circus Fire in Hartford, CT on July 6, 1944, put an end to the days of the canvas tent, so Jay simply changed the viewing venue by putting his acts on display on top of a large portable stage. It was a perfect set up in front of drive-in theaters or the grandstands at ballparks where everyone had an excellent view of the show. His circus traveled on the primitive roads throughout the entire Midwestern Region including, in later years, huge cities such as Minneapolis, MN and Chicago, IL. Gould's outfit was large, hiring an array of acts, including a few of his nine musically talented children; his leftover "gems." Jay hired some of the best acts in the country and entertainment-starved audiences were both overwhelmed and amazed by his spectacular operation.

Jay Gould & Robin

He also owned several carnival rides, with a good sized midway where people could buy cotton candy, popcorn, souvenirs, and snow cones. They could play games and take in one of the

numerous sideshows. He made it easy for a small-town soul to get lost in the crowds and escape from their humdrum daily routine. An array of animals traveled along with the show which included elephants, bears, lions, Leo's numerous dogs, and ponies, and believe it or not, a couple of chickens. Jay's outfit was consistently billed as, and was a "clean show." He never failed to open the program with a prayer. It was easy for strangers to spot Jay in a crowd because he was always dressed in a white suit, sporting a matching white hat, with a red boutonniere tucked in the front pocket of his suit coat. People knew it was Jay outright.

Jay turned the suspect mummified body of John Wilkes Booth, President Lincoln's assassin, into a profitable venture. The postmortem career of John Wilkes Booth which nearly every showman who exhibited the mummy was ruined financially besides the eight people killed in the wreck of a circus train in 1902, on which the mummy was traveling. Two books were written in 1937, one on Lincoln's assassination and the other on John Wilkes Booth helped revive interest, bringing curious spectators from miles around to view the body. First Jay invited local undertakers to view the body for free and then sent them away dumbfounded. With a certificate of authenticity signed by a Judge, Jay offered a thousand dollars to anyone who could prove it was a fake. Because of Jay, "John Wilkes Booth on Tour," appeared in the Saturday Evening Post, and Reader's Digest did a reprint. The articles revived an extensive debate throughout the country, focusing on the real fate of John Wilkes Booth. The cursed mummy once bought and sold, traded, leased and held under bond was for the first time profitable.

Jay was also the one responsible for giving Lawrence Welk his first job in the entertainment industry. Welk and his partner Lincoln Bouldes showed up one day in Jay's office asking for a job. Jay auditioned them in front of a live audience and they traveled on Jay's show for about six months before going on to bigger and grander things. Years later, at a dinner in Jay's honor, Welk credited Jay for giving him his start in show business.

Leo toured with "The Million Dollar" circus that holiday season and then entered a partnership with Jay which lasted the next several years. Jay's investment in Leo paid off in more ways than he could ever have imagined. His original goal had been to hire a replacement for his dog and pony act, but he struck gold the day he hired the man with a creative mind and a handy hand. Shortly after the end of the season, Leo traveled to Jay's storage facility in Marseilles, IL where he was hired to paint all of Jay's trucks with showy lettering and colorful circus themes. Now that his trucks resembled those of the big circus names such as Ringling Bros. and Cole Bros., Jay booked his circus in the biggest towns in the Midwest. Leo also built and carved every display used in the Christmas parades, an idea originally given to Jay by Leo. Years earlier, Leo had teamed up with a man out of South Dakota, Warren Anderson, who'd put on some very primitive circus parades, and Leo's goal was to create a much more elaborate display for Jay. He exceeded Jay's highest expectations, creating colorful holiday floats, beautiful circus wagons, and caged animal carriers!

Each float and wagon were given themes: Land of the Midnight Sun, Fairyland, Miss Merry Christmas (a sleigh pulled by eight reindeer flying over a house) and Happy New Year (a large float with Father Time and a newborn.) Leo also constructed an airplane, complete with detachable wings, Santa sitting in the cockpit depicting the modern-day Santa Claus. And, he built a long, colorful bandwagon that could comfortably fit 60 musicians. By the time he had finished his artwork, the parade of colorful circus trucks, hand-carved circus wagons and Holiday floats stretched well over half a mile. He didn't realize it, but Leo had built the last circus parade on the American Streets; all made possible because of Jay Gould.

Jay's most beautiful and talented gem and the star of his vaudeville show, was his daughter, Gloria, a stunning woman with her long thick, jet-black hair, a face prettier than Elizabeth Taylor's and a sumptuous body that caused a man to blush. During the show, she would take a

sexy stroll out into the audience, pick out a handsome face, and sit on his lap while singing her dreamy number. "Give Me a Little Kiss, Will Ya Huh."

Despite Jay's strict Christian rearing, at an early age, Gloria met and dated an older man, Ernie Stibal, a drummer whose band played at a dance hall outside their hometown of Glencoe, MN. But, while seeing Ernie, she was also secretly involved with his brother Tom. Gloria affected men like an aphrodisiac, and it soon became apparent that both had fallen under the influence of her spell. The two-timing activity continued until she got pregnant at 17. After it was determined that Ernie was the perpetrator, her parents bluntly demanded, "by God" that they get married. Then their first child, Gloria Anne Stibal was born. Ernie and Gloria's marriage started on shaky ground and never had much of a chance of being a joyful union. Neither set of parents liked or got along with the other. The Stibals being farmers and the Goulds show business people, the two families mixed like oil and water.

Gloria and Ernie

Having married into a circus family, it was only logical that Ernie joined them on the road. He and Gloria became a team, traveling with the show performing all the musical numbers for the parades and the performances; she on the calliope and he playing his drums. But even though Ernie was far away from his family, their marriage didn't go the way Gloria had hoped it would. The Goulds were a loving and close-knit group, so Gloria had always been accustomed to giving and receiving outward affection daily. But Ernie's personality was quite the opposite. He was a very reserved man and seemed incapable of showing her any tenderness. Rather than settle for an unfulfilled marriage, Gloria soon looked for affection in other places. With the conflict and stress it caused in their relationship, sadly, little Gloria Anne was raised in a very dysfunctional home.

She grew up on and off the road, in and out of several homes and schools. One year, she attended seven schools. Her only stability in life came from Grandpa Jay, Grandma Mabel, and her aunts and uncles. Sometimes, it seemed as though the circus acts and flunkies loved her more than her own parents. Despite her irregular upbringing, she was as talented and as beautiful as her mother, kicking off every show with her lovely voice at the tender age of 11. Jay took his granddaughter under his wing and had her professionally trained as an aerialist performing an act called, "The Swinging Ladder." She'd gracefully pose while swinging upside down, her foot inside a cloth loop tied to the top rung of the ladder. Gloria Anne blossomed early and soon was considered the star of the show; billed as The Glamorous Gloria Decardo, A Star of Ravishing Beauty, "America's Aerial Queen." Around this same time, she met a man who Grandpa Jay had hired for that holiday season, the colorful Sonny Albright, who performed an amazing act with his showy, white ponies and white Alaskan Huskies.

Sonny owned a semi sized circus truck before he reached his 21st birthday, his partner a pet monkey riding alongside him in the cab keeping him company between the long hauls. Because of their seven-year age difference, he and Gloria Anne were just good friends, but little did Sonny know that she had been smitten with him since the day they met. Sometimes he would invite her to ride along in his truck, he at the wheel, monkey in the middle and she on the passenger side. When they'd pass by a pretty girl, Sonny would reach up, grab a hanging rope and trigger a loud Wolfe

whistle mounted on the hood, making Gloria Anne madder than a wet hen. Over the next several years, she grew into a beautiful woman, Sonny took notice and a romance between them eventually blossomed. Soon after though, he had to leave Gloria Anne and the circus life he loved, to join the military, but he vowed to keep in touch.

With the Korean War raging, he had been forced to join the military in 1951 after receiving his draft notice. He was not interested in the army and the only appeal that the marines held for him was their sharp uniforms, not a good enough reason to choose that branch. But the navy seemed like an ideal fit because he loved to travel and learn, and especially loved the adventures it promised. In his mind, it didn't seem that navy life would differ greatly from the circus lifestyle, other than the Cracker Jack uniform and the rigid guidelines. And, even though he'd already traveled from Texas to Canada and as far west as the Rocky Mountains, he had never been to the Pacific Ocean. So, he looked forward to seeing the rest of the world and the new experiences that lay ahead.

He sold his prize circus truck to Jay, handed over the dogs and ponies to his dad and hopped on a train headed for Naval Recruit Training Center, Great Lakes, IL. Toward the end of boot camp, he chose Aviation Airman School in Memphis, TN. While attending school there, he put in for Aircraft Engine Mechanic, was accepted and stayed for another three months. Graduating second in his class, put him second in line for orders, ultimately choosing a squadron with an elaborate title he thought had "aircraft carrier" written all over it. But to his surprise, it turned out to be a large aircraft transport squadron in Moffett Field, CA.

Sonny and Gloria Anne stayed in touch through letters and visits while he was home on leave. Meanwhile, back in California with Gloria Ann forefront on his mind, he worked nights for the navy and picked fruit at the local orchards during the day, saving enough money for her wedding ring. Before his second transfer to Barbers Point, HI. while home on leave, he gave her the engagement ring, officially proposed and they planned for a Hawaiian wedding. Three days after she graduated high school, Gloria Anne was on an airplane headed for the tropical island paradise and to the man she had a crush on since before she was a teenager. During his tour in the navy, Sonny advanced quickly attaining the rank of E-5, or Aviation Machinist Mate, Second Class Petty Officer, besides logging many flight hours to "Islands in the Pacific Ocean." For Gloria Anne, Hawaii was a wonderful fourteen-month vacation filled with sun, surf and serenity. Her tropical vacation ended during the fall of 1954 when Sonny was honorably discharged from the navy. They headed back to Minnesota to visit the family and to look for a job, Gloria Anne six months pregnant with Mike.

When the newly married couple returned from the Navy, Sonny's dad was waiting with big plans for them, "Albrights Attractions." The strategy was to build a large portable stage similar to that of "Jay Gould's" and to have everything in place before the following fair season started. Now that Sonny had a new pregnant bride to support, he jumped at his dad's proposal. Leo set out on the road that fall and into winter booking the show while Sonny cashed in his savings bonds and put the attraction together. He bought two used busses. One he converted into comfortable living quarters

Albrights Attractions Stage Circus

and the other into an animal carrier with a room in the back for some of the hired help. He then singlehandedly designed and constructed the entire portable stage, stripping down one of the long circus vehicles to the chassis and building the fold-out stage, complete with lights, sound system, and scenery. He completed this huge project with only a hammer, a saw, and an electric drill. The brand-new stage took three people, less than an hour, to set up the whole shebang a third of the time to set up Jay's stage and using one less man to boot.

They hit the road as scheduled with Sonny playing the role of MC, acting as the magician, performing with the dogs and ponies and during the holiday season, playing the role of Santa Claus. Leo alternated his wire walking and chin balancing routine. Gloria Anne was back up in the air doing her swinging ladder act between pregnancies. Uncle Dave did a skillful sharp shooting and balancing act... The highlight of the performance was shooting at an ax blade with two balloons on either side, the bullet splitting and breaking both balloons at once. Even little Uncle Gary did an act with his trick pony Silver.

After that first fair season, Sonny and Dave, came up with an idea to promote the show in a manner much easier than their dad had done all the previous years. They had the towns come to them. Every year each state would hold fair conventions at a hotel of their choice. Committees would congregate there to hire the entertainment for upcoming festivals and celebrations. With Sonny and Dave's new strategy, booking town fairs and celebrations became an easy sell, enabling them to schedule enough shows to fill the entire calendar season. First, they rented a room in the most visible location in the same hotel. Next, they set up a large display on a tripod just outside their door, drawing attention to "Albrights Attractions" in all its glory. The final trap unfolded inside the hotel room where they had a case of whiskey, along with all the mixes and buckets of ice, and a modern-day slide projector that would loop through large, beautifully colored photographs of all their different acts, the stage, and the crowds. Once the committees entered their quarters it was all over but the shouting. Sonny and Dave, dressed to the nines and smelling of heavy aftershave, would offer them whiskey as they treated them to a very professional presentation.

- **America's Most Beautiful All White Dog Act**
- **Don Leon, Master of the Silver Strand**
- **The Human Seal - who can balance just about any object, including the thin end of a bullwhip on his chin**
- **A Magician**
- **Dave, the sharpshooter**
- **Aerialist Gloria Decardo - the swinging ladder act**
- **Trained Dogs and Ponies - ending in a comedy riding mechanic act involving the local children**
- **The Grand Finale, "Rex" the World's Highest Diving Dog**

And they would hire other entertainment to supplement their acts.

- **Dot and Sonny Burdett - table foot juggling, rolling globe, slack wire and devil sticks**
- **Barth and Maier – pole balancing act**
- **Yo Yo the Clown - comedy trapeze, along with tap dancing on six-foot high stilts (If you got him you also got to see his gorgeous daughter, Arlene, who did rolling Globe, Contortionist, and Trampoline.)**

The town holding the festival had access to the stage for anything they desired. For example; one town utilized the stage for a beer judging contest and another, for a beauty pageant. There were also many dignitaries and politicians who took advantage of the stage, the crowds and a microphone, including the State Senatorial Candidate, Hubert Humphrey, and Gubernatorial Candidate, Orville Freeman. Bringing in two to four hundred bucks a night, depending on the package, was a sweet deal for both "Albrights Attractions" and the city. The Chamber of Commerce would get all the credit for putting on a free show for the town. The stage show brought many people over great distances spreading their money around the local stores and restaurants.

The show was highly in demand drawing the largest crowds from far and wide, being billed as "always a fast moving, clean show." Leo was also told by many professionals in the entertainment business that their stage was the best-looking outfit on the road. The town that Leo enjoyed the most was Baraboo, WI home to Gollmar Bros. and Ringling Bros. Circuses. Not only was the show an enormous success in a circus town, but Leo got to meet the 92-year-old Gollmar who passed on the circus bug to little seven-year-old Leo while showing in Belle Plaine in the late 1800s. But as they say, all good things must end; it did as well for Albrights Attractions.

On a parallel track with the success of the stage circus, was the coming age of modern conveniences such as television and air conditioning. And state, city, and municipalities imposed strict regulations and guidelines on circuses making it difficult for them to operate. People watched the entertainment on television sets right in their cool living rooms and the crowds disappeared. The days of the numerous traveling shows faded into the sunset of the American historical landscape. Sonny faced the reality of the times and retired from the circus for good in 1959. In the five short years of their marriage, Gloria Anne had given birth to as many children, Mike, Theresa, Tom, Dale, and Mary. I was the only one of the five that was born while they were out on tour, and it was not intentional. Glo was

Angela, Theresa, Sonny, Leo, Gloria, Mike

visiting the circus while they were on the way to play Medford, WI but they only got as far as White Hall before she went into labor. No doctor was available in the small, town so they found a veterinarian who helped with my delivery.

When Dad was seeking employment, Mike was getting ready to start kindergarten. Mary and I were still in diapers. Fred, a childhood friend and now part owner of Keup Chevrolet/Buick in town had always told him, "Sonny, if you ever need a job come and see me." Sonny started at the bottom painting cars, working the lube rack and doing light mechanics. Now with a steady income, he bought an old four-bedroom house on a nice city block in Belle Plaine for $4,500.00. Three years into the job, Sonny's future got a little brighter with his advancement to Service Manager, but poor old Grandpa Leo couldn't let go of the past.

Grandpa Leo, along with sons Dave and Gary went out each summer with a bare-bones outfit. Mike was older and lucky enough to travel with them when school let out for the summers. The

rest of us kids would dread the day the show left because we hated seeing our beloved grandparents leave us for so long. When the caravan of trucks and trailers would 'intentionally' drive by our house heading for Iowa each summer to wave goodbye, we would all sit on the curb and cry our eyes out. After a long summer, Mike would be back in our lives a little older and a little cockier than he was before he left. This time he had been out on the road as a real circus flunky selling circus souvenirs during the show and cleaning up the lot afterward with a broomstick tipped on one end with a nail.

He'd bring back many circus souvenirs: tongue whistles, flapping birds on a string and even rubber spiders, and he had complete control of who got what. Mike also tried to teach us this strange sounding language, "Carney" that he learned while out on the road. Mom and dad used to speak it fast, so we couldn't understand what they were saying. To the novice it was very confusing;

- Deazoo yeazoo weasant teeazo geazo teeazoo theeaza sheeazo? DO YOU WANT TO GO TO THE SHOW?

- Weeazat eeaziz yeeazor neeazame? WHAT IS YOUR NAME?

We were hoping to master the language, so we could show off in front of our friends, and we also wanted to know what the heck mom and dad were talking about. Mike had little patience with our young brains, normally ending our speech lessons a minute or two after they began. The rest of us would practice Carney between ourselves, but never could figure out just exactly where to put the Zs' or the Es.' We did not master the odd speech well enough to impress our neighborhood friends, nor well enough to keep up with the speed and the ease at which our parents spoke.

One year, the little ones normally left behind, piled in the family car on our way to Iowa to visit both sets of grandparents and witness our family circus for the first time up close. It was both interesting and enlightening watching Grandpa Leo performing his skillful acts in front of the large crowd, doing the same things he did with us kids down at the circus lot, but with a little more showmanship and a little more spring in his step-in front of the awestruck audience.

Albrights Attractions thrilled the hometown crowds three times, starting off in 1957 with the stage circus set up in front of the grandstands at the baseball park. The event was sponsored by the Men's Club of St. Peter and Paul Catholic Church, all the proceeds going toward the nuns' new convent, yet to be built. They brought in over $2,000.00 during the two-day special showing handing over every last dime to their beloved Catholic Church.

The second appearance was in 1963 when "Albright's European Style Circus" performed under the big top, thanks to local businessman Louis "Louie" Lieske who owned and operated the Sinclair Service Station situated right off HWY 169 and right across the street from a large grass filled softball field. Louie put on the FREE CIRCUS as a customer appreciation event, advertising long before the crowds gathered at the canvas entrance or Grandma Angela sold her first cotton candy. He decorated his service station island with large blow up green dinosaur balloons promoting Dino Beach Toys with the single word 'Sinclair' written in red block letters stretched across its side. Out in front of his service station was a strategically parked trailer holding up two separate large banners advertising in big colorful circus lettering, 'Free Circus' and 'Customer Appreciation Day.' Louie also mounted a large Dino dinosaur on the top of his Volkswagen car, draped it with a large banner that read: 'Circus Tickets Free' and drove around town promoting the big event. Not stopping there, he advertised further by hanging up stylish circus posters all over town which said:

The circus is coming to town, Albright's European style circus will perform two shows under waterproof tent, Softball Park across from station, Belle Plaine, Saturday, May 11th.

The big event even made the front page of the Belle Plaine Herald receiving publicity the same week of the circus. Louie handed out over 1400 free tickets, with 814 people attending both shows. That's not too bad, considering Belle Plaine's population was a little over 1500. Louie was so proud of his achievement and had such a wonderful time with the entire experience he put together a scrapbook complete with newspaper clippings, original tickets, an advertising poster, advertisement photographs along with photographs of the performers up on stage. The promotion was so successful that Louie invited our family back to perform for the last time before the hometown crowds in 1967. By this time, Albright's Circus traveled via a scaled-down version of the portable stage they used during their heydays of the 1950s.

Great Grandpa Jay Gould and wife Mabel accompanied them that year with an antique Merry Go Round and a few worn out kiddy rides. Jay and his wife were both over 80 years old and so was the 81-year-old Merry Go Round operator from New Prague, MN. The aging couple planned to finally call it quits after the season. Ironically, Jay's Maker had the same plans! Towards the end of the season, Jay got very sick and was hospitalized in his hometown of Glencoe, MN. Nearing the end, he scribbled these words on a piece of paper: **I was conscious always that I was in the presence of a living manifestation of God.** Grandpa Leo took that as a sign to throw in the towel after 50 years out on the road, but he could not give up on his slack wire or balancing act, and not his headquarters down at the circus lots.

Most town kids knew of the magical circus lot on the edge of town, many attended their own private circus showing regularly. Neighborhood children often gathered with their bikes on the edge of the gravel road, in front of the water trough waiting for the white performing ponies to come up for a drink so they could get a closer look. Once the local children discovered Grandpa Leo was there, upwards of a dozen of them followed him around like puppies as he practiced his act on the slack wire, balanced several objects on his chin or worked on his prized circus wagons; adorned with hand carved wooden scrolls, lion heads, flower patterns all painted gold along with artful shaped mirrors sitting in front of brightly colored side panels. When he completed his work, it was their turn to practice their circus skills, pretend to ride in a circus parade or listen to a circus story. Handing out pieces of hard candy, Grandpa Leo would gather the excited children around the prairie grass and tell them of his adventures to faraway lands and some of the interesting performers he met along the way. He took them with him on a journey to a very different place from their little world, painting the stories on an imaginary piece of canvas, deep in the fantasy portion of their young minds. They listened, they laughed, they clapped, they went home happy, and they dreamt about the magical circus lot and storybook character who they all new as Grandpa Leo.

The Old House

As I walk through the refuge of our alleyway, I think of all the fond memories that took place in the old neighborhood over the years. With a Marlboro cigarette tucked secretly in the cuff of my hand, I reminisce at each house or yard that triggers an image here or a recollection there. Peering between those houses towards Meridian Street, I try to recognize the cars cruising up and down the main drag. It is Friday evening in the small town of Belle Plaine, the start of the weekend and everybody will be out and about looking for a beer bash or a party at someone's house. Then again, they might cruise around town all night with a carload of friends and occasionally, head out onto the country roads to down a few beers or smoke a little weed.

The sun is low in the sky causing my shadow to appear slightly taller than my 5'4" height. Everyone says I take after good old Grandpa Leo, which is about the biggest compliment in the whole wide world. I study my long blonde hair bouncing off my broad shoulders in perfect beat with Led Zeppelin's "How Many More Times" that I had listened to before leaving our new house down at the old and magical circus lots. My shadow fades and reappears as I make my way across Park Street and onto the alleyway of our old block.

Dale

When I reach the third house on the left, I stop, take a last deep drag off my smoke and study our old house at 241 South Willow Street. Even though we moved from there only a few years ago, it seems like so much longer now. The house is unchanged, except for the color on the exterior. Missing is the old shed used to raise pigeons. Now a garage stands on the side of the house where the alfalfa field used to be, and the cement dinosaur was supposed to be built. Staring at the window above the back porch, looking back at what it was like when the six of us kids lived there while growing up in that big old drafty house.

Dad first woke us clamoring for his clothes and yelling, "Where did I leave my shoes?" as his shadow disappeared down the stairwell, the door slammed against the side of the house and tires squealed halfway down the block. That and the high-pitched whistle blowing from on top of the old firehouse building downtown announcing to the entire borough there was a fire burning

somewhere! Screaming fire trucks grew louder as they headed toward our side of town. Then one by one, the high-pitched sirens stopped, only a few blocks away from the back side of our house. Curious about what all the excitement was at this unusual hour, we climbed out of bed and gathered in the upstairs hallway. The orders and shouts of men echoing into the humid summer night drew our attention to the open window at the top of the stairs. There we huddled together and stared through the lower part of the window screen at black smoke billowing above an eerie orange glow. A battle was being waged over there against a thirsty monster that was swallowing up the shifting streams of water arching toward it from the street.

We all knew that Dad was out there during the action, risking his life and tackling the toughest assignments. Normally, he was the first one to the firehouse giving him first crack at the fire details and giving him first choice of the truck used to fight the fire. Dad was always seen driving one of the big fire trucks as they sped through town on their way to the emergency. When that fire whistle blew during work hours, he was always the fastest man, beating four other firemen who worked at the same Chevy dealership across the street. He may well have missed the action and the excitement of the circus and the navy, but as a volunteer fireman, he found he could feel the thrill of danger and the rush of exhilaration each and every time a call came in. Even though he had driven big rigs all his life, nothing thrilled him more than speeding through town in a big shiny red fire truck, sirens a-blowin' and lights a-flashin'!

He wasn't around all that much at "The Old House" on Willow Street, a little over a block away from where we now live. Between acting as a volunteer fireman, working at The Garage, driving the tow-truck after hours or "wrecker" as we called it, and his many civic duties, Dad was left with very little time to be at home. Maybe he designed it that way, a house full of six mischievous kids was enough to get on anyone's nerves. Still, he provided whatever extras he could. Raising six kids required additional income even back in those simpler times. Dad utilized his skills as a sign painter often. Most of the downtown businessmen hired both Dad and Grandpa Leo. At one time, most storefronts were designed and painted by them. Dad would also climb the 90-foot-tall light towers at the ballpark to replace burnt out floodlights at $1.00 apiece. The high salary offered was because nobody else in town wanted to climb the tower. The tower shook and swayed at the top as you reached for the burnt out light bulb. He replaced about fifteen to twenty light bulbs two times a year adding another thirty bucks to his income. Every 'after hours' wrecker run, brought home 50 percent of what The Garage took in. This was the money he used to pay the taxes on the house each year.

Even though we didn't know it, we were a poor family living in a big old house filled with second-hand furniture. We watched one black and white television set and wore mostly hand me down clothes. There were no sugary food or drink products in our cupboards or refrigerator, only Mom's occasional baking which consisted of rhubarb desert in the summer and apple pie or apple crisp in the fall. And when they shopped for food, they would load us all up in the old station wagon driving all the way to Target in the Twin Cities and filling the back with groceries bought by the bulk just to save a few bucks. If we told Mom we were hungry or thirsty, her answer was always the same, "Eat a piece of bread or get a drink of water." We couldn't afford regular milk, so Mom bought the powdered stuff and mixed it with water, which was not the best tasting. The same thing with potatoes, Mom bought the dried up flakey ones that you added water to. She swore that we couldn't taste the difference, but we could! They were the worst and we all knew they were phony the minute we saw their slightly yellow pasty appearance laying flatly in the pan. Although we ate Dad's favorite liver and onions on Fridays, most days Mom cooked up some good wholesome meals. Regardless, Dad's steady job at The Garage and living in a big house in town gave us the impression we were well off.

We all bragged to the neighborhood kids that our house was the tallest one in a four-block area totaling three stories with dormers on the west and south sides of the full sized attic. It was possibly even one of the tallest houses in town, we would boast. The Old House had a nice three season porch on the front where we kept Grandma Gloria's piano so she could play it when she came over for a visit. There was also another porch as you entered from the side rear, perfect for buffeting dirt from a bunch of kids running in and out of the house all day. It was a big drafty four-bedroom house built around the turn of the

The Old House - 241 S Willow Street

20th century without a level floor in a single room. The most dangerous place in the old dwelling lay on the floor in the family room. A large six by six metal grate situated directly over a gas firebox provided heat for the entire house.

When the furnace was lit during the frigid Minnesota winters, we could look through the metal grate and see the flames down below. The large six-foot grate would get hot when the furnace was cranking and the little kids would burn their hands or feet on it if they stayed in one place more than a second. We'd all lie around it before school in the morning hoping to get in just a few more minutes of warm sleep before heading out into the cold. The upstairs was always chilly, heated by open vents in the upstairs floor relying on heat rising up from the downstairs. After sledding down Townsend's hill or skating on the ice rink, we would sit around the large steel menace as if we were sitting around a fire warming our numb frostbitten feet and hands. As both thawed and the feeling slowly returned, along with it came that first painful tingle and then a burning sensation so intense that it made us cry. Dad would tell us, "There is nothing you can do, just don't warm them too fast or it will hurt even worse." And he was right!

Fireman or citizen, you could call Dad fearless, never backing down from anything or anyone. One of the toughest drunks in the town known for his bar fighting skills and time spent in jail was at the local swimming pool, 'drunk' and trying to enter through the women's locker room, causing a ruckus with several adults and children present. Dad was driving by when he witnessed the incident unfolding and immediately jumped out of his car and positioned himself between the troublemaker and the rest of the local citizens. He demanded forcefully and loudly, as if he was a deputized sheriff, that the drunk leave the area and quit causing trouble, at once! Luckily, he backed down but swore he would get Dad back for crossing him before he staggered down the sidewalk back up to the bars from where he came. We feared for Dad's safety for months and worried that any day the tough guy would make good on his promise, but it never happened. He was probably so smashed he didn't even remember the incident the next day. Dad did what he thought was right even when nobody was looking.

On a sunny Sunday afternoon, the family was driving in the car down CR 3 from New Prague, MN. Several local men, including our cousin, were standing just off the road urinating, as they had been on a beer cruise and half in the bag. They were feeling cocky and waved as we went by. This

was a large mistake on their part because Dad quickly slammed on the brakes, got out of our car and chewed their butt because there were women and girls in our car; Mom, Grandma Angela, Theresa, and Mary. Dad took his principles seriously and publicly didn't hesitate to take action if he believed that it was warranted to do so. Maybe he was wired that way, but perhaps his life experiences while traveling on the road with his father played a major role.

Years before when showing with Grandpa Leo in Oklahoma, the owner of the circus he was traveling with was arrested after a young girl told the authorities he made a move on her. Right before the afternoon matinee was about to start, an angry group of men drove up to the circus in pickup trucks and demanded, "Tear that rag down and get the hell out of town." In the urgent scramble and confusion of putting things away, one of the hired help got into an argument with another and was hit over the head with a tent stake knocking him unconscious and exposing part of his brain. Grandpa Leo sprang into action, grabbed one of the angry town men with a pickup truck and demanded he transport the Oklahoma boy to a hospital! Because grandpa's circus truck was the first one loaded, he and Dad followed the truck to the hospital.

While outside waiting for word of the boy, a solemn, but a still stressed crowd gathered in front of the circus truck. Grandpa Leo jumped up onto his running boards and addressed them: "Gentleman, we have an Oklahoma boy we brought in to see a doctor. This is my son, and we are from Minnesota, but I belong to the Legion. I'm a vet and this boy is a veteran, and I'll do everything I can to help save his life. I don't believe what they said about my boss because I know him to be a good man. When he finished, the mesmerized crowd slowly dispersed and left. His boss was found to be innocent after the girl admitted to authorities that she made the story up. But the circus did not show again until they were out of the State of Oklahoma. At the entrance of every town, there was a policeman blocking the way telling the circus trucks to keep on moving.

Dad gave us more reason to look up and admire him the morning after a horrific head-on collision out on HWY 169, where an entire family had been killed. He told us the story as we took bites out of peanut butter toast and sips of our hot chocolate milk. The family was hit by a drunk driver going down the wrong lane who lived through it. Anyway, a small crowd had gathered, as it normally does during these accidents, but one particular guy was laughing and joking about it no doubt trying to impress his buddies. Sonny had enough and took control! All dressed up in his fireman's firefighting attire, he grabbed the guy by the scruff of the neck and forcefully shoved his head inside the window of the burned-out vehicle. "You think this is funny Mr.?" He said as he held the strangers head inside the car long enough for him to grasp the gravity of it all. The previously cocky young man quickly ran about 20 yards, relieved his stomach on the side of the ditch, and then shamefully left the scene altogether. I don't know why Dad told us young children of these details, but it provided us with the realities of life at an early age and at the same time, may have been therapeutic for him. There are numerous other examples of his bravery, but there are also a few examples of the prankster within him as well; a man who loved to pull one over on his coworkers and friends and even a few of The Garage's customers sometimes.

Although Dad was the service manager, he always participated in or dreamed up some prank or a good joke. An old bachelor would bring his vehicle to Keups, he was a skinflint, tighter than a drum with his money, and always watched the mechanics working on his car to make sure he was getting what he paid for. Before his scheduled appointment, Dad and co-owner, Paul drilled a deep hole in the cement floor of the shop where the old guy usually stood. Then they brazed, or soldered a long piece of metal rod to a fifty cent piece and drove it into the hole. Sure enough, when the old man saw it he tried to move it with his cane, and then put his foot over it to hide the coin. Everybody went upstairs for a coffee break and when they came down the coin, the rod, the whole thing was gone. Dad said laughing, "Looks like the old bastard got it. "As they turned

around, the old guy was standing right by his car and heard the whole thing. The cheapskate never brought his car to The Garage again.

Another tightwad came into The Garage because the choke on his carburetor was sticking. He watched the mechanic take a chisel and a hammer and bend the linkage just a tad which fixed the problem immediately. When the tightwad went to pay the bill, Fred told him the cost would be $20.00. The guy made a big deal out of it and said, "It took your mechanic less than five minutes to fix my choke, all he did was hit it with a hammer." Dad told him, "Yea, that's 50 cents for the labor and $19.50 for knowing how to fix it." The man continued to argue over the cost, so Dad reached in his pocket for a quarter, threw it to him and told him to get the hell out and never come back.

Years later, brother Mike went to work at the same garage doing clean up and helping on the lube rack, etc. Well, the Capaul brothers from rural Belle Plaine bought one of Ed Gein's trucks for hauling livestock when he went to prison. (Ed Gein, the guy that dug up dead women, ate parts of them and made things like lampshades and coin purses from their skin.) All day Dad, his brother Gary who ran the lube rack and Paul, told Mike this truck was coming in for a lube job and he would be the one cleaning the windows and sweeping it out. They told him all about the butcher, Ed Gein that had owned it. Finally, the truck came in and as he was sweeping it out, he found a bloody finger under the floor mat, a rubber one that the guys had planted. At first glance, it looked like the real deal and Mike let out a yelp! The guys laughed for a half hour.

Fred never participated in the games the boys played daily, but he rarely stepped in and told any of them to stop the pranks. He may have been amused by the comradery of the guys and probably felt it helped the overall work environment. They got Mike good that time. But Dad's next prank, pulled one over on a couple of hundred smelt fishermen north of Duluth, MN...

Smelt are silvery thin fish, usually no longer than 12 inches that run or lay their eggs and spawn in streams and rivers draining into Lake Superior in the early spring. When they run, fishermen wearing their waist-high waders, walk out into the stream and rake their metal nets towards the lake in hopes of scooping up a few. When the smelt get running and you hit it right, catching a dozen to two dozen at one scoop is not uncommon. We would travel up there every year, most times in the back of an old pickup truck with a camper shell over the top. Dad would always let us bring one friend along usually picking somebody without a father of his own. One year we brought back three large trash cans full of the smelt and it took the entire family all afternoon to clean and freeze them all. The only thing we didn't look forward to was Dad's cooking. His idea of a good meal was pouring three soups together; split pea with ham, chicken noodle, and vegetable beef. It didn't matter if it was those three as he would have grabbed randomly three others and used them just as well.

This year we were at Knife River hanging out in the back of a pickup truck with a crude camper over the back end using a kerosene tent heater to take a little bite out of the air. The smelt fish normally run upstream at night, and the time came for us to climb out of the back of the warm truck and head to the cold riverbank with our nets and containers. All the fisherman were standing on the bank waiting for the run to start with only a few people dipping in the river. Out of nowhere Dad says, "Wait here kids, I'll be back in about ten minutes or so." Sure enough, a few minutes later we could hear a familiar voice in the distance, "Here they come, here they come!" Everybody scrambled to get their nets. There was even a guy dressed in a wetsuit who dove in the river with his dip net. Dad showed up a few minutes later laughing his butt off. He had climbed up onto a railway bridge which crossed the river downstream shouting out from there.

As I said, Dad wasn't around much, but when he was, he took the time to fix the yard up or work on some family project. He welded/built a giant swing set and buried a large tractor tire halfway into the ground for us to climb on. We used to run, then jump over the tire while one of us

pretending to shoot with a baseball bat (we imagined it was a bazooka) to see who could simulate the most realistic death. Another time Dad built roman shields and even fashioned solid steel swords so we could engage in mock battles. Both Mom and Dad painted them up looking like shields out of ancient times, even painting a crest of each like the Knights of England. It was amazing none of us were ever injured. He also put up a sturdy wire fence encircling the large yard to keep the little kids from straying and to help give Mom some piece of mind.

Gloria Decardo the glamorous circus aerialist was now just our mother Gloria or Glo for short. We all just called her mom or ma. A few years earlier she was featured as "America's" Arial Queen thrilling crowds daily and now she had six kids to look after, most born within a year of each other. Joe was the latest addition to the family born a whopping four years after little sister Mary. Having all those kids, the first five, so close together, resulted in her developing an array of health problems. Despite her illnesses and tight family budget, she always made sure we had three squares a day and always made sure we were dressed nice.

Mom, and Dad liked to show their kids off to friends and relatives because we were a diverse and cute bunch. Out of all six of us, none of us looked like either parent or another sibling, unlike some families who all looked alike. Each one of us even had different color and consistency of hair. For example, my thin blonde hair turned white in the summer sun and Tom's just the opposite, thick dark brown. Theresa kept her hair rather short as Mom grew Mary's beautiful hair long and would put curls through the entire length. Mike and Theresa were rather tall, and Mary and I were fairly short with Tom somewhere

Mike holding Joe. Tom, Theresa, Mary & Dale

in-between. Tom possessed all the physical attributes of the Stibals on Mom's side whereas I possessed all the physical attributes of Grandpa Leo on Dad's side. The only thing similar to all was certain mannerisms as with most families. The four years younger, Joe was still a baby and a very cute and well behaved at that. I'll never forget the day that Mom brought him home from the hospital and what a big deal it was for us kids. Just watching Mom take care of him was a wonderful learning experience for the rest of us.

At times, Glo would dress Theresa and Mary alike, and she would also do the same for Tom and me. She called Mike and Theresa the big kids and the rest of us the little kids. Dad was happiest when we were happy, and he was constantly seeking our approval when the opportunity arose, "What do you think of this kids? Or, "What do you think of that kids? Huh?" "Are you kids having fun yet?" Huh… And then, if we responded in a positive manner, he would ask us again with a wide grin so he could hear our response again. Dad was happiest when everybody was having fun and getting along, but if we weren't, look out…

Just satisfying imaginations as huge as Grandpa Leo's was a never-ending challenge for Mom. Back in those beginning years, we fascinated with the monster movies on TV such as Dracula, the Wolfman, Frankenstein, the Mummy, and the Creature from the Black Lagoon. Mom bought grey plastic, put together models, and then she painted them up all scary looking. Dracula even had blood dripping down the side of his mouth! We brought all our friends over to look at the display, and they thought they were awesome.

Besides the huge task of keeping track of us all, she was constantly at work baking, cleaning, cooking, or making us costumes. She made Mike and me our Batman/Robin superhero outfits and she made or picked out all of our Halloween costumes. Every holiday was made extra special by Mom, even with the limited household income Dad was bringing in. She was Santa Claus, the Easter Bunny, and the Tooth Fairy. She was also the expert we turned to when we wanted to fill out and mail in special offers for toy dinosaurs featured on the back of cereal boxes. That part where the company allowed two to three months for delivery was a stinger, and we'd watch the mailbox a month into the wait, bugging Mom daily until it finally arrived in the mail.

Although poor, we were never bored! Grandpa Leo, Mom, Mike and Theresa ensured us little kids would have a childhood filled with fantasy and wonder, like the time we tried to catch the tooth fairy. One of us little kids had lost a tooth, and the big kids derived a plan sure to discover where the tooth fairy lived. Mike found an ink pad and set it on the floor with the tooth next to it as bait. The fairy would think the ink pad was a trampoline and take a break out of her busy schedule to have a little fun. Little would she know that as she jumped up and down, she was getting ink all over the bottom of her shoes? We could then follow the footsteps left behind leading us to her hideout. Sure enough, the next morning the tiny ink footprints were there on the floor. The tooth was gone with two quarters replacing it. We followed the tiny footsteps all the way to the outside front step. Unfortunately, that is where the footsteps ended leading us to believe that is where she flew away. Oh, the fairy size shoe prints, one of Theresa's Barbie dolls.

Another time Mike told the little kids he had planted a "small candy tree" and a few days later the big kids tied candy on the branches after we had gone to bed. We all offered proudly the magic candy to our neighborhood friends extremely jealous at our good fortune. Every kid did not have a candy tree growing that produced red striped gum and butterscotch wrapped in plastic.

Grandpa Leo's stories of little leprechauns living underground in the roots of our trees stretched our imagination to the extreme. We even baited the little people with food and anxiously waited with a canning jar in our hand in case one of them appeared. The big kids had spotted them several times, but by the time we got there, the little creatures had gone back underground.

The same thing happened with Santa Claus and the Easter Bunny. One of the big kids would say, "There they are!! Dang!! You just missed them." Rainbows had a pot of gold at the end. Snowflakes resulted from pillow fights between the angels. You could catch a robin if you could sneak up to it with a salt shaker and sprinkle some salt on its tail, and the end of the horizon is where you could jump up onto a cloud. All true because Theresa told us so. One magical day it even snowed towards the end of summer as we played outside in relatively warm temperatures. Another time it only rained on the other side of the street. If that isn't mystifying enough on its own, try explaining that one to your five years old... At that age, our block was our world so next time we thought it would rain on our block and not the one across the street.

As it is with most dreams, our biggest and grandest never came true. After one rather successful night of storytelling and feeling a little boastful, Grandpa Leo announced that he would build a large cement brontosaurus dinosaur in the alfalfa field next to the house. It would have ladders on the inside and slides on the outside. It would really be something! I think he intended the announcement as something for us to dream about that night. But, the dinosaur story grew into a monster that was talked and dreamed about by us kids along with the entire neighborhood. "Sure you can come over and play on it after its built," we would say. "Grandpa said he was going to build it as tall as the house, and it's going to be as long as the alfalfa field," we would boast. "Yeah, we're all gonna sleep out in it during the summer." Every time grandpa came over for a visit, one of us or one of the neighborhood kids would pester him about it, "When you gonna start building the dinosaur, grandpa?" The answer was always, "Oh, next year," or "Sometime after the winter." He gave us the most vivid picture of just how big and grand it would be. Like a fish story

over time, the dinosaur got bigger and bigger!" "Will the tail be big enough to go inside grandpa?" Or, "Grandpa, can we put a secret chamber in the leg that only we will know about?" The dinosaur story went on for so long that we eventually stopped thinking or asking about it. The one-time dream to build a house-size dinosaur slowly faded along with our childhood.

Halloween at the old Albrecht house was a highly anticipated event by every kid in town. Each year they knew they'd be met at the door with a frightening new prank conjured up by Dad and Mom. One year Dad rigged a wire running directly over the front door from the attic to a tree in the front yard. A weighted hilex bleach bottle hung from the wire, covered with a long, white sheet. When trick or treaters would approach the house, he'd release the "ghost" and at that moment would rub a thick piece of wire with "rosin" to create a screeching sound as the spectacle sailed loudly over the front step to the porch.

Another time he took a windshield's large cardboard box from work, painted it black, and placed lighted candles around it on the front porch. He lay in state in the improvised coffin dressed as a ghoul. As kids would arrive, Mom dressed up as Frankenstein's wife escorted them over to the makeshift coffin where he'd sit straight up, eyes glaring and hand them their candy. But one year his pranks went too far.

He dressed in a costume, sporting a rubber monster mask from Keup's Garage, used to wear while undercoating cars. The mask by itself was scary enough, but the liberal coating of the tar undercoat jazzed it up. Two kids edged toward the door for treats, when Dad suddenly appeared in his "greasy getup," with hands out as if to grab them. One boy ran away immediately, the other was trapped in the porch. He shrieked, dropped his bag of candy, ran between Dad's legs, and out the door; his screams trailing behind him into the night.

After we would see the scary exhibition that Dad and Mom had come up with, we would head out and do a little trick or treating on our own. One of the first places we'd head was to Edberg's Dairy. They lived on the end of our block. We couldn't wait to get a small container of delicious chocolate milk. Some parts of town were better than others and we kept track of who gave the most candy or the best caramel cornball. Even back then, stories of apples with razor blades or pins in them and open candy laced with LSD were real and we took them seriously, even though we thought that most folks in town were honest. And watch out for the Fahey boys because instead of going door to door, they bullied kids into giving up their candy. As much fun as Halloween was, we always looked forward to Christmas.

Christmas at The Old House was by far the family's favorite holiday for several reasons. Mom would make the house all up for Christmas with decorations while listening to Christmas records play out of the old phonograph. During the 40's and 50's, some of the best Christmas music was put down on vinyl and it seemed like Glo had the most popular albums. Getting the decorations down from the attic was one of the rare times we got to go up there and explore the cold haunted space. Dad always picked up a real Christmas tree from downtown somewhere and Mom decorated it with large Christmas colored lights, a ton of ornaments and a bunch of tinsel. The smell of that real Christmas tree flowed throughout The Old House reminding us of our vacations to Northern Minnesota while camping out under huge pines.

The city of Belle Plaine hosted a contest and gave out a winning prize for whoever could decorate their house and property the best. Many residences participated in this yearly event and each year they would come up with something new to take home the prize. On Christmas Eve we'd drive around town and look at all the houses made up with brightly colored lights and different Christmas scene settings. Then we'd cruise by the Nativity Scene that Grandpa Leo built and painted for the town. It was the largest display in the state and was so popular that Greyhound bus drivers would stop and let the passengers out to have a closer look. Grandpa Leo even built

and painted two 17-foot-high Santa's that greeted travelers entering on either side of town. And then it was back home and into bed hoping Saint Nicholas would soon be there.

The next morning it was finally Christmas. We skipped downstairs to presents brought by the big guy himself who never failed to eat half of a chocolate chip cookie, drink a half glass of milk, and leave a thank you note signed Santa, Ho! Ho! Each gift marked with our name in giant letters. We didn't always get what we wanted, but he had somehow slipped inside our house undetected leaving us gifts and that's all that mattered to us. After playing with our presents, we would all get ready for church, load the car with all the gifts, and then head to Grandma Angela's house afterward... The church was always decorated beautifully and the choir was always at their best, but we couldn't wait for the lengthy Mass to end so we could hurry up and get to our Grandparent's house for the food and the fun.

We could tell it was Christmas the minute Grandma Angela opened the side door as the warmth and smell of her holiday cooking swept over us. A loving hug and a Merry Christmas greeting to each one of us six, as we walked in the door one at a time. First grandma's hug and then Grandpa's customized handshake. Our hands would start from a distance away while we formed a cup in our shaking side. Then we'd bring our cupped hands together in a playful clap. If everything went according to Hoyle, the impact would make a nice loud pop and he would say, "Ohhhhhh that was a good one!"

Grandma Angela & Grandpa Leo

We'd answer, "Heyyyyyyy, way to go Leooooooo!!!!" After a short visit, we'd sit down to a tasty old-fashioned turkey dinner made with Grandma's homemade delicious dressing and Aunt Arlene's famous roaster full of sweet tasting baked beans. During the Christmas dinner, Grandma never sat down throughout the entire meal and was constantly attending to every one of our needs. Before dinner finished, Dad had talked Grandpa Leo into a shot of schnapps to warm him up for the present opening ceremony soon afterward.

After the traditional turkey dinner, it was downstairs to her basement with spackled walls painted pink no less, where she had a three-foot-high ugly, fake Christmas tree sitting on a table decorated with red and gold ornaments, candy canes and no lights. My Grandmother was a traditionalist true to the core, but she had this ugly, modern-day tree. A stool was set up "center stage" next to the tree, and one by one we would open presents from Mom and Dad; all those once a year new clothes. Then we'd open the fun presents from Grandma and Grandpa and Uncle Dave and Aunt Arlene. There were always slide photos taken with those big, blinding flash throw away bulbs which practically filled the garbage container when all the pictures were finished. If Santa had not brought the present we wanted, and if it didn't cost too much, Grandma probably had it under the fake tree. Christmas was as always magical at grandma's house and so were our yearly family vacations.

All year Dad would pinch his pennies and plan in microscopic detail where we would go on vacation and how much it would cost. At the dinner table, Dad would pull out a map and show us which sights we would see and what our camp spot offered in the way of trails or monuments nearby. He often bragged to both friends and co-workers at The Garage how little money the whole trip cost. The few expenses he inquired were gas, campground fees, and entrance fees to different exhibits and State Parks. The vacations varied from staying at campgrounds in northern

Minnesota, touring Mark Twain's home in Hannibal, MO, to viewing the caves of Meramec Caverns in AR. And just as we'd get out of town and hit HWY 169 on our way out to our yearly dream, Dad spoke the same famous words every year, "Kids, let's get the hell out of town!" Dad could tell us exactly when we had traveled a mile without looking at the odometer, and he could tell us just before the traffic light would turn green. We always played games to keep us occupied like how many state license plates we could spot or draw a squiggly scribble on paper and have someone draw a picture out of it. Brother Mike was always pointing out the wildlife he spotted to the rest of us. We'd travel down the highway with Dad's homemade family trailer in tow.

He built the trailer from the chassis up in the upstairs of Keup's Garage complete with bedroom, storeroom and Glo's kitchen featuring a drop-down table and fold out shelves. We all went to The Garage to either give him a hand or check on our progress. Dad and Mom had the luxury of their own private bedroom with a queen size bed and a real mattress on top. It was cozy, even sliding doors for the shelves above the head of the bed used for extra storage and a screen door to keep out the mosquitoes. When it was finally finished, he painted it blue and white, the same color as the car and it didn't look too bad going down the highway.

Mary helping Mom in front of Dad's trailer

Mom packed a week's worth of food and all the pans and utensils to do the cooking out of Sonny's cleverly built kitchen. Our parents were masters of this type of travel having done it professionally most of their lives. Grandpa Leo went with us a few times and would sit for hours in the car just taking in the sights, no doubt envisioning he was back on the road going to the next circus town. We would stop at rest stops and mom would go back, set up shop and make the family sandwiches or fix a quick snack. Then it was back in the car to continue on to our destination, and in the true spirit as circus people drive for hours on end without stopping. Once our campsite was all set up, Mom would make large complex meals cooking them over a small four burner propane gas camp stove.

The place we loved to vacation the most was northern Minnesota because we got everything: Lake Superior, tall pines, birch trees, hiking trails, and an abundance of wildlife. Driving alongside ocean size Lake Superior was always beautiful as we would try and count the number of long Iron Ore ships that dotted the horizon. We all loved to camp in true camping fashion and that meant all of us kids sleeping in a blue eight-man tent. We even had bunk beds for the two girls and Tom and me. Joe had his own cot set up between the bunk beds and Mike in true woodsman fashion, slept on the floor or slept in his own tent.

Our family vacation to Kawishiwi Campground, Superior National Forest near Ely MN laid the framework for Mike's interest in deer hunting four years later. The family was hiking a trail in the pine woods when what Mike thought were two big dogs busted out of the brush in front of us. As they trotted down the trail, he realized they were deer; the first he'd ever seen. Later that day near our camp a big buck with a full rack walked across one trail at close range. Mike was so awed that he fainted to the ground and laid on his back, stunned at his good fortune. We were more stunned at seeing Mike go down rather than the big buck which just crossed our trail.

Besides those fun-filled family vacations, every year we would travel to some relative's home, park or cabin for a reunion with mom's side of the family. Every fall we would go to Grandpa Leo's brother Chris's cottage on Maple Lake to rake his leaves for him. The cottage was named by lakeside residences, "The Castle on the Lake" because of its flat, grey stone exterior and castle looking structure designed and built by Chris himself over a twenty-year period. He designed and built it for his wife Rose, but she never slept

Uncle Chris's castle on the lake

a night in the place. Why, we don't know, but it was beautiful with a huge cedar lined great room that featured vaulted ceilings, a huge fireplace and a very large crystal chandelier hanging down the middle. The master bedroom even had a fireplace, goose down bedspreads and antique furniture. There was even a little round tower on the end facing the lake. It was a huge yard with leaves a foot deep. It would take all day to clean them up, and that cheap, old, rich bastard never gave us a dime for helping. I discovered how cheap he was after Tom told me about his experience up at the castle. One time I was supposed to go up to the lake with Grandpa Leo and Chris for a fishing trip, but I got sick and Tom went in my place. Tom had to eat the fish he caught, off the same paper plate he had pancakes and syrup on earlier that day for breakfast. That was the one time in my life, I was glad I got sick...

The Little Corner

Belle Plaine was a small farming community with a population of around 1,750. Just about everyone knew everyone else... and their dog. It's about halfway between Minneapolis and Mankato, the northern edges running parallel along the banks of the Minnesota River. A quaint little town known as the "only Borough west of the Mississippi," also for its wide streets that run north-south, east and west, and infamous for its eight bars in the downtown area. Belle Plaine always had a reputation as a "wet town." When Grandpa Leo was a boy, the population of around 1,200 souls sported 13 saloons!! On Friday and Saturday nights the town buzzed with activity until the bars closed at one a.m. For some, the party continued till dawn. Dad always said, "Take a 50-foot rope, tie it to your rear end, and you can touch four different bars and not run out of rope."

Our childhood block consisted of roughly twenty homes all built around the turn of the 20th century. Ten homes each separated by a gravel alley with a worn down patchy strip of grass and weeds running through the center. When most houses were built, garages went up in the back of the homes as automobiles became more prevalent. Homeowners drove through the center of the block, or alley to park inside their garages. It also served as a path for large farm tractors that would appear each spring, tilling and spreading smelly cow manure used for fertilizer on top of the large German and Irish gardens which dotted the neighborhood. The manure made the whole block stink for weeks on end, but boy did that stuff work. The alley was also a big deal to us because that's where all the action took place near the larger back lawns, around the gardens, on the sheds, and in the trees. Because our house sat three doors down from the southwest end of the block, we all called the corner there "The Little Corner" and we claimed it as our own because it was so close to our house. So, it's only natural we named the corner at the opposite end "The Big Corner" because it was so 'far' away. Belle Plaine was not a large or populated town by any means and everyplace essential to us spread over four blocks from where we lived.

Grandpa Leo and Grandma Angela's house was only two blocks away, as was Dad's work and the downtown area. The South Park was a mere two blocks over behind the high school, and the public swimming pool right across the street from The Big Corner. And if Mom couldn't make it downtown to Huber's Red Owl to pick up a loaf of bread, she would send one or two of us across the active Meridian Street (the main drag) to pick up a loaf at Barney's Hamburger Joint. We loved going to Barneys because the long counter was filled on one end with much penny candy kept inside large glass jars. Sometimes we'd get two twisty strawberry licorice pieces for the price of one, and if we spent a nickel we were splurging! Everybody's favorite penny candy was the perplexing sweet/sour powder inside the pixie sticks, not only because of the tizzling taste, but they lasted for more than a minute or two. And, even though our house was located smack dab in town, we got a little taste of wildlife at our Great Uncle Harold's beautifully maintained wild yard. Great Uncle Harold lived down the alley a little more than a stone's throw from our house.

The 30-year high school English teacher tutored Mike on many wildlife subjects which included birds, edible mushrooms, local plant life and the Minnesota woods in general. Not only that, but Harold loaned Mike several of his wildlife books and records to study and learn from. He once provided Mike a record with recordings of many birds singing, tweeting and even buzzing. For example, the narrator would articulate in a dull monotone voice, "The Tufted Titmouse," and then the sound of the bird recording would play out for about 30 seconds, give or take a few. One of the funniest birds sounded like a loud three-second buzzer! bzzzzt...bzzzzt. We couldn't help but roll on the floor laughing as we would all tilt our hip to one side and lift our leg up in perfect sync with the noise. Harold seldom showed his personal side or displayed any affection for anyone

other than immediate family, but he took a liking to Mike. Harold even let down his guard one day opening a cotton lined box full of mothballs, he revealed a tiny, dead male Ruby-throated Hummingbird that had flown into a window at the local high school where he taught. Every time Mike would go to visit Harold at his home, he would beg him to show it to him.

The rest of us kids learned about the different species of birds after Dad put a bird feeder at the edge of the yard by the alfalfa field between us and the neighbors towards the big corner. We would watch the many species of birds at the feeder for hours on end; Mike pointing out which birds were which. He also tacked tallow to a tree in front of the outside kitchen window during the winter months which attracted upside down nibbling Nut Hatches and charming little Chickadees. But as much as Mike was enthralled with the songbirds, Goldfinches, Cardinals, and Orioles all fell to his Daisy BB gun so he could study them up close. Not exactly the homework assigned to him by his tutor! And, Harold's endless variety of flowers attracted more than bees, hummingbirds, and songbirds, it also attracted young nephews in search of trouble.

Brother Tom and I used to meander down the alley to his house and play a risky game of hunting for large, fat, yellow jacket bees and long body, stinging wasps with mason jars in one hand and a screw top tin lid in the other. Our goal was to see who could catch the biggest and the most, sometimes the most variety. The trick to catching bees wasn't catching the first one but catching about number four without letting the other mad, buzzing bees loose when the top of the jar's lid was off while taking a stab at another. Once we finished catching all the bees, we'd give the jars a good little shake so we could watch the battles unfold inside the captive glass and listen to the fierce fights through the holes punched in the top of the tin lid. Often, the girls would tag along during these pursuits so they could observe our fearlessness from a short distance away and then look closely at an insect capable of inflicting excruciating pain. Tom and I would proudly display the captured bees to the girls, even giving the jar another little shake before holding the tin lid close to their ear so we could laugh at their frightened facial expressions. The most dangerous part, which required extreme precision, was letting them go after they were battle-scarred and ticked off. The secret was to open the jar, toss it as far away from us as we could and run full speed in the opposite direction. One by one the pissed off bees would leave the jar. Later, we would sneak up slowly to see if they had all departed before gathering the jars up for use some other day. Sometimes our pursuit of something new got us into a sting, like the time Tom and I launched a massive offensive on a black hornet's nest.

We were overjoyed one summer day to find a foot-long black hornet's nest hanging on the branch halfway up a tree, located right next to the detached garage on The Little Corner's property. Well, we threw rocks at the rounded grey paper nest trying to knock it down so we could study it after all the bees had departed. With each rock ripping through the nest, the bee swarm around it grew. I was lucky to be standing in the alley farther back, whereas Tom was much closer to the nest and making all the direct hits. As the swarm was increasing in size, so were the number of bee scouts sent out in search of the rock throwers behind the unprovoked attack. Tom was a better shot. He caught their attention more than I did. When his rock made a direct hit at the top of the nest, he knocked their entire dwelling to the ground. It exploded into a menacing dark cloud of bees that headed directly for wide-eyed and open-mouthed Tom. He raced towards The Old House at full speed as the tornado of bees took aim and zeroed in. Poor Tom swatted, twisted, grimaced, and screamed, "ouch, ouch, ouuuuch" all the way inside the side door of our house. I ran down the alley as far away from the hornets as I could and stayed there for a good fifteen minutes. When I arrived back at the house, Tom was swelled up like a balloon and headed to the clinic with Mom! Unfortunately, Tom discovered that he was allergic to bee stings and feared them ever since. No more bee collecting for us.

We also attempted to capture hummingbirds, coming within inches of the little flying fairies. Tom and I believed that we had one in the jar. We scooped it off a flower while hunting for bees down at Harold's flower gardens and quickly rushed home to show Mike. He identified it as a species of large moth with many similarities to the hummingbird; such as the long thin snout and the vibrating wings.

Both Mom and Dad were a little more than lenient for housing creatures of all kinds around various parts of the house. We had them in our room, in our basement, in the closets and even had them in the kitchen. We would have four or five mason jars lined up against the wall in the back porch. One held a caterpillar who spun a cocoon on a cozy branch we cocked to one side, later emerging as a beautiful Monarch butterfly. In another was a big black spider we caught while hanging around Grandpa Leo down at the circus sheds. We would feed it a fresh fly each day and watch the spider pounce on the prey and go about its trade twisting it into a tiny ball before taking the first taste. Still another jar held a trophy-sized yellow jacket which Tom and I had captured a few days before the hornet's nest incident. Besides the jars, we found a salamander under a rock beside the house and that too went on display in a baking pan right next to the slithering Garter Snake sitting there sticking out his smooth slippery tongue.

Dad even built us a glass aquarium ant farm, filled it with dirt and ants. One time, after feeding the ants some sugar, one of us kids forgot to put the rubber plug back into the access hole drilled in the top and all the ants escaped ending up all over the house. Mom maintained a tropical freshwater fish aquarium in the family room next to our fiery furnace. While cleaning it one day, she accidentally spilled a few fish onto the floor and some fell through the metal grate and fried.

Our desire to capture creatures of all kinds did not stop with mere insects and reptiles. We drowned out baby gophers and placed them in a cardboard box. We found six baby wild rabbits and built a crude cage for them in the backyard. We had baby birds, and even brought back to life two half froze baby raccoons. Mom baked them in our oven at 150 degrees Fahrenheit for a few hours with the oven door left open. Add to the list frogs, toads, and turtles, too. Perhaps we had ourselves a real menagerie, just like they had on the circus. I guess that's why Mom and Dad didn't mind our zoo all that much because they grew up around them, too. They almost encouraged it. One day, they brought home a tiny chameleon lizard that changed colors. We put a little leash around his neck, hooked him up to an eight-inch chain, pinned him to our couch and fed it flies by hand. Simultaneously they picked up little turtles and put them in one of those molded plastic containers that even had a ramp where the turtle could crawl up on an island topped with a plastic palm tree. "

The most wonderful living gift I ever received as a young boy was a domesticated baby rabbit who I named "Bunner." On the morning of my fourth birthday, I was awakened by all my brothers and sisters saying, "Happy birthday, Dale! Get up and look at your present!" Mom and Dad were smiling as they watched from the doorway. Still in bed, half asleep, they handed me a black and white pattern rabbit that barely fit inside the cup of my hands. We would let him run around the house. After a little romp, we put him back into his cage. Then we'd go around and pick up all the little round droppings he left in his favorite spots. As Bunner grew, I kept him in an empty cage that Dad had originally built for Uncle Gary's real prize pigeons that was next to the shed in the backyard. I bought him a collar and leash so I could walk him around the yard and the neighborhood. Sometimes we'd all take him out in the backyard to watch him run full speed kicking up his heels, zigzagging as he went. The older he got, the faster he became until one day he ran away from us and kept on running.

After a heart-wrenching week of searching, we put an ad in the Belle Plaine Herald describing him, our plea for his safe return and contact information. Sure enough, a few days later the phone rang with Lester Otto's mom on the other end. Lester had found Bunner while visiting his

grandparents three doors down the block and had seen the Ad in the paper. So, within a half hour, Lester and his mom showed up at our side door with my black and white birthday present, Bunner tucked tightly in his arms. I could tell the kid had a hard time giving him back to us, but he knew it was the right thing to do. We kept Bunner for years and even though he was officially mine, the rest of the kids all took ownership of him. We were also very fortunate to reside in a unique area of town with kids of all ages running and playing about.

We practically lived outside during those fond summer days, always curious about what was going on with all the neighbors. A young family of four lived directly across the alley behind our house, another family of four, the oldest my age, were two houses down from them and still another younger family of three resided kiddy corner across the street from our house. Kids of all ages, shapes, and sizes were constantly outside playing, but their childish games bored us, so we always gravitated toward the older boys who lived on the block; the ones that made life a lot more interesting.

Our next door neighbor, Jack, lived on the other side of the alfalfa field that separated the two properties and he was a lot older than us, maybe 17. He used the alfalfa field for his shooting of the bow and arrow. But the big event we all anticipated the most from our older neighbor was the Fourth of July. Jack would spend the entire year putting together large magnificent models of ships, trucks, tanks, and all kinds of cool things. On the Fourth of July, he would plant cherry bombs in each of his models and one by one, blow them to smithereens! The cherry bombs sent pieces of plastic everywhere, even out into the street. He would also put varying amounts of explosives under a tin can to see how high up he could launch it. It was quite a show, we all loved it, except for Dad, who had put together and built a few models of his own and could not understand why Jack blew his up. Dad would watch out the window, look slightly down and just shake his head from side to side in disbelief. Instead of Jack's younger brother, Don, spending his days working on a constructive hobby like his older brother, he was the quintessential serial killer of all living animals and crawling creatures.

He was a big fat kid. We used to laugh at him riding by on his bike with a banana seat, skinny tires and butt cheeks extending way out on each side. Don would get a big bowl of potato chips, watermelon or whatever and lay on the sidewalk eating his snacks while burning nightcrawlers and worms with a magnifying glass, using the sun as the source of his enjoyable entertainment. Once the worms were well cooked, he would lay sideways with his head resting on his hand as he carefully placed them with his other hand on an anthill, only to watch the ants go about their busy work on the wriggling burnt flesh. This guy was plain evil, purely no soul. He once tied the tails of two cats together and hung them on the clothesline wire to watch them claw each other up. He also liked to catch live birds, squirt a little lighter fluid on them, tie a fuse to their legs, light it and throw them into the air watching them burst into flames and drop from the sky. He came up with many senseless ways of torturing animals, birds and crawling creatures and no one was more attracted to it than brother Tom. Whenever Tom would see Don's big body lying on the sidewalk with a magnifying glass in his hand, he would run outside to watch the gruesome games unfold.

On the other side of Jack and Don's house was a couple other older, cool guys Tom and Jerry. They were well liked and respected by everybody in the neighborhood. Unlike neighbor Don, Tom followed his older brother Jerry's hobby by learning how to play the electric guitar. Tom used to practice with his band "Vas Diferens" in the basement of their house. When we would hear the loud rock music from our house, we'd head over, peek through the basement window and watch them play. Tom and Jerry would often join us in a softball game in the alfalfa field next to the house. I wasn't old enough to play. I didn't understand the game, but I discovered what a softball felt like when it connected with the solid end of a hard wooden baseball bat.

I walked into the back side of the batter's box just as big 200 lb. plus Don took a swing at the softball. The bat hit me hard with a deafening thud directly across my left temple. A high pitched steady squeal rang inside my head for what seemed like forever and thousands of little shiny lights shot off in all directions. I thought for sure that I was a goner. All the kids ran from the horrific scene, all that is, except Tom and Jerry. They stayed and practically carried me into the house where our babysitter, Mugs Schuman, put a cold ice pack on the side of my face and waited for Mom and Dad to get home. I sported a huge shiner which turned several

Dale sporting a black eye and baseball bat imprint

colors over the weeks it healed. This act of kindness showed the entire neighborhood a lot about Tom and Jerry's character.

Another example of Tom and Jerry's character mixed with an unexpected quantity of courage came the following year. It happened right across the alley where the younger family of four lived. Their father, Wayne, was an overly strict disciplinarian and was hard on his kids, often locking them in a little shed for hours as one form of punishment. Once he left his eldest son locked in the shed all night long with nowhere to sleep but the cement floor. The day after the incident, we asked the young boy why he kept yawning and out of the mouths of babies, he spilled the beans. Wayne was also a bully to the neighborhood kids and would come out of the house after us if our ball rolled into his garden. We were terrified by him!

One day Tom and Jerry were playing ball with us, Jerry was a senior in high school, growing into a man and had enough of our "mean" neighbor. He purposely rolled the ball into the guy's garden and walked right across the alley, stepping over the staked-out twine encircling the garden and grabbed our ball. We expected him to get out of there quick, but he waited till "Wayne" the mean neighbor came out yelling and screaming. Jerry calmly walked up to him, grabbed him by the neck and told him in no uncertain terms, "Leave us alone from now on, or I'll clean your clock!" We never were bothered again, and Jerry became one of the neighborhood heroes. We were all sorry to see him leave for the armed forces a few years later after he received his Vietnam draft notice. Everybody in the neighborhood was gathered at his house around their picnic table as the large dull green military truck pulled up next to the curb. Jerry threw his bag up to a few guys standing in the back of the box, jumped up the back end, waved and was gone.

Five boys close to Tom's age lived within a three-block area from our house. They usually flocked to our place because our family always had some exciting project in the works or were engaged in play that hadn't been tried before. And each boy was enchanted with and drawn to our colorful circus heritage, and we all shared the same legendary grandfather, "Grandpa Leo." Some of us were even blood brothers, cutting the bottom of our hands and pushing together the bleeding wound, we made our lifelong pledge just like the American Indians did.

John Stier lived across the street from the little corner. He was sister Theresa's age and his parents and grandparents were well-respected businesspeople in town who owned and operated Stier's Bus Company. And they owned a couple of farm bulk tank trucks which they used for transporting dairy milk from local farmers to the Creamery. John's Grandfather would make the daily walk down our alley from his house at the end of the block on the way to his bus sheds, always giving us kids a friendly greeting as we played outside. John had an older brother, younger

brother, and sister, but out of them all, he clearly was the most daring. His immediate goal, which he bragged to the boys would happen soon, was his attempt to climb to the very top of the water tower located right across the street from The Big Corner, as all Stier boys had done in their once in a lifetime pursuit to become a man. The thin slippery steel rungs rose 90 feet to the top of the tower, an exploit we believed was worthy of the rite of passage. John would attempt this daring feat during the middle of the night, climbing blindly above a bottomless ground, making the treacherous climb even more terrifying. All the boys were excited about the prospect of climbing the tall tower too, and committing the same daring act required of all the Stier boys, but we still had doubts about its legitimacy and regularly pressed John for the truth. Anyway, he was always busy working on the big orange school buses and around their huge bus shed. The same shed that almost went up into flames while Tom and I were playing with him in a sandbox located right beside it.

John got little free play time, but when he did, he made the most of it. The army battle scene looked realistic enough with the little green plastic men scattered on sand hills, in the ditches and even in water pools. But the display was missing one element that would bring it to life, fire and army men burnt during the imaginary war. John grabbed a gas can out of the bus garage and a book of matches from inside the house. Our dads were both volunteer firemen and John had been taught all about fire safety from his dad, so he thought he knew exactly how to safely carry out the chore as if he were an explosives expert on a Hollywood film set. He poured a little gas in two areas of the sandbox, put the gas can at a 'safe' distance, lit a match and threw it onto the gasoline. The field was now real and to make it even more realistic, we threw a few veterans soldiers into the flames and watched their faces, arms and legs melt away. Everything was going according to plan until the fires died down and our 'explosives expert' was far from finished having fun.

Well, one thing John's dad had not taught him, probably because he never thought John would be playing with gasoline and matches. Fire, like water, takes the path to least resistance and it does so quickly. Good old John squirts more gasoline on the fading fires to make the flames many times larger. He stood a 'safe' distance away, but as the stream of lethal liquid hit the smoking sandbox, a flame traveled rapidly back up the downward stream of gas, skyward to the can and flickered on the red plastic pour spout. The fuse was lit with one-third of the can full of gas and the other two-thirds filled with the explosive fumes. Our dangerous child's play was a ticking time bomb that had instantly become a real fight for our very own survival. Each of us looked at the other in horror and disbelief! But, instead of throwing the can and running for our lives, we blew on the flames as if we were trying to blow out a birthday candle sitting in frosting on top of a dynamite cake. It still blazed, but we didn't run, we couldn't run because we were worried more about what our parents would do if they knew we were playing with fire, rather than think about the reality of third-degree burns or losing our lives.

John remembered one lesson that his father taught him about a fire, he remembered that if you take away the air, the fire cannot breathe and therefore will be extinguished. He quickly grabbed gob-fulls of sand from the sandbox and threw them on top of the softening spout. The explosives expert had saved the day and the entire city block, we thought. We all talked and bragged about that nearly catastrophic incident for years and despite the slightly shriveled red plastic top of the gas can, our parents never discovered a thing. Well, maybe the whole city block wouldn't have gone up in flames, but we would have. John's dad Lornie was a good man and a good father as he proved to Tom and me one nasty, stormy night in July.

We always loved to sleep outside at night because we thought it was an adventurous thing to do, and we could stay up much later than we normally did when we slept in the house. Sleeping out was more fun than dragging large empty furniture boxes down the alley from behind Hennen's Furniture store and cutting in windows and doors making them into cardboard forts. Besides

sleeping in tents or Stier's truck camper, we would occasionally sleep out in the trailer that Dad built. The queen sized bed could easily hold three young boys in sleeping bags.

Finally, one day in July, John was granted permission to sleep over at our house in the trailer that Dad parked unsecured in the backyard. We stayed up late, as usual, playing cards, joking around and telling stories by flashlights and by candlelight. Come midnight the block was dark, quiet, sleeping and the night belonged to us. We scurried to and from the neighbor's gardens eating our fill of carrots and green beans before we retired back inside our temporary quarters for the night. Finally, crawling in our bags with our bellies full of garden fresh veggies, we laid back and closed our eyes. As the late night talk died down, the first few outer wind bands of the approaching thunderstorm started to gently rock the trailer. At first, it was no big deal, even kind of exciting to be sleeping out on a stormy night. But heavy rain soon pounded the flat top and strong gusts of wind started us a rocking and it felt like the old trailer was headed for the land of OZ. John looked out the small window that Sonny had built into the side of the plywood door and could not see his house through the driving rains. There was no way he was running home in that downpour and besides, we thought we would be all right inside the safety of Sonny's stronghold.

None of us would ever admit that we were just a little afraid, and there was no way that John, Tom, nor I, would be the first to chicken out and run home to Mama. Besides, both of our families were fast asleep. We did not want to wake them. Suddenly, we heard a hard knock, knock, knock on the trailer door along with the sound of John's dad yelling, "Hey boys open up. John, John, are you in there?" We pushed the door open against the wind and there standing under a shifting waterfall was Lornie wearing a dark green, full-length raincoat, topped with a bucket style rain hat and a bright flashlight beaming from his hand. To say I was a little bit relieved to see him standing there, would be an understatement! He shouted over the noisy storm as he explained to us, he could see the trailer shaking wildly from his house across the street and that we better head inside before it blew away with us in it. As much as we hated to face the humility of telling our friends the next day we chickened out because of a measly thunderstorm, we all knew that Lornie was right and none of us questioned his wisdom or his authority. He gathered us all up as a drill sergeant would barking out orders to move quickly and do it now! He steered Tom and I to the house just as Dad was heading our way to grab us, each giving a quick shout out before Lornie left with John tucked under his arm trotting through the neighbor's yards and disappearing amongst the wind and the rain. Although the trailer was still standing the next day, Lornie had actually done us a favor by giving us the cover we needed to call it quits the night before! Now, we could tell everyone "Yea, we were going to tough the storm out, but John's dad came over and ordered us into the house." And John's mom, Shirley was too nice for Tom and me to appreciate at a young age.

Although the same age, John's next door neighbor, Bob and he were always at odds. Tom and I were often forced to choose sides. Who's ever side we took, the other would be ignored altogether for as long as the feud continued. John and Bob were really whaling at each other one afternoon near The Little Corner. John's right knuckle had connected with one of Bob's teeth opening a bloody gash on his fighting hand. Bob's face was imprinted with bloody knuckle marks on the front and left side from numerous direct hits thrown by John, but Bob got in a solid blow occasionally. Tom and I saw the whole thing unfold while watching from the family room bay window and darted outside to relish the prize fight up close. But, just about the same time we arrived, John's mom Shirley came running out of her house and broke up the fight while several neighboring boys watched and cheered from the street. She then lectured all the boys, reminding us of the Golden Rule; right out of the big book itself. "Do unto others, as you would have them do unto you." We all thought it was corny and we used to laugh and joke about it. We were more inclined to go along with the saying, "An eye for an eye, a tooth for a tooth, a hand for a hand."

But, after we got to know Shirley's virtuous and friendly way, we realized that she was speaking straight from her heart, so we tried to live by the words of the biblical quote. At least for keeping the special bond that all the boys shared with each other in the neighborhood.

John's neighbor Bob lived in a small basement house on the south side toward the circus lots. Basement houses are built below ground with a flat roof about two feet above with just a tiny entrance standing alone on one end. His widowed mother, Fran worked all day at the local plastic plant and was also elected town judge. She'd hold court down in her basement house at all hours of the day and night. Her sons would relay to us what comical case took place the night before and how she handled it, and if there is one word for Fran, its "creative." There were six kids living in that small little basement house: four sisters, Mugs, Midge, Marilee and Marcy along with older brothers, John "ruler of the neighborhood," and younger brother Bob. They also had two older brothers who were military career men living away; one in the air force and the other in the army. We saw them both maybe once in all the years growing up while they were home on leave. Back to the house, to get to the living quarters, you had to go through a door at the top entrance which they all called, "the landing," walk down the steps and enter the house through another door at the bottom. There was one large room in the center with the bedrooms and a bathroom on the outer edges. On the right was their kitchen with a table and four chairs, and on the left was their living room. John slept with Bob in a small room where they had to turn sideways to get by each other. Bunk beds to the right and a dresser across took up most of the room. The girl's room was bigger, but I only saw one large bed in the room, so I don't know where all four slept. Naturally, Fran had the largest and nicest room in the square. The place was always smoky because Fran and most of her kids smoked cigarettes beginning at age 12.

Their flat roof, which practically begged and called to us, "Run across me!" got us into trouble with Fran on more than one occasion. You could hear her screaming below us as we made the mad dash across the flat surface, "Kids get off that damn roof!" and we'd keep on going after we jumped to the ground on the other side. She never came after us, but her shouts were intimidating enough we only made the daring move across once about every few months. Between those runs, just to get an extra dig in, we'd stand on the alley and launch rocks onto the roof. It's not like we didn't like Fran, we just liked to hear her roar from under that flat roof of hers. Another thing that got us into trouble with the flat-roofed house was picking bubbles that formed during the hot summer off the freshly tarred roof while sitting on the edge. Fran had a sixth sense about that roof, almost as if she could see through it. Now basement houses are considered a poor man's house, but the way the Schuman's used to get around this myth was to tell everyone, "The best thing about living in a basement house is that we don't have to worry about tornadoes." And everyone I knew was petrified at even the mention of tornadoes so, after that pronouncement, everyone wanted to live in a basement house.

Bob was a natural smart ass and he would do anything to get a laugh in any setting. He was also a devious little devil where he could be just nice as he could be in front of Mom one minute, only to do something stupid behind her back the next with a barely noticeable smirk on his face, relishing the naughty nature within him. Bob also did certain things not in accordance with the law, and he didn't mind taking a chance or putting his life on the line, like the times he sat with me 60 feet up inside an empty silo on rotted boards lying loosely across the top of the silo at Townsend's farm. Tom and I shared Bob equally and he was hanging around one or both of us, all the time. Every day he came over to our house to watch the Flintstones cartoon or Gilligan's Island before we'd head outside to find something to do. The only time he went home was to eat and sleep, and sometimes he ate and slept at our house. His mom and sisters ruled the roost over at the basement house, and with John gone most of the time, he liked our place because the numbers

favored the boys, plus he liked teasing the girls and Glo. Because he was two years older than me, I learned a lot from Bob.

He and his entire family just loved our family and Grandpa Leo because we sort of adopted certain pieces of them. Grandpa Leo used to let the oldest girl, Mugs ride on one of his trick circus ponies all the time telling us he was giving her horse riding lessons. In actuality, he was letting her ride one of his star ponies because of her expressed interest and desire and his kind heart. This made us kids slightly jealous, but we all understood why he gave her attention and love. They had no father figure in their life and Grandpa Leo thought it important that they do. Grandma Angela even taught young Marce how to embroider. Dad took Bob along smelt fishing up past Duluth, MN and sometimes he would have him tag along for other events. We would always give Fran two packages of fresh smelt upon our return from up north. Tom had two nicknames for Bob because he was such a character, he needed more than one.

At first, he named him Flapper because he had rather large ears and because the Schuman's called the top of their stairway entry 'the landing.' Every time Bob would open the landing door Tom would say, "This is where Flapper comes in for a landing." Over the years, Tom changed his nickname to Wile E. Coyote, or Wile for short as in the cartoon, "The Road Runner" because Tom thought that Bob looked and acted as Wile E. the coyote in the cartoon series. And Tom also made up a little saying just for Bob. He would sing to him upon our first meeting of the day, or if he hadn't seen him in a while: R – O – B – E –R - T Robert, Robert Schuman. S – C – H – U – M – A - N, Schuman, Schuman, Schuman. After that first song introduction by Tom, the entire family joined in and sang it to Bob every time Tom kicked it off; sometimes even Mom joined in.

There were three other boys Tom's age living within a football field from our house who would occasionally cycle through the four of us. Frank Krushkie lived on the other side of Bob's basement house, Lee Blume directly across the street from him and, Donny O' O'Brien on the far end corner from Lee. Each was different, but we all shared the same interests and we all sought after adventure. All the boys in the neighborhood played rough. One of our pastimes involved gathering as many of our neighborhood buddies as we could rustle up. We were all "armed." Those with the good fortune to own a Daisy BB gun brought it, others had the 10 cent slingshots bought at the local five-and-dime store. The ammo used for this was kernels of hard dried field corn and rocks. If we did not have access to these preferred weapons, we used hand thrown dirt clods, green apples or, tiny plums. Yea, the baseball bat bazooka and fake deaths weren't doing it for us anymore, so we used real weapons. We would pick sides as if choosing kids to play opposite sides of a baseball game. But our play was all out war for the two opposing groups. It was based on the many WWII movies and TV shows we watched and idolized. We played these war games in the yards and alleys in our neighborhood and in later years, "Hoddy-Boddy Land." Getting hit in the butt or leg, hell, anywhere with a BB or a projectile of corn hurt a lot and many welts were raised on various parts of our anatomy. We wore these battle scars with honor and took personal pride in taking the pain, and more importantly dishing it out. It was a miracle nobody lost an eye while engaging in these realistic battles. But, dodging flying bamboo poles took the rough play to an entirely new level, and the odds of losing an eye increased exponentially.

We had an old shed in our backyard next to the alley that Dad utilized for storage on one side while Uncle Gary used the other side for raising domesticated fancy pigeons. We were playing a made-up game which involved Mike throwing a 12-foot long bamboo pole, (spear) over Theresa, Tom and I as we lay flatly on the roof with our arms covering our heads. The spear was something Mike picked up from watching a Tarzan movie on TV. Well, just as 'Tarzan' released his spear, I stood up in protest, put my right hand out in front of me and said, "Hey Mike wait a minute." Too late because the pointy end of the spear was on its way and before I saw it coming, Bam!!! The spear hit and stuck for a moment on the inside corner of my left eye. My world went into a hazy

green fog! I put my hands out as a blind person would in an unfamiliar setting trying to find my way off that roof. The roof, where seconds earlier I was a native tribesman taking cover from Tarzan's dead on spear throwing, was now a captive island in the sky with my brothers and sisters screaming and jumping up and down all around and below me. Between squints and tears mixed with blood, I made my way to the end of the shed towards Bunner's cage and by that time, Grandma Gloria who was over for a visit heard the screaming, rushed over, crawled up onto Bunner's rabbit cage and with a terrified look on her face carried me down. Mom rushed me to the clinic as Mike thought for sure he had taken my eye out. Sobbing uncontrollably and kneeling by a lilac bush behind the house, he prayed to God I wasn't blind.

It was a miracle because the pole struck the top of my nose and directed the spear to the left corner of my eye. Another quarter of an inch and it would have hit the center! Dr. Hallgren dug out the fragments of wood, stitched up the cut in the corner and, placed a large bandage over the eye. It hurt like heck, but at least I would not be blind! A week later he took off the bandage, but something hadn't felt right since the day he placed the bandage on. It felt as if something foreign were still deep inside my head. I kept feeling for whatever it was, kept working at it and finally discovered the problem. I pulled out, nice as you please, a two inch long narrow piece of the bamboo pole that Dr. Hallgren had missed on his initial exam. I was not only lucky that I still had an eye, but luckier still to be alive... But our risky games didn't stop with realistic battles or even bamboo pole spears. Eventually, we'd find a way to use them while engaging with flying bats. The ones that somehow creep inside your closet and fly around your living room with Mom screaming at the top of her lungs.

Right around dusk in the summertime, the neighborhood boys would gather outside under the streetlight in front of our house equipped with 12-foot long bamboo fishing poles. We'd try to knock flying bats out of the air while the girls screamed as they watched the night-time sparring unfold. Sometimes Tom and I would bounce a golf ball high in the air while Mike waited with the pole. The bat, thinking it was a juicy moth, would dive toward it... and bam, down it would go. As we got more creative, Mike taped a small badminton racket to the end of the pole, simultaneously trying to obtain a larger striking surface and confuse the bat's radar. It worked out so well, it knocked out one flying mouse. It lay unconscious for a few minutes, time enough to examine the weird critter's thin-skinned bony wings attached to the body of a rodent. We ran into our crude cave basement, put the unconscious bat into Mom's now empty glass fish aquarium, fit the top with quarter inch mesh wire, and a heavy rock to hold it down just about the time it awakened from the dead. Learning rather quickly that a bat can squeeze through the tiniest of holes, we watched in horror as the creature crept up the side of the glass as a spider would, and before our dumbfounded eyes, morphed oddly through one of the tiny squares. To us, it was as amazing as watching Hollywood legend Bela Lugosi transform into a bat during the original 1930s vampire movie, Dracula. A creature that can accomplish this feat is not of this world so, we ran up the steps as the faint, fleeting bat disappeared somewhere into our cave and, was never seen again. But, the bat wasn't the only living being that escaped into unknown parts of our crudely poured concrete foundation.

We hounded Mom and Dad for a replacement kitten after the shocking death of our first one, "Butch." Butch was rescued out of a dilapidated shed from the neighbor down the alleyway after hearing his faint meows while walking by. It was an adorable little grey and white long-haired kitten only a few weeks old, and despite its poor health, fleas, lice, and constant oozing out of its left eye, we all passed around our kitten with loving hugs and kisses just the same. Little Butch was left unattended and unknowingly sleeping peacefully under the tire of Dad's car as we played in the backyard. After Dad's usual noontime meal, he climbed into his car, started the engine and, started back for work. That was the end of the little fuzzball Butch except for the heavy dose of

ringworm he left as a parting gift to each and every one of us. Now, we all thought that because of Dad's guilt, he would find us some cute little lovable replacement we could play with and adore as we truly did Butch.

Instead, he went out to Lloyd Schulz's farm and picked up this wild, full-grown barn cat that had never seen the inside of a human dwelling. He brought it home in a cardboard box with holes poked in the side, so the cat could breathe. He wrapped twine around the outside, so it couldn't escape. That big cat was so feral that Dad didn't want to let it loose in the upstairs, so he brought it down into the bat cave to release it there; at least until it 'settled' down. We never discovered if it was a male or female, the color of its eyes, how old it was or anything else. We glimpsed the large cat's light orange fur with darker tiger stripes running about the body. Dad gingerly opened the flaps of the cardboard box, and that beast sprang out of there quicker than a jack in the box. It streaked twice around the basement walls (defying gravity running halfway up the wall) in less than five seconds, before disappearing into a discrete opening in a cement crevice leading to parts unknown behind the foundation. Before we had time to react to the fleeting feline, it had vanished, never to be seen nor heard from again! To this day, nobody knows where that crevice leads, but we were all sure that it didn't go to the outside. Poor cat!

There was always something happening around the block, and it usually originated at our house. Our family's colorful character ensured the neighborhood was kept as active as a three-ring circus during the daytime and kept guessing on what we would do next during the evenings. But, little did our friends know, or anyone else but our immediate family, that behind the scenes, Mike was planning something so big that it only took place in the movies or on TV. WWll battles, blowing up models, and knocking flying bats out of the air was fun, but those things didn't compare to living the life of a real-time Super-hero.

Mike and I were both so fascinated by the 1966 TV show "Batman" that we talked Mom into sewing us replica costumes. She was very creative and by the time she finished, we had very realistic looking costumes. Mom would have to keep the secret that Mike was Batman and I, Robin, 'The Boy Wonder,' from the world. The only missing piece to my uniform puzzle that Mom couldn't place was Robin's pair of green gloves. We searched everywhere for them and then one Sunday morning coming out of church, like manna from heaven, they were staring at me from inside a box marked 'Lost and Found.' I swear those gloves were designed especially for that uniform because they were made of Swede green leather ending half the way up to my elbows, just like Robin's gloves on the TV show.

Mike and I knew all the lines from the show and he would speak in a robotic hesitant tone just like Adam West's character, Batman on TV. "Wait a min_ute ____ Robin, get pre_pared to ____ drop one of the bat ____ bombs. We ____ will show this Joker ____who gets the last ____ laugh" And I would answer in a factual military manner, "Roger that Batman, preparing to drop the bat bombs." Yes, we were the Batman and Robin of Belle Plaine and

Belle Plaine's Batman and Robin

had collected all the weapons that we would need to battle the bad guys. We modified and painted a bicycle flat black, then filled our utility belts with ladyfinger firecrackers, smoke bombs, and bat ropes. Our "GAS GUN" was a baby bottle filled with flour. We enlarged the hole in the nipple, so when we squeezed the bottle, flour would shoot out. As a second grader only recently told there was no Santa Claus, Easter Bunny, or Tooth Fairy, I became 'Robin,' the Boy Wonder every time I dawned the mask. The imaginative Mike easily moved from one character to the next, this time he just was "Batman." We'd suit up after dark and ride the bat bike, Batman in front and I in the back on the banana seat, and streak through the well-lit main street. Our identities were secret, but one of our neighborhood friends eventually discovered the "creative kids behind the masks," and snapped a photo of us, proudly sporting our costumes in a superhero action pose…

Hoddy-Boddy Land

As we grew a little older and ventured further from the confines of the neighborhood, our explorations into the woodland began in a very special place not far from our house. A mere ten-minute walk brought us to a wild little ravine system below the Oakwood Cemetery we called "Seven Ponds." A beautiful, rambling creek ran through this ravine, and seven ponds of various sizes and depths lay undisturbed along its bottom. In the summer, we would get a group of neighborhood kids to scrounge what food they could and talk the girls into cooking us fried potatoes, bacon, and onions over a campfire. We caught salamanders, frogs and striped skinks in the lush grass and moss that bordered these water holes. Forts and crude tree houses were built, and many hours were spent playing Tarzan.

Naturally, Mike played the lead role as Tarzan, King of the Jungle, Theresa played Jane, I played Boy, and Tom or Mary played Chita (a chimpanzee) or a native tribesman. Mike talked Grandpa Leo into carving him a large wooden knife; a replica of the one that Tarzan carried. He carefully painted the blade silver, the handle red with gold trim becoming the ape-man every time he had the weapon in his hand. Mike could even yodel just like Tarzan, "Awe-awe-aye-awwwwe, awe-awe-aye-awwwwe!" We would beg him to do it when we were back at The Old House and finished with our play.

The Seven Ponds area was considered such hallowed ground by all the neighborhood kids. It was given another special name by our older neighbor Tom, "Hoddy–Boddy–Land." It's a name he dreamed up after watching an old black and white Tarzan film. The natives were singing and chanting in the village scenes. The sound they were making sounded to him like the made-up words, Hoddy-Boddy. We all immediately took a liking to the name and Hoddy-Body Land was born. We used to build reed huts there in the fall, genuine Hoddy-Boddy dwellings just like Tarzan and the natives. Whenever we could find the right tree, we'd hang a rope and swing on it imagining we were in the dark, African jungle. If we followed the Seven Ponds ravine system far enough, it would take us into a larger ravine directly connected to the Promised Land itself, "Pine Grove."

Our travel into the Seven Ponds ravine provided our early days of innocence with the rare opportunity to live out fantasies and dreams while receiving an education that cannot be bought or bartered for. We learned about life and we learned about death. We watched fish turn into frogs, and eggs hatch into baby birds. We learned to run from skunks spraying their stink from underneath their striped tails. Mike and Bob's older brother John, taught us many lessons in woods education, like what plants were safe and which ones burned, how to handle a snake without getting bit, what wild animals to look out for, how to check for a live electric fence, but more importantly, we were taught how to go virtually undetected in the woods. We also learned communication techniques we believed were unnoticed by any stranger in our woodland domain. A certain bird whistle or a light tap on a tree meant different things to us that no one else knew.

Tales of Robin Hood and his Band of Merry Men hiding in the Sherwood Forest, dressed in Lincoln green garments was too much for Mike to pass up, especially with Hoddy-Boddy Land a mere few minutes from home. His earlier Batman and Tarzan characters somewhere, he was eager to try out in his next role as "Robin Hood" leader of his Band of Merry Men. The 1930s movie starring Errol Flynn caught enough of his interest to read the book Robin Hood by Henry Gilbert. In his version, besides the standard fare of the legend, he incorporated two tiny Woods Folk, or elves, Ket the Troll and Hob O' the Hill. These mystical characters, one third the size of a normal man were Robin's friends and helpers. They too dressed in Lincoln green, poached the King's deer, and did much of Robin's spying against the sheriff of Nottingham and his soldiers. Ket and Hob were masters at avoiding detection and they were thought to have magical powers. Just like us.

Mom bought Mike a used pair of army green pants and a green sweatshirt. He would dress up in his cammies. Then, it was off to Hoddy-Boddy Land with older neighbor, John and three of us lagging behind. While the two of them stalked birds and squirrels, they sent Wile E. and me up a tree and stuck brother Tom on a hillside to be their lookouts. Our orders were to be on the lookout for elves, or any kid that wandered into our territory. Some entire afternoons were spent up in a darn tree swaying in the wind waiting for Robin Hood and Little John's return. They would announce their arrival with coded whistles. Sometimes it was a hoot, hoot, hoot and we would have to follow that with, "Halt who goes there?" testing our alertness and previous attention to their lessons.

John was three years older than Mike, and could easily have declared himself Robin Hood, the leader of the band, but he wanted to keep the band as realistic as the book version. John was a lot taller than Mike, as was Little John in the book and the movie, plus John's name in real life was John. Mike looked like a good Robin Hood and dressed the part in his green woodland outfit. Little John even wore a long brown burlap sack and carried a solid wooden staff any time we traveled through Sherwood Forest. More important, anyone that tried to get to Robin Hood had to go through Little John first; a duty he relished. Although Mike was insubordinate to John in real life, as Robin Hood Mike played the leading role well, giving "Little" John orders as spoken in the book, and as he had with me while playing the role of Batman. We practically lived in the woods all day during the summer, off early in the morning and not home until dinner time. Our Robin Hood band built a hidden, "secret fort" about 200 yards from Grandpa's circus lots, in a tiny ravine across from Townsend's barn. It was camouflaged perfectly and only the boys in the band knew of its existence. But one fort and a couple of tree houses were not enough for our creative minds. We wanted several secret locations to escape to and hide in if the King's men were on our trail. Robin Hood and Little John brought us to Townsend's barn so we could build a hidden hay fort there, but little did we know as we entered through the basement hay shoot, we were not alone and danger lied in wait under the shadows of the stacked hay.

The band went to work pulling hay bales out of the way and measuring the size opening when Robin Hood and Little John noticed movement at the opposite end of the barn. Most of the band had seen the movement and those that didn't see it, acknowledged the nod by Robin Hood and Little John in that direction. We all froze for a moment, speechless and stared in shock and disbelief. We squinted amongst the hay dust that now filled the old barn and blinked at the shadow of a man emerging from underneath the hay, expressionless but staring at us as he slowly brushed hay from his untidy clothing. At first, we thought we were busted by the owner of the property and cringed. But there was something eerily different about this stranger and we knew right away that he wasn't the owner, but possibly a bum or worse yet some murderer hiding from police in the barn!

Grandpa Leo had told us stories about bums from back when he was a young hobo riding the rails around the turn of the 20th century, and some of them were very dangerous characters. We'd also heard stories of serial killers and men who took children and tortured them for their pleasure. My mind raced with several possibilities. Suddenly, the man made his way toward us silently, clumsily stepping over and on the bails, tripping on every other one, but incessantly making his way toward us. There was only one quick way out and that was through the eight-foot-high trap door which had brought us up from the basement floor below. We had climbed the steel rungs to get up into the barn, but we wouldn't have time to use them on the way down. Our only chance for a successful escape rested within the courage and leadership of Little John. The man was making his way to block our exit when Little John made his move!

A square beam of sunlight from the lone window on the east side, shined down through the moving dust lighting up Little John as he positioned himself between his band and the attacker. He

looked like Moses in his brown cloth robe, parting the Red Sea with his rod held high in a commanding and determined manner. Little John was now living the genuine role of protector as in the book and the sun on his face beamed with delight. Little John's role was to protect Robin Hood from the sheriff of Nottingham's men at all costs, even his life. With his other hand motioning forward he yelled, "Everyone move. Jump down the shoot!" The hay shoot was only ten feet away, the bum now twenty feet beyond it, and it took a mere second to get there while keeping an eye on the figure clumsily heading our way. We jumped, two at a time, without hesitation or worry about broken bones, or bumps on the head. Tom, who was deathly afraid of heights and wouldn't jump from anything over four feet, didn't think twice beating me to the cement floor below. When my turn came, I didn't stop to plant my feet on the barn floor but dropped from two stacked bales above adding another four feet to my journey below. When I landed, I rolled along the cow stalls and up onto my feet heading for the freedom and light shining through the sliding basement door. The last one down and right behind me was Little John dropping to the pavement with staff still held firmly in his grasp. His knees barely bent six inches as he sprang into a gallop, the burlap sack waving goodbye to the scary figure left up inside the barn.

We gathered back together as a band in the openness of the pasture huffing, puffing, and all spoke over each other about our close call and our successful escape. Along with our success returned our confidence and our talk soon turned from that of relief to that of revenge. We regained our courage and our temper gathering weapons of rocks and sticks and headed back to the barn. This bum wouldn't have a chance against Robin Hood and his Band of Merry Men. Little John planned to go directly into the hay barn from the front door this time giving us easier entrance and an easy exit if things went awry. We quietly snuck up to the barn walking tightly along the wall anticipating the capture of one of the sheriff of Nottingham's fiercest soldiers. Little John took the lead, giving us a quick wink, he swung open the barn door, and it hit hard on the side, making us flinch. With sticks and stones in hand, we waited at the ready for the word to attack, but the signal never came. The barn was mysteriously empty? The bum, murderer or torturer of children had vanished into thin air! We never figured out what the man was doing in that barn, but we all believed that he wasn't coming to help us build our fort. After that incident, we carried BB guns with us for protection from evil doers who lurked in and around our Sherwood Forest.

"John taught me how to climb trees," I'd proudly tell all the boys in the neighborhood. Everyone within a four block radius of our house looked up to John. Every time I went to hang out with Wile E. Coyote, I'd hope I'd get a glimpse of big, bad John who was our real-life characters "Branded" and "The Rifleman." In the true western classic TV series "Branded," Chuck Connors played the part of Captain Jason McCord, West Point graduate and decorated cavalry officer. As the sole survivor of the Battle at Bitter Creek, an Apache Indian massacre, he is judged to have deserted the field of battle and is stripped of his rank. During the theme song at the beginning of the show, he is shown standing at attention as a senior cavalry officer cuts off his buttons and stripes from his uniform with a sword. The former captain is branded a coward and a disgrace in the eyes of the world. But he is unafraid to take on any task and through his strength and will, he can overcome whatever odds are placed before him. Chuck Connors also played the lead character in our favorite western TV series "The Rifleman." He looked like cool Chuck with the same, tall skinny shape and same long handsome face, and even possessed the same color hair. Those two fictional characters fit John to a T, unafraid, wild, and rebellious all the way to the end.

John's only physical flaw was a habit where he curled his tongue under the top side of the roof of his mouth. This gave the appearance as if his face were stuck on the pronunciation of the letter "L." Brother Tom made the horrible mistake of asking John about this one day, "John why do you

hold your tongue like that all the time?" Oh, John took after Tom. "None of your business little shit." And then he chased seven years younger Tom all the way inside our house. Poor Tom couldn't get a break from John to save his life.

John's job as Little John was not only to protect Robin Hood at all cost and steal from the rich, but it was to train Robin's bandits as well. In his mind, learning how to climb trees was essential to being a good bandit so we could see the entire woodland from aloft. He taught me everything he knew about climbing and showed me how to bear hug up the tree and how to grab a limb to get up over the top. More importantly, he taught me how to prevent myself from falling by ensuring that I had at least one limb anchored before moving upward or downward.

Little John was a great climber and I felt sort of special having a much older guy like him teaching me his craft. My lack of fear of heights and natural climbing instincts were more than Little John had hoped for. He was surprised and impressed at the ease at which I went up that first tree. "Get up there as high as you can Whitey, and if you see anybody coming, give us the signal." He complimented me and bragged to Robin Hood about it, "Whitey can really climb, he makes for a good scout in the forest." Little John's words and compliments only encouraged my pursuit of overcoming dangerous settings of all types. Within a few weeks, I could bear hug straight up a steel flagpole, no problem. I could and would climb to the top of the barn rafters and on the top of the silos, both inside and out. And, I would dare a bull to stick me with his horns as I ran ahead of him and slipped under the barbed wire fence near Hoddy-Boddy Land. Mike's little brother had become, for all intents and purposes, bold and fearless because of Little John's training. But Tom just couldn't prove himself worthy in the eyes of Little John.

One night we were after pigeons in Townsend's silo located across the pasture about 200 yards from the circus sheds. We were catching them to use in a display as one type of bird for our zoo that we planned to put together for the neighborhood that weekend. John taught us an effective pigeon-catching method. One of us would shine a bright flashlight directly in the eyes of the pigeon as it rested for the night at the top of the empty silo. Then someone else would climb 60 feet up the metal bars with a fishing net and scoop one up as it sat blinded on the semi-rotted boards. Once the pigeon was captured inside of the net, it was dropped from above to the rest of the group waiting on the ground, who would then throw it in a pillowcase. John had the procedure down to a science. We caught two pigeons and two starlings that night. At any rate, John knew that Tom feared heights, so he wanted him to climb the embedded steel silo ladder anyway, to possibly give him a little confidence, and overcome his fear. But, no matter how much coaching and taunting John and Mike did, Tom wasn't going up there for all the tea in China. So from then on, John had little to do with Tom.

We did, however, use the captured birds for our animal zoo charging attendees 10 cents admission to see the large variety of mammals, reptiles, bugs, and birds with a piece of paper displaying their species printed in black crayon on a label ahead of each one. Nobody around was doing this type of thing, so our zoo brought kids from as far away as the other side of town. It was a huge success, as was the carnival we put on in our backyard. Now, a carnival is something that we knew a thing or two about.

In those days Jerry Lewis carnivals were a big event and many kids in town put them on. We would put on one of Jerry's carnivals ourselves sending away for a packet which contained a roadmap on how to carry out the task. The packet also contained information on where to send the money once the carnival concluded. Grandpa Leo helped a lot of kids organize their carnivals because the kind-hearted old man admired the children that so freely gave to such a worthy cause. But after viewing the packet of instructions, we changed our mind. We didn't want to follow Jerry's stupid rules, we didn't want to put on the same old boring games, and we did not want to give Jerry any of our hard earned cash. Instead of seeking Grandpa's help, we kept our carnival a

secret from him because we didn't want him to think any less of us. Tom and I, assisted by Theresa and Mary, and our friends would have our own carnival. Besides, all the kids would come because we had put on such a successful zoo display. This carnival thing was right up our circus alley and we would prove to the town kids that Albrights Attractions was back in all its glory. If we advertised as we had our zoo, kids from all over town would show up and it could be huge. And, while we planned and prepared, we prayed that our loving Grandfather wouldn't come by the yard and discover what we were up to.

Nevertheless, Grandpa Leo somehow discovered the upcoming event and thankfully, saw nothing wrong with putting on a show and learning a little about capitalism. He even volunteered to help us put the display together. We put on a carnival that outshined Jerry's any day. We had bottle toss games, and balloon and dart games. We handed out prizes found in our junk drawers and penny candy purchased at Barney's. We dressed as clowns using the makeup that my parents still had left over from their circus days, and we put on performances. We even cleaned out Dad's side of the shed making it into a haunted house as a sideshow with a nickel admission to attend. We strung up blankets making it dark while one of us led the children through the maze of scary displays. Hands reached for them from behind the blankets as they walked blindly through the web of paths. With cold, wet spaghetti noodles as brains and skinned grapes for eyes, we placed them in a bowl behind a dark blanket. We even put on a magic show borrowing a few of Dad's props used during the days of their Stage Circus. We put up bike ramps, and obstacle courses, and by the time we finished, the backyard was completely taken up and filled with kids from all over town having a blast. We brought in more money than Jerry's carnivals, plus we got to keep the dough.

Little John's feelings toward Tom took a turn for the worse one day in the front yard of the basement house after Tom threw a softball high in the air, and waited for it to come back down into his baseball glove. The high throw was about ten feet off target and it came straight down landing directly on the top of Little John's head. Little John ran over and picked that ball up, took careful aim, his mouth open with his tongue tucked under the roof, "Why you little shit ass," and threw it as hard as he could, hitting Tom square in the back between his shoulder blades. Nobody messed with Little John, especially a punk kid like Tom. And Little John wasn't afraid to fight with anyone around his age. We discovered what type of fighter he was up close and bloody right next to our house on the alfalfa field that same summer.

Little John and older neighbor Tom got into an argument that led to a challenge, and acceptance for a bare-knuckle fist fight the following day. Better yet, the fight would take place right next to our house in the alfalfa field! How we could be so lucky was beyond words. Everybody in the neighborhood was there to witness the colossal event because the fight had been announced ahead of time, just like a prize fight between Ali and Smoken Joe. Both fighters were lean, but John had the height and reach advantage plus the experience. This was to be Tom's first fight, but John's fifth or sixth. The match started fast with a flurry of blows and it was over before we knew it. Bloody lip, bleeding nose and bruised body, Tom, sat humiliated, as he held a red-stained white towel beneath his nose in front of his bloodstained white sweatshirt. But he was cool about it and held nothing against Little John. They shook afterward and Little John had asked mom for a cold wet towel for his friend. Little John had won the fight outright. He had done so fair and square and was still "King" of the entire neighborhood. With that fight, his influence over the boys in the neighborhood grew and we all looked to Little John for excitement and direction.

For doing anything slightly dangerous or illegal, Little John was eager to teach us the proper way to carry out the task. He not only taught me how to climb, catch pigeons, and crack a few gardens, he taught everyone in the neighborhood how to steal the annual pea harvest from the big man himself. Every year Green Giant contracted with area farmers to lease their fields for

planting, harvesting, and processing peas in their factory in Le Sueur, MN; a town 12 miles away. These peas when ripe were another highly sought after item of plunder. Though we all snuck into the pea fields to have our fill of these sweet peas, it was much more fun to risk it all and snatch them right out from under the Green Giant's nose. Brainstorming with Little John eventually brought about a slick way to steal the peas. Here's how it worked... First we learned the routes the filled trucks would use coming through town on their way to HWY 169 in route to the pea canning factory in Le Sueur. Then we all sat lined up along the curb and simply waited.

When a truck approached the stop sign, Theresa or Mary would roll a ball into the street in front of the truck. Then they'd merrily skip after their stray ball while two or three of the boys snuck behind the truck with rakes and pull vines full of peas. It all took place in about five seconds. The trick for the boys in the back was to avoid being spotted in the rear view mirror by the driver preoccupied with the vulnerable children in front of his truck. Leaving the vines on the street, we returned to the curb until the truck rounded the corner and headed out of town. We'd all pick up the vines, sit on the grass in our backyard and eat for hours. We became very efficient pea thieves often changing the distraction, or just running from behind a nearby tree, grab a few vines and take off so fast we were a mere blur to the driver. While munching on the delicacy, we even graded which year had been more successful than others. Mom knew we stole them, but she went right along with us, often helping clean and put the peas in freezer bags. She figured Green Giant wouldn't miss a little in the big scheme of things. What's that they say about stolen grapes tasting sweeter?

We didn't think twice about stealing from the big man, but stealing from our very own neighbors never entered our young minds. The majority of our adventures were pure fantasy, but we did a fair amount of raiding local gardens at night, sneaking raspberries, strawberries or melons. Little John taught everyone in the neighborhood how to raid neighbor's gardens at night. I vividly remember the first night I tasted the thrill of evasion of adults and that all night adrenalin rush as we traveled the back alleyways while the small town slept. We ruled the night!

We got permission from our parents to sleep out that night across the street from The Little Corner in a fort on the side of Stier's bus shed. Our explosives expert had taken possession of an old storage shed, cleaned it out, put a few personal items in there and called it his fort. Everybody had to have a fort to call our own and hang around in, so we could plan our future schemes. Little John and Mike set up the time to meet us in their tent put up in the backyard of the basement house. When the minute hand touched 11:30, Tom and I along with a few of our neighborhood buddies visited the tent next door. The first thing we knew, Little John was giving us a lecture on what we would do, how we would do it and how not to get caught. After explaining our objective, Little John then went into ten ways to operate while out after curfew on the small town streets. We were told earlier that day to report to the tent, wearing dark clothing. Anyway, Little John's Ten Winning Rules of the Night were:

1. **Always dress in dark clothes**
2. **Never talk out loud. Whisper or use sign language**
3. **Move slow so you can see and hear everything**
4. **Always walk through the alleyways when at all possible**
5. **If you see headlights, announce it and hide before the driver spots us**
6. **Before crossing the road, look left and right for any movement or any car lights; at least twice**
7. **Cross the street one at a time and once on the other side, get behind something or lay on the ground while waiting**

       for the others to cross
8. **Avoid open areas and lights unless it's the last resort**
9. **If confronted by a cop or an adult, run for your life!**
10. **If you get caught, keep your mouth shut…**

    Little John had scoped out all the best gardens ahead of the big raid, so we followed him and the older boys to the first and most sought after stronghold. It was only two houses down from the tent directly across the alleyway, but the delicacies would come at a cost. The large garden was protected by a seven-foot-high steel fence fitted with a paddle locked entry gate. To make things more difficult, the garden was right behind the caretaker's open bedroom window. There was a reason that the owners went to such extremes to protect it, behind that steel fence grew the best fruits and vegetables in town. The older boys, under the direction of Little John all climbed the fence as the rest of us trainees watched them carry about in systematic silence under the light of the silvery moon. We requested certain delicacies from the outside as they pulled and stomped on the vegetation so carefully placed in straight lines earlier that spring. The prize was a large head of cabbage pulled out by the roots and hurled over the gate almost taking out John Stier as it landed with a dull thud six inches from his feet. We went from one garden feast to another until wee hours in the morning. Most were left in literal ruins. Those poor old people that had spent all summer grooming their gardens and watching their crops mature, must have had a heart attack the next morning when they first glanced out their backyard window and saw the trampled vegetables and empty holes.

    After the raids were finished, we assembled inside the older boy's tent and learned about some of the other things they did when everybody else in town was fast asleep like John Stier's conquest of the water tower, climbing the fence and taking a midnight swim at the local swimming pool, stealing ice cream from the freezers inside garages, and stealing chocolate milk left on the steps by the milkman before the town awakened. Everyone who participated in that first taste of stolen fruit and vegetables from Belle Plaine's finest gardens on that famous moonlit raid talked about it for years. This was our plunder, our form of poaching the King's deer and hiding from the sheriff of Nottingham and his soldiers in Sherwood Forest. That night, all night, I felt I was more than a little kid and the touches of rebellion teased at the corners of my soul, and I craved for more. Little John's Ten Rules of the Night carried us successfully through all our nighttime activities from then on. But the next adrenalin rush didn't happen at night while tearing up gardens, but rather at the Seven Ponds ravine where avoiding the sheriff's soldiers and their beast was always a challenge.

    A good part of the Seven Pond property belonged to a local home builder. He had two sons known to run other kids off with BB guns and by "siccing" their dog on them, a fierce looking Boxer that accompanied them and their buddies into that area of Seven Ponds. A very big part of our adventures was mostly a product of our imagination, but keeping our eyes open and doing our best to steer clear of the owner's two sons and their fierce dog was real. For the most part, we avoided them, but one day we came face to face. It was the first and last time and resulted in a standoff with both groups leveling BB guns at each other. Little John now looking like Chuck Connors "The Rifleman" told them, "Keep the dog away, or we'll perforate its hide with BB's!" It worked, he called their bluff, and we had no problems with them or the boxer again.

Building our Animal Kingdom

The day we tore down Grandpa Leo's circus sheds brought with it a mixture of emotions. A big part of our captivating childhood was torn down along with those tin sheds. On the one hand, we hated to see the buildings that served as Grandpa's headquarters for so many years disappear, but then again, we were excited to finally build the house we talked about and planned during noontime meals for over two years. Dad purchased half the property from Grandpa Leo for $1,500.00. Grandpa had used the large sheds to house his hand-carved circus wagons, and circus vehicles. He even trained his dogs and ponies during the bitter cold Minnesota winters in them. The entire block had been a barbed wire fenced-in pasture for his beautiful white performing Shetland ponies. It also served as the burial place for many circus animals throughout the years: goats, dogs, even a monkey or two and the star of his circus for years "Jimmy, the pick out pony." Grandpa also had a garage connected to the large tin sheds he used as a workshop where he created all his artworks. He taught many of the neighborhood children how to paint pictures and carve figures out of wood inside his self-proclaimed art studio. He

Grandpa Leo balancing six chairs in front of circus sheds

also created many of his own rubber molds casting figures made of fine sand and cement giving each one a smooth and unblemished finish. His passion was casting the heads of Jesus Christ and the Virgin Mary, painting them gold and giving them away to his family and Christian friends. The sheds came down, but Grandpas art studio was in the way of our future home, so it had to be relocated about 100 feet down the hill on the left side of the property line.

Dad and Grandpa Leo jacked it up on all four sides, put long boards across the bottom so we could position a moving wagon underneath, and slowly transported it to its new location. His old workshop would be a storage facility housing his remaining circus wagons and many other circus treasures. Out of all the wagons, he kept only the coronation coach, (the one that took him five years and 2000 hours to assemble,) a wagon cage, and a cute little Cinderella coach that Dad built back in the early 1950s.

Grandpa Leo divided the huge lot into three plots of land; half for us, a corner for Uncle Dave's future body shop and the rest of the southeast side to Lornie Stier who planned to expand his bus and transportation business.

Just preparing for the destruction of the tin buildings turned out to be a huge task as Grandpa Leo had accumulated years of circus equipment and memorabilia. And the ground still held onto the winter cold anchoring some of his coaches in thick ice. Dad and I along with my brothers, ripped the tin sheds apart nail by nail, starting at the roof and working our way down, using hammers and crowbars before hauling most all of it off to the dump. The remaining sheets of tin and lumber were intentionally held back for material to build our new stockade fort and horse and hawk sheds. The girls stayed at home to help Mom get everything ready for the big move down the block.

We practically made daily trips from The Old House on Willow Street to our new lot. We eagerly watched the progression as the land was readied, the foundation put in place, and the walls

and roof erected. Like two skillful surgeons, it was the steady hands of the electrician and plumber who brought our house to life. Building our new home was almost as exciting as watching a canvas tent raised to the top of the tall center pole. We learned the plumbers' first names 'Amo' and 'Darrow' and often joked about them upon our return from the latest inspection. Their names were actually Emil and Darrell, but Uncle Gary pronounced their names by unintentionally skipping the ending letter "L," so in a mocking and comical way, we'd horse around with our newly discovered dialect, "I saw Amo and Darrow today."

The boys, who had run kids off their land with their fierce Boxer, were now older and working for their dad building our house. As the house neared its final completion, every one of us did our part to help get the place ready to move into. Once it was finished, it had a real clean, new look and smell to it, and Dad was, to say the least, "pleased."

The brand spanking new house cost around $30,000.00 with a 30-year payback to the State Bank of Belle Plaine. Dad showed all of us kids the payment book from the bank, and it seemed as though the pages lined with numbers went on forever. The mortgage principal and interest were almost incomprehensible to every one of us, so he broke it down in terms we could understand; around $100.00 a month for 30 years. A lifetime.

We moved into 125 West Raven Street in the summer of 1969. The Apollo astronauts had just landed on the moon. "Operation Breakfast," the secret bombing of Cambodia was underway. Hundreds of thousands of people were participating in the Vietnam antiwar demonstrations across the entire United States. Some were attacked by helicopter with skin-stinging powder by the National Guard in California. It was also the summer of "The Woodstock Festival" and the release of "Led Zeppelin's" first studio recorded album, while the most influential rock band in history, "The Beatles" were breaking up. "Midnight Cowboy," an Oscar-winning John Schlesinger film opened along with "Butch Cassidy and the Sundance Kid," directed by George Roy Hill and starring Paul Newman and Robert Redford. That year, the news media extensively covered the Manson Family who killed Leno and Rosemary LaBianca, wealthy Los Angeles businesspeople. In our short lives, we had witnessed the assassination of President John Fitzgerald Kennedy, the assassination of Dr. Martin Luther King Jr., the subsequent success of the civil rights movement, and the rise and fall of the King of Rock and Roll, "Elvis Presley." These were momentous events in American history, but our focus and attention was Building Our animal kingdom and neighborhood hangout... Besides, I was more fascinated with Grandpa Leo's period in history, the romantic era during the first part of the 20th century.

Pine Grove

In my mind, Grandpa Leo's former circus lot was in the best part of town, situated at the very edge of the southwestern side, bordered by three roads; Raven to the north, Willow to the west and a gravel road to the south that led out into the country. About a mile down that gravel road to the right was our favorite woodland paradise we called, "Pine Grove" (750 acres of fields, woods, valleys, hills, creeks, springs, with an abundance of wildlife). For young explorers, it was a paradise. "The

Wooden Fence" located right next to the gravel road as it rounded the mile corner was the gateway marker into our vast playground. We would always say, "I'll meet you at The Wooden Fence." The constant hum of Highway 169 droned on about three hundred yards beyond the gravel road, with only pasture and crop fields between our house and its hypnotizing sound.

Across Willow Street sat a small wooded lot the size of half a city block that had several hastily made tree houses with their walls insulated with thin cardboard. Little John and our old neighbor Tom constructed them around the time of their prize fight on the alfalfa field. One tree housed two forts with a wooden ramp centered between them. It was the best treehouse in and around town. The neighborhood kids put up a thick rope in a tree at the top of a rounded dirt hill. We could swing way out over the small dip in the valley; one of our Tarzan vines. As children, we dug pits in the ground on the trail near them. We covered the holes with reeds and grass and tried to catch each other as we unknowingly rode bicycles over them. It was a wonder no one was hurt. Directly across the gravel road from the wooded lot was a steep hill on Townsend's farm where we would go sledding once the winter snows arrived. The barbed wire fence at the bottom of the hill was always an obstacle that had to be avoided, most times by ditching the sled or toboggan before getting creamed. While still living at the old house, we would stay out in the Minnesota cold until our limbs could take no more. Then, we'd limp home to thaw out before the menacing furnace. Minnesota winters seemed to last longer than any other season. Spring took a long time to arrive. The spring floods were a yearly event we always looked forward to because the floods signaled the end of the drawn-out winter and the beginning of a short spring.

On warm spring days, we could see the shrinking snow form little streams on Townsend's hill and off we'd run to announce to the neighborhood boys that the long-awaited floods had returned. The water traveling through the ravine at warp speed. It was quite the yearly spectacle, filled with both excitement and risk. The water grew so deep it barely slipped under the ten-foot-tall metal culvers tucked under two roadways not more than two football fields apart from each other. We'd travel from one to the other studying the fast current rushing in and out of them. One person would stand on one end of the culvert and throw a stick in the fast-moving current, while the person at the other end would yell when and if they saw it come through. That way, we could judge the speed at which it traveled. Some flood years were better than others, but just watching the small creek grow to the size of a raging river sent chills and thrills up our spines.

Tom's curiosity got the best of him in the Seven Ponds area when he tried to get as close to the rushing water's edge as possible. He lunged three feet over standing water onto what appeared to be a solid sheet of ice frozen around a tree stump. But when he landed on it, the tree stump along with four sections of the ice broke away. The ice island, along with Tom headed toward the raging waters mere inches away. He quickly turned around and lunged for our outstretched arms and urging Cries. Tom landed two feet short of his original launching pad in thigh deep, freezing cold water. We grabbed his begging arms and pulled him up and out just as the ice island shot for the Minnesota River. Then, we quickly headed for the warm, menacing furnace.

Once settled into our new dwelling, Dad would come home from The Garage a minute or two after the high pitched squeal of the noon whistle, grab a quick bite to eat. Then he would lie by the stairs with his head resting against the wall to admire his new home. From his vantage point, he could see the kitchen, dining, and part of the living room. If he lifted his head and sat upright, he could see part of the downstairs fireplace. He could also look up and admire his tall slanted ceilings with neatly built-in wooden beams spaced between a sparkling ceiling texture that was brand new to the market. The sparkling ceiling made the house look ritzy and gave the upstairs rooms twinkling character. There were only two things that Dad didn't get in the new house, no, make that three things. He didn't put in a two-car garage. He didn't install the balcony that was

supposed to run the entire length of the back upper level, and he didn't get the bulldog we had all agreed upon and picked out of a lineup at The Old House during several dinner discussions.

The 2000 square foot ranch featured a walkout basement, four bedrooms, a bath upstairs and down, and one car attached garage. Some features we thought were luxury items, besides the slanted sparkling ceilings and beams was a light brick, wood burning fireplace featuring a huge half round rock hearth standing proudly in the corner of the downstairs family room. The precise brick pattern continued upstairs passing through the dining room partially open to the kitchen. The rather large living room had a triple size window in the center viewing the front of the property facing Raven Street and the neighbor on the other side. The pink carpeting/drapes and furniture made it look like a "French whorehouse," but boy did Mom think it was fancy. The hand-built oak kitchen cabinets matched the wainscoting which went around the dining/kitchen room, including the entire wall leading to the downstairs. The stairs themselves were crowned with a solid oak railing running around the two sides leaving an opening that led to the inviting basement below. None of us had ever experienced the luxury of the carpet before, but almost every room had it on the floor. The basement was finished with wood paneling and solid white ceiling tiles which gave it a clean, finished look.

The house was built on top of the torn down circus sheds, which meant all that land the ponies used to roam on was now our playground and zoo. Our new, large yard was also the perfect location for all our friends to hang out. One of the main reasons was our "stockade," a very unique structure which was the envy of all our friends and every other kid in town. It made the double tree house across the road look like a rundown shack sitting next to the Taj Mahal. Dad designed the stockade straight out of his creative mind. Tom and I helped him erect it from that material we salvaged from Grandpa Leo's tin circus sheds. It was basically an eleven foot by eight-foot tin fort, sitting firmly on top of railroad ties. A solid wooden step ladder made from two by fours led to the opening of a three-foot-wide covered balcony that ran the entire length of the front end; the balcony he didn't get in his new home. An entry door hinged at

The stockade

the opposite end of the ladder opened into a room that could easily hold six or more young teenagers. The seven-foot-high ceiling had a built-in slant starting at the front of the balcony roof and ending at the rear. The three other walls held solid tin windows hinged at the top, so they could be pushed out and lifted up. To keep the windows open, we inserted a piece of wood cut to the correct size. We covered the wood floor with varied colors and textures of scrap carpet we retrieved from Hennen's Furniture Store trash bin.

To us, the structure resembled a lookout tower on the inside walls of a 19th century army post; just like the ones we saw on our favorite TV western shows, but the stockade turned out to be so much more. Many a night we slept in the stockade. It amply served as the headquarters for our daytime and night-time adventures, which often included experimentation with alcohol and the entertaining of young ladies. We almost needed a calendar to keep track of whose turn it was to sleep out. Between two sisters and four brothers, there were sometimes 20 to 30 kids and teenagers milling around the large property. Better still, even though the old circus lot was on the edge of town, the downtown area was still only three blocks down the alleyway.

Our yard was also an ideal setup for Mike's future hawk training activities. It took a lot of wide open space to train these hunting birds. In our expanded backyard, he had the room to teach the instinctive predators to fly to his fist, chase lures, exercise them and let them soak up a little sun while sitting on their handmade perches. Mike and his hunting buddies also had an improvised archery range set up, where they practiced with their recurve bows to get ready for deer hunting. The backyard archery range became another hang out for Tom, and me and our buddies. Besides Mike and his hunting friends, up to a dozen kids sat on and around a primitive fence Dad built out of saplings. All eyes watched the

Tom showing good form with the recurve bow. Dale turning toward the camera. Our friend Bob waiting to shoot.

arrows being released at a life-sized deer which was painted on a large cardboard box sitting ahead of hay bales. The house was always busy with young kids and loud rock music coming from Mike's garage band or Moms 1950s phonograph which he now claimed as his own.

Our property was so large there was ample room to put in a decent size horse pen near and around Grandpa Leo's relocated workshop. Dad tentatively agreed to both mine and Mike's continuous urging to get a horse and a hawk. He lived up to half of the agreement the day we all scrounged up the remaining tin and lumber and put up the buildings to house them. We extended the tin structure about ten feet out and along the entire length of Grandpa Leo's old workshop. Then we divided the shed into two halves; one 10 feet long for my future horse and the other six feet long for Mike's future hunting birds. Dad built a horizontal split door on the horse end facing the highway and a solid tin door on the hawk side facing the house. We painted it the same color as Great Grandpa Jay's old circus trailer, "white" that now was permanently parked alongside the front of the new zoo buildings. Grandpa Leo had tons of circus posters and memorabilia stored throughout the old trailer and he was always rummaging through the mess, no doubt reliving his circus life. He'd spend hours in there trying to hold onto a little of what he once had!

Mom and Dad finally approved, (aided by my brothers and sisters) and gave the go-ahead to acquire a new pony. Behind the scenes, Dad was looking forward to having a horse around the property. He had been around them his whole life on the circus, so I think he sort of missed them, but I could have been wrong. He made numerous conditions and ensured that I knew what I was getting myself into as far as caring for the animal and all the costs associated with the purchase and upkeep afterward. I had saved roughly $150.00 from working at the downtown bowling alley setting pins, bailing hay alongside brother Tom at local farms, working at the carnival during the local Bar-B-Que Days celebration, and working part-time at Anabelle's Café as a night-time dishwasher. My parents allowed me to work at Anabelle's till ten o'clock at night during the week and all night on weekends. So, preparations began for my long awaited pony.

Dad and I rounded up the round wooden posts and barbed wire needed to build the fence from a few farm auctions held one Saturday morning. Grandpa Leo gave me some of his leftover horse harnesses and equipment I would need, but I had to come up with a saddle and they were expensive. Fortunately, our old neighbor Tom had an advertisement in the paper selling two and gave me a good deal on a beautiful suede covered saddle in blue and grey tones. With all the

pieces finally in place, complete with a freshly stacked set of hay and straw, anxiety set in as the day neared to pick out my horse.

Dad knew everyone in and around Belle Plaine from working at The Garage all those years and he knew of a pony farm not too far from my new pasture. So, Dad borrowed Ellis Johnson's truck and horse trailer, picked up an excited Grandpa Leo, and we all headed to the pony farm to do a little shopping. "Which one do you want Dale?" Dad asks me as I'm watching thirty to forty wild ponies of all shapes, sizes, and colors moving in unison back and forth throughout the small wooden corral, tucked in front of an old rundown barn. Although springtime, the ponies still wore their thick winter coats making it hard to discern their true colors. Instead of watching the herd, I looked for a horse that stood out from the rest and saw her running faster than the others as she led the way. She was a good size Welsh pony, (*the next size down from Quarter horses.*) I pointed her out to Dad who told me she was a strawberry roan color, meaning a reddish brown with white hairs mixed between. A white patch ran the length of her face starting at the top of her forehead and ending just below her nostrils. Her lower legs matched the color of her face patch, and she was adorned with a long blonde mane and matching tail. She cost me $32.00, and I gladly laid down the $6.00 difference to get the next size up from a Shetland pony.

Catching her was extremely difficult and time-consuming because she was so high spirited and wild, as they all were. The female pony made me a little nervous because I knew that I would be the one to break her in later that day, which was fast approaching. Thank God I had Dad and Grandpa Leo there to handle her because I sure had no clue what to do. It took two ropes, a blindfold, and three men to get her inside the horse trailer which made me a tad more nervous than earlier. Grandpa Leo could see the uneasy look on my face and assured me she could be tamed, and I never doubted Grandpa. He opened her mouth and looking at her teeth judged her to be between three and four years old, which meant she was set in her ways. I already had a name picked out for the wild beast, "Sheba," a name with an ancient theme similar to the era of the name "Turak" which Mike would use for his first Red-tailed Hawk. I thought it was a nice fit; Sheba the horse and Turak the hawk.

Sheba munching on hay. Wooden corral and stockade ahead of Townsend's pasture

When we arrived back at our new Kingdom, the entire family was on hand to watch me get my ass kicked by the Queen of Sheba. We prepared to let her run in the pasture we had laid out for her, so she could get a feel for her new home before putting weight on her back. Sonny and I had built the entire fence line together digging every hole with a manual post hole digger and put up all the barbed wire one strand at a time. The pen was roughly the size of a quarter of a city block with ample room for the horse to run but not enough for her to get her fill of grass in the summer. Dad built a rudimentary wooden corral around a wild area inside the pasture where the circus animals were buried. The permanent resting place for the circus animals was almost as sacred to us as American Indian burial grounds and something to be respected. The stockade stood just beyond the corral close to two, nice sized trees situated on the corner next to the road that led out to The Wooden Fence. The pasture's crowning jewel and gateway to the rodeo stood erect in the center of the pasture facing

the rear of the house. The opening featured two, ten-foot tall posts with a five foot solid old wooden board nailed across the top looking like something straight out of the old west, especially with the deer horns that Mike placed in the middle of the top plank. Our new kingdom was really something special; brand new walkout basement leading to a large backyard, complete with a horse pasture and housing area for the horse and hawk and our famous stockade sitting solid and erect in the southwest corner of the lot. It's no wonder that all our friends wanted to hang out there.

We let her loose to explore her new home and as soon as we did, the crazed horse ran full speed toward Willow Street. She soon discovered that not all fences are made of wood! Just as she reached her max speed, her head and body ran smack dab into the three-layered barbed wire fence, stretching the wire to the extreme and straining the newly placed wooden poles. When she hit the wire, it acted as a spring jolting her backward and knocking her half off her feet causing her to stumble before regaining her stature. We all looked at each other in disbelief as the horse experts ran over to her and tried to calm her down. Her eyes rolled up high underneath her lashes. Now the previously unblemished pony had a nice eight-inch jagged cut that started above the middle of her eyes and traveled upward to the top of the white-faced patch. Grandpa Leo assured me she would be OK. It would heal on its own, and I always believed Grandpa Leo.

We thought we would break her right off anyway to get some of the wild out of her. It was as exciting as having a real rodeo right in our own backyard! Grandpa Leo put on her harness and put a straight bit behind her teeth, tightened up the straps on the saddle while pushing his knee into her stomach to release the large breath she had intentionally taken in. She was smart, thinking she could then release her breath after the straps were tightened and while nobody was looking, but Grandpa Leo was smarter and he knew every trick in the book and then some. With Grandpa Leo in front of the horse and Dad blocking her right, I jumped on her and got ready for what I knew would be the ride of my life. They let her go and she did not disappoint, bucking, rearing, and running, but I kept hold tight of the reins and saddle trying to keep her in control. Everybody was cheering and yelling and it all happened so fast, I thought I stayed on her for longer, but there I was lying on the ground watching Sheba circle the entire length of the fence. Theresa had ridden horses before and got up the nerve to give her a shot. With Grandpa Leo in the front and Dad on the side, she jumped on and got the ride of her life, ending up on the ground as I had. Dad's weight and experience won the day, but when one of us lighter kids would get on her, she'd still try to buck us off at every chance she got. And if I carried a passenger behind her saddle, she would rear back every time trying to throw them off her back.

As spring slowly turned to summer, she settled down and gradually lost her thick winter coat. A barely noticeable scar formed over the cut from the barbed wire. Grandpa Leo had been correct on both counts! She turned out to be the color I hoped she would be; short-haired darker red with the white liberally mixed between. She now revealed the tight muscular body and the secret to her speed. Sheba grew to know and love her new home where she was now the center of everyone's attention, getting fed sugar cubes and corn cobs by all. The once untamed female even allowed me to crawl underneath her without getting startled. She was a real beauty, and I felt proud walking her around the streets of Belle Plaine and the gravel road leading to The Wooden Fence. The leader of the herd cost me almost my entire life's savings, but I finally had a real horse to ride and a new best friend. Our next obsession was getting hold of a baby crow. We anticipated teaching it to ride on our shoulder as we rode our bikes or on Sheba's back. As much as I bugged Dad for a horse, Mike was constantly trying to convince him he was ready to take up the ancient traditions of falconry. As I now had my horse shed occupied with Sheba, Mike would eventually obtain a hunting bird to put on the other side of the shed.

Crow School

Sitting on the balcony of the stockade, "The Night Raiders" wait for the lights to go out in Mom and Dad's bedroom window. Jim and I are reminiscing about our best days attending "Crow School" when Sister Marianne was our sixth-grade teacher. With our black pullover masks at the ready, we wonder whatever happened to the energetic nun who had stormed into Belle Plaine's St. Peter and Paul Catholic School fresh out of college and soon after captured the hearts and the minds of the entire student population, only to mysteriously disappear the night before the end of the year picnic. Some students thought she might have been called home because of a family emergency while others felt she had taken ill, but nobody knew for sure. When our class discovered she wasn't coming back to teach the following year, questions swirled around her covert exit. Most everyone in the school thought the old Crows and the priest were the ones responsible for her disappearance. Even if they were not directly involved, they still treated the young nun like a doormat the entire school year, probably worse than they treated my brothers and me and for that alone, their feet should be held to the fire. The holiest among us were not practicing the teachings of the New Testament. Their condescending attitude and a swift hand to the face ticked off a lot of kids who attended their school over the years, 'especially me.' My Night Raiders provides the perfect medium in which to capture their attention and give them something to think about before they lay down and pray themselves to sleep. Our first mission is to pay back the institution where we spent so many years.

Our entire family was raised as strict Roman Catholics. We all attended the same parochial school that Dad and Grandpa Leo had gone to as boys. St. Peter and Paul's school was a three-story, straw-colored, brick building located directly behind the church. The school and the church both took up half of the city block. Besides the old rectory, the rest was mainly playgrounds. The parish utilized four of its six school rooms; two on the first floor and two on the second each separated by a fifteen-foot-wide hallway. A large wooden staircase took up a good chunk of the main hallway on the lower floor. The nuns further divided two of the four rooms into two classrooms, so they could simultaneously teach two smaller grades in the same room. Tom was always a grade ahead of me. Mary was always a grade behind, so sometimes we shared the same classroom. The population of the entire school was less than 150 making us a tight-knit group of kids who stuck together even after graduating and transferring over to the public school.

The parish priest was from the Franciscan order wearing a long brown robe, cowl, and a pair of sandals. The nuns were from a Religious order women called the Poor Handmaidens of Jesus Christ, also wearing the traditional ankle-length black habit with a huge rosary tied around their waist. The only skin showing on their entire body was their hands and lower part of their face. The upper half was overtaken by a white rectangle forehead extender beginning just above their eyebrows. It traveled sideways to their temples and extended upward four to five inches. A long black flowing veil attached at the top front part of the rectangle hung heavily to the back of their knees. A white cloth slightly overhung the rectangle and then traveled tightly down the sides of their face covering their ears. This tight-fitting habit holder outlining their face gave the nuns the appearance of having a tight peek a boo

Crows

look. Because the headwear blocked their peripheral vision, the nuns were forced to turn their entire body 90 degrees to the left or to the right to get a straight-line view of what was going on around the edges of the playground. The Crows side to side shuffling began the minute the kids hit the playground and didn't end until the last kid was safely back inside the old schoolhouse. The entire outfit looked like an uncomfortable and burdensome thing to wear every day, especially, during sizzling summer days. But, there was something strange and intriguing about these long robes and other garments. It was as if time had stood still, and we were stuck in the Middle Ages.

Every day before the start of school, we had to attend Mass daily. Beginning at 7 a.m., each grade level marched up the center aisle of the church in two rows, a boys' line and a girls' line, side by side. One nun had a little hand clicker, (we called it a cricket) the type used to train dogs. Once we reached the pews, (*wooden benches with a padded kneeler in front*) the clicker would sound for us to genuflect, another click to turn and walk in the pew and a final click to either sit or kneel. Once Mass was over and we were back in the classroom, we'd start off with an hour-long lesson in religion. We learned about sins, Saints, studied the meaning of the daily scripture and prepared for first Communion and later Confirmation. At any rate, I attended the Catholic school from the second to the seventh grades. Mike, Theresa, and Tom all had to endure the eighth grade, but thank God, the school dropped that grade toward the end of my seventh-grade year sparing me their misery.

Even though we went to church every school morning, Mom and Dad made us attend Mass either on Saturday afternoon or Sunday morning, no questions asked. Going to church six days a week month in and month out was worse than Chinese water torture for the likes of me.

Back during those simpler times, many Catholic families wanted one or more of their kids to become a priest or a nun. Little girls dressed in freshly purchased white, frilly dresses to celebrate their first Communion. The boys especially had to dress up in little cassocks, surplus and skull caps for Christmas or Easter services. We were trained as altar boys or servers, so we could assist the priest during mass. This consisted in bringing the priest cruets of water and wine, ringing bells,

carrying a big crucifix or candle during processions, lighting and extinguishing candles and lastly holding the patten or gold plate under parishioners' chins. The patten was used to catch any fallen crumbs of bread while they received communion. After communion, the priest would mix the fallen crumbs from the patten with the leftover wine into an ornate chalice and drink it in front of the entire congregation. After downing every last drop, he'd then wipe out and polish the inside of the chalice with a special silk embroidered hanky. Every once in a great while he'd accidentally drop an entire host or round wafer of bread on the floor and everybody would step back like someone had been shot. Then the priest would grab a cloth and put it over the spot where the bread of Christ fell so he could clean it up later with, I suppose, some special holy water mixed in with a particular prayer chosen from the Catholic doctrine. But most days nothing happened at communion time and the wafers got placed on people's tongues. No pieces fell on the floor, so it was boring.

To spice things up and have some fun, we servers would hold the patten, rub our shoes back and forth on the carpet to build up a static charge of electricity before one of our buddies came up to receive communion. Then, all it took was a light touch of the patten on the kid's chin or neck to give them a nice little jolt. Next time, he'd be up front and return the favor. We did it back and forth as a running joke. It was a tough trick to pull off because you had to make sure the priest didn't see you creating the charge with your feet or intentionally touching your buddies chin with the patten. We kept a lot of things from the priest and the nuns figuring that what they didn't know wouldn't hurt them, or us.

The holy wine was kept locked on the left side of the sacristy inside a James Bond type cabinet hidden behind two dark blue felt curtains. Watching the priest open the cabinet was like watching a magician perform one of those hidden compartment tricks. First, he'd move the curtains with flair to the side revealing beautifully patterned brass doors. Then he'd fit a fancy key inside the special lock, turning it in a certain sequence while mumbling a little prayer we couldn't quite pick up on. That's when you had to pay close attention because two sets of doors (one outside the other inside) opened so quickly and in such an unusual pattern it was hard to discern if the inside or outside door opened first or closed last. Behind the magical brass doors sat a fancy wine bottle featuring an ivory horse head spigot where we'd fill the cruets with wine from the horse's mouth. Before and after Mass, most of us would take turns watching out for the priest, so we could down a few shots for ourselves, always refilling the bottle with enough water so no one knew that we'd been pulling on the jug. Heck, the priest mixed water with it anyway, we thought, "What was the difference?"

It was still common to get slapped or knocked around by the teachers for misbehaving in class, parochial school or public, it mattered not, you got it twice, once at school and then at home after your parents discovered what you got in trouble for. To say that discipline was stressed and enforced was an understatement. As for getting slapped, having a ruler rapped across your fingers, or getting dragged into the "cloak room" to get worked over with a long wooden pointer at the hands of an angry nun. It could happen anytime for any reason. Some of us were always looking around to dodge a swing here or a blow there from a ticked off nun. The worst thing that could happen to any student was a call to the priest from the principal requesting assistance for special cases of misbehavior. What we lived in was a constant state of fear and apprehension while in class, and it was the same once you got home. Most of us got slapped, whipped, and thrown around regularly. It was just part of being a kid back in the 1960s. How it affected us and what it did, was made us real sneaky, and real fast to escape getting clobbered. We boys were professionals both at home and at school in dodging and avoiding a good whack, whereas our sisters were just the opposite. They both graduated Crow school as pure and as innocent as the first day they walked in the front door.

When I entered parochial school as a frightened little second grader, I witnessed firsthand who Mike had been warning the rest of us about for years. She was tall, mean and a particularly ugly old nun who taught seventh and eighth grades named sister Michael. She had a beak on her like The Wicked Witch of the East, buck teeth and a hunched over back. Though we all feared her, everybody called her 'CROW' behind her back. Not only because of her physical features, but the long black habit made her look very similar to an old crow bird. The Catholic school was called "CROW SCHOOL," plain and simple. Mention the term and instantly everyone in town knew what you were talking about. One of Crow's jobs was ringing a big, brass bell to start the beginning of school, recess, and lunch hour and the end of each, but more importantly, her job as a head nun was to keep the old school running like a military unit.

The girls had to wear dresses of a very modest length, no sleeveless blouses, and as a rule of thumb, show little or preferably no skin, anywhere, PERIOD!! In the winter, the girls had to wear long pants or leggings under their dresses. I'm not sure if it was to keep them warm or to keep the boys from seeing a little skin. At any rate, Mike discovered the true meaning later in a big way.

Some kids were having the usual snowball fight, pelting each other every time Crow's back was turned. It was the regular child's play we all remember, stuff a little snow down your buddies coat, hit him in the back of the head with a hard-packed snowball, etc. Mike was getting into it and the same as you'd put a handful of snow down somebody's jacket, he threw a snowball under a girl's dress. It was purely innocent with no sexual connotations, but Crow saw him, came up behind him and nailed him on the top of his head with that damn brass bell, grabbed him by the ear and hauled him into the classroom. After getting a couple more shots at him, the tongue lashing came next and she must have chewed him out for 10 minutes and was still at it when the rest of the class came back in from recess. He thought that was it, but it wasn't by a long shot. He had to stand up in front of the class and get it again. Finally, Crow told him he was "dirty and rotten to the core." Mike was an innocent, impulsive kid having some winter fun, but the old Crow made it out to be something sexual and dirty.

Now when Crow lit into somebody, they got it good! She was what you might call thorough in her delivery of the combination ass chewing/skull cracking. Two of her favorite expressions during the tongue lashing was "I'll box your ears," or "If you don't like it, pack your doodle sack and beat it." What the heck was a doodle sack? Nobody knew. Getting chewed out from and skull cracked by her was a long drawn out affair usually done in front of the entire class to cause a good, old-fashioned helping of shame. As for the actual method of clouting you, she wasn't particular using many techniques and instruments of pain to work you over; bare hand, ruler, her heavy brass bell, in cases of gross misbehavior she'd march you into the 'cloakroom' and thrash the hell out of you with a long, wooden pointer. I don't know why it was called the cloakroom, nobody we knew owned or wore a cloak, not even the nuns. They wore shawls. I suppose cloakroom sounded better than shawl room. Supposedly, she had a two-inch thick wooden paddle in her office complete with drilled holes through it to lessen the wind resistance and had been given permission from the parents to use at will, if need be.

There was also a dress code for the boys required to wear their shirt tails tucked in, a belt and absolutely no blue jeans. It seems the nuns expected us to restrain ourselves even at recess and they were constantly shifting from side to side on the lookout for any erotic advances from either sex. In their minds wearing blue jeans would cause us to play a little too rough by possibly rolling around on the grass or sliding into second base. They thought that wearing dress pants supposedly prevented that sort of thing. I still can't see why they didn't understand. We did it anyway, dress pants be damned! It was the late 1960s and by then we had been listening to bands like Hendrix, Zeppelin, and Cream, etc. Naturally, a guy admired their fashion statements and wanted to look cool too, especially Mike.

Once Mike got a job at the Garage, he bought his own clothes and he found these great checkered pants (jeans actually,) and a lot hipper than salt and pepper corduroys. He had them a couple weeks before he got up the nerve to wear them to school. Crow herself was his teacher that year and he was taking a chance of not only being sent home but cracked along the side of his head as well with that solid brass bell. Everybody saw his new pants when he walked into the room, but they escaped Crow. Maybe she was distracted by something else or her eyes were getting bad. She looked like she was a hundred years old. Well, he did pretty good all morning until she told him to go to the blackboard and solve a math problem. His buddies all looked down at their desks because they knew he was about to be busted and he was, as soon as he got up. "What, you're wearing jean pants?" Crow asked. "Not me, these are my new dress pants, sister." "Get over here, let me see them," "Yes ma-am." "They look like jean pants to me," says Crow. "No, they aren't sister," Mike gulped. "Well just make sure you don't start rolling around outside at recess, you'll ruin them." Mike couldn't believe that she bought his explanation, no lecture, no fisticuffs! After that, he got himself a nice pair of striped bell bottoms and black Beatle boots. The rebellion taking place in the upper classes was studied by all the students, but no class crammed for the final exam harder than our young class.

As altar boys, we all stole a few sips of wine now and again when the priest wasn't looking, but halfway through my fifth-grade year, a few fellow classmates stole two quarts of blended whiskey from "The Knights of Columbus," who had them stored in a cabinet down in the church basement. We found them while skipping out of church one morning and hiding out down in the basement below until morning mass was over. We buried the bottles in a snowbank behind the high school and invited all the 'drinkers' in class to join us in a few shots the following Friday night's high school basketball game.

Before the basketball game, close to a dozen boys and a few girls, gathered behind the high school standing in foot deep snow, passing around and taking sips off those two bottles of adult beverage. We did the same thing at halftime and again at the end of the game until the bottles were empty. Most of us were half in the bag by then, but my dear friend Joe who was the ringleader of the bunch drank way more than the rest of us and didn't quite make it home that night. He ended up passed out in a snowbank, mere footsteps from the front door to his house. Lucky for him, a local cop found him lying there while making his late-night patrols. Joe was in the initial stages of hypothermia and he would have died had the cop not spotted him. The theft of the whiskey and subsequent plans to drink it were kept under tight lip by our young class right until the cop happened upon Joe. The police finding an eleven-year-old kid drunk out of his mind and nearly at death was big news in a small town and word traveled quickly. The priest was determined to get to the bottom of the theft and uncover anyone who was involved in the actual drinking the whiskey. One by one, six of the most troublemaking boys were summoned to see the priest for questioning. We all kept quiet and none of us admitted to anything, including Joe. That single, momentous incident gained our class a reputation as one of the rowdier ones around town, so it was beyond me why our unruly class would be blessed with a nun straight out of heaven the following sixth-grade year; the one and only Sister Marianne!

There was a feeling of anticipation running throughout St. Peter and Paul Parish during the summer of 1969 when word spread that a new "young" nun was coming to the convent to replace the much dreaded and feared Crow herself, Sister Michael. A young nun fresh out of college could bring some new and updated ideas along with her and hopefully breathe a little life into the old brick schoolhouse which seemed stuck in the Middle Ages along with the costumes priests and nuns wore. We all felt that things would change for the better once the new nun arrived? They did for my sixth-grade class anyway because she was miraculously scheduled to be our teacher! A popular movie called "The Singing Nun" aired in 1966 starring a young-faced Debbie Reynolds

who sang and strummed on her guitar, as did a hit TV series the following year, "The Flying Nun" starring Sally Field; another cute young face tucked under an unusually large winged white habit. Most kids in the parish had images of those two female actors fresh in their minds and everyone was more than eager to see what the new nun would look like once she arrived for duty at the convent steps. Every Saturday or Sunday Mass we'd look for her hoping to get a glimpse finally putting our curiosities to rest.

When Sister Marianne arrived, she was the talk of the town. All the boys thought she was good-looking, and all the girls just drooled over her in admiration. She was the complete opposite of the nuns we were used to seeing roaming the church grounds. Somebody in heaven must have screwed up and assigned her to the wrong place because this young energetic nun seemed way too cool for our little town, let alone our class numbering thirty. She didn't look like a Debbie Reynolds or a Sally Field, but she was a fresh and exciting diversion after years of the same routine. She owned her own unique look. Unlike the older nuns, the front part of her jet-black hair waved proudly ahead of her modest length, black veil that was fitted neatly just 'behind' her ears. She looked like one of those Jewish women you see in the Bronx of New York, the ones featuring skin as white as New York snow accented with black eyebrows resting above pretty dark eyes.

Sister Marianne

She dressed more modern than her counterparts wearing a bright white shirt boasting ruffled ribbons which filled the entire front, "I suppose 'excuse the expression sister,' to draw attention away from her large breasts." Her black skirt ended at the knees instead of the tops of her shoes sinfully exposing legs barely hidden behind black see-through nylons. She was more than friendly that first day before class when a few of my sixth-grade buddies and I intentionally arrived early to get a close look at her for ourselves. She sat cautiously behind her new desk studying our youthfulness as we joked around with each other and threw her a stupid question now and then. She answered pleasantly enough and asked us a few ordinary questions of her own while pretending to straighten and tidy her desk. She probably wondered to herself during that first encounter if she could teach the likes of us anything or if she could even tone down our assertiveness a notch, maybe two. The bell sounded and we all took our seats with everyone trying to sit close to the new teacher sitting upright and saintly behind her desk. At any rate, she was excited to begin her first day as a teacher where at the end of the year she would take her final vows to become a full-fledged "Poor Handmaiden of Jesus Christ." She had to go through us first and survive.

Sister Marianne was a novelty in all the grades, not just our own. Because of her background in biology, she spent an hour each day crossing the hallway to teach Tom and Theresa (7th and 8th graders) math and science while we had to put up with Sister Cyril's history and reading lessons. Even though Sister Marianne was the youngest nun ever to serve the St. Peter and Paul Parish and wore an updated uniform, she was all business for teaching; more so than I hoped for initially anyway. But I would much rather be staring at her teaching in front of the blackboard than Mrs. Krava or the two other Crows teaching Theresa, Tom, and Mary in the other classrooms. For the first time in all my years attending Crow School, I was excited to be there. The thought of having her the entire school year was almost too good to be true. How could we get so lucky?

Our tight-knit class resembled Sister Marianne's somewhat rebellious and non-conformist ways, making me wonder if that screw up in heaven might have been planned for all along. We were all pleasantly surprised to discover that she could play the guitar and sing better than Debbie Reynolds did in her starring role as the Singing Nun. After school, she taught four of my classmates Mary Kay, Shari, Pam, and Susie how to strum the guitar and sing upbeat modern Christian songs and they occasionally joined her playing for the school's morning Masses. Once they were ready, she asked and was given the opportunity to lead guitar Masses on Saturday afternoon right up front and center of the congregation. They sounded fantastic together and livened up the previously monotonous musical selections. It didn't take too many Saturdays before the pews were full of the younger generation and some older folks mixed in. And her love of music didn't end with the guitar lessons or the Saturday afternoon Masses, she assembled a 5th through 8th-grade choir and trained us to perform at the annual high school Christmas program. Even rebellious and troublesome, I wanted to be a part of the excitement radiating all around her, so one day after class I nervously tried out for the choir and was accepted into her fold. To say I enjoyed Sister Marianne's company was an understatement, even when she was marching me over to the rectory to see the priest or chewing me out for stepping out of line.

Despite her breakthrough with the youth, her energetic involvement at the church and teaching passion inside the classrooms, it seemed as though she was constantly bumping heads with the older nuns. I suppose some of the dim-witted things we pulled under her leadership didn't help her standing with them, and I of all classmates probably did her the most harm. Besides my open classroom wisecracks and mouthing off during our walks to and from the church, the little stupid things got me and Sister Marianne into trouble.

One day while feeling cocky and daring, I poured some pencil shavings out of the pencil sharpener, grabbed some lined writing paper and rolled up a real looking cigarette. Then I lit the end and took a few drags to show off to my classmates while Sister Marianne was out and about somewhere. Smoke and laughter resonated throughout the classroom and out into the hallway. Neither escaped the noses or the ears of the older nuns. I threw the self-rolled pencil shavings out the window, but by then it was too late. There was an immediate scramble to find the culprit and the principal, Sister Roselia (the head nun) was the one leading the charge. As I said, I did little to boost Sister Marianne's standing, and she suffered the most. I was punished at home, but poor Sister Marianne had to live with the very nun that chewed her out that day. And so, the little foolish pranks continued, and I discovered that some of the innocent things I did were just plain unacceptable.

Joe and I were enjoying a little free time during a break in the classroom looking out our second-floor open window when this high school girl walks by and both of us loudly whistle, "Whew whoooooo!" Sister Marianne knew she was in for it because she didn't leave her seat behind the desk, said no word, just buried her head in her hands and shook her head back and forth. It wasn't a minute later Sister Roselia came storming in the door and chewed her out in front of the whole class. We were always pulling some stunt or craze and had anyone other than our sixth-grade class known about our latest experimentation into the unknown, Sister Marianne would have been history.

I don't know how it started, but our class became obsessed with a new craze that involved hypnotism and intentionally making ourselves pass out. The girls experimented with hypnotizing each other while the guys were consumed with assisting each other to the state of unconsciousness. While crouched down low with our head between our knees, we took ten deep breaths of air holding the last one. Then we stood up quickly as another classmate picked us up from behind, squeezed hard and shook the hell out of us. Some guys would pass out on their own

just by standing up, so it was the shaking person's responsibility to catch them as they fell to the ground.

The experimentation eventually worked its way into the classroom when it was too cold to go out for recess and when Sister Marianne was preoccupied with something else. The boys began with the blackouts while the girls were tucked in an abandoned classroom connected behind our own doing the hypnotizing thing. One girl hypnotized another so well that when they attempted to bring her out of it, they couldn't! The girls panicked. Mary Kay and Susie ran to get Sister Marianne who came charging to the rescue with a puzzling and somewhat frightened look on her face. She shook the girl and called out her name, but the girl was so out of it she couldn't get her to wake up. Sister Marianne eventually got her to come around by slapping her in the face several times. Until that point, we guys thought the girls were faking the hypnotizing thing but realized afterward that it was for real and never messed with it again.

With the head-butting over at the convent and no family or close friends in town, Sister Marianne buried herself in her schoolwork and into her music. She also poured her heart into her sixth-grade class taking sole possession of her disruptive little darlings. She treated us as an older sister would, forgiving us for being the kids we were despite the embarrassment we caused her on so many, many occasions. Even though there was more than a decade of an age difference between us, we connected with her on a personal level. She even found humor in my classroom antics which she admitted she admired because acting out in front of a crowd was something she never did.

On rare occasions, she would open up to us as she would a close friend. One night after choir practice, she took off her habit and revealed her long black hair to a select few girls. We thought it was forbidden by the church, possibly even a cardinal sin. Had the older nuns discovered her sinful exposure, she would have been disgraced and isolated even more than she already was. I respected her after that, even though the move was purely innocent, it was rebellious and sneaky all rolled up into one. But that was not the first time she unveiled her long black hair when she was forbidden to do so.

While attending college in Milwaukee, after a math class at Marquette, she went into a public restroom, changed from her habit into her "civvies" and joined one of the civil rights marches taking place throughout the country. Because of the times, this was big news and the march was covered by the local television stations complete with footage of all the marchers including Sister Marianne's lovely black hair on display for the entire world to see. The march topped the evening newscast reaching as far away as the nuns Motherhouse in Indiana and to the startled eyes of her superiors. She was chewed out good for pulling that stunt. Anyway, the girls who witnessed the colossal event all thought they were so special. They bragged about it and talked about it the rest of the school year. But, there probably wasn't a lot of talking taking place over at the convent once the school doors were locked.

The nuns lived mostly in silence, speaking only if it was necessary. Every once and a great while Sister Marianne would ask them for an opinion on how to handle a certain situation (probably me) only to be told that she'd figure it out on her own and then silence. Throughout the year, the neglect and the isolation took its toll.

Three-quarters of the way through the school year, we all sensed that she was feeling low. We discovered just how much so the day she brought in a tape player so we could listen to her favorite song. It was titled "Bridge Over Troubled Waters" written and performed by Simon and Garfunkel. The song started to be a modest gospel hymn about comforting a person in need but became more dramatic as they put it together. If there was any song in the world that described Sister Marianne's feelings, it was that one. Throughout the song, we watched the range of emotions pour out of her inner self as if she were the person they had written about.

Then her solemn look changed into an expression of hope as she sang along with the final two verses with the tempo building and lyrics changing to words of hope. Her dreams not yet fulfilled but would soon be on their way.

By the end of the song, we all realized what Sister Marianne had been holding inside for the better part of the school year. We felt so honored that she entrusted herself to us and from then on, we didn't look at her as a teacher or nun, but rather as one of our own. And I think she saw us in a different light as well because despite all our youthful indiscretions, she protected and shielded us under her "would be" heavenly wings.

Nearing the end of an interesting and fun year with Sister Marianne, I wanted to give her something to remember me by, so I gave her a personalized postcard where on the back side it read:

<u>SR. MARIANNE,</u>
WE ARE ALL SORRY TO
SEE YOU GO. I HOPE YOU HAVE BETTER
LUCK NEXT YEAR TEACHING THAN YOU DID
THIS YEAR. I'M SORRY FOR ALL THE TROUBLE
I CAUSED YOU.

GOOD-BYE AND GOOD LUCK.
YOUR (**XXXXX**)
STUDENT,
DALE ALBRECHT

P.S. HAVE A NICE
VACATION THIS
SUMMER!

On the front side, Theresa drew a picture of Sister Marianne sitting behind her desk holding a pointer near the top of my devil horns as I stood behind my desk squirting water at her with a squirt gun. On the blackboard behind her, my name topped the list of four, each with check marks numbering the times we got into trouble. There were five check marks behind my name whereas my nearest competitor only had one.

Our year spent with Sister Marianne was better than we imagined it would be the distant summer before. Although difficult, she passed the grueling test given to her by her sixth-grade class winning us over and teaching us a little something along the way. Now she could concentrate and look forward to taking her final vows to become a Poor Handmaiden of Jesus Christ. But, while everyone else in school was looking forward to the annual end of the year picnic, Sister Marianne was awaiting a response to a letter she wrote to the Motherhouse where she requested a meeting to talk about her next assignment. In Belle Plaine, she wasn't involved in the community as much as she hoped, and she had studied to be a high school math teacher, so she was not doing what she was trained for and she wanted to express her thoughts in person before taking her fast-approaching final vows. The negative response she received back about floored her! Briefly, it read, "If you're having second thoughts now, there is no need to talk, just pack your bags and leave."

It was the end of her life as she had dreamed it would be since she was the age of twelve when she began her journey to serve her Best Friend Forever, Jesus Christ. She felt like she had tried to give her life to God and her gift was being rejected. The thought of abandoning her darlings without a chance to even say her goodbyes cut deeply into her wound. Many tears were shed, many questions went unanswered and probably still are today. But, she kept in touch with my parents through an exchange of yearly Christmas cards.

Every time I think of Sister Marianne, I remember her as she was the night of the Christmas concert standing before us proud and joyful mouthing the words to the song "Do You Hear What I

Hear," while her hands kept in perfect rhythm with the priest fingering the keys of the piano. I can see shades of Debbie Reynolds as The Singing Nun gracing her lovely face.

The following year, the school was back to the way it was before Sister Marianne arrived and lovingly guided us through the last stages of our youth. We spent one more painful year with a nun cut from the same cloth as the Crows we had before, the little beast herself, Sister Cyril. She may have been a tiny woman, but it appears Sister Michael's spirit lived large inside her. She didn't laugh or even smile often and when she did, it was usually done in front of an adult. She was obsessed with and detested any kid who didn't take care of their bodily odor. She taught on her feet and constantly moved between the rows. Sister Cyril used her nose, like a bloodhound, to sniff out smelly body odors. And when the smelly aroma touched the insides of her nostrils, she'd come to a complete stop and pull out her book of matches. The little leprechaun would light a match, blow it out, and as the smoke rose from the end of the matchstick, she'd wave it up and down saying, "It stinkith in here!" The smoke should cover up the bad body odor, at least for a little while anyway. This overdramatic display would be followed by a lecture to the entire class on body odor and the need to bathe often now that we were in our teenage years, all the while standing directly in front of the embarrassed stinker. Her favorite saying was, "Patience is a virtue and very few people possess it," and she sure as hell wasn't one of the few! It seems like every old nun had one saying or another. Sister Marianne was the only nun who didn't have a stupid saying and did not similarly inflict her students with it.

Throughout all our years attending Crow School, the best part came when summer vacation rolled around. Three months away from the old girls was something that we all looked forward to the most. The nuns even lightened up the week before school's end, but they followed a rigid set of procedures for closing the classrooms. Those days we had the old-fashioned desks, several in a line, the metal 'runners' bolted to long pieces of wood. After cleaning the wooden parts of the desk, we had to get down on our knees and clean and polish the runners. After all the business was taken care of, it was outside for the picnic. Hot dogs were grilled in the huge fire pit. Mom packed us 'Brimful' pop, Frito corn chips, cookies, Hostess Snowballs, and the nuns even made grape Kool-Aid; some boys smuggled in cans of beer. When the final ringing of the brass bell echoed across the playground, we were on our way to junior high school to join with the Trinity Lutheran Kids and the public-school kids too. All of us melting into the class of "1976."

Mom and Dad were both heavily involved in the church besides their having to deal with their troublemaking altar boys once or twice a month. Dad was a member of the Knights of Columbus and a lector while Mom led the church in song every Sunday morning and volunteered to help clean the church and the rectory a few times a week. They also invited the priest or the nuns over to our house for dinner twice a year. Despite the uncomfortable setting and embarrassment it caused us, kids, we always tried our best to put on a good showing for our church loving parents. Mom would bake the priest his favorite dish "baked smelt fish" caught by Sonny and his four sons earlier in the spring. Father would devour them by the cookie sheets full. I swear the guy would eat thirty-five fish himself as if they were crunchy Lays potato chips. Before and after the meal, he sat in Glo's pink French whore house smoking cigarettes and downing her steady diet of heavily mixed drinks. By the end of the evening, the whole ashtray was full of cigarette butts, and the man of the cloth could hardly talk. I don't know how he pulled it off, but the priest always drove back to the rectory without crashing into something or falling asleep. The nuns were complete opposite the priest, always on their best behavior and never drinking as much as a shot glass of wine. The nights were a bust, but Tom and I always made the best of them by downing a few shots of hard liquor on our own when Mom and Dad were preoccupied with the priest or the nuns in the living room.

One would think that the Albrecht kids would get special treatment at school for all of Mom and Dad's involvement in the church and all the times they had the priest and nuns over for dinner. That and that our circus had put on free shows handing over all the proceeds toward building their convent and all, but we never got a lick. It seemed like it was just the opposite. Because Mom and Dad were so tight with the priest and the nuns, I think that they felt they could get by doing anything they wanted with us. I never quite got over this twisted thinking, especially the way some of us were treated at the hands of the priest/nuns, so I took matters into my own hands, formed the Night Raiders Club, and then planned my revenge.

I asked one of my Crow school classmates, Jim if he wanted in on a little fun and take out a little revenge on our beloved old school. He was a viable candidate because he had been in on the fifth-grade whiskey heist and every other dastardly deed undertaken while attending Crow school. I had known him since kindergarten, slept at his house, and even attended one of his birthday parties. I told him that our first mission was to gain the Night Raiders some recognition while having a little fun with the nuns stationed over at the convent. As I described our costumes and told him about our first mission to be carried out while most of the town slept, he laughed and said, "No way." I don't think that he thought I was serious about the whole thing. But as he was wondering if I would really pull this thing off, I was getting things underway and working on my note to the Crows.

I enlisted Theresa to help put our costumes together which consisted of black dyed tee shirts, black pants and black dyed pullover masks made of old pillowcases with holes cut out for the eyes. Theresa could always be counted on to keep everything we did secret, and it didn't hurt she was a wiz with the sewing machine. Because she alone was in on our gig, we considered her a charter member of the club and kept her abreast of our latest happenings. Once the costumes were finished, we hid them in a small trunk buried under the ground in Grandpa Leo's old art studio just in front of his ornate coronation coach. All superheroes changed into their get up in special places like the bat cave, or in a phone booth, ours was the mystic art studio. The buried trunk was a stone's throw from the stockade making it easy to slip into and out of quickly.

```
Twenty minutes after the house falls dark, we dawn our black
pullover masks, quietly crawl out onto the balcony of the
stockade, slip down the wooden ladder and start towards St. Peter
and Paul convent as The Night Raiders. Normally, we'd navigate
the alleyways where it is relatively safe, but under cover of
costume, we walk boldly on the sidewalks instead. Other than the
local cop making his boring rounds, the streets are usually void
of cars this time of night. After traveling about a block and a
half, we become even more emboldened and walk down the center of
the road ironically in front of our old house. Then the beam of a
car's headlights approach from the front, but we don't run or
hide like we normally do, instead we stand in the center of the
street and watch the lights come to rest in front of a local
businessman's home. "Come on Jim, let's see what this guy will do
when he gets a load of us."
    "Follow my lead," as I hunch over to disguise my height and
walk with a limp to disguise my walk. Jim bends over and slightly
drags his right leg following alongside me until we are standing
directly inside the headlight's beam. The man sits there with the
engine running for the longest time before he looks up and
```

notices two masked men standing bent over in front of his car. He is taken totally by surprise and fidgets wide-eyed inside his car possibly searching for something to defend himself with, before shutting off the car and running full speed for the inside of his house. We both stand there laughing, for less than thirty seconds, until the sound of the police sirens and red flashing lights head our way. We can't believe that he called the cops and that they were responding so quickly.

We momentarily panic and take off running in the opposite direction of the sound and the lights out into an open field directly across from the high school. I made a grave mistake by breaking more than one of Little John's Ten Winning Rules of the Night and now I had rendered ourselves vulnerable running blindly in an open field. Had I thought for more than a second, I should've headed deeper into the residential blocks where there were plenty of places to hide and would have put us out of his direct search area. Instead, we run blindly behind these cut-out eyes trying to suck air through the pillowcase fabric. Jim turns to the right heading for the high school just as I turn to the left heading for the safety of the Seven Ponds ravine. We collide hard tumbling to the ground. This is worse than getting hit by an open field tackle on the football field because it's so unexpected.

As we lay there in the darkness stunned and in pain trying to gather our composure, we notice that the red lights are circling in front of the businessman's house. It will be but a minute or two before that cop heads our way which gives us roughly thirty seconds to disappear from the open field and put us on a safe path to the Seven Ponds ravine. "Come on Jim follow me. We'll head past the elementary school and then backtrack to the stockade."

Less than ten minutes into his tenure as an official Night Raider, Jim is already experiencing the thrill that the rest of us feel during our many cat and mouse chases with the local cops launched from our stockade on the edge of town. Even though Jim is sweating badly and worries that he'll be caught, he seems to be enjoying the whole experience. We spring to our feet and make the record-setting run across the open field to the tree line bordering the edges of the Seven Ponds ravine before the cop's searchlight rounds The Little Corner of our old block.

Hell, that small town cop is probably more frightened than we hoping that the two masked bandits will be far away by the time he finishes taking down our descriptions from the businessman. Catching kids stealing vegetables out of 'housewives' gardens is one thing, but men in black costumes boldly hassling the locals is something a little bit out of this man's league. After watching him encircle the block for several minutes from the tree line, I guide Jim through the Seven Ponds ravine, up the other side, through a small graveyard and end on

the gravel road leading to The Wooden Fence. We are practically home free! "Looks like we'll have to scrap the mission Jim, let's lay low for a week or so before heading back out." We turn left and follow the gravel road back to the circus lots and into Grandpa Leo's art studio, where we change back into our street clothes and crawl up the ladder leading to the stockade. We will fulfill our original mission, but it won't be for another two weeks...

The second try, we are again dressed in our now 'mold' covered Night Raiders costumes, but this time, we take a direct route to the sacred church grounds. We are also a little more cautious this outing following Little John's Ten Winning Rules of the Night to the number. A set of bushes on the front corner of the church provides the perfect cover to hide and launch across the street to the convent. The convent is dark, and the nuns are more than likely tucked in their beds fast asleep dreaming up new ways to keep their students under control. Jim seems to enjoy this second outing as a Night Raider, so much so he insists that he be the one to deliver the note. I will not argue with him as he grabs the note from my hand, runs across the street, sneaks up to the convent steps, stuffs the note in the outer screen door, rings the doorbell and runs back to our space. Hiding behind the bushes, we both keep our eyes fixed on the convent door and nervously wait for one nun to answer the bell. Soon an outdoor light switches on, the door opens. She pulls the note from the storm door, reads it over a few times and quickly ducks back inside. The note reads:

"Dear Crows, keep your schoolhouse brats off the streets this summer because the Night Raiders are in town."

We giggle behind the cover of the bushes and wait for something, anything to happen, but nothing does. No sirens blaring, no lights flashing, no lightning bolts from above! I guess we are expecting more. Disappointed and bored, we head a few blocks north of the church and vandalize a few yards before heading back to the old art studio. We stuff our moldy costumes back in the trunk where they are probably still buried today. We wait for weeks to hear any news of the note written to the Crows but never hear a word. So much for putting a mark on the town and getting some recognition, we got none! But, we got the satisfaction of giving back to the old parish a little of what they had given us all those painful years of attendance. And I'm sure those old Crows lay awake a few nights with one eye fixed on their bedroom windows while they say an extra prayer or two.

After discovering that the costumes made little of a difference while roaming the small-town streets and were more of a burden than anything else, "The Night Raiders" tenure died the same death as Mike's "Scarecrows."

The Race

When Dad finally finishes with the evening meal, I start work separating the dirty dishes left solely for me to clean up. He is always the last one to finish eating, often spending fifteen minutes to a half hour gnawing every last bit of meat and marrow off everybody's steak bones. As I move between the dining room table and the kitchen sink, I keep my eyes looking out both sets of windows surveying our expansive backyard, admiring my mature horse pasture and our tin stockade fort standing proud, just beyond the old wooden corral over in the far-right corner.

Turak scanning the neighborhood

Mike's young Red-tailed Hawk, Turak perched just below the kitchen window, stands erect keeping her eyes keenly focused on anything moving in the neighborhood and anything flying miles into the sky. I am proud of Turak, that I had acquired her for Mike when she was but a little hairy fuzzball, and now she is growing bigger by the day and looking more and more like an adult Red-tailed Hawk. She's now old enough to live in the hawk shed built onto the side of Grandpa Leo's old art studio. The shed, along with Great Grandpa Jay's trailer sitting alongside it, makes the left side of the pasture appear a little junky. The steel cage which we erected on the back side of the old studio last year does little to improve the otherwise lovely view of the yard and beyond.

Tom and I successfully raised an abandoned pair of baby raccoons inside that very steel cage until they were old enough to fend for themselves. The mischievous nighttime robbers were playing, sleeping or eating. There was no in-between! That pair of masked critters were fun to raise and fun to watch. They played together like Tom and I use to play as rowdy little two years olds wrestling on the floor all the time. We also got a big kick out of the way they used those magical little hands to wash and play with their food. They always ate next to the water bowl so they could wash their food before juggling it around and then making it disappear into their long cat-like mouths. Tom's raccoon was mild-mannered and loved human contact all the way

until the day we let them go, but mine grew a little meaner the older he got until I stopped handling the little biter altogether. As the late summer called the large raccoons back to their wild, they began to grow anxious. As with most of our wild pets, we used and learned from them, loved them a little while, and then ceremonially set them free.

Mike gave us the word it was time for them to fend for themselves, so we let them go the next day. I suppose we should have taken them out beyond The Wooden Fence somewhere in Pine Grove to let them free there, but we were still attached to them and not entirely keen about never seeing them again. Instead, we let them loose in my horse pasture and the two little critters headed straight up one of the two trees standing next to the stockade. They huddled in the nook for a few days, before their hunger drove them to God knows where or who. During those few days, it pained us to watch them beg for food, especially right next to our home away from home. However, we knew that if we fed them, they would never leave and therefore always depend upon us. During the fourth night, as one would expect of masked thieves, they disappeared and were never seen again.

Dale and baby raccoon

It figures, that I'd get stuck with the kitchen clean-up duties because Mom had put together a full course meal as usual; including rhubarb dessert. She often cooks using every pan in her arsenal and is infamous for leaving the pans for us with layers of food baked on the bottom. It usually takes a good hour and a half to clean up all the mess! And then the kitchen must be inspected before given permission to leave the house. Our daily work schedule hangs inside the long cupboard door next to the refrigerator. Dad titles it, "Help out Glo List." Once or twice a week, one of us gets stuck cleaning up the entire kitchen and doing all the dishes for the whole family. We all dread when Mom puts on one of her dinner parties for the priest, nuns or friends because there is no mercy shown or no help offered, even though the mess is three times as large.

Upon immediately hearing that either the priest or nuns will be our dinner guests, we run to the long cupboard door, open it, and view Sonny's neatly laid out schedule to see who the lucky sole is on dish duty that evening. If it lands on my watch, I always try to talk Theresa or Mary into giving me a hand in exchange for helping them out the next time. Occasionally, they pitch in and lend me a hand without even being asked. Besides

cleaning up the kitchen, each one of us must clean our rooms, take out the trash, do the yard work, weed the garden, besides the six other items on the 'Mom's' list. I have the additional daily responsibility of taking care of Sheba out there in the pasture. Try as she might, poor ol' Sheba continues to nibble off the grass that never seems to grow any taller than a half inch.

Her once beautiful long blonde mane has shortened to about three inches due to her constant reaching through the barbed wire for taller grass on the other side. She is a big responsibility and expense. Dad had made that very clear well before I purchased her. I keep up with her costs, take good care of her, and know she is worth all the work. The once wild pony who led the way for the rest of the herd inside that small wooden corral has tamed, but she still has a bad habit I can't seem to break, and one I continue to pay the price for.

While running full gallop, she takes an unexpected left 90-degree turn jumping in the tall grass along the ditch, causing me to fly over the top of her and land in the middle of the gravel road. I always get up, examine my scrapes and feel for any broken bones. Then I brush myself off while looking at her munching nonchalantly on the tall virgin grass. I scold her, but a month later I find myself once again, on the gravel. Despite flying over the top of

Dale, Adrian & Sheba

her head at 30 mph and her occasional bucking, she is everything I always expected in a horse. As with most animals, they are best when sleeping. Sheba lies near the stockade next to the wooden corral that houses the graves of the circus animals while she awaits our return from our nightly adventures. Often, I lay there beside her under the stars, amongst the fireflies. The sound of thousands of crickets and the hum of HWY 169 filling the night. I fantasize that Sheba chooses this spot because she feels at ease with the spirits of the circus animals buried inside the corral, especially Jimmy, the pick-out pony.

The spirited Welsh pony is like a big puppy with lots of penned up energy. Occasionally, I take her out of the pasture to run a little spunk out of her and stretch out her muscles to keep her fit and fast. We always head out toward The Wooden Fence and

just as we pass Townsend's farm, I kick her in the side of her ribs taking her as fast as I think she can fly. I know she is fast because I have raced her against a few other horses in and around town and beat them easily, but one day Sheba met her match with a horse who fit his name, 'Gargle Axe.'

My rebel friend Mark thinks Sheba is fast as well but curls his left upper lip and follows with, "Swans, Gargle Axe can beat her in a race any day." Then he snorts backward up into the far reaches of his nose and throat, collects the snot on the middle of his tongue and shoots it out the stockade window as if to put an exclamation point on his words! While sitting on the patched carpet floor, we shoot our smoke rings toward the top of the wine bottle sitting in the center, and Mark tells me all about the infamous Gargle Axe and Swans' Jessenland farm tucked along a hillside overlooking the Minnesota River bottoms. If Gargle Axe is anything like Swans, Sheba is in for some stiff competition!

Swans is my age. He hangs out in Belle Plaine on weekend nights. He catches a ride into town with one of his two older brothers on the way to their favorite bar, the Red Door. His brothers are friends with Mark's older brother Donny, so Swans hangs around with him in the downtown area, most notably, the bowling alley. All MacGuire brothers are rough and tough as nails, and their influence has been studied and adapted by Swans. He relishes in being the youngest rebel of the family. I like Swans because of his silent toughness, and the fact that he is the only guy Mark won't challenge. Mark wisely teases him just enough to get by without causing a battle. Even though Swans attends Henderson, MN school, he fits in with our group better than his own classmates and fits in especially well with his prototype, Mark. The two wild teens blend better than Seagram's whiskey mixed with 7 UP soda pop. Along with being the same age, either can give a crap what people think of them, both have the same disregard for the law, and both share their older brother's thirst for alcohol and never-ending desire to get into trouble. Swans stands about two inches taller than Mark but is built solid as a rock. No doubt from all his hard work on the Jessenland farm.

The MacGuire boys all possess the same rugged look. Each has wide, squinted deep brown eyes tucked below thick frowning eyebrows, a wide rounded bottom nose, gradually flattening toward the top. But what really makes them stand out in a crowd are their lips. They are permanently held in a kissing position, like that of a little boy stretching his lips to meet his vagrant aunt's cheek. Swans has all those same rugged looking features, but more of a handsome version looking very similar to Micky Dolenz of the band "The Monkees." Like the rest of us, he has grown his jet-black hair down to his shoulders. His thick strands resemble that of an American Indian. And like a silent warrior, he hardly ever initiates a conversation, usually only answering

questions posed directly to him. When he speaks, I have to watch and listen closely because he mumbles just above a whisper, half through his teeth and the other half through the upper part of his nose. Every time I see Swans downtown, I inquire about Gargle Axe and bug him about getting together to go riding some day and to possibly discover which horse is faster. However, Swans lives two miles beyond Blakeley, which is four miles beyond my boundary line, so the chances for a race are slim to none; I think.

The farthest I can take Sheba is to Stoppleman's Creek where the gravel road meets up with the tarred Blakeley road which is four miles short of his farm. I would never take the chance of riding her on the narrow, winding, and shoulderless black top with cars traveling upwards of 50 MPH, but Swans doesn't seem to have a problem with it, so The Race is on. We plan to meet at the Blakeley road on Friday afternoon, ride our horses back to my pasture and then go uptown and raise a little hell. Swans will spend the night up in the stockade, and Gargle Axe will bed down with Sheba in the pasture. While planning, it all sounded reasonable and a fun thing to do.

I ride Sheba the three-mile stretch of loose gravel out past The Wooden Fence, beyond the creek at Oldenburg's valley, around the corner at Edberg's Horse Ranch, and head the final straight mile towards the Blakeley road. I have never placed eyes on Gargle Axe, but Mark described him in good detail that day up in the stockade, and Swans mumbled a word or two about him. But, I'm

The old Corvair driving on the gravel road to The Wooden Fence

more than taken aback when Swans, already four miles into his trip, trots towards me on this muscular, sweating, black beast a little taller than Sheba, and twice as thick. He also displays a very visible nasty flesh toned jagged scar starting five inches below his mysterious black eyes and extending to the top of his massive forehead. Gargle Axe is much more intimidating looking than I had earlier imagined. He's snorting loudly and gasping for air like a bull entering the ring. This midnight monster belongs in Hollywood, where he can be a stand-in for the horse riding beneath the torso of the Headless Horseman.

I'm also impressed to see that Swans is riding Gargle Axe bareback atop a red wool blanket, that nicely offsets the sweat-soaked red bandana rolled tightly just above his eyebrows. He's wearing a white sleeveless T-shirt, revealing his large biceps, thick chest and a slim waistline. His faded jeans are torn at the knees matching Gargle Axe's flesh-toned scar. The rider also wears the face of an American Indian warrior about to engage in battle, and I think to myself, he has his race face on. Swans is the perfect match for the likes of Gargle Axe looking almost as intimidating as his prized brute trotting heavily underneath him.

I can't say I blame her, but at the first sight of Gargle Axe, Sheba rears back, lets out a loud whinny and comes down hard on her front hoofs. She shifts nervously below me while I hold her back with the reigns and wait for their arrival. Gargle Axe runs with his head sideways, fighting the bit digging into his jaw, anxious as well to get on with The Race. It's obvious from the start that neither horse like each other. They size each other up, holding their heads proudly in the sky as they shift restlessly from side to side beneath us. Swans mumbles out a few words to his horse, acknowledges my friendly greeting with a devilish grin and we start back the way I came, bound for the old circus lots.

Just as we reach the top of the incline, Swans, impatient to see which horse is faster and not one to initiate conversation, kicks Gargle Axe into the only gear he knows, ultra-fast. I need not tell Sheba that The Race is on because she quickly takes off after the front-runner who now has a ten-foot lead. I stand in the stirrups, hang onto the saddle horn for dear life, while the rows of corn streak on by me. I am bouncing at a speed the old girl has never taken me before. My Sheba loses no ground and gains some as we near the end of the half-mile run but can't quite catch the horse built solely for speed. And even had she pulled within his eyesight, the veteran probably had another gear or two left in him. Not only that but, Swans had just run the hell out of him most of the way to Stoppleman's creek. Mark is right, Gargle Axe is the fastest horse around, and it's thrilling racing on horses that run like the wind! Sensing victory, Swans pulls back on the reigns and slows things down to a trot allowing me to catch up and walk alongside. Both horses are soaking wet, breathing hard, and arguing back and forth all the way to the pasture. Swans says little, rather lets his horse do all the talking for him. I am thinking that letting Gargle Axe share Sheba's pasture wasn't such a clever idea after all.

Eager to get downtown, we let both horses loose anyway to see how well they will take to each other, especially after their bickering back and forth the entire ride home. Their argument picks up where it left off and intensifies now that they roam inside the barbed wire ring. This is Sheba's home territory. She doesn't want to share her space with the horse she couldn't seem

to catch on the way to Edberg's Horse Farm, and one in which she disdained ever since their first meeting at the Blakeley road. The fight for dominance of the pasture begins and each taunts the other to engage in a competition of power instead of speed. They rear, scream, run, and kick testing each other's will and temper and at times, coming within inches of contact. Worst still, there isn't a thing Swans or I can do about it, but watch. Where is Grandpa Leo now? I can just picture trying to explain to Mom and Dad I let the horse of the Headless Horseman into the pasture without their permission and the nightmare attacked and maimed poor Sheba. Well, as luck would have it, the fight ends without a blow and they each part their separate ways, Sheba's lips back to the green grass and Gargle Axe scoping out his temporary quarters. I hope and pray that they won't get into a fight while we are away raising hell downtown.

Swans throws a few personal items and a change of clothes up in the stockade, we make a final check on the horses and then head downtown to look for Mark and my other friend Greg. We take the usual alleyway and as we walk, I brag to him about all the cool stuff we did as kids tearing up the old neighborhood. I show him our old house and where Wayne the mean neighbor kept his son locked up in the shed. He gets a kick out of the time Jerry went up to Wayne and put him in his place. And, he even lets out a slight snicker when I tell him about Don, the quintessential serial killer of many critters. My first impression of Swans has proven to be correct; a silent proud American Indian warrior who need not say much of anything. He just walks alongside me with a slight grin and puffs on his cigarettes, one after the other! We search for Mark and Greg, but they are nowhere to be found. Instead, we use Mark's recently taught method of stealing booze and cigarettes out of unlocked cars. It pays off in a big way for Swans and me.

After searching the cars parked in front of the stores lining the main drag, we begin looking behind the bar's parking lots. Wouldn't you know it, we strike gold the last place we look behind Krant's Bar. A case of Grain Belt Premium sits for our taking tucked behind the driver's seat of an unlocked Buick Riviera. We pull the case from behind the front seat, flip open the two top flaps and count 12 unopened bottles of beer. Bingo, six bottles a piece! Overjoyed, we cart the bulky cardboard down the dark alleyway, and just to be extra cautious, stay clear crossing busy Meridian Street, travel an extra block and go through the culvert, which floods Townsend's pasture in the springtime. From there, it's a hop skip and a jump to the safety of the stockade.

Both horses are bedded down for the night. Sheba is near the wooden corral next to the stockade and Gargle Axe up on the high side next to the gravel road. It's the same place Grandpa Leo puts up his huge telescope in the fall. We spend the rest of the

night sipping on the champagne of beers out of the extraordinary, clear, glass bottles. Of course, I am the one doing 95% of the talking. I tell Swans all about our childhood adventures with Little John, how he named Pine Grove and how he looked just like cool Chuck Connors. And when I opened my fifth beer, I open up and tell him the story about how we discovered Little John's death on a frigid day in November…

Fifteen minutes after arriving to work on Monday morning, Dad returned home from The Garage with a shocking announcement. The sheriff who worked there part-time told him about the tragedy. I guess he felt he should be the one to tell us the shocking news rather than we hear about it second hand. We all were getting ready for school when he walked into our room and said that he had some bad news to tell us. He announced Little John's demise, similar to the delivery of a nightly news broadcaster reporting on a gruesome street scene killing in Minneapolis, with little emotion. But, he spoke with a downward pout and when he finished, he looked further down, turned, and went back to work leaving us with that "kicked in the teeth" feeling. We couldn't believe it, Little John along with two of his friends, were killed in a car accident last night by Jordan, MN. Little John, the King of the entire neighborhood, the one who taught me how to climb trees, the one who emboldened my fearlessness, was dead at 19.

I was proud of Mom the day Fran showed up at the side door, fighting tears, asking her if she would sing at Little John's funeral. Glo handled the uncomfortable situation cool. I wouldn't have known what to do? I watched the surreal scene unfold before me, almost as if I were witnessing it as a soul that leaves the body and watches events unfold from above. She gave Fran a big hug and told her how sorry she was and how she felt honored to be asked to sing. When Fran said her goodbyes, Mom again hugged her for a long time, and I think took a little of the hurt away.

We were all prouder of Mom when just a few days later, sang "How Great Thou Art," John's favorite gospel song from up in the choir loft in the back of the church. Now, Mom has a professional, clear voice, but she did practically lose it a few times, although the barely noticeable wail, in key spots, put real emotion in the song. Almost as if she had planned it that way. It made the song so much more real and so much more beautiful. Over half the church was in tears.

I tell Swans as beautiful and touching as that song was, I like to remember Little John by his favorite rock song instead, "Bad Moon a Rising" by Creedence Clearwater Revival. Every time I hear it play, I think about Little John's memories and the dead cedar trees, still standing proudly at the top of Pine Grove.

Cool Sisters and Cold Steel

I neatly fold the kitchen towel, carefully place it on the counter and call Mom to inspect my handy work, where it is usually met with her 'glowing' approval. Then, I head outside to check on my girlfriend. As I approach her, I yell "Hey, Sheeeebaaaaa!" in a long deep voice, and she comes trotting over answering with an expectant nicker, with a second nicker for good measure. "Oh, you're a beautiful horse. That a girl." talking softly while brushing her. She presses her velvety nose against my shoulder and snorts softly in approval of my affection. I slip her two sugar cubes and a stroke behind her soft ears. I kiss her goodbye, playfully pat her on her back and head into the house to get ready for the big Friday night on the town.

Theresa and Mary are both primping in the upstairs bathroom, as they always do, before heading out for the evening. We all have plans for the biggest night of the weekend. Theresa is meeting up with Young Buck after he returns from his pigeon hunt with Jim, Mary will go walking around town with four of her regular friends, Tom has plans to go driving around town with Tomato, and Joe is in a bubbly mood because he'll have the place all to himself for the night. We all plan to meet back at the house after we get home from our nighttime escapades so we can share in a pan or two of Theresa's famous Cheeset Cubes. The combination of bread squares dipped in egg and topped with cheese and parmesan baked for ten minutes at 350 degrees is the perfect snack prepared for the second late night party. It's common for us to all gather back at the house staying up late on Friday nights watching Johnny Carson or Benny Hill while Mom and Dad sleep in their bed. Sometimes Tom makes a huge batch of his famous sugar popcorn. He puts it in a big turkey roaster pan, and we all sit around the basement and tell each other what is going on in our world. My exploits always top everyone else's!

The girls take great interest in knowing what their uncanny brothers are doing with their exciting and adventurous lives. Mike is now into falconry and banging on his drum kit alongside the phonograph in the basement, me running with the devils downtown and always in some trouble in school, and then there's Tom, who is proud of his gopher killing club and a teaser with a nickname for just about everybody in town. But the girls are not immune to mischief and even have participated in a few of our shady deeds over the years. Both are even willing to help us out with anything from illegal winemaking to sewing our nighttime gang wear. They helped me pierce my left ear aided by an ice cube, a thick sewing needle, and a potato. Theresa even gave me one of her cool turquoise earrings, cast one of her good luck spells on it and sold the idea to Mom and Dad before it met their

eyes. Her spell was a huge success! Mary is even willing to go out of her way asking some of her friends if they want to join me in a game of "spin the bottle" or "make the rounds" up in the stockade. Our sisters are opposite most sisters I know. Instead of running to Mom and Dad to squeal about our unruly behavior, they keep quiet, cover up and even lie on our behalf. I think they are enthralled by our colorful personalities and our bad boy ways and for that, we cannot have asked for better Sisters!

Where Mike keeps us all entertained by his ever-changing characters and roles, two-year older Theresa remains the constant nurturer to all the rest of us. She is often the first and only one sought in the family for her advice on everything from spiritual matters to suggestions on how to handle relationships. The advice given or solutions offered by her is normally accepted outright. Before going out on weekend nights or special occasions, one by one, we parade before Theresa seeking her approval as she makes final adjustments and suggestions to our wardrobe. Never one to turn down a request for help, she often trims our hair and makes our jeans a little tighter at the top and a little wider at the bottom. Maybe it's because she wants her brothers to look as cool as she does, but I rather think that's just the person

Theresa and Mary

she is. Something that makes her unique and special is her dabbling and experimentation with witchcraft and her natural gift of special powers. She believes in the power of crystals, cast spells on jewelry and holds an occasional seance; nothing too harmful or serious. Still, we are all spellbound with our sister Theresa and so is Mike's bow hunting buddy, "Young Buck!" He shows up almost daily to witness Mike's training sessions with the hawks, but more important he is there to impress our smoken hot sister.

Theresa changed in both looks and attitude ever since she left Crow School and joined Mike in the rebellious movement all-encompassing the United States. Over the past couple of years,

the straggly, skinny, short-haired, Catholic school girl has morphed into a beautiful, tall, slim blonde with high, tight hips, long legs and a nice pair of breasts. She's a literal poster girl for the 1970s! To my friends, Theresa is like a Goddess and they all drool over her behind her back. Whenever she comes into the room, she is immediately the center of everyone's attention. Not only because of her good looks but because of her warm outgoing personality and quick sense of humor. And her wardrobe is some of the coolest in town altering many of her jeans and tops on Mom's old sewing machine in the upstairs utility room. She wears low waisted, high, tight jeans with some of the widest elephant bell bottoms around that ride just above her butt along with tiny tank tops showing off her thin flat stomach. Theresa is in that elite category hanging with the most popular and successful girls in high school. Not that she seeks to be the most popular girl in school, but perhaps she is anyway. Unlike me, she is a great student involved in lots of school activities, often appearing in plays. Theresa and Mike shared lead roles in a melodrama when Mike was a senior. She also sings at school ceremonies and performances with the lovely voice she inherited from Mom. More than living up to the Albrecht artistic background, Theresa is always lauded by teachers and family for her creative and clever artworks.

One year, she and I took first place at the downtown Halloween Store Window painting contest. She designed, drew and painted almost the entire Casper the Friendly Ghost Theme titled, "Make Your Halloween a Friendly One." I got half the credit, and all I did was hand her brushes and paint. I feel it an extreme privilege to have Theresa and Mike as older siblings because their huge popularity automatically transfers down to us younger kids.

Mary is just the opposite, from the rest of us, we think anyway. Whereas Mike, Theresa and I are all colorful counterculture or rebellious, Mary just kind of goes with the flow and has her close circle of four friends. Tom

Theresa's 'Make Your Halloween a Friendly One'

dubs them, The Grey Hooded Sweatshirt Gang because the girls each wear grey hooded sweatshirts when they walk around town; seems like all the time. And even though Mary keeps tight with The Grey Hooded Sweatshirt Gang, she is a fun person to be around, so she

has at least a dozen more friends she can call on in a minute's notice; all but a select few carried over from Crow School. She is a quick study, and it didn't take her long to figure out that Mike, Theresa, and I are at odds with Mom and Dad all the time. She has seen the consequences of those tussles and realizes that it's not worth the risk. Mary lives a happy and simple life where laughs and giggles come to her easily. She too wears altered bell-bottomed pants but doesn't fashion some of the more hippie and revealing clothing that her older sister does. She is three years younger than Theresa, still growing through her awkward years and trying to figure out what makeup looks good on her. Although there is three years between them, the roommates are close. And like her older Sister, Mary gets good grades in school and is involved in after-school activities.

Like all the Albrecht's, she is popular and well-liked by everybody in school. But instead of acting in plays, she took up cheerleading and made the "A" squad for both wrestling and football. Mary has even gained attention from some of the older boys in school and for some dumb reason, Tom and I can't figure it out. Even though we're kissing her girlfriends down at the stockade, we don't look at little sister Mary as we do our older sister Theresa. She is always just little sister Mary to Tom and me. So one would imagine how shocked we were the day John Stier pulled up to our driveway on his motorcycle with Mary riding on the back! Funny, there was a time growing up in The Old House when Mary and I were the only ones who could understand each other.

Being the youngest of the original five, we stuck together tightly well before Joe was born, calling each other Shocky and Jammy because of the dangerous game we played with 110-volt electricity. We used to stick butter knives in electric outlets and stick our fingers in open light sockets. We didn't know that electricity can kill and thought that the buzz traveling throughout our entire body, felt sort of stimulating. Mary and I had another shocking experience while attending the Minnesota State Fair with the rest of the family one year.

We were all grouped together walking down the midway when Dad spotted a magic act out of the corner of his eye. Dad, the consummate magician himself, stopped to watch the show. Mary and I were around four and five years old, smaller than everybody else, couldn't see the performance, so we moved up to the front to get a closer look. After the magician laid down his final card, the crowd gave him a round of applause and dispersed out into the midway. Mary and I turned around to join the rest of the family, but instead looked at each other in amazement and disbelief; there was no one to join, our family had abandoned us! They forgot about the two little ones and moved on without us down the midway. Mary and I, standing way up front, didn't notice them departing way in the back. Meanwhile, Mom, Dad, Mike, Theresa, Tom, and little Joe took in the sights and dodged the large crowds out on that bright sunny day. Apparently, they didn't notice that the two little ones were not following behind them for a good 20 minutes. By then Mary and I were long gone...

After a brief search near and around where they last left us, Mom frantically reported me to the lost and found department, ten minutes before they noticed that sister Mary was missing. Mom quickly shuffled back a second time to report her missing as well. The lost and the found

department was more than concerned with the first report of a missing child, but when Mom returned to report a second, they peered strangely as if wondering to themselves, "What kind of parents are these?"

So, little Mary and little I were alone amongst the crowds of people passing on by us, lost inside the Minnesota State Fair which covered hundreds of acres and hundreds of displays. After looking for our family in all four directions, and asking each other if we should contact an adult, we decided to search for our car on our own. We both remembered walking by a large billboard which featured a pair of large blue coveralls somewhere close to our parking spot. We also remembered that the family would meet back at the car for a picnic around noon featuring Glo's baked chicken and homemade biscuits. Dad would not spend a fortune on the numerous food concessions that the fair offered, especially after all the hard earned money he spent on gas and entrance fees. Our Guardian Angels must have been with us that frightful day because Mary and I somehow found the coveralls and then walked up and down the rows of cars until we found our old blue station wagon. Then we merrily sat on the rear bumper and simply waited. About an hour later, the family headed our way, Mom in the lead doing a fast version of the Glo tourist shuffle. They couldn't believe that the two little ones had found their way out from the middle of the State Fair, all the way to the parked cars and were sitting on the back bumper smiling from ear to ear! Mary and I couldn't believe it either…

"Remember that Mary?" as I turned laughing and headed downstairs to clean up and change into my nighttime street garb. But, as I enter my room a rush of reality sets in. An empty reality.

The bedroom feels abandoned now that Mike is living in Grandma's upstairs apartment with Lena. Our once lively room has become rather boring without his multiple personalities around keeping me company, and I already miss watching the entertaining performances he used to put on for me. Although he often trains his hawks here at the old circus lots and he practices with his garage band occasionally in our basement, our family will never be the same. I can easily picture Mike as the many characters he portrayed throughout the years, but I have a hard time facing up to his having sprouted feathers and left our nest.

What I miss the most are all the cool things he collected over the years neatly on display in our room. As a consummate reader, he had a three-tier shelf filled with all his different books. I was going through those books just before he moved out and came across one he purchased all about the Woodstock Festival. I didn't read the book but fingered through the pages to look at the photos of all the rock legends who performed there that weekend: Jimi Hendrix, The Who, Santana, Janis Joplin, and many others. I came to a page which made me stop and fixate on a close photo of a young Grace Slick of Jefferson Airplane. I stared at her for a long time studying her dark wavy hair, sexy look, and big beautiful eyes highlighted by thick black eyeliner and heavy mascara. Unfortunately, he took that Woodstock book with him, but her image remains etched in my mind.

It seems like just the week before, he was anxiously waiting with a record spinning around on Mom's old phonograph and a

blonde horn handle switchblade glittering in his hand. He tucked the blade into the side of the handle, stuffed it in his back pocket and sits me down on his lower bunk bed so I can watch his latest performance.

He cranks up the volume on the 1950s phonograph, waits for the tubes to catch up after a turn of the knob, the front speaker to hum loudly before he sets the needle down on the record featuring a five-minute drum solo performed by "Ginger Baker" of the band "Cream." Then he slumps against the bedroom wall as if standing against a streetlamp post in a city slum. A scowl slowly forms on his eyebrows as he transforms into a hoodlum straight off the pages of our favorite gang books. He looks the part with his long bulky brown hair parted neatly to the side, dressed in tight blue jeans and a tight black T-shirt. The same type that Ponyboy's oldest brother Darry wore in the "Outsiders" book when the Greasers were heading out for a rumble with the Socs. I study my older brother closely and wonder what has become of that kid wearing a weird green woodland outfit barking out orders to his men while exploring Belle Plaine's Sherwood Forest with Little John at his side.

Although Mike is four years older than me, we are close, and we share similar qualities. I am his ever-eager student with all things wild accompanying him 90% of the time in the woods and I am his ultimate falconry partner. I not only climb the trees to secure his birds of prey, but I help with the

Mike holding Turak 1 above Dale's head

training process. Both Tom and I kill most of the wild game he feeds to his carnivores. Although his imagination slightly exceeds mine, he admires my boldness, fearlessness, and desire to do what he cannot. And I think he revels in the fact that I'm willing to follow in his rebellious ways. But, I also learn things from Mike I can never learn from my friends because the crowd he hangs with is his age and older. Mike keeps nothing from me because of my teenage youth and speaks as if speaking to someone his own age on subjects ranging from sex to drugs.

Mike is a perfect example of someone bore out of the rebellious 1960s, cut from the same cloth of nonconformity. He not only looks the part but has a magnetic, leadership quality about him that seems to attract people of all ages, especially females. As a sophomore, he stood only five feet nine, with a small build, but now a strapping six foot one, 185 pounds. He not only draws attention from most girls in our high school but also many who'd already graduated years before him. Yes, Mike is handsome. Often, I hear girls compare his looks to sexy Jim Morrison of the Doors. And he bears a striking resemblance to Jim; same hair color with the tousled shag cut, similarly shaped eyes, and nose, with only the slightest difference in the lips and jawline. He dresses like Morrison too; tight blue jeans, tie-dyed t-shirts, wearing a unique, American Indian beaded headband. And, he echoes Jim's public persona; showy, arrogant and rebellious, all characteristics that add to his overall appeal.

But Mike also has a dark, exciting side that holds plenty of appeal to the "more adventurous" girls. His hometown idols are those who have the longest hair, listen to underground rock music and resist authority. And the string of infamous adventures he created in his young life add to the fascination; organizing the "Scarecrows" in 64 and the "Green Hornet" in 66, the "GADFLY Caper" of 70, drumming in a local rock band in 71; plus his legendary run-in with Sister Michael in Crow school. While the years pass and times change, so do the characters he plays. As a young boy, it was the Scarecrow; Portraying Dr. Syn by day and Scarecrow (the most famous smuggler on England's south coast) by night. For now, it is Mike the falconer, in the daylight hours and a ladies' man after dark. And, if you are a girl in our small town, you know each facet of every Belle Plaine boy's life. To Mike life is a half-written book, with him invariably starring in every lead role writing the next chapter. And Belle Plaine girls take exceptional pleasure in following "dreamboat Mike" through his many actions and characters throughout the years. Most girls are turned on by what they observe. So, even if they aren't fortunate enough to have a romantic relationship with him, they settle on being Mike Albrecht's friend or any association really, just to be in his presence.

Mike not only has it all going on with his looks and attitude, but he is also a talented actor (appearing in several school plays) writer, musician, and sketch artist. As a child, I watched, mesmerized, as he drew cartoon action heroes in only a few minutes. They were so perfectly rendered, you'd think they had jumped right off a comic book page. He also plays drums in the high school band and in several garage bands. He often practices to various rock records alongside Mom's old phonograph in the storeroom basement. He can play "Jimi Hendrix's" Purple Haze as good as his drummer "Mitch Mitchell." I guess you could call Mike somewhat of an extremist though because when he becomes

interested in something, he'll take it to the max. For instance, regarding his fascination with falconry, once he got started, he didn't stop until he's now an expert on the subject. And so it goes with every other topic that captivates him. He is also quite the character in school and a wise ass which makes him even more popular. Sometimes he'll pull a stunt just to see if he can get away with it.

He once wore a self-designed t-shirt to Rhinehold's class, with a picture of a rhinoceros wearing a cape and mask, beneath that, spelled out in big block letters read, "CAPTAIN RHINO." Well, Rhinee didn't find it amusing, to say the least, and pulled Mike out into the hall to give him a good takedown. Afterward, he was sent home to change the offensive shirt and ordered to report back to his classroom after school to face punishment. Old Rhinee began by drawing a circle high on the chalkboard and forced Mike to stand on his tiptoes, keeping his nose inside the circle. I know from personal experience that after about 39 seconds your heels begin to drop causing pain on the lower ankle as Rhinee whacks it hard with his pointing stick, sending that nose rubbing back up to the center of the

Rhinehold

circle. He then commanded Poor Mike to do a series of pushups. Every time his ass got too high, Rhinehold would hit it with a wooden pointer that had a sewing needle taped to the end. Arriving home later, he found that his "Fruit of the Looms" were speckled with tiny blood spots from the countless pinpricks. But, Mike figured it was well worth the discomfort when his popularity in school skyrocketed as a result. The incident continued to be the "tale of the school" for the rest of the school year.

Another episode that boosted Mike's standing in high school was the "GADFLY" Caper. Some of the upperclassmen came up with publishing an underground newspaper. The perpetrators were all popular and considered leaders in the senior class. Although Mike was only a sophomore, they included him in their group, and for good reason. He was an excellent writer, a non-conformist and had a refreshing, cut-through-the-bullshit attitude. And, it didn't hurt that Sonny had a printing machine in our house, owned by the Knights of Columbus. Mike somehow convinced Mom to type, and Dad to print and assemble the weekly newsletters. So, much to Mike's credit, the GADFLY came to be.

Most of the material written was a sarcastic parody of the school, teachers, and principal, Mr. Delgahousen (appropriately nicknamed Booger D, as he had absolutely no inhibitions about picking his nose in public.) The first issue was written fairly quickly, and the plan was to distribute it as soon as possible. But how to get it into the hands of the students, undetected, was the question?

Well, Mike left a window unlatched in Rhinehold's classroom. That night he slipped it open, crawled through and then opened the rear door for his friend Randy; one of the upperclassmen. They put copies under every classroom door, in the bathroom, under the principal's office door, in

the library, etc. The next day the shit hit the fan and the entire high school was buzzing about it, students and teachers, especially the name of the little publication. A "gadfly" is actually a type of blowfly that harasses mainly cattle by laying its eggs on a moist spot of their body. The egg hatches quickly, descends into the stomach and grows. Then the one inch, adult maggot eats its way out to the hide of the critter and drops to the ground. One gadfly buzzing around can actually stampede an entire herd.

The second issue was distributed in a similar manner, but this time Mike never left the school. He took all the wet paper towels out of the big trash can in the boy's locker-room during volleyball practice, climbed in and Randy covered him with trash. He waited until everyone left the building and went about the distribution the same as before. On the third and final issue, Mike and Randy hid in a secret compartment behind the auditorium stage (it was a tunnel system for checking the boiler room pipes.) Unfortunately though, by that third issue, the English teachers had identified the writing style of each author and they got busted (bye-bye GADFLY.) But, to their credit, they never turned Mike in, and he wound up being the only subversive to escape without punishment.

When Mike entered the public school system, he found their dress code was like that of the Catholic school. Sometimes he wouldn't tuck in his shirt or wear a belt and got called in the office to be straightened out by our principal. Soon a few of his classmates grew their hair long, wore tie-dyed t-shirts, bellbottom jeans, and Beatle or as we called 'em' girly boots, with nice pointy toes, high heels, and a buckle. These boots zipped up the back. Mike customized all his shoes having the local shoe store put steel cleats on the heels, so they clicked on the hard floors when he walked the halls. Later, when Kids got into rumbles giving someone a kick in the face was called, "Putting the clickers to them." There were maybe six to eight guys in the whole high school that adopted this style of dress and they got sent home often for violation of the dress code or a haircut. The phy Ed teacher, a drill sergeant sort of guy simply hated long hair on guys. Being one of the first in his class to have long hair, he singled Mike out in the locker room whenever he felt like it, calling him Michelle and asking him where his purse was. Well, the students just put up with it, but right after they put out The GADFLY, things began to change. A lot of the students rebelled and started wearing what they wanted. There got to be so many dress code violations that the principal would have had to close the school which resulted in the end of the dress code--for good! Man, it was great and very liberating to be at the tip of history and I for one benefitted from his young and courageous Waterloo.

I sit down on Mike's old bottom bunk wearing the same pair of patched jeans and Jimi Hendrix sleeveless shirt I wore to school imagining him with the switchblade tucked in his back pocket leaning against the bedroom wall… With the tap of Ginger's drumsticks to his snare, the performance begins: three city hoods approaching Mike as he slowly pushes away from the street post and narrows his eyes to

Mike practicing on his drums in the basement storeroom

meet his oncoming enemies. He mouths words and argues in silence, addressing each using facial expressions that would give top Hollywood actors a run for their money. The three circle around him, he circles one way and back the other way, peering intently for the first one to make a move. Just when the drummer works in a steady smooth beat, Mike is struck with a left fist causing his face to jolt sideways and he goes down. But when he hits the carpet floor, he quickly rolls once in sync with the tap of the high hat, back kicks an attacker coming at him from the rear and then crouches in a fighting stance with the switchblade knife held at the ready in his right hand. A thrilling high hat roll accompanied with light foot pedals to the bass provides the suspense for what happens next. He presses the button centered at the top of the blonde horn handle and the blade blurs out from the side. The light reflects off the four-inch blade held street style in his outstretched hand, and now he smiles with confidence and taunts the hoodlums by tickling the left fingers towards his blade. The drumsticks roll on the snare and edge of the drum as Ginger's feet slam hard into the double base increasing the tempo every five seconds. Mike fights in a right rhythm, working around each one of the three attacking from all sides. Ginger is working clocklike around the skins and brass as well in an ultra-fast and methodical beat. Mike is keeping in perfect sync. The best drummer in the world now sounds like twenty, hitting each drum and symbol at different times as Mike is but a fighting blur amongst the noise blaring out of the old full range speaker. I have to admit that I am a little nervous watching the engaging fight before me because I actually think he might accidentally stick himself with the switchblade. The drum solo and fight finally end with two taps to the high hat accompanied by two thumps to the base as the rest of the band "Cream" joins in... One hood lie dead on the street and the other two running away from the cold steel blade now stained in blood.

He finishes breathing hard and asks me to grade his performance. I am speechless! What can I say other than, "Wow, that was cool?" I don't know why Mike puts on these demonstrations for me because I already know he is skilled using any knife, whether skinning a deer or using it to protect himself. Maybe, it's just to show off in front of his little brother? He is lucky to end his routine with only a single cut bleeding out the side of his left eyebrow, but it wasn't from the performance in our room. It was from me in the backyard shortly after.

Mike practices knife fighting stances a lot with Tom and me. Most people would use a rubber or wooden knife, but at mid-teens, the thought never occurs to him. I am often his sparring partner in these mock battles, and he is still in a playful mood. Only minutes after his performance in our room, he follows me out the back door, and into the backyard where he pulls his switchblade

on me. We immediately act out our routine. I'm small and skinny, but also fast and agile. Before Mike knows it, I kick the switchblade out of his hand. The knife's tip flying into his face. A dandy cut oozes with blood out of his left eyebrow, coming within an inch from losing his left eye. I follow him into the downstairs bathroom where he dabs the cut with Kleenex and admires my handiwork in the mirror, viewing the cut from several angles as he thinks it makes him look tough. He looks like he has just been involved in a knife fight in the city slums! The near miss to the center of his eye might be just a lucky fluke as mine had been years earlier when Tarzan released his spear as I stood in protest on top of the pigeon shed in the old backyard; then again it might be divine payback? After that close call, we toned it down and eventually dispensed practicing with a real blade, but Mike still uses his prized switchblade for staged choreographed knife fights to music!

Grandpa Leo's stories of riding the rails as a hobo included telling us that the only weapon he fears is the cold steel. Whenever he witnesses us playing with knives, he either leaves or asks us to stop while he cringes, turning sideways and partially covers his eyes behind his shoulder and paint-stained fedora hat. He never reveals to us why he fears the knife. We can only imagine that he witnessed them being used on people in the hobo jungles along the railroad tracks deep in the south. So in our minds, this gives the knife a mystic it did not have before and no doubt entices us to want to possess the weapon and play with the steel blades even more.

Little John had a switchblade that his older brother brought back from the military and gave him while home on leave. Mike offered to buy this knife every chance he could, but to no avail. One day John was short of cash and needed a cigarette in the worst way. Mike gave him the money for a carton of smokes and the knife was finally his. It became his pride and joy. Eventually, he wore the damn thing out flicking it open repeatedly, especially while watching the TV series Garrison's Gorillas. His next switchblade came from our Uncle Dave, and he soon wore that one out. Our other Uncle Gary and a friend went on a road trip to Mexico when Mike was 15. Mike begged Gary to smuggle him a new 'Switch' across the U.S. border. He said he'd see what he could do. Mike sat on pins and needles until Gary's return to Minnesota, and true to his word he smuggled out two dandies, one in each of his cowboy boots.

Knives were cool and the better we were with a knife, increased our standing among our friends. Mike taught Tom and me how to handle them with precision. He coached us as we threw knives back and forth to each other, sometimes at 10 to 15 paces. Our favorite throwing and catching knife was a dagger with a small ivory covered handle with a unique curved Egyptian blade. Sometimes Tom and I would just sit around the basement talking with our friends throwing the blade around like it was part of the conversation. We also learned how to make a knife twist and flip as we would throw it up and try to catch it on the handle; twisting and turning on the way down. We all carried some type of knife or other and sometimes carried two to three at once. When hiking in the woods, we always had a long-bladed knife housed in a shield hanging off our belts. A pocketknife with everything from a bottle opener to a tin can opener was parked in the front of our jean's pockets. The switchblade was always a concealed and a hidden weapon, we

normally kept it slid inside the top of our sock but protected and hidden from our boot. Switchblades were illegal and if caught, we would face felony charges...

I was caught up in all this rough and dangerous play because Mike had been telling me all about his rumbles, fights and nighttime exploits since I was five or six years old. I was pumped up after reading "The Outsiders," by S.E. Hinton, and then he introduced me to another book called, "Durango Street," by Frank Bonham. Rufus Henry got busted for grand theft auto and had to serve time in a work camp. After he gets out, he is assigned a Parole Officer and given a job, but with nowhere to live but his Mom's house on Durango Street in the projects, he is forced to join the Moors rival gang of the Gassers constantly on his tail. With his position in the gang secure, he'll be all right for a while on Durango Street, but when the Gassers catch up to him.... There are street fights, switchblades and the book was almost as good as the "Outsiders." One of Mike's rumbles involving a switchblade could have been a scene read straight off the pages of Durango Street, but the incident took place one night on the dark track field when Belle Plaine was playing Le Sueur in a high school football game.

There was always a rivalry between Belle Plaine and Le Sueur both on and off the field of play. Even though Belle Plaine comprised people from all walks of life, such as farmers, businessmen, athletes, and underprivileged, they rarely fought amongst themselves, at least as a group anyway, but took their penned up aggression out as one fighting unit on the surrounding town's boys. Since Le Center was so close to Le Sueur, some boys from there came to backup their buddies for the rumble with us. The Belle Plaine boys met their opponents behind the white wooden fence between the football field and high school to get ready for the fight they would have across the street by the track field (no lights.)

Mike was partnered up with longtime Crow School friend Dave getting into position to face their opposing fighters. Both were wrapping their wide leather belts around their fists, in order to lay on a little extra stiff leather on their rivals and protect their knuckles from getting cut and bruised. This bigger kid walked up directly in front of Mike looking cocky and says, "Trying to keep your right-hand warm man?" The next thing he knew, the guy pulls out a nine-inch, black handled Italian switchblade and stuck the bayonet style blade against his chin. I listened intently as Mike watched the reaction on my face as he told me the most suspenseful part of the story. Once he finished, I could only envision a wide-eyed Mike staring at the moonlit steel, with fear in his eyes, but amazement. He described the switchblades length, color, shape and even the sound of the blade shooting out the side in stark detail. No doubt he was scared shitless. But Mike was well-versed in the handling of all edged weapons. He had studied the blades features closely while the Le Center kid gripped the black handle as a street fighter would, holding his thumb tightly on the top of the handle and pressing it a little tighter against the skin; just to show he meant business. Both Mike and Dave slowly unraveled their belts, backed away and ran to the safety of Hoddy-Boddy Land just below the bordering line of trees behind the track field.

Dave later told Mike the knife guy's name and said he was from Le Center and that it was a good thing he didn't mess with him. They figured later, the only reason the guy let them get away was that he recognized Dave to be his brother's friend. The rumble never happened and a few weeks later Mike ran into Switchblade Sam at another football game being played this time in Le Center. He told Mike it looked like him and his buddy would pee themselves when he pulled out the knife, and then he laughed. Then the guy showed the knife to Mike and said his oldest brother had gotten it in the navy and passed it down to him. Mike offered to buy it but he wouldn't part with it, however, he put him in touch with a guy with a similar switch with a blonde horn handle and he bought that one for $25.00 which was a small fortune in those days.

I hop off the lower bunk bed, throw on my green army coat, walk upstairs to say my goodbyes to Mom and Dad, who reminds me of my 10:30 curfew. As soon as the side door to the garage closes, I reach into my boot, pull out a half pack of Marlboro reds and make a beeline for, as always, the alleyway entrance. It has been less than two months since my famous climb to obtain the baby Red-tailed Hawk and little do I know that I am about to make a mistake that will cost me the entire summer and some of the fall.

No Way Back

It's finally Friday night, I need not worry about school or homework until Sunday evening, but I have to be home in time to make Dad's imposed 10:30 curfew. That gives me roughly three hours to have a little fun downtown and hopefully catch a little buzz. I must pack a lot in these three hours and that's what I intend to do. I'm eager to get where there is usually plenty of action taking place around all the bars scattered throughout the downtown area. At the intersection of Main and Meridian Street, the downtown extends only about a block in all four directions and on North Main, it is only a couple of buildings. One would never know that little area contains eight bars.

Each one of the eight bars feature a different theme drawing diverse types of crowds and personalities from Belle Plaine and beyond. A drinker isn't out of choices for the palette of saloons ranges from distinguished to destitute. For example, Krants Bar caters to the more high-class business types who prefer martinis and Manhattans, whereas the Red Door draws the young adults and riffraff who drink cheap glasses of tap beer by the pitcher. The athletic jock or popular young adults in town gravitate towards John's, located right across the street from the Red Door. There is even an old bar next to Hahn's store that doesn't even have a name, where the 70 and above town's folk drink whiskey and talk about their younger years. During the annual weekend Bar-B-Que Days celebration and on St. Patrick's Day nights, the bars are filled, and the crowds flow out onto the

Four corner center of town - Burney leaning against the light pole

downtown streets. Seems like all the drinkers go from bar to bar in search of friends who have since moved on and to check out the action going on in each one of the eight venues. My great, grandfather once owned Carlson's hotel and bar at the four-corner area directly across from Krants. Grandpa Leo and his brother Chris managed the pool hall inside the hotel for a few years back in the 1920s, so the bars have sort of a nostalgia about them.

Although the bars bring in plenty of tax revenues for the city, they are looked upon by most in the town like X rated movie houses. Church-going citizens, such as my beloved Grandma Angela, keeps her eyes looking forward and steers almost to the curb when walking by the bars. Even though they blend in nicely with the brick front abutting stores, the insides are hidden from public view behind solid wooden doors and covered windows. If it weren't for the signs out front displaying the bars name and a fluorescent beer advertising light in front of the shades, you would never know that it is a place of ill repute. The only time we get to peek inside the adult world is when one door unexpectedly opens and reveals the darkened watering hole with stranger's shadows sitting on the bar stools. The smell of stale beer flows along with the smoke out into the streets. When the door closes, they again go stealth. Many patrons, some closet drinkers, prefer their privacy often parking their cars in the back alley and slipping in through the side or back door. A few bars even have a dance floor where the drunks get to show off their best moves and show a little more. Brother Mike coined the term "Pissy Pants Drunk" because every weekend some guy gets so intoxicated that he pees his pants and keeps on dancing away with some corn fed young woman hard up for companionship; who pretends not to notice.

The bars are off limits to anyone under the legal drinking age of 18, but some bartenders bend their rules for friends or family depending on the particular mood they're in or if an entire wedding party shows up unannounced. Out of the eight bars, younger teenagers can only hang out in two, Porky's and the bowling alley because they only sell 3.2% alcohol beer and no hard liquor. Those two places suit my friends and me well because both allow us to loiter and smoke cigarettes. Basically, just hang out if we behave and spend a little money now and again.

Mark's misconduct landed him out of Porky's Bar more times than I can count on my hands, including the time he was chased out by an old man with a cane. The quarrel continued out onto the city streets and ensued for another block and a half. Mark chided him moving in close and backing away as the old guy swung blindly his way, me apprehensively following the embarrassing scene ten feet behind. I kind of felt sorry for the old guy as his cane never got within three feet of Mark. I have to admit, it was funny as hell, but I didn't laugh a few weeks after. I stopped into Grandpa Leo's house to pay him a surprise visit and that same old man was visiting with him in their living room. I didn't stay long.

Normally he gets kicked out for mouthing off to old man George who tends the bar during the daytime. Mark always taunts him in a little girl voice, "Georgy porgy pudding and pie, kisses the girls and makes them cry," repeatedly until George runs after Mark with his bar wiping towel swinging it all the way to the

front door. Mark always waits a few days and then goes back inside to apologize just so he can hang out in there again. George won't sell us any 3.2% beer over the counter, but he slides a pack of cigarettes to thirteen-year-olds, always giving a quick glance up and down the bar before throwing the pack on the top and grabbing the money without even a thank you. But I can't afford to buy any cigarettes this night because my wallet holds a single dollar bill and my left front pocket two nickels, just enough to buy a 10-cent postage stamp. I'm saving that dollar for the entrance fee to a beer party if there is one going down somewhere in town.

I dodge a beautiful thick floating ring of smoke and then look back to admire my handy work spin, bend and disintegrate into the slight breeze of the alleyway as I near the basement house. Had it not been for my friend Chip's constant coaching in the fine art of smoke ring blowing, I could never make them swirl and float as well as they do.

Very few smokers go through the rigorous training process required to become good enough at blowing smoke rings to impress even the most seasoned smokers. Just as a fire eater on the midway causes people to stop and look, so do good smoke ring blowers out in the public. We practice almost our entire smoke ring blowing up inside the stillness of the stockade, whenever we are fortunate enough to have cigarettes on hand. Chip is without a doubt, the King of the perfect smoke ring blower largely in part because of his uncanny ability to make his jaw shift downward and backward so effortlessly. I swear he has a disconnected joint on the back part of his jaw because he can snap it downward and backward all in one motion without even moving his head. I have to jerk my head back as I drop my jaw to give the ring the final push it needs to accelerate. Although I study harder at blowing smoke rings than I ever do on English or math, it still took six months to a year for me just to blow a halfway decent circle. Getting the half second hard push of air to work in chorus with the action of the jaw along with the placement and movement of the tongue is a tricky thing to master. Once we learned that most difficult part, we perfected the skill to where we can aim at and hit just about anything at the speed at which we want it to get there. The real challenge is not only to shoot them well but also to look cool as you blow. Both Tom and Chip's brother Tomato look like a goldfish peering out from inside a round glass bowl during their few futile attempts.

Our newly acquired skill of smoke ring blowing has become as addicting as the nicotine itself, normally pushing out two or three rings after every drag. We consider ourselves fairly skilled because we can shoot out a thick circle of smoke that swirls as it moves and stays intact for upwards of 20 seconds. Now we can even blow a large thick floater and then shoot several smaller, thinner rings directly through the center, the last one

breaking up the first. As one of our past times, we hold smoke ring blowing contests up in the stockade to see who can get the most rings to float and sink down over the top of a wine bottle from up to four feet away. The shooter that can get that ring to travel down the entire length of the bottle and break apart as it hits the carpet floor always receives a round of applause. But more importantly, blowing a perfect smoke ring at 13 gives us instant adult stature and proves that we are seasoned smokers and not just out trying to impress friends; which we are proud of. To us, blowing perfect forming smoke rings belongs up there with some of the better things enjoyed in life like the sound of a switchblade knife or the acceleration of a motorbike.

At the end of the old alley, I turn right, walk the remaining half block and hop on the sidewalk right next to Meridian Street. The four-corner center of town is now well within my view, and I too, become part of the small-town streets. I slump a little lower and strut a little harder showing the face and actions of a defiant young teen with no regard for the law or authority. Just like the characters in the Outsiders. Hot Chevrolet Camaro Z28s, Pontiac GTOs, and Ford Mustangs, along with chopped motorcycles, make their way methodically up and down the five-block strip, honking, waving and waiting to pull a U-turn at both ends. An unfamiliar 1970 Monte Carlo SS 454 package slips in behind Spankies 1968 Chevelle Super Sport, pushes the clutch pedal to the floor, the other foot on the gas opening all four barrels of the carburetor revving up the powerful engine in a taunting and challenging way. By the time I reach the four-corner center of town, both disappear, along with half of the cruising cars. No doubt they are headed out of town, across the HWY 25 Minnesota River bridge, up over the hill where the starting point for the one-mile race is crudely spray-painted white across the well-known dragway. Win or lose, the opponents always park in a vacant lot near the downtown streets and proudly describe their Positraction Rear Ends, Quick shift manual transmission kits, along with the horsepower, rpm, and foot-pounds of torque available within their powerful engines.

Warmer days have finally arrived in Minnesota, and with another school year nearing the end, the town is a buzz of activity. All the diagonal parking spots in front of the stores and bars are full as are the sidewalks with people and the main drag with cars, trucks, and motorcycles. The stores stay open till nine O'clock on Friday nights and the bars don't close until one in the morning so for that prime period of time, the little town is hopping. There is excitement in the air and I'm in for another fun filled night scoring some booze or best ever, a real beer party!

Another block and a half brings me to my regular hangout, the local bowling alley. The bowling alley is spread out on the basement floor below the old movie theater. It features six

bowling lanes on the left side of the room and a large bar room on the right side. At the bottom of the wide stairs, I hang a right and head through the bar room opening. There, I find my rebel friends, Mark and Greg sitting in their regular booth, playing poker, smoking cigarettes and listening to someone else's selection blaring out of the jukebox. As usual, Mark has an unwelcoming expression written across his face.

Mark and I are about the same height, but I'm built a lot more solid thanks to Grandpa Leo's genes. I inherited Grandpa's broad shoulders, well defined deltoids, and carved triceps, whereas Mark has none. Don't let Mark's thin frame fool you. He'll spring at you like a viper, and you'll never see his fist connect with the side of your face. Mark's hair is blonde as mine and he too wears it almost as long. But whereas my face is soft and gentle looking, his is sharp as a wolf. My eyes are blue as the sky and his are grey and cold. Our eye colors match our personalities to perfection.

I slide up beside Greg because Mark is the very last person to make room for anybody. Greg is another fatherless teen who hangs out downtown and is the youngest of four reputed rowdy older brothers. The brothers are all known for getting into trouble, fighting, and dropping out of school, most before reaching the eleventh grade. Greg is almost opposite the rest exhibiting a soft mannerism and a desire to finish high school. He too wears his straight brown hair long and is constantly throwing his head to the side to get it out of his face. He is a little on the heavy side and walks with a slight limp. Greg never initiates trouble but joins in once the games get started, especially after he drinks alcohol. Because we are all in the same grade, we often hang out as a group.

I love hanging out down here because the owners don't mind if we smoke, even selling us packs of cigarettes right over the long bar counter. The room easily houses two pool tables, a foosball table along with several booths lining two sides of the room. The joint is always loud from bowling balls slamming into pins and shouts of cheers emanating from the bowling league teams. I got my first job here at 12 setting pins for 13 cents a game. Whenever I got hit by a flying pin while sitting on a stool in the middle of the lanes, the bowlers would throw me an extra nickel or two to help ease the pain. My parents never step foot in the place, so I get to arrogantly smoke freely out in the open. The bowling alley is off limits to most teens my age because it's considered a mainstay for underprivileged boys who routinely get into trouble. I'm not an underprivileged boy, but I like hanging with the troublemakers since they are a hell of a lot more fun.

Because drinking is all a part of growing up in Belle Plaine, young teens always get their hands around a glass of beer or a pint of whiskey. The cheapest and easiest method is beer

parties. They're held almost every weekend either at the sand pit, someone's farm or a house in town. Some are put on in a secret countryside setting hiring several local rock bands and usually start on Friday night and go on all weekend mirroring The Woodstock Festival. One of the main reasons they are so popular is because a single dollar bill buys you a bottomless plastic cup which you can fill up with freshly tapped beer all night long and party alongside some of the most popular teens and young adults in town. Even though the beer party's entrance fee is only a buck, the person that sponsors the event normally makes money or at least brakes even. The boys drink the hardest, the girls drink the fewest; except for a few looser ones in town. Most girls don't like the taste, instead come for the party atmosphere.

Beer parties are the talk of the town and my friends that attend, tell me all about them like who was there, who got drunk, who passed out or who got laid. I always feel like I have missed out on something big? Both Tom and I have tasted keg beer before, sneaking a glass or two with friends at the annual fireman's picnic and we also sucked down a few free ones in the early morning hours taken from the beer garden during Bar-B-Que Days. From the very beginning, we discovered there is nothing like the taste of cold keg beer sipped out of a clear plastic cup.

The three of us always find a way to get our hands around a few bottles of Strawberry Hill wine or a six pack of beer. Between Mark's older brother and Greg's older brothers and relatives, it's easy. Either Mark or Greg enters the bars from the dark alley through the rear door looking for a willing accomplice, hands him the money, then we wait in the darkened alley for our brown paper bag. I like drinking with Greg and Mark but don't much care for Mark's cockiness once he gets his drunk on. The lip licking, teeth dragging and lip curling slow down, but his mouth doesn't, and he becomes louder and cruder than before. I'm not afraid of him, but his quick anger followed with a fast fist to the face is something I want no part of. Friend or foe, he treats everyone equally. Once he starts a fight, he intends on finishing it and quickly! That's something I don't do with my 'friends,' especially when they are in need of assistance.

Take for instance, the night Mark, Greg and I each drank a bottle of Strawberry Hill wine in the North Park. I'm worried enough about arriving home half in the bag and facing the possibility of coming face to face with Dad when I check in for my curfew. Instead of giving me breath mints or a cup of coffee, Mark plays a little mind game with me he had apparently planned with Greg earlier.

When it's time for me to head on home, Mark says "Hey Albright, Greg and I will walk you to the four-corners," grinning and obviously eager to conduct his experiment. As we come to the first corner, Mark blocks me from crossing the street saying in a

snide way, "No Albright, you're not going home yet, you're gonna stay here with us and your gonna miss your curfew and Sonny's gonna be pissed."

The wine has gotten to Greg as well because he puts on a tough act and blocks me with a straight face just the same. I try to act cool about it and try walking around them, but they move in front of me and laugh. After about a minute into the game, they let me go and say, "Alright Albright, we're just kidding." Then they walk alongside shooting the shit like nothing happened. When we reach the four corners, they again block me and put on the same tough act, Mark watching closely for my reaction? Instead of attempting to go around them, I stand my ground and say to them both, "Hey man, that's cool. I'll miss my curfew and then I'll be grounded, and you guys won't be able to mess with me anymore." It works! They let me go and never pulled that crap again.

Even when he isn't drunk, Mark always talks tough, teases me a lot about my curfew and my strict parents. He does it in a childish sort of way teasing in a giggly voice and always ending in a devilish grin. I know just about every aspect of his tough guy act and teasing is mostly all for the show, especially in front of the downtown tough boys. When we're alone, he is a normal teen, just like me? He backs up his tough street fighter image by holding an unbeaten record as a Golden Gloves boxer besides all his out of the ring victories in the schoolyards and on the streets of Belle Plaine. Although he thinks knives are tough, he never carries the cold steel, instead, he uses his lightning-fast hands to take care of business. If he takes a punch, he just gets more pissed off whereas most guys twice his size have never felt the sting of a fist on their nose. Once they discover what real pain feels like, they lose any nerve they have, and the fight is usually over. Because of Mark's small size and lack of strength, he has to get the fight over with before it goes to the ground where he will succumb to the other fighters grappling. Mark often applies karate and judo techniques on his opponents and brags to me before school one morning about a fight he just had with the new kid in town.

He tells me that the new kid, who is a grade behind us, six feet tall, has a big mouth, and how he chops him down to size three and a half. Mark waits for the kid by the State Bank of Belle Plaine. When he walks by him on his way to school, Mark marches right up to him, reaches up, grabs his head with his hands, pulls it down and slams it into the upward blow of the right knee. The tall kid doubles over and falls to the cement sidewalk, and Mark walks on to school as if nothing happened. The reason for the attack is none other than the kid has a mouth on him and doesn't back down from Mark when he harasses him at school. That was a premeditated strike because Mark had thought the entire fight through and planned it right down to the

snarling and spitting at the end of his knee after delivering the devastating blow.

Mark constantly challenges me to see if I possess the same qualities that have earned him his defiant reputation. I think he finds it amusing that I am almost as wild as he is, even though I have to contend with one of the strictest dads around town. It's almost as if Mark deviously thinks he has some kind of psychic control over me. He seems to study my reactions to his mental manipulation and continues to place me in less than legal predicaments. However, as he studies me, I study him as well and discover a little bit more about who that young rebel teen is behind that scowl.

Growing up without a father forced Mark to rely on his older rebel brother Donny for guidance. I found that he doesn't respect too many people, but he does respect Dad and never mouths off to him. Even the time Dad walked downstairs at one in the morning and found Mark and I sucking on two beers last winter. Dad said to Mark, "What in the hell are you doing here at this hour? Get the hell out now!" Mark said no word, just put on his coat and walked out the basement door sipping on his beer, but stopped, turned around and grabbed the remaining two cans and carried on as he had before. Mark loves very few, but I think that he loves good old Grandpa Leo.

Sometimes, I bring Mark along with me for a visit to Grandpa's and that's when I get to see the little kid come out in him. Grandpa Leo radiates the inner glow of Santa Claus bringing out the child in anybody, even Mark. All that penned up aggression and anger, left at the doorstep, Mark's face and personality change into one of an innocent little boy just at the sight of Grandpa. Mark seems to soak in a little of that circus magic the entire time he's there.

Grandpa Leo leads Mark far away from his troubled young life taking him back to an innocent time before his father left the family when he was a very young boy. I swear Mark never even wrinkles his nose the entire time he is there, nor does he bite his lower lip or curl the other, just all smiles and wide eyes. And when Grandpa balances something on his chin for Mark or tells him a funny story, Mark looks at me and gives a long forced fading laugh and then turns his attention back to Grandpa.

Grandpa Leo knows that Mark is a no good kid and in trouble all the time in school and with the law, but he never tells me to stay away from him. Maybe he feels that Mark needs not only a halfway decent kid for a friend, but he also needs a little love too. You have to understand the wisdom and the tolerance of Grandpa Leo and know that he lives by his actions and by the words he speaks, "The love in your heart wasn't put there to stay, love isn't love till you give it away!" Once we reach the sidewalk, the scowl returns and Mark changes back into his former rebellious self.

"Alright Albright, it's your turn this time," he says after discovering an open carton of Pall Mall cigarettes in an unlocked car parked in front of Lee's bar. Even though I'm sweating brass tacks and rubber nickels, I put on my Outsiders face, walk casually near the car and wait for his signal. Once given, I quickly open the door, lift the carton, stuff it inside my green army coat and walk away like nothing happened. The adrenaline rushed through me similar to the time I walked out the front door of the hardware store with Wile E.; a pack of .22 caliber rifle shells strategically tucked in the front of my underwear. Boy, I thought, if Mom and Dad knew what I was doing with the bad boys downtown, they would have a cow.

"There's a party at *The Hill* tonight Albright, you wanna go?" Mark asks with a smirk and then studies my look for a response; his psychoanalysis kicking into overdrive. I keep on a poker face, look down for a minute and then look back up at him. "What and where in the hell is *The Hill?*" Apparently, everybody who is anybody knows what and where The Hill is but me. The Hill is on Swan's farm at a well-known spot that everybody calls "*The Hill*" because it sits on the flat top of a hillside overlooking the Minnesota River Valley. Mark and Greg are both planning on going but must catch a ride there sharing the bed of MacGuire's pickup truck with two kegs of beer. Let's see, it's only eight o'clock which gives me two and a half hours to get back to town, but still, the distance way out in the country bothers me. I have a ride there, but more importantly, I have No Way Back? My 10:30 weekend curfew is again interfering with my attending one of these long-anticipated beer parties. "Man, I'd love to go, but let me think about it for a while." I can tell that Mark is enjoying the hell out of my internal struggle. Greg even joins in the chorus, "Come on Albright, we'll have a blast out there." I keep them guessing right until the truck is getting ready to pull out.

"Well, Albright are you coming or not?" Mark says while sitting in the back of the pickup truck with two 16 gallon kegs of beer on either side as if they were nothing more than two bales of hay. I can't believe the balls on this kid, 13 years old sitting between two kegs of beer right in front of the Red Door Bar and doesn't care who sees him. Unlike Mark, I worry that someone might see me, and the thought of getting back to town later weighs heavily on my mind. I tensely look up and down the street at least twice before taking the giant gamble, "Hell ya, I'm comin." I jump up over the tailgate and awkwardly duck down pulling my army coat around the sides of my face and hope and pray to God Almighty that no one sees me.

Mark and Greg look over at me and laugh as we make our way down the busy main drag and turn left onto the Blakeley road. The truck travels through the lawless town of Blakeley, out across the Minnesota River Bridge, turns left on the Jessenland road

before making a right turn onto a gravel road just before reaching MacGuire's house and farm buildings. It then heads up the steep gravel road towards the top of a hillside overlooking the valley, but before reaching the top, the truck turns right onto a grass path and goes through an open part in the barbed wire fence.

The spot is well chosen because of its concealment from the road and large flat space that provides plenty of parking for all the cars, motorcycles and pickup trucks that usually fill up once the party gets rolling. Ironically, "The Hill" is only a mile or two from the Red-tailed Hawk nest I climbed earlier this spring. The truck backs up next to a huge fire pit ahead of a big metal tub filled with ice awaiting the beer. Both Greg and Mark have been through this routine often, so I follow them around and mimic their every move. They each hand Swans a dollar bill, I do likewise. We are each handed that long-awaited plastic cup and we make a beeline for that freshly tapped half a barrel of beer. Sitting on a large log next to the bonfire with that heavenly liquid close at hand is where my butt is planted. I have roughly an hour and a half before I have to find a way home in time to meet my curfew, and I take full advantage of the dollar as time ticks on by while filling my cup one after the other.

I lose all track of time getting caught up in the excitement and the drink and my curfew time comes and goes. By 11:00 I downed nine beers and stumble from one blurred person to the next looking for a ride back to town. Mark comes up from behind, grabs me, and spins me toward Connie, our neighbor who lives right down the street, "She's heading back to town Albright and she said she'll give you a ride back along with her friends." I remember little of the ride, but she's even nice enough to take me directly in front of our house. But, as she pulls up next to my driveway to let me out, her eyes widen with horror.

Dad's running full bore towards the car yelling, "Hey you! Stop. Don't you dare move!" Connie and her friends practically throw my drunken butt out of the car and take off, tires squealing. Dad gives a brief chase on foot, turns around and then turns his fury my way. "Dale, where in the hell have you been? It's way past your curfew." He notices I am drunk and then he loses his temper, "Get your ass in the house," as he kicks me in the rear end so hard that I roll to the ground. I get up stumbling and catch a fist to the back of my head and fall again. Pulling me up by my long blonde hair he screams, "Get up and get in the house!" I wobble into the house to await my doom as he jumps into his car and speeds down the road in search of my generous neighbor. Dad is bound and determined to figure out this midnight foolishness. Who in the heck was it that dropped his young drunk teen off after midnight and well after his weekend curfew?

After an unsuccessful attempt locating Connie and the girls, he returns and begins his interrogations as I sit in the corner chair of the living room, Mom quietly sits in the other corner and lets Sonny do the questioning using the old "good cop, bad cop" routine. "Where did you get the beer Dale? Were you at a beer party? Who was it that dropped you off? How much did you have to drink?" Sitting there in a drunken and I might add a rebellious frame of mind, I speak little and tell him nothing. (Drunk or sober, I'm not a snitch.) Before sending me to bed, he makes one last attempt at getting me to squeal on my neighbors and friends. "That's it!! If you don't tell me where you got the beer, I'm calling the cops!!" I think he's bluffing, "Go ahead and call 'em, I ain't talkin'!" He roughs me up more before I stagger downstairs to the safety of my room.

About three thirty in the morning, I am awakened by Sonny along with the man the size of a grizzly bear, Chief of Police Fred Wieger filling my bedroom doorway. "Come on Dale, get dressed, you're going to jail." I can't believe it, Sonny actually called the police around three am because his kid got drunk at a beer party. He must have laid awake thinking about it until he started his crusade and made the call. They bring me upstairs, put me back into the interrogation chair and fat Fred takes a crack at me. "Where was the party, Dale? Where was the keg?" In an act of sobering rebellion, I say, "It's up in the tree, man." Oh, that's not what they want to hear, "Alright get your shoes on, you're heading to jail."

By now it's around four in the morning, I feel like hell and just want the game to end. The beer party is long over? "Alright, it was at "The Hill." Never in my wildest dreams did I think this cop would know what or where "The Hill" was, but with those two words, the big man loses "all interest" in jailing me and is out the door before you can say "Rumpelstiltskin." Little did I know the implications of that confession until Mike and Theresa tell me what happened the next day. They spoke seriously and compassionately and both tell me they have a bad feeling that the family has not heard the last of this little episode, and there is trouble brewing under the big top.

Just so happens that at 4:30 that morning the party wasn't over and it was busted by the cops. It was not only busted, but they found the local dealer passed out in his car with an ounce of marijuana sticking out of his front pocket, and they carted him off to jail. He was not only popular, but a big supplier in town and everybody who smoked pot was ticked off. Yes, I was grounded, but it didn't matter because my name and reputation were known all over town as the NARC (Narcotics Police Detective) that busted The Hill. My life turned into a real living hell. Very few beer parties ever got busted so this was a big, big deal and it was my entire, stupid fault.

Then we discovered what that trouble brewing under the big top was when Sonny went public with a cause that would put an end to these parties where 13, 14 and 15-year olds could get their hands-on beer. The following week, a big front-page newspaper article appeared in the Belle Plaine Herald quoting Sonny and his plans to put a kibosh on this out of control behavior. That very week, signs went up all over town calling for Sonny's head. Our family woke up to beer bottles and cans scattered across our front lawn on more than one

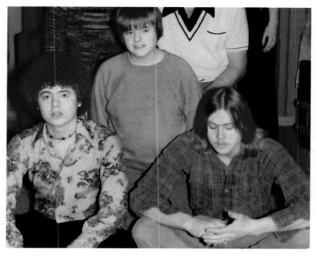

Tom, Joe, and Dale

occasion. Horns blew, and the yells of profanities wailed out in front of our house both day and night for weeks on end. I was forced to lay low almost all summer and didn't dare go out in public where I could be seen and harassed. Hell, my brother, Tom didn't even want me hanging out with him and physically pushed me away when I tried to tag along with him and our friends a month and a half after the incident.

It was bad enough I couldn't hang out with our childhood friends, but brother Tom's rejection, hurt more than just about anything in the world!

Tom is just a little more than a year older than me and I consider him both a blood brother and a best friend. We've grown up almost as inseparable twins doing everything together, and we both enjoy similar interests. We are always competing against each other and our competition often ends in a drop down drag out fights, like the one for all the marbles as four and five-year old's next to the grapevine at The Old House. Though we fight hard and fight to win, we never ever hit each other in the face, instead, hitting on the shoulders, back and arms or wrestle to the ground to see who can stay on top. We always put our differences aside and eventually, we are again, thick as thieves.

Tom possesses the exact look of Mom's brother in law Tom Stibal who was the spitting image of the debonair Hollywood movie star Clark Gable. Tom and I both have our own soft look and although our eyes are both blue, his is a lighter shade of grey. He wanted to grow his thick 'Gould' brown hair long like mine, but when he tried, it looked so shabby that Mom made him cut it to a tamer length. He stands about three inches taller than me and again likens the Stibal build, tall and skinny. And like Mark, he has a habit of wetting his dry lips all the time and biting his lower lip or chewing on the edge of his clothing. Even though Tom is a handsome young man, he has little interest in

taking on a steady girlfriend because he is having too much fun with his friends.

My three older siblings each possess their own unique characteristics: Mike and his never-ending cast of characters, Theresa the consistent nurturer and Tom the teaser and needler. Our family is never bored with the top three, especially with Tom around. He is more fun to hang around than all our friends combined because he is quite the comic with a quick delivery and a mouth that won't quit talking. He also has a sort of a narcissistic personality in the way he needs to have everybody's attention and he needs something to do to fill the empty moments, like chewing on the corner of his sleeve or the top of his tee shirt. At any rate, he is an interesting individual to watch because he is constantly pushing his needling envelope to the extreme

Tom holding his gopher club

with both family and friends. He is teasing someone, commenting on something or singing his little made up songs and rhymes, like the Bob Schuman number or singing theme songs from our favorite television shows, like Gilligan's Island or the Flintstones. The only time my beloved brother can keep his mouth shut is when hunting or sitting in church and even then, he's still fidgeting. And just to get a laugh, he'll walk around with his tongue pushed up against the top of the inside of the mouth making fun of his tormentor, Little John. But what makes Tom stand out more so than anybody is his uncanny ability to hand out the best nicknames in town to friends and family, and even our cat.

He calls our cat both "The Northern" and "The Mink." Grabbing the cat underneath her arms and legs, he stretches her out in front of him saying, "Theresa, look, the Northern" and then wraps the cat around his neck finishing with "The Mink." Theresa always laughs and says, "Oh give her to me" in a childish munchkin voice. Then she grabs our cat from Tom, wraps her around her neck and says, "Oh I much prefer the Mink" and keeps up with her entertaining chitchat as we all have a good laugh.

Once Tom gives someone their particular nickname, it fits them so well that everybody calls them that henceforward. The proud recipient of the nickname tells all their friends the name that Tom had given them so they can be addressed as such. Besides bolstering Tomato's nickname, he names another classmate Bino because of his fair skin and white bleached hair. Young Buck, who by the way was nicknamed by Tom, has a younger brother Jeffrey. At first Tom called him Jefferies with emphasis placed on the last part of the name Reeeeeese, eventually dropping Jeff altogether. After Reese took a fancy to Reese cup candy bars, Tom permanently changed the name to "Reese-cup." Still another Crow School friend, he names "Jags" and yet another "Knobby." He gave this young boy the nickname Alice and it stuck with him for life. Alice grows to be six feet four inches tall and weigh upwards of 250 pounds, but Alice wears the name like a badge of honor because the name was given to him by Tom. He also nicknames several family members and some are given two: Mike is named "Bo-he" or sometimes "David," Theresa, "Daunte Heel the Magician" and he calls younger brother Joe, Pony Jonesy. Because Tom calls Mom and Dad, Sonny and Glo, we all follow and when teasing Mom, he calls her by her stage name "Gloria Decardo," emphasizing the "car" and "do."

Unlike Mike, we both like and participate in sports, not organized school sports, but more side yard stuff with the neighborhood boys. We play catch with the baseball, shoot hoops, organize football games and practice with the frisbee. Nonetheless, we love professional sports and so does Dad bringing his boys along to a few Minnesota Twins games and a few Vikings games. He also took Tom to see the Vikings practice at their site in Mankato.

There is nothing more thrilling for us than watching as our beloved hometown heroes compete against the opposing towns. We go to basketball games, wrestling matches and especially love to watch the outdoor football games played under the floodlights in the fall. Tom holds the record length for riding a two and a half block wheelie on his bike and carries on the family's circus tradition learning how to ride the unicycle that Grandma and Grandpa bought us; one I never had the patience to learn.

Because we are only one grade apart, we are paired up in the same classroom both at Crow School and again in high school. Probably the most memorable class was when we were both in Rhinehold's Accounting class and we got caught cheating on an assignment that wasn't due until after Christmas break.

Four of us copied Lee Blume's homework, but the first one in line forgot to copy the last page and the rest of us followed. It was easy for old Rhinee to figure out. I could just imagine him when he made the delightful discovery. Better yet, he now had rebel Mike's younger brothers trapped like a hawk in a snare on top the "BAL-CHATRI" noose cage.

I'll bet you he steamed and beamed, with a Grinchy grin, as he schemed and dreamed up the perfect punishment for the Christmas trouble we were in. And the more he thought of this punishment thing… He came up with a wonderful idea, a wonderfully awful idea. Rhinee thought he could make this punishment thing last well into spring.

His speech before the class began pleasant enough by extending compliments to Lee Blume who, "Due to the snowstorm," completed his entire assignment before it was due. All four of us joined in with the class as everyone all gave Lee a round of applause. But, then Rhinee changed into the cruel Christmas cartoon figure we had all grown up to fear, and he told the rest of the story that the five of us did not want to hear.

Maybe his shoes were too tight, or maybe his head was not screwed on just right, but the man with garlic in his soul made the cheating announcement with a Grinchy frown. Then he smiled with delight as he called us by name, enthralled with the sight of our belittlement and shame.

After class, we all lined up before his desk as he flinched and he twitched, he snarled and growled, he spattered and stuttered, like the crocodile he was, demanding our rebuttal.

We admitted our guilt, and awaited our fate, as the cheaters we were, what a character trait!

The side of his mouth twitched once and twitched once again, and then it changed into a toothy smile as he handed down a two week prison term of detention in the Grinch's cruel style. He was the master at savoring every last drop and keeping us guessing if he'd tell Mom and Pop.

Rhinee took extreme gratification watching our mental torture drag on for the rest of the school year, often gleefully reminding us of the incident and making us wonder if he would fail us right until we received our grades. The last time he had this much fun was when he was pricking Mike's ass with a needle tied to the end of his pointer. He was the King of sinful thoughts, definitely smoke in his atheist soul, and I have only three words for old Rhinee the King of Trolls, stink, stank, and stunk!

Tom and I are always trying to pull one over on each other and one day I got him but good! We were hanging around the basement of the new house one afternoon when the phone rang. On the other end of the line was Grandpa Leo asking for one of us to help bail out his brother Chris who had a flat tire on his car. Chris was located a ways away and the round trip would take two hours. Neither Tom nor I wanted to go and fought about it while Tom held his hand over the phone. Finally, I said, "Lets both go" and Tom readily agreed. "Sure Grandpa, Dale and I will be happy to lend you a hand." We waited for Grandpa Leo in the front lawn and he was there within ten minutes, parked along the curb and waited in his car. As we approached the car, I told Tom, "I'll

take the front seat, you take the back" I even opened his door
for him. He crawled in, I closed his door, opened the front
passenger side and said to Grandpa Leo, "You guys have a safe
trip now, bye" and closed the door. Grandpa Leo batted no eye! He
threw the car in gear and pressed on the gas. Tom was shocked and
from what I could tell, speechless. The last I saw of him, he was
looking at me through the back window with a puzzled but pissed
off look upon his face. I must have laughed for an hour after
they left. When Tom returned a few hours later, he could only
laugh as well and vowed to someday pull one over on me as good as
I had on him that day…

I dreaded going to school right after The Hill incident
because I got eyeballed in the hallways and called NARC by teens
up to five years older than me. Mark was always quoting the Belle
Plaine Herald article, "Leo Albrecht, a concerned citizen, said
that 13, 14 and 15-year olds are going to beer parties," in a
sarcastic manner and made sure that everyone around him heard his
quote. And then he would say, "Put it in the paper," and then
laugh his ass off loudly inviting others to join in. Hell, the
only reason Mark shows up for school occasionally is to relish in
this type of provocation. Thankfully, there were only a few weeks
left on the school calendar before it ended for the summer break.

That long lost summer turned out to be the worst one of my
young life. I was grounded forever and was told what friends I
could hang out with and which ones I couldn't. Mark was the first
one scratched off Sonny's list! Are you kidding me, nobody, my
age and older were my friends after 'The Hill!' If not for
helping Mike with his hawks, tending to Sheba and teaching a cool
younger neighbor, Pat who lived in the house on Townsend's farm
all that I knew about the Seven Ponds ravine, I would have gone
crazy.

Over time, my brothers and sisters pled my case to their
friends or anyone that would listen attempting to get my version
of the story out, which helped to some extent. And, Sonny's
extreme actions in the weeks that followed sort of helped me.
Most everybody thought that going public the way he did, was over
the top so some even felt a little sorry for me.

Sonny and my relationship became very strained. I would regain the trust of my friends and
convince everyone I could of my resistance against him and the cops that drunken night. Waging
public war against Sonny was one of the toughest things I ever had to do because besides being
my father, he was one of my childhood heroes who took on the bad guys and rescued people from
burning buildings. I had a lot of admiration and respect for Sonny because he was Grandpa Leo's

eldest son who trooped on his own at the tender age of fifteen. As a young navy man, he had flown numerous missions to islands in the far Pacific. He used to bring me along with him on wrecker and dump runs and on weekends brought me with him to The Garage, so I could hand him wrenches as he worked on the family car. He even carried me around for a few days two summers back when my feet were so swollen and infected after the scooter accident in the driveway that I couldn't walk. Besides his occasional bad temper flares, he was a good father trying to raise unruly young teens the best way he knew how. Now he had to contend with his 13-year-old son drunk as a skunk at an illegal beer party.

Defiant teenager

I almost felt like Peter when he denied Jesus three times the night before his crucifixion, because I would talk bad behind Sonny's back and tell everybody what a nut case he was. Inside my teenage wasteland, all the good that Sonny did, and the mountain of a man he was, didn't matter now. All that mattered was remaining focused on my comeback. Dad had always taken his principles seriously and publicly. He didn't hesitate to take action if he believed that it was warranted to do so. Dad hadn't changed, but I had. Regardless, behind his back, I vowed to myself that he wasn't gonna break me. I would go on about my life, only being more careful from now on. If I got caught, I got caught, but I would make it difficult to ever get caught again. I would not take the gamble I did the night I hopped in the back of that pickup truck and headed to "The Hill." From now on, I would have a plan that would bring me back home. It took a long time, "as the truth normally does," but eventually most everyone realized that the kid who busted The Hill, was defiant almost to the end. Still, I did NARC and that is something you don't do in a small town.

By late summer things got back to some normalcy, and I was back to my old rebellious self. I was once again hanging out with the same friends who participated in my demise the spring before. Life at school returned somewhat back to normal. I continued to attend my regular detention due to bad midterm, smarting off to teachers or cheating! At least I wasn't stared at in the halls and called NARC anymore. Mark put the word out on the street that I was cool and could again be trusted, even if I was "waterboarded" for information. Even though Mark was on Sonny's blacklist, I still hung out with him every time I went downtown but had to keep a lookout for Sonny during the day because he was always testing cars or heading out on wrecker runs for The Garage. And as he tested and gathered cars, he always kept a sharp eye out to see if he could catch one of his young teens doing something that he had forbidden. I used to cringe while hanging out on the corner of Meridian and Main Street when Sonny would drive by, slow down, give me a mean ass look, roll down his window, and tell me to get the hell off the corner.

Beer and Bar-B-Que Days

Follow me Albright" Mark says just before ducking into a narrow opening between Porky's bar and an abutting business. The foot and a half wide walkway lead us to the back alleyway running parallel with the businesses lining Main Street. When we reach it, he takes a left and walks me another 30 yards before turning onto the connecting alleyway which runs through the middle of the block bordered by Meridian and Willow Street. This is the same alley I use all the time when heading downtown from the old circus lots. He stops less than 50 yards away from Porky's bar right next to a nicely placed set of bushes roughly five feet from the loose gravel. Looking toward Meridian Street and then squinting down at his wristwatch, he pronounces with a half-cocked grin; the kind that James Cagney does so well in his gangster movies, "Here she comes Albright, isn't it a thing a beauty?" I look over my right shoulder and see a beer truck taking a left off the main drag obviously heading toward the back of Porky's to make a delivery, "Yea it is, what about it?" I'm a little puzzled. "That's our next target Albright, easy pickins." As he watches the large truck pull up to the back of the bar, he reveals his plans to steal beer out of this very same truck next week.

Mark has carefully thought out every detail of his beer heist having monitored the truck's movements for several weeks. He has the driver's timing down to within minutes knowing exactly when the truck arrives and how many minutes we have before he finishes with his business inside the bar. Mark also picked out this perfectly placed set of bushes where we can hide until the time comes to head for the back of the truck's opening. He completes the alley tour by leading me to a surprise little opening two doors down from Porky's where in-between two businesses there is an open area roughly the size of a one-car garage. Tucked deep inside is a dilapidated lean-to, five feet deep and just as wide. "This is where we'll hide the beer," speaking coolly as if he's spelling out plans to hide Easter eggs in an upcoming church festival. "We'll make the hit next week, this same time" curling his lip up on the left side while studying closely my noticeably apprehensive facial expression.

Although his plans to steal beer out of the delivery truck is risky, I can count on him to come through because he is just so damn good at eluding the law. Even though he has done everything as illegal as his older brother Donny, he never gets caught in the act, only a suspect afterward. Even at a young age, Mark is as streetwise as an old owl. And his proposal sounds like it could well succeed. The bushes are the perfect hiding place because we will be hidden from public view, yet still able to watch both entrances to the alleyway lining the backside of the

businesses. And, even though I walk by the hiding place all the time, I didn't even know that it existed until just a few minutes ago. Mark's narrow grey eyes beg for my response, but I'm still thinking about everything that can go wrong, especially trying to pull this theft off in broad daylight when the downtown is as busy as it is now. And, even I have limits. The petty thievery that we've been doing snatching beer and cigarettes out of unlocked cars is one thing but stealing beer out of a delivery truck is out and out robbery bumping up the penalty if we got caught, two big notches. Then again, all the good times we can have with that much beer at our disposal sounds tempting and the timing cannot be any better, especially with the recent completion of our new party spot which Tom calls 'Chink Valley.' The valley is named after three oriental girls who moved into town last year.

Two of the girls are classmates and friends of Theresa and Mary and the third is in my grade. They are a novelty in town because Belle Plaine is anything but diverse. It is made up of ninety-nine and one-half percent white Germans and Irish parentage. Tom and I are also friends with the two younger girls because they hang out at our house all the time and they like to party as much as we do. We've even kissed them a time or two. To some extent, we built the party spot to impress the girls, so Tom thought it only fitting to name our secluded spot after their slanged ethnicity, but not in a derogatory way; it just sounds cool to him.

Chink Valley is tucked away in a little gorge across from Townsend's barn only a stone's throw away from our old Robin Hood Fort. Our newly claimed piece of real estate is fitted with flat rock steps leading roughly fifteen feet down to the valley floor. We dug a hole deep enough to house a trash can for the ice and the beer covering it with sticks and tall meadow grass, not far from a good-sized fire pit. The little indent in the hillside is hidden from the gravel road leading out to The Wooden Fence and unseen by the cars and trucks buzzing away on HWY 169 two football field lengths across from the open crop field. Once we get the beer, we can show off our new spot and impress the girls, along with others.

"You want in Albright?" edgy for an answer, licking his lower lip and dragging his teeth across the bottom of his mouth. Then he spits through his front teeth aiming for and making a direct hit on a winged grasshopper sitting in the middle of the alleyway. The thought of having that trash can filled with tons of ice cold beer is just too good to pass up, and besides, I don't have the guts to turn down Mark. I'd rather face the punishment if we happen to get caught, than be looked down upon by him so by, by, conscience, "Count me in!"

The following week we take up our position behind the bushes next to the alleyway and then simply wait for the truck to

arrive. Mark lights a cigarette and glances down at his wristwatch and says, "Well Albright, he oughta be here in about five minutes give or take a few seconds. Here have a smoke and relax," handing me one of his Marlboros and lighting the end for his partner in crime. Yea, I'm relaxed all right? Inside I worry most about the worst-case scenario of Sonny test driving a car from The Garage located less than a block away or heading out on one of his many wrecker runs. We will be exposed to his direct line of sight from the time we snatch the beer all the way until we duck inside the back of the stores. Often, we run the other way when we see the menacing truck with a crane fixed to the back end heading in our direction knowing that nine times out of ten, Sonny is behind the wheel manually shifting the gears keeping a wary eye out for his troublesome teenager.

Mark's timing isn't exactly on the money, that or the driver is a little bit early because we're not halfway finished smoking our Marlboros and sure as there is a day and a night, the beer truck makes an intimidating left hand turn off the main drag and roars for the back entrance of Porky's bar. The driver gets out, rolls up the back door of the truck, stacks several cases of beer on his dolly and wheels it care-freely toward the back door. Both of us scan our surroundings looking for anybody who might be out or about, before Mark drops his cigarette on the ground, snuffs it out with his tennis shoe and whispers, "Time to move!" We make a mad dash for the truck, which now looks as big as an eighteen-wheeler. My heart is pounding so hard I can feel it in my throat. We each snatch two brightly colored twelve packs featuring a wildlife scene of a flock of ducks with 'Schmitt Beer' in large letters spelled out across the top. Then we run to the narrow opening between the two stores, duck inside, and out of sight. After stacking the twelve packs under the rotting lean-to, I bend over placing my hands on my knees to catch a breath. "Whew, that was too easy. I can't believe we made off with the beer without anybody seeing us. We got a case each!" Again, looking down at his watch Mark disgustedly barks out an order like a drill Sergeant, "Come on Albright, we still have time to grab a couple more, let's go!" Again, racing back to the truck, we each grab two more 12 packs, stack them under the lean-to, cover them up as best we can with some old flattened out water-stained cardboard boxes and step out onto Main street looking as innocent as kids hunting for those Easter eggs.

"I wonder what that delivery driver is thinking right about now," Mark laughs out loud while looking down at his wristwatch one last time knowing that the driver is probably standing at the back end of his beer truck scratching his head. When we reach the four-corner center of town, we cross over Main Street and head to our bowling alley hangout to bask in the glory. Mark says, "That sucker is probably wondering, what the 'F'" then laughs loud enough for half the downtown to hear him, but I don't join in his

laughter because the theft went down so fast, my heart is still pounding hard and my mind is still racing.

While at the bowling alley, his euphoric celebration eventually turns into worry that someone might find our beer resting under the cardboard and claim it as theirs. Perhaps the driver looked closely around and discovered where we hid his beer or maybe someone was peeking out their window as we ran the 50-yard dash along the alleyway carrying the two colorfully designed cardboard boxes. Will the beer still be there for tomorrow night's transportation down to Chink Valley?

When I tell Tom and a select few friends that Mark and I have eight twelve packs of beer hidden away downtown, we're treated like heroes. This is big, big! We've made our own wine, stolen plastic cups of keg beer from the annual fireman's picnic, and even snatched a beer or twelve from the gas station across the highway, but this blessed encounter with alcohol is by far the greatest and grandest success. Four cases of beer waiting for our taking! If only Little John could see us now!

Mark and I enlisted Tom and "Never Say No," Chip to help us transport the beer from smack dab in the center of the downtown all the way to Chink Valley. We figure that making only one trip instead of two will double our chances for success. First things first, we must get permission from our parents to sleep out in the stockade which is usually not a problem. Though they are strict on most things, they're both liberalists for sleeping out in the stockade. Sonny feels sort of proud that he built the fort for his boys and that we are always so eager to make such effective use of it. Little does he know what mischief takes place inside those four tin walls, and if he discovers, he'll take a wrecking ball to the place before pulling a rabbit out of his magician's hat?

The following night, the four of us wait in the dim candlelight reflecting off the tin walls in our fortress sitting on stilts smoking Marlboros, wine tipped cigars, playing poker and telling jokes.

"Did you hear about the truck driver and the parrot?" Mark snickers licking his lips a couple times to get ready to tell his joke. "This truck driver had a parrot that used to travel with him on the road. In the back of the truck, he was hauling chickens. Well, the truck driver would stop for women walking along the highway and ask them if they wanted a ride. Once inside the truck, the driver would ask, 'Do it or walk.' If they would say, 'Walk,' he would angrily tell them to get out and give them a rough push on their way out the door. Finally, one woman said, "I'll take the ride." The driver threw the parrot in the back of the truck alongside the chickens and started traveling down the highway in search of a nice spot to park his truck to have a little fun. But, he didn't get too far before he saw police lights right behind his truck, so he pulled over. The cop came up

to the driver and said, "Did you know that you have chickens scattered all over the road?" The driver followed the policeman to the back of the truck and sure enough, the back door was open and a butt load of chickens was flapping around the highway. He looked inside the truck and saw the parrot grabbing chickens by the neck and saying, "Do it, or walk" and when they would say qwalk, he'd throw them out the back end." The Stockade erupts into laughter!

At 10:30 sharp the lights in the kitchen switch off followed by the master bedroom lights meaning that Sonny and Glo are now tucked under the covers. "It won't be long now boys," I say standing in the shadows next to the open tin door peering at the darkened back end of the house. We wait another hour just to be on the safe side going over every detail of our mission while reminding ourselves of Little John's ten winning rules of night-time travel. We take nothing for granted knowing that Sonny might be peering out the darkened bedroom window trying to catch his son's shadows walking in front of the moonlit tin background.

On hands and knees, we sneak our way across the balcony floor behind the cover of the tin sheet nailed across the bottom of the front end, slip down the ladder and on past a sleeping Sheba lying next to the wooden corral. We then run for the cover of the Stier's bus sheds and take up our position along the wall of Uncle Dave's body shop. We scan for car lights and listen for any sound or movement before slipping across the roadway, one at a time, to the safety of the darkened alleyway. Then we start covertly moving toward our hidden pots of gold. The next two blocks go routine, but as we approach the back of the stores, streetlamps light up the entire area; an obstacle we had not considered before this night. One of Little John's cardinal rules is never to expose ourselves under any light source unless we have no other choice. Oh well, we took the beer during the daylight so moving it at this late hour with an all but dead town asleep, is definitely worth the risk.

Again, we gather before heading vulnerably under the light watching and listening before making our move. One by one, we run full speed toward the narrow store opening while praying that the four cases of beer will still be there. Sure enough, our hard-earned treasure still lies beneath the weathered cardboard just as we had left it yesterday afternoon, but now comes the challenging part of transporting eight twelve packs of beer back to the empty trash can which lies in wait underneath the valley floor of Chink Valley with nobody seeing us. We each grab two twelve packs and again one at a time, in ten-second intervals, slip out of the narrow opening, dash through the lightened area and disappear into the darkness and into the safety of our beloved alleyway. We walk silently, 40 yards apart from each other just in case one of us gets caught, the rest of us can scramble or hide.

When we reach the old circus lots and cross the gravel road behind the stockade, we are home free! From now on, if we see headlights heading our way off in the distance, all we have to do is lay down in the tall meadow grass until the car passes us by. We need not whisper or use hand signals anymore either, and we are all in a triumph-full and vociferous mood. I've never seen Mark happier. He beamed with delight while sucking on the free cans of beer after our arrival and toast to Chink Valley. After filling the trash can with the sports packs of Schmidt beer, we salute to our success under the star-filled night sky while planning our first big beer bash during Bar-B-Que Days. The local celebration of Bar-B-Que Days is in a few weeks. Perhaps we can somehow tie the two events together…

The most anticipated event for everyone during the summer is Belle Plaine's annual Bar-B-Q Days festival. This traditional celebration stretches over three days. It begins on Friday evening and ends on Sunday night. The festivities are held each year during the third weekend in July. Just about every little town around us has their own carnival, each unique to their own theme. Le Sueur boasts a festival called "Corn on the Curb" days. Henderson owns the rights to Sauerkraut days. 'God bless em,' but we have the most attended shindig in the five-county area, "Bar-B-Que days!" The popular celebration is well-known for its delicious roast beef sandwiches, grand carnival, and great entertainment. Many people, who have long since moved to other parts of the country plan their yearly vacations around the popular Bar-B-Que Days get-together. They come back year after year to enjoy the entertainment, visit with family, reminisce with old friends and give thanks for growing up in this special little town.

The celebration is also widely known for its beer garden where every year stories are born of some poor local peeing their pants or throwing up all over the dance floor in front of God, Country, and three-quarters of the town. The Belle Plaine Herald always posts the pounds of beef sold and how many kegs of beer the Beer Garden goes through, and every year the Beer Garden sells more kegs than they did the year before.

The barbeque beef flavor is a secret recipe conjured up by the first-year steering committee who passed over the responsibility for preparing the beef in quantities measured by the cow instead of the pound to the local volunteer firemen. The beef has its own unique barbequed flavor. It is so tender it almost melts in your mouth. It is as if the mouthwatering scent of the beef roasting can actually be tasted way before one enters the park grounds. The Spiekerman brother's dad supplies the delicious buns that are cut and ready to be filled by the ladies working behind the hot and steamy barbeque stand counter. At 25 cents apiece, we order them by the dozens and gorge on them from the beginning of the festival to the end. As kids, Bar-B-Que Days was like living out a three-day dream filled with fun, friends, and food.

One of the many things that makes the occasion so special for us is that during the planning stages of the second year's celebration in 1960, Sonny and Glo recommended adding Klein's Carnival to the Bar-B-Q Days event. They knew the Kleins from back in the day when they were out on the road touring with "Albrights Attractions Stage Circus." They would often recommend

them to cities and towns looking for good carnival entertainment. And the Klein Carnival has a squeaky-clean reputation and is run professionally by both Mr. and Mrs. Klein, who are formally addressed as such by all their employees. Always dressed like they are heading to a Broadway production. They stride about the grounds, he in his red suspenders, and she in her white ballroom dress, inspecting the set-up of their many rides, games, and concessions. Their operation has a strict set of rules and standards that apply to every person who works for them. Most importantly, all employees are expected to present a good public image. The hard-working, greasy guys we watch putting up their rides in the morning are clean and presentable by show-time, proudly manning those same rides at night. Because of Klein's wholesomeness and the large variety of entertainment, the city of Belle Plaine continues to invite them back year after year…

The first four years, the carnival was set up directly on the pavement in front of the downtown stores, blocking two major throughways. The bars got overcrowded and rowdy. And with the July heat reflecting off the tar, too many people would take refuge, loitering in the local merchant's stores and shops. Those complaints eventually put an end to the downtown location, so the celebration was moved to its new permanent location at the South Park.

In younger years, while living at The Old House, Tom and I would traverse the alley to Meridian Street and sit on the curb across from Skelly's gas station for days before the carnival arrived, trying to glimpse the trucks rolling into town. Just as Grandpa Leo did as a boy watching for lanterns that would guide the circus wagons over the hillside 65 years earlier. Often our friends would join us or 'look-out' from the town's other entrance and whoever was the first one to spot the carnival trucks and correctly identify the carnival ride, owned bragging rights for the rest of the year. Most years we could see the trucks turning onto Meridian Street from HWY 169, slowly making their way down the three blocks towards us on their way to the set-up location. As the trucks would pass us by, we would study every inch of steel trying to determine which unassembled ride was tucked away so neatly and cleverly in the back. Then we'd spread the word to our neighborhood friends that the yearlong wait for Bar-B-Que Days was officially over!

Once all the trucks arrived, town kids would show up, hanging around looking for work helping to set up the carnival rides and games. Seemed like every year the same kids would appear, asking to work on the same ride they'd set up the year before. The pay was determined by the difficulty of the job. For instance, the Ferris wheel was the toughest, so the older boys on that crew made more money than the younger kids helping set up the games or kiddy rides. The Carneys always seemed to have wads of cash in their pockets, readily available to hand out to some lucky kid looking to make a buck to blow on the upcoming weekend.

After the carnival set-up was complete, and the Kleins settled inside the comfort of their luxury trailer, Mom and Dad would make their way there to pay them the yearly visit. Usually, they'd bring a few of us kids along to show off to Jenny Klein. "How many children do you have now Gloria, I keep forgetting you have so many?" And just like clockwork, toward the end of the visit, Jenny would grab a large roll of ride tickets, unravel a dozen or two per kid, and hand them to Glo. The wider our smiles, the more she'd give out and by the time we were ready to leave, there'd be enough tickets for each of us and our friends to ride for FREE all weekend. Throughout those three fun-filled days, we never failed to point out Mr. and Mrs. Klein to all our friends, proudly letting them know that they knew Mom and Dad. The Kleins enjoyed coming to Belle Plaine, not only because of our family, but their carnival was always so well received, and they made great money here.

After sunset, Tom and I would again sit on the curb, only this time we had a front row seat to the carnival a mere two blocks buzzing away in the center of downtown. As we watched the streaking fluorescent lights, we could also hear the muffled sounds of the carnival off in the

distance. Festive Polka music resonating down the street, rides throttling up at full speed, and girls screaming as they rode the Octopus, Scrambler or Tilt O Whirl.

Another thing that makes Bar-B-Que days extra special is that our parents put on the "Family Night Talent Show" every year. This is the last event of the festival ending on Sunday night just before the Belle Plaine Queen Coronation, and it grows in popularity every year. One year, Dad performed the same magic routine he did on the stage circus back in the 1950s. You could tell he did this in his prior life because his professional style and smooth showmanship was as skillful and grand as those performed on the Vegas strip. Grandpa Leo and Dad always worked in volunteers from the audience to participate in the acts and this time he picked out two 'over-eager' young boys.

He started the magic act with "color cards." Showing the audience three big cards with the colors red, green, and yellow written on them and then asked the two boys to remember them in that same order; RED, GREEN, YELLOW. Then he neatly tucked them in a folded newspaper and asked the boys for the first color. They pulled out the RED. Asked for the second color and pulled out the GREEN, asked for the next color, and the kids both yelled, "YELLOW," but he pulled out a card that said WRONG and also showed there was nothing else inside the paper. They yelled, "Turn the card over" and he just turned it end for end. They said, "No the other way," so he turned it around and the card said, "WRONG AGAIN."

The magician told the audience that little Johnny and George would assist him in his many amazing magic feats while holding a black wand in his hand waving it around to ensure everyone's attention. Then he asked one of his eager assistants to hold the wand for him so he could ready his next trick. The boy smiled as the magician let him hold the magic wand giving him the power of magic itself, but when the young boy took possession of the magician's wand, it went limp into 12 sections and lay bowed below his outstretched hand. We all knew how the wand worked, but this poor kid had no clue and gazed dumbfounded out in the audience. The sound of the laughter from the audience was the signal for Sonny to stop and turn his attention back to the befuddled boy. Sonny was very empathetic to the young kid handing the wand to him stiff as a cane three times, but every time the kid snatched the wand, it would again go limp, and each time getting a round of laughter from the audience.

Next was the "Passe Bottle" where he showed two empty tubes, put a bottle under one and a glass under the other. He waved his "magic wand" and the bottle and glass mysteriously swapped places. After that, was the rope trick which I could never figure out even after Sonny showed us kids, how it was performed. Anyway, he had one boy cut the rope in two and the other boy tied it together which made two knots directly in the center. With flair, he wound it around his hand, told one of the young lads to blow the knot away, and when he blew Sonny said, "I said blow, don't spit on it!" He then unwound the rope and it was amazingly in one piece minus the knots, so he threw it out into the audience for them to see it was the same piece of rope he started with. No one could tell it was a mere inch or two shorter than before he started; the knot resting in the bottom of his black magician's dress coat.

He also had a water pitcher fixed with a false compartment in it, filled with water and a small ball inside. He told one boy to catch the ball, then he turned the pitcher and the ball rolled out without the water. He did this three or four times and each time a little farther away than the time before. Then he tipped the glass over one of the boy's hands and the ball stayed inside, but this time, the kid got a hand full of water instead.

This magician was good, but his next trick was so mind-boggling that it left the audience and me wondering. He took an ice pick, "poked" an imaginary hole in Johnny's head, put a funnel over it and poured some water inside. He turned to the audience and said, "Now Johnny has 'water on the brain." He had the kid put his finger in his ear, held a funnel under his elbow directly over

an empty bucket while George pumped his other arm. As he did, water flowed down through the kid's head and came out through his elbow as it poured into that empty bucket. Sonny showed us how some of his tricks worked but kept others a secret leaving us guessing along with the rest of the audience.

Even though these were all stock tricks anybody could purchase at any magic store, the perfection and timing of each trick coupled with the exchange and banter of the locals put the act over the "top."

Glo starred in the same show as well singing a few selections only attempted by the gifted few; like the song "The Impossible Dream" composed by Mitch Leigh, with lyrics written by Joe Darion:

The audience sat spellbound during her performance and applauded wildly at her powerful ending, but the song wasn't over, and she cranked it up a notch and went through the song again twice as powerful as the first. Glo, up there singing away, how she hypnotized me. Soon she wasn't Mom, but the gorgeous Gloria Decardo of yesteryear, up on the stage opening Jay Gould's Million Dollar Circus with her lovely voice and once again, wooing the crowds. We were so very proud of her powerful delivery, cool stage presence, but most of all, her lovely angelic voice. Our church congregation new of her God-given talent, but other people in town had no clue. She could have sung professionally at the very top levels. On a starry moonlit night, in mid-July, a star was reborn in the sleepy little town of Belle Plaine…

Besides putting the Family Show together, Mom and Dad always MC'd it. And every year they would try to outdo the previous. After the Family Night Talent Show was in the bag, planning for the next year's "really big-shoe" had begun. Some ideas they dreamed up were clever and one even had a hometown theme. Grandpa Leo came up with the idea to build a fictional character named 'Bucky Borough' and introduced him to the city of Belle Plaine during the Family Night Talent Show starring Mike and Theresa.

Grandpa Leo named him 'Bucky Borough' because Bucky was a mule, and Belle Plaine was the only Borough west of the Mississippi. Grandpa Leo had seen this publicity stunt on a circus he traveled with years before. Mike took up the inside of the front half of Bucky which consisted of a large mule head. Theresa took up the blind rear in charge of the long mule tail. She was also responsible for keeping in perfect step with Mike leading the way. Mike was able to see out the front through a small screen set in the neck painted the same color as the rest of the body; grey, airbrushed with a bluish/green highlight. Both Mike and Theresa had on the same pants, made of the same material and color of the rest of the newborn Bucky. They practiced their routine in the backyard of The Old House with Grandpa, Sonny, and Glo all giving orders and giving advice as they ran through their funny routine in front of Dad's homemade blue and white trailer.

**Bucky Borough; Mike in front
& Theresa in back**

Come show time, Bucky ran heavily around the stage with Theresa's hands holding firmly onto Mike's hips crouching down to keep Bucky's back nice and parallel to the ground. Bucky would shake his head and stomp with his feet as Dad would ask Bucky questions, just as Grandpa Leo had done with his trained pick out ponies. Young Bucky even sat down on a chair during one part of the number; Mike sitting on top of Theresa's lap. Introducing Bucky Borough to the town of

Belle Plaine was as with everything else that Sonny and Glo put together, an enormous success bringing laughter and screams from the entire audience. Bucky Borough was also showcased the following week in the Belle Plaine Herald.

In 1969, good old Grandpa Leo and I performed our acrobat routine titled "80 and 11" in front of the hometown crowds. Only thing was, I wasn't 11 for a few more weeks and some big mouth girl in my class shouted out loud enough for everyone to hear, "You're not 11 years old, you're only 10!" I cringed… Grandpa had insisted on my age being 11 because, in his mind, it made the act sound more challenging for him: as if it wasn't challenging enough for an eighty-year-old. Grandpa's strength, at that uncanny age, left people scratching the top of their heads wondering if he had stumbled upon the fountain of youth. Despite being nervous performing in front of my friends and my classmate's cringing comment right before the act, the performance went off without a hitch. We were the only act that year to end up with two photos in the next week's Belle Plaine Herald.

After the Talent Show, the final event of the celebration was the Miss Belle Plaine Queen Coronation. The candidates each represented one business in town, but if chosen queen got to proudly represent the city for the entire year. In 1974, Theresa was fortunate enough to place runner-up, although we all thought she should have been crowned queen. But she took on all the queen's duties for most of the year because the original Queen studied abroad as a foreign exchange student.

The town looked to Mom and Dad when the pool show replaced the Family Night Talent Show in the late 1960s. They always put together an entertaining show even acquiring the high divers who performed at Valley Fair in Shakopee, MN. They dove off an extended 90-foot platform into the 12-foot end of the pool. Sonny extended the 12-foot-high dive ladder helped by John Stier. As with the Family show, Sonny and Glo always picked the best talent around and came up with clever acts of their own. One year Sonny performed as an odd and funny character called "The Whistler" after seeing something similar while on a cruise ship.

The Whistler wore a huge black wide-brimmed hat that rested on Sonny's shoulders covering his head and like Bucky Borough, a small set in screen, painted black, allowed him to see where he was going. The Whistler's face filled Sonny's exposed hairy chest and round stomach designed perfectly for whistling. The poor Whistler had no chest or stomach of his own, only a set of long legs under his chin. He was just all hat, head and skinny frog legs. Glo cleverly created a child-friendly face using the same clown makeup left over from their days on the circus. After preparing Sonny's faceless chest and stomach with white clown cream blotched with white powder inside a nylon ball, she painted large friendly eyes around his nipples, a nose that took up the center of his torso and brought the Whistler to life. Next, Glo artistically drew a wide happy mouth which started on one side of his belly and went all the way to the other. Sonny made that character whistle in perfect sync with the tune sent out to the audience over loudspeakers. He sort of crouched down a certain way to get that horizontal fold of fat in line with his belly button. As he walked, those big blubber cheeks blew a catchy tune right out of his belly button as the mouth jiggled open and closed. The entire act was funny and well executed drawing huge laughter from the entire audience. No one laughed louder than his proud kids. But, as usual, one year Sonny went a little too far, in a scheme he dreamed up. He kept the secret from everyone but the local dentist Dr. Miller who MC'd the show, a few select Firemen and the ambulance crew.

During the mid-part of the pool show, this raggedy dressed drunk started clumsily climbing up the steel ladder of the water tower located right next to the pool and yelled out to the MC, "Miller you tooth puller, I'm gonna get even with you, I'm gonna dive in the pool!" All the way up he stopped, stumbled and slurred, "I'm gonna jump in the pool from on top of the water tower. I hate Bar-B-Que days." The mayor was on the stage and rushed over to Dr. Miller and yelled at him to

get the guy off the tower, but the MC responded that it was all part of the show. The mayor's response was, "Why wasn't I told about this?" Whereas Dr. Miller said, "Well if I would have told you, you wouldn't have approved." By this time the fire department and the ambulance arrived on the scene with the sirens screaming. Anyway, the drunk kept climbing skyward toward the top almost losing his footing a time or two, high above the screams of the audience below him. When he reached the top platform, he stood on it and said, "I'm gonna show you how to dive in the pool" whereas Dr. Miller nonchalantly said, "Go ahead and jump, I'm gonna continue on with the show." The drunk slurred back, "Hey you old tooth puller, I'm gonna jump anyway." All heads were tilted upward toward the drunk and no longer parallel with the pool show. And like a magician, Sonny disappeared behind the big silver tower and within seconds leaped from behind and headed for the pool, but landed in a thud far short of his goal on the grass filled ground on the side of the audience, his head rolling backward toward the water tower.

The entire crowd was filled with horror and most screamed or ewed and one poor woman fainted. The fireman and paramedics immediately threw the limp and lifeless body in the ambulance, retrieved the severed head and took off out of there leaving the poor woman to be revived by her family and left everyone else in complete and utter shock. The show somehow continued and the stunt went off exactly as Sonny had planned. Dad stayed hidden on top of the boards he placed there the night before with the dummy and he didn't come down until well after the crowd departed. The local doctor discovered the gag from the mayor and went up to Dr. Miller and said, "Are you guys trying to make business for me?" That memorable Pool Show kept the entire town talking for weeks, but the mayor wasn't talking. When all was said and done, he was so mad at Sonny for not letting him in on his gag, he never spoke to him again.

Sonny and Glo may have ended their circus days back in 1959, but their desire to continue performing in front of a large audience and their love of the spotlight was renewed every year those carnival trucks turned off HWY 169, slowly passed by Tom and me heading for our heavenly three-day playground...

With a little over 'seven' twelve packs of beer now secure under the valley floor, we head for Anabelle's café to pay Tomato a visit. He is working the graveyard shift as the head cook. Mark is especially excited to get a freebie off the big man. He didn't know that we always plan to visit Anabelle's after a successful night out having some small town fun. And that we are always welcomed by both Tomato and the waitresses.

Visiting Anabelle's café is one of the boldest things we do while roaming the streets at night because getting to the screen backdoor proves to be challenging. With two flood lights standing on the front and side, one in the back and cars cruising right next to the frontage road on HWY 169, the place is lit up as bright as downtown Minneapolis. In addition, we must cross an open field, the street, and a back-parking area before we make it to the back door. The ten seconds of well-lit exposure is a rare gamble we normally do not take. Not only that, but one of our biggest threat is the local policeman who frequents the joint. Once, he was out front filling his fat face while we were munching away in the back of the kitchen. Another huge obstacle is Anabelle's son who watches over the place like its Fort Knox.

He had been a naval officer and after his stint, invested his hard-earned money into building a liquor Store under his home, kiddy corner from his parent's cafe. His post is one place we have to pass by on the way to the back door. This guy was actually spotted by the waitresses lying on his stomach in the cemetery across HWY 169 peering at Anabelle's with binoculars, no doubt trying to see if things were going kosher when no one was around to supervise the place. So, we really must be careful navigating around his house because he is always on the lookout for food thieves raiding his parent's cafe. And like the local cop, no doubt there have been times his eyes were behind the binoculars while we were tucked in the back feasting on his parent's free food.

Our arrival is right on time because the bars are not yet closed and the drunks who normally fill the place to capacity have not yet arrived. Any time later, Tomato would not have the time to tend to our palette of desires. We each order up the best piece of steak that Anabelle's offers along with a bowl of her famous chili on the side. And we especially like arriving here in the wee hours of the morning, say around three after the crowds leave, when Tomato is just putting the finishing touches of frosting on the day's supply of delicious donuts; a perfect snack after building up our appetites from a night of mischief. I don't know why, but for the luck of the Irish or the blessings of the Lord, we never got caught going in or out of the back-screen door of Anabelle's Café.

After we fill our bellies and before the crowd of drunks arrives, we make our way back to the old circus lots, slip up the stockades ladder, crawl into our sleeping bags and lay awake bragging about how great the food was and how it compared to other times we ate there reminding us about the time Grandpa Leo pretended to be asleep while the "lock cleaners" bragged about cleaning out the local jewelry store when he was a tramp. I eventually drift off to sleep with a belly full of free food and stolen beer.

Our first big beer bash at Chink Valley held during the Bar-B-Que Days celebration was an enormous success, but it was the last time we partied there. It's not that we didn't have a wonderful time drinking the stolen beer and showing off our new spot to "many" girls who gathered around the fire pit, but on our way to and from the celebration we could see the orange glow radiating above the gorge, and we didn't want to take the chance of anybody seeing it. The firelight could easily be seen from both HWY 169 and the road leading out to The Wooden Fence and we feared that someone would call the Fire Department to the area, and the first ones to arrive on the scene would be Sonny and Lornie Stier. The word of Chink Valley spread around town, and the beer we had remaining in the buried garbage can was gone the next time we went back to polish it off.

We never heard a word that any beer had been taken from the back end of the beer delivery truck, so we got away with the beer heist scot free. That was the last time I pulled off anything that big with Mark because stealing beer from out of the back end of a delivery truck was a once in a lifetime thrill. Whereas Mark pulled this illegality all the time. More importantly, I didn't want to risk the chance of getting caught and grounded, if not put in reform school.

Our nighttime escapades with the neighborhood boys and friends from every part of our little town piled up, one on top of the other. The legend of our stockade fort made from tin and boards tucked in the corner of our majestic circus lot grew tenfold. Young teens sleeping out under the stars always visited the place where Grandpa Leo's trained ponies once roamed.

The Budding Falconer

Standing on Jessenland's grassy hillside, our eyes scan the dying elm tree one last time before making the second attempt. At the top of the tree resides Mike's long sought after baby Sparrowhawks. He has seen the tiny falcons in the area before but couldn't locate the actual nesting tree until he happened to just glimpse the female disappearing into one of the tree's cavities a few days before. The tree is a 60-foot snag which has two large dead nubs both at the 50-foot level along with a few newer branches growing out of them near their base. The top of the tree is already dead and had broken off years before. About two feet below the jagged top are two woodpecker holes a foot apart, one of which the hawks are

Dale climbing the Sparrowhawk tree

using. I had been up as high as the nubs yesterday but was forced to abandon the climb when I ran into a problem. I was using climbing spurs and a rope to ascend as a telephone pole climber does, but when I reached the rotted nubs, I was in a quandary. I found I couldn't get past the nubs and live branches without untying my safety rope. Normally, I would just grab a branch and pull myself up over the top, but the tight rope held me back. I needed both hands to untie the rope to continue and there was no safe way to do so, especially at that height. Even if I grabbed a live branch and pulled a Houdini type move through the rope, there was no way of getting back down.

We abandon the tree, head home and think of a way to overcome the obstacle. Mike's solution is to utilize two screw-in tree steps commonly used by deer hunters when erecting portable tree stands, placing them about three feet below the clump of nubs and branches. I can stand on them, lean against the tree or possibly grab a live branch with one hand and untie the loose rope with the other. Then I can easily climb up over the branches and get to the woodpecker holes eight feet beyond. On the way down, I can grab a living branch, lower myself to the steps, then tie the rope back around the tree and continue down.

With the tree steps in my butt pack and climbing gear in hand, I put on my lineman spurs and start up the tree to achieve our objective. I ascend about 40 feet when a surge of panic overcomes me as I attempt to dig in with my right spike and the

side of my shoe hits the tree. Something is not right! I look down in dismay and see that my spike has come unbuckled and is hanging as loosely as I am. The blood rushes to my face and the hair stands up on my arms as I momentarily freeze in the state of shock and disbelief. With my left climbing spur buried in the bark, I hold on tightly to my lifeline. Trapped 40 feet above the ground, I stare into the grooves of the bark as my life flashes backward to a simpler time as a young boy without a care in the world...

"One day, Gramma and I loaded up the horse and buggy, picked up all you kids, and we went for a picnic in the deep green forest. We drove through the lush forest until we found a nice place with huge trees and soft green grass to take a break and eat. While we were sitting there, I heard a noise... and it sounded like this." Grandpa Leo took his hand and put it behind the couch and scratched slowly on the back of the fabric three times. The look of interest appeared on his old wrinkled face as he raised his eyebrows and cocked his head to one side. "Then, I heard it again..." he did the same, three scratches on the back of the sofa. "And I went over to find out what that noise was," his voice trailing off, "Then I saw them... elves in the forest hiding behind the trees, only about this high..." he held his hand a foot off the floor. Our eyes grew bigger. "The little people turned out to be very kind and they invited us into their home, inside the mountain. One of the elves pushed a button hidden behind a tree and a secret door opened up the side of the mountain. We drove the buggy through the door and into a huge cave opening which was stacked neatly with large fruit. The strawberries were the size of watermelons." He held his hands open about a foot apart, "The elves filled the buggy with all different kinds of the giant fruit and we drove the buggy home. We had plenty of food for a long time, and every once in a while, we would go back to visit the little elves and they became our good friends."

We couldn't wait for that old circus man to come over to our house to babysit and tell us stories. Our earliest recollections in life are that of old warm-faced Grandpa Leo telling stories. Before bed, we all crawled up on the couch, listened and watched as he stood before us "center stage" and acted out the tales. He told us about the circus days, little people who lived in the roots of trees and our favorite, his days as a young bum riding the rails around the turn of the 20th century. We'd make him carry us around on his shoulders, balance things on his chin, bounce us on his knee, teach us how to stand on our head and we wore his coat and hat and pretended to be him...

We took advantage of his calm demeanor and taunted the old guy sometimes. We would get on his nerves every so often and he would pretend to get mad, "You want a taste of this belt?" he would say as he pulled it from its designated location behind the closet door and held it out in front of him. Brother Mike boldly walked up to Grandpa and called his bluff, licked the end of the belt and pretended to taste it, "Sure put a little salt and pepper on it, will ya!" We all laughed... That old circus man kept busy entertaining us kids from the time he arrived, till the time we went to bed, and he never tired.

Our grandparents lived through the depression in the 1930s and because money was so scarce and they were so poverty-stricken, they wasted no food after it was over. They always thanked God before the meal and cleaned their plate whether they liked the food or not. We all knew his weakness, "not wasting food," so we always came up with pranks designed to see how far he would go to not waste any. I think it was my brother, Tom, who came up with the idea, but

basically, it involved him sucking on candy, throwing it on the floor and then Mike intentionally rubbing it into the floor with his dirty sock right in front of Grandpa Leo. "Grandpa, I can't eat this candy now that it's been stepped on, I'll have to throw it in the trash," Mike said with a devilish grin. No sooner than the word trash finished, with sleight of hand, he snatched that candy up off the floor and stuck it into his mouth so fast we didn't see it go in. We all laughed again. "Ha, ha, ha!" The whole thing had been planned and staged ahead of time by all of us mischievous kids. Almost as if we were in a huddle during a football game and going over the play called.

We again tested his weakness while vacationing with him up in Canada one year. Dad bought some, what he thought were fruit rolls and when we bit into them, found they had weird, nasty tasting meat inside. We all threw ours in the lake and Grandpa Leo fished them out and ate them. "Never waste food kids." And then he would give us a little lecture on the depression and what it was like living through it.

By the time all us kids came along and got to know Grandpa Leo, he was already an old man in his 70s. But there was something puzzling about his age that didn't square with the rest of society; he looked old as all the other old men in town, but unlike the 99.9% of them, he had a young body and sharp mind. He could still do pushups, pullups, jump rope and even run well into his 80s. And he could still do most of his circus acts like the walk on the slack wire and balance an 85-pound wagon wheel on his chin.

Grandpa Leo was always trying to talk Tom and me into going into the circus business and we'd play along and tell him we would after we graduated high school, but both of us knew it would never happen. Grandpa Leo even helped Tom and I acquire two goats who we named Thursday and Friday. He let us keep them in a hay room at his circus sheds. Thursday was my goat, and she was multi-colored browns and blacks and even had a little white on her face extending down to her long chin hairs. Friday was Tom's goat and she was white as the snow. We thought it was cool that both the goats had horns about a foot long and their knees had no hair from always kneeling. But most of all, we liked the way they sounded with their dwarf like baby baaaaaaas.

He had plans to train the goats to do tricks, and he would also use them to cart our wagon around from house to house come harvest time selling goods out of Grandma Angela's garden. Tom and I would make a percentage of any profits. He drew a picture of what the goats would look like with the harness installed and hooked up to the wagon. But neither idea ever materialized, sort of like the cement dinosaur promise in The Old House. The goats were interesting pets and they stuck close to each other. If you tied Thursday to a long leash, Friday always stayed within about ten feet of her even though she could roam. We had the goats for a couple of years, and we would travel daily to visit and take care of them. Then one summer morning, our goats were taken from us in the most brutal of ways.

We got a call in the early morning hours from our neighbor Mr. Staubs who said that he heard a pack of three to four dogs going crazy over on our property around one o'clock in the morning. He said that he fired two birdshot pellets towards the ruckus to scare the dogs off. He ended with, "You might want to check on your goats." Sure enough, the dogs had been there the night before leaving Thursday dead and Friday with a broken leg and several puncture marks about the body. Sonny immediately called Grandpa Leo over in a flash and the decision was quickly made. Because of her injuries, Friday would have to be put out of her misery! Tom and I were still in shock and silently said our goodbyes as Sonny retrieved the 22. Caliber rifle from the house loading it with a bullet as he walked back our way. We took Friday inside the tin shed originally built for Sheba and backed her up against the rear wall facing the doorway. Sonny took careful aim from only a couple feet away, pulled the trigger and hit her dead center of her horns, but it just knocked her head backward for an instant. He reloaded, recalibrated by lowering the gun an inch

and fired again. This time it was fatal, a few small squirts of blood ran out of the wound and down the snowy white face, Friday stumbled and fell to the ground as dead as Thursday. The whole family was so pissed off at that pack of dogs. Tom and I vowed to find them and get some payback, but we never located them. We buried the goats in the corral along with all of Grandpa Leo's circus animals.

Grandpa Leo still tried talking Tom and me into taking out a little circus, never a big one, just a little one. Both Tom and I knew that the numerous circuses, part of the landscape back in the first part of the 20th century, had dried up and would be no more; as much as old Grandpa Leo pretended otherwise. Television and air conditioning along with strict guidelines and restrictions imposed by different states counties and municipalities had killed the small-time circus back in the 1940s and put a nail in the coffin in the 1950s. Well, Grandpa settled for second best and taught me how to do an acrobatic routine with him called "80 and 11."

He was the strong or anchorman and I was the acrobat doing all the moves. The act really showcased the enormous strength for a man of his size, but more important a man his age. He had a scheduled time when we would practice our routine together. We would run through the whole act at his house with Grandma Angela there to critique us. She made our ties up flashy and ensured that our wardrobes matched giving us a crisp professional appearance like performers from the days of Vaudeville. I didn't mind performing the tricks because I thought they were all good except for the last one. Grandpa Leo would hold his arms in a circle, crouch down on one knee and I would run from like 20 feet away and jump into his circle with my right leg bent back in the shape of a V, finishing with my other leg and both arms held straight out. It seemed a little too feminine, but both grandparents assured me it wasn't and that it was a good closing for our act. We trained at an easy pace and over time we got the act down to perfection. He knew all these different acrobatic moves, and he would try them out on me and just about every other one of us. Perhaps he used his grandkids as props.

Sometimes Grandpa Leo would get some gig and tell me when and where it would be. We traveled via bus and the driver always had a puzzled look on his face as grandpa waited wearing a straw hat, with a bullwhip in his hand, and three colorfully painted chairs sitting on the sidewalk next to him. We showed in several places including the Stillwater State Prison and the Rochester Hospital. Rochester Hospital was featuring what people did beyond their 80 years. The man who went before us blew up a balloon to show how he still had air in his lungs, I guess. Then Grandpa Leo and I came on and did our act and just blew the crowd away. The sight of that little old man throwing this eleven-year-old kid around with such ease just dazzled and amazed them. After our act, he does a solo balancing routine with the bullwhip, a borrowed broom and the three colorfully painted chairs we brought along. He would start the routine off with the borrowed broom balancing it in

80 and 11 performing at Stillwater, MN State Prison

several positions including laying on his back and getting up again. Then, he balanced the thin end of the bullwhip on his chin followed by a straw hat on the tip of his nose ending up on his head with a slight move forward. I handed him a chair, and he balanced it on his chin in several

positions and finished his routine by balancing all three chairs at once. To close out the act, he sang a powerful opera song, as if the audience wanted to hear it (which they all did.) Yes, the man could still sing opera at 80, unlike most opera singers who lose their voices in their 50's.

Grandpa Jay Gould thought he could make a million bucks off Grandpa Leo's voice alone, but unfortunately he never lived to carry out his idea. After the show, he was sought by many because everyone wanted to meet this talented and ageless circus man. Most of our audiences were groups of people gathered for a specific reason such as the Golden Agers out of Minneapolis which was an African American Senior Citizen group. Sometimes we would put on our act for a large event such as hometown Bar-B-Que Days and a huge outdoor celebration in a park in St. Paul, MN. Grandpa Leo and I were featured in the Minneapolis Star Tribune, The St. Paul Pioneer Press, Belle Plaine Herald, and the Stillwater State Prison Mirror. The most thrilled and appreciative audience was the prison population who drank in all of Grandpa Leo's goodness and the wonder.

Grandpa and Grandma were both great teachers and role models for promoting good family values and possessing a good, strong character. They were both very religious. Grandpa Leo made us kiss the cross of Jesus sitting on a shelf every time when we went down into his basement. He was also knowledgeable in the celestial bodies, and each fall when it was clearest, he would put up his huge telescope that Uncle Chris built. He would angle the telescope on a slight rise toward the southern end of his circus lot and show us the rings around Saturn and the moons around Mars. He tried to help us understand how far the distance of a light year was and tried to explain the meaning of forever. **"If a little sparrow flies to the top of a mountain once a year to sharpen its beak and over the millions and billions of years it takes for that little bird to diminish that mountain to nothing, that is just the beginning of forever."** He pointed out this example when discussing our soul and where we wanted it to end up after it departed our bodies. **"We are but dust, only on this earth for a blink of the eye compared to eternity."** For a man with a sixth-grade education, he knew quite a bit.

Even at a young age, we knew that Grandpa Leo was a novelty around our small town. Although he left Belle Plaine for the thrill of the circus life, he always called it his home and kept his circus headquartered there. He had good family roots in the town of Belle Plaine and was admired and respected well before the start of his circus career. As he grew much older and accomplished numerous charitable tasks for the community, he became embraced and loved by all. He was constantly in the newspaper for either something he did, defying his age or some volunteer work he was involved with somewhere else in town. With Grandpa's "larger than life" storybook character and Grandma Angela's unconditional love and support, we all felt so privileged that they were ours. Starting life off with loving grandparents such as those two, was special…

Dale fixing loose spur

A slight tingle felt on the inside of my elbows quickly erases those pleasant childhood memories with my grandparents as I realize the dire situation I'm in. I yell down to Mike, "I have a major problem up here! My buckle on my right spur came

loose." He yells back up to me, "What?" I repeat, "My damn, right buckle came loose!" "Can you fix it man?" He sounds worried. I wonder that myself. Can I fix it? I am using both of my hands to steady myself with the rope and don't feel like letting go of either hand, especially with only one foot dug into the tree. "Man, I don't know about this Mike. Let me think." I have no choice but to put my faith in the good Lord above and slowly ease my back tightly against the rope. I tilt slightly to the left to off balance the lack of footing on the right and let go of my lifeline with both hands. So far so good. Wow! I breathe a slight sigh of relief! Then I ever so carefully bring my right leg up as I lean slightly down just far enough to retie the straps. I awkwardly balance for at least a minute or two fixing my loose spur and then quickly stick the spike back to where I intended it to go. "OK Mike, it's fixed, I'm heading up." "That's gonna make for a cool picture Dale, I got you hanging there working on your spur."

I ascend another 10 feet bringing me eye level to where I intend on inserting the tree steps. Then digging in tightly with both of my spurs, I again lean against the rope and go about my work screwing in the steps. At least this part goes smoothly and they seem solid enough to hold my weight. I pass on by them until my arms are about even with the dead nubs. One by one, I step out of the tree and onto my new steps, grab hold of one of the two living branches, slip out of the rope, and throw it over the dead limb. After that, I simply climb up on the rotten clump, stand straight up, and head for the woodpecker holes above me.

However, as I near the holes in the tree, the protective parents start their continual dives towards me sounding off with their displeasure through shrill screams. They come in at me fast from the side instead of above, as one would imagine. Mike is down below witnessing the show of a lifetime and I can hear his oohs and awes at each close encounter. I reach up into the hole and then deep down inside the cavity before I encounter the five babies. Not only are the kamikaze type dives getting closer to my face, but the little ones inside are coming at me with fury. I feel several sharp pains as the pointed beaks and tiny talons tear at my hand, puncturing tiny holes everywhere as I pull each one out for inspection. The little hawks are fierce! Shew, wind from the little falcons attacking wings brush against

Dale throwing the peace sign before heading up to the woodpecker holes

my face as they go streaking by. I have been exposed to Great horned Owl and Red-tailed Hawk displays of hostility before, but none comes anywhere close to the aggressiveness of these little falcons.

The babies are older than I expect, all feathered and within days of leaving the nest. I pick out the prettiest color male and a gorgeous female with the most dynamic brown pattern against her white breast. Like always, put them in a cloth sack, tie the nylon rope around the top and lower it down to Mike. Then, I grab onto the branch, hop back down onto the steps and gladly away from the attacking little birds. Then I re-tie my safety rope and descend back down. Our plan is a success, despite the "little" hair-raising incident on the way up and the puncture wounds that still bleed from both my hands.

This is not my first successful climb for my brother, The Budding Falconer, and not my last. He has a burning desire to obtain many hawks and owls so he can either train or study from them to increase his ever growing knowledge on the subject. I am his constant companion in the woods, and I too learn the habitats of these fantastic birds of prey.

With the woods, wild birds or animals, Mike is a walking encyclopedia. He knows every bird by name, color, sound, and habitat and can quote facts about birds and animals that would make your head spin. He tells Tom and I which are the songbirds that should be spared, but unprotected species such as starlings, and house sparrows, can be taken for hawk food. These birds compete with bluebirds and other cavity nesters for the prime real estate, forcing songbirds out of their nesting spots. Every time we go out into the woods, we learn something new from him. As a woodsman, there is nobody better than Mike, and he is often sought for his advice or handed some creature found here or shot there from total strangers. Mike knows every inch of the Seven Ponds and Pine Grove better than the person who owns it. Pine Grove is not far from the Seven Ponds. We have only to ascend a hill and cross a cornfield and we are in the very grove of trees that gives the place its name. We climb "The Wooden Fence" often entering into our Pine Grove paradise where wildlife and adventure are never-ending.

Our trips as children to the Seven Ponds were frequent with always some exploration to engage in; search for an owl nest, look for deer sign, check our traps, etc. On one hike through a grove of cedar trees Mike heard a sharp "cackling" sound and immediately the shadow of a fairly large bird passed swiftly overhead and landed on an oak snag 25 feet above us. It remained only a second or two, staring at us with hot, piercing red eyes before it let out another shrill cry and sailed off into the cedars. The memory of that fierce, brown streak breasted bird remained imprinted in Mike's memory. Later, he found its picture in one of his bird books and discovered it was a "Cooper's Hawk" which is considered the miracle killing machine of birds of all types. This encounter was the start of his interest in birds of prey and not long after, the start of his quest to become a falconer. His next close-range encounter with hawks happened on a fall squirrel hunt with Sonny.

Sonny and Mike were climbing up the side of a ravine when Mike spied a large hawk perched on the edge of the woodlot. He told Dad he would take a shot at it, but Sonny grabbed the barrel of his little single shot .22 caliber rifle, "No, you won't shoot this bird or any you see, ever. Hawks and owls eat mice and rats that destroy grain. Most people, especially farmers like to have them around." So they proceeded to the car, but Mike kept seeing that large regal bird in his mind and out of the corner of his eye for weeks.

The Walt Disney episode that aired in 1968, "The Owl That Didn't Give a Hoot," teased Mike's interest even further to become a falconer. Basically, the episode was about a boy who found a baby Great Horned Owl that had fallen out of its nest. He raised and hunted with it in the manner of the falconer. Mike was fascinated with these birds of prey and longed for the day he could see one up close.

The day arrived when he got to see his first owl, but it wasn't quite the way he had planned it. Neighbor Don, and friend Arlie showed up at the back door of The Old House. They had shot a big owl while squirrel hunting and wanted Mike to identify it. It was a beautiful barred owl with dark round black pupils surrounded by a distinctly bright and colorful feather pattern that circled outward giving the eyes the appearance of being huge. After they left, Mike went to his room and cried. Despite his condemnation for their unjustified act, he almost mimicked their brutal crime while doing a little squirrel hunting on his own the following year.

After concealing his 250CC Harley Davidson motorcycle in a thicket near The Wooden Fence, he climbed up on over and headed for the hills and valleys of Pine Grove to do a little squirrel/rabbit hunting. Walking in, he saw an American Kestrel (*Sparrowhawk*) perched in the top of a dead snag along the field. She sailed off her perch and for some strange reason, he brought up his .410 shotgun and fired. She was so far off he never dreamed he could hit her, but she dropped in the bean field running and screaming as he gave chase. She bit the hell out if his hand, as he inspected and found no injury. As soon as he returned home, he called Grandpa Leo who found where a single shotgun pellet had bruised one of her wings, that was all. Mike never could figure out what compelled him to take a shot at something he held so dear, but he had a falcon. He named her "KEE" after our cousin Chris. He was very young and couldn't pronounce all his words. If you asked him his name, he'd say "Kee Daywa" Chris David.

When Grandpa Leo told Mike the female Kestrel had been hit only with one pellet, he breathed a sigh of relief and as long as he had help, affixed the jesses (*a short leather strap that is fastened around each leg of a hawk*) to her legs, and attached a swivel (*a freely rotating metal device which attaches the leash to the jesses which prevents twisting*) and a leash (*a long, narrow, leather strip one end of which is attached to a hawk's jesses via swivels and the other end secured to a block or perch.*) Then they fashioned a temporary perch out of a large cardboard box with a broom handle running its length and newspapers lining the box to make cleanup of her mutes (*droppings*) easier. About two hours later, when she seemed settled down he tried to feed her tiny bits of squirrel meat, but she only flicked them away and screamed at him. Mike told the folks he couldn't go to school in the morning because he had to "man" (*accustom a hawk to people, to handling, and to strange sights and sounds*) his new hawk. Mom told Mike the principal said in all his years he never had heard that excuse for being absent from class. That's because the principal never dealt with a circus family before...

If he had any time, he'd do his homework but usually let that slide till morning study hall. After working with Kee for three weeks, her wing was healed but not strong enough for sustained flight. Kee would fly to his fist at a distance of only 10 feet. The little falcon seemed to trust him completely. She no longer would "bate" (*fly off his hand and hang there flapping wildly*). He still was keeping her in his room, but Sonny and Mike were also putting the finishing touches on the hawk house on the back side of Sheba's new home. Mike spent many hours proudly walking Kee

on his gloved hand, into the woods and fields close to our house. Over a short period, he had gained a sort of celebrity status, people were used to seeing him with a hawk perched on his fist.

As her wing became stronger, he increased the distance calling her to the fist, and although he still kept her on a creance line (*a long leash*) she was progressing well. Since she was doing so good he became careless. On windy days he'd let her wings catch the breeze and she'd fly and hover with the creance line attached. He reasoned that exercising and strengthening her wing was good for her. Since she had shown no desire to fly away, he gave her first free flight. Big mistake!

He had her in the field behind the house on a very windy day, set her on her perch, unfastened the swivel and creance, stepped back about 30 feet and called her to the fist. As soon as she spread her wings, a gust of heavy wind caught her and she sailed up above tree-top level and drifted away with the wind. He ran, blew the whistle, called her name but by then she was several hundred feet in the air, a tiny speck that grew smaller as she gained altitude. Soon, she was gone and he was sick. It was his fault, not the birds. No sleep for him that night. He kept going over and over in his mind the entire episode, but that only made it worse. He lost his hawk, plain and simple. Sadder still, sooner or later the jesses would get tangled up in tree branches and his bird would die a slow death. He took off school the next day and spent most of it searching for his lost bird.

Later in the afternoon after searching in vain, Mike went bow hunting for deer at Pine Grove to get his mind off losing his prized Kestrel. After assembling his gear, he strung his bow and headed out of town for the walk to the deer woods. He hadn't gone more than a few blocks when he noticed a Kestrel perched on a telephone pole along the gravel road leading to The Wooden Fence. Quickly bringing up his field glasses, he saw the jesses dangling from the bird's legs. Running to the pole, he tried to coax the bird down, but with no meat, whistle or gauntlet (*a stout glove with a long loose wrist,*) Kee just sat looking down at him. As he ran home, he feared the bird would fly off.

When he neared our house he saw me riding a motor scooter around the yard and yelled for me, "Dale, I found the hawk and I need your help ASAP." After hastily grabbing his gear, some meat, and Sonny and Tom, we all headed back to recapture his new bird. Mike tried luring her down by whistling and offering her meat to no avail. Sonny suggested someone climb up the telephone pole and naturally, I was elected and started up the pole bear hugging my way to the top. The climb was easy as telephone poles are perfect for getting your arms and legs around. As I looked up

Kee

I could see the hawk peering down as the pole wiggled and shook. When I neared the top and made a grab for the jesses, Kee sailed off to the next pole. I went up after her again, the same thing happened, just as my hand got close enough to make the grab, the hawk opened her wings and made for another perch. So it went for close to an hour, the hawk going from pole to tree to pole, everybody following not far behind. Just when we thought we were licked Kee must have gotten tired because she flew down to a fence post. Here, too, she played the musical perch routine when Mike got within a foot, off she'd go. She then caught and ate a few grasshoppers which was a good sign she was hungry. We all sat down in the pasture hoping she might think about the gopher meat on Mike's gloved hand.

After sitting in the long grass for about another hour, Mike got up and slowly made his way towards his bird talking to her in soft, hushed tones. Step by step he closed the distance, all the while holding out the meat garnished gauntlet. Soon he stood a mere three feet from the bird and to everyone's surprise, she hopped onto the glove and fed. With swivel and leash secured to the glove, we all made our way back to the house. Because Kee's wing was probably not recovered, it possibly had just plain tired her out. The weeks passed by and with another winter approaching, the cold weather set in quickly.

Mike moved his bird out into his new "hawk house" and for a solid week sleet mixed with the rain came down. One day after school he went to check on his hawk and found her hanging limply from her perch. She appeared to be very weak, so she was brought back into his room to her cardboard box/broom handle perch. After a week of warmth and tender loving care, she seemed her old self, but the reason for her illness could not be explained. In case she was still not fully recovered, Mike decided not to tether her to the perch. That day after school, he opened the door to the hawk house and was surprised to find her nowhere in sight. At first, it looked as if she vanished, but a glance towards the ceiling revealed the back half of her body. The little falcon's wings, head, and shoulders were stuck in a small opening between the wall studs and tin covering. Apparently, she saw the light and attempted to try for this chance at freedom. Now, she was gone for certain, dead, because Mike had made another bad choice. He had learned the hard way, and he took it hard. With his hawk gone Mike seemed lost. The daily, familiar routine of working with his bird, now over, left a deep void in his life. He did not even have a photograph of his bird, only memories of the pleasures of the short time he had with her. Regardless, his quest to obtain hunting birds continued and intensified.

In grade school, Mike was friends with two brothers who lived on a farm north of town and would occasionally invite him to spend the day exploring the ravine system and creek that ran through their property. Once he arrived for Saturday's fun and was floored when his friend showed him a young Great Horned Owl they had found in their pasture. They even let him feed the owlet a few gophers and a snake! Each time he visited the bird was bigger, no doubt they fed it well, and soon it was winging its way around the farmyard. To everyone's dismay, it eventually went off on its own.

But later that winter, they captured another adult grey phase Screech Owl in one of the hen houses with a flashlight and landing net the night before. They knew of his burning desire to have a bird of his own and offered him the Screech Owl as a gift. They told him if it was still there after school he could take it. After getting permission to show up late for work at The Garage, he

Mike holding Screech

caught a ride from Grandpa Leo and proceeded to get his new bird. They arrived at his friend's farm so quickly that he had to wait for their school bus to arrive. Sure enough, the owl was still in the little outbuilding where it had spent the night. This time, with more experience handling

raptors, the jesses, swivel, and leash went on the new owl quickly. After giving his pal five dollars for his trouble, it was back to town with the new bird. The Screech Owl ounce for ounce is one of the fiercest little birds on the planet and it fought him with both beak and talon.

Once they arrived back at the house, Mike set his new Screech Owl up in our room using the box/broom handle type perch that housed his first Sparrowhawk. He left the bird to settle in and went to work. While he washed cars, emptied trash, and swept floors, I shot a sparrow and had it waiting for Mike's return. After work, he partially plucked it before offering it to the owl. The poor thing must have been half starved because it tried to grab the meat from his gloved hand. Unable to free it, the owl nervously ate, pulling morsels of meat, off the carcass, its beak covered with blood and feathers. Though his new owl was keen (*hungry*), it still snapped its bill at us between mouthfuls of the sparrow. After the feeding, he took it on the glove and attempted the manning process. In the next few days, he found it best to attempt these sessions during daylight hours, as the sun glaring off the bright snow seemed to put the little owl in a trance as it sat on his hand with eyes half closed as if sleeping.

This bird was not friendly and like a horned owl, it snapped its beak at us when we brought it mice and sparrows for dinner. Though we did a good job of cleaning up the bird's droppings and disgorged pellets of undigested bones, fur, and feathers, mom was not happy with the owl having free reign of his room. When she would enter to get us up for school, the owl, usually perched on our curtain rods would snap its beak at her for invading his space. We gave him the name "Screech" and brought all our friends over to show the owl off. While there, we would play the radio for them and one particular Budweiser beer commercial seemed to interest the little owl as it would stretch its body erect and open its eyes wide each time he heard it. Another thing everybody thought was cool was the way the owl could turn its head entirely around.

Mom eventually tired of the beak snapping and stated emphatically that a Screech Owl would not have free reign in the house, period! So we moved the owl out to the hawk house and let it fly free inside. Mike had since repaired the opening that had caused the death of his first Sparrowhawk by covering it with insulation board.

Unfortunately, we didn't learn until later that Great Horned and Screech Owls must be obtained as babies while their eyes are pale blue for them to be good pets as their vision is not very good at this age. When the eyes turn yellow they see well. Getting them before their sight is developed assures that the owl will imprint on the first thing it sees; a person or an adult owl. Any bird acquired with yellow eyes remains wild and untamable. In Mike's excitement of getting a new bird, he ignored the fact that this owl, whose eyes were as yellow as could be, had imprinted on the parent owls and was therefore, untamable. Still, he persisted stubbornly for two weeks trying to win over the affections of the owl. She seemed docile during the day, but at night her repeated attempts to escape along with her shrill wailing prompted Mike to set her free.

On an overcast day, we walked the mile to Pine Grove, climbed over The Wooden Fence and headed far out into the open meadow. Mike held the owl while I took off the jesses. Because of all of my help, Mike handed me the little owl. I flung it high in the air, we both watched it wing its way towards a stand of thick cedars. On the way back home, we both promised to remind each other that any owl with yellow eyes would be left alone. We concluded we'd stick to hawks from now on unless we found a baby owl that had not imprinted on its mother. Who knows, someday all the stars could align, and we could feasibly find an active nest with baby Great Horned Owls in it. Although apprehensive, he knew that an old woodsman might be able to help him out.

Right across the alley from The Garage, a little piece of wildlife habitat surrounded a house, barn, and several sheds. The yard held a grove of apple trees, hedges, thick bushes, a large garden, and many birdhouses/feeders. He had seen the old timer that lived there out and about the property while he was working part-time at The Garage but never got up the nerve to speak to him. One day

Sonny took him over and introduced him to the man everyone called "Bump." When dad told him that Mike liked birds, they became instant friends. It seemed Bump and Mike had a lot in common. They both liked birds of all kinds, hunting, and everything about the outdoors. It was a strange friendship, he being 70 and Mike 14. Then again, he had a similar relationship with Uncle Herold years before. Every chance he could, he'd sneak away from washing cars and sweeping floors to talk to Bump about all things wild, especially Great Horned Owls and hawks.

Meanwhile, he found several resources where books on falconry, hawks, and owls, could be obtained. Mike sent for several catalogs. Great Basin Labs in Utah sold falconry supplies, including traps and leather to fashion your own gear. There was even a place out of a Florida Pet Ranch, and a zoo supplier out of North or South Dakota where actual birds of prey could be purchased, including the now rare Harpy Eagle for $1,200.00! It may as well have been 12 thousand dollars or even a million as he only made 50 cents an hour at The Garage. Mike did "start" saving money for a Prairie Falcon. Its price was $62.00 which was another small fortune, but he often fantasized about the possibility of having one anyway.

Between his studies and daily visits with Bump, his book knowledge grew, and he was also making his own falconry equipment; hoods *(a leather cap which covers the head and blindfolds the bird thus keeping it calm and quiet,)* jesses, leashes, perches *(a structure upon which a hawk is placed,)* and lures *(an object which is made of leather/feathers, and garnished with meat to which the raptor is trained to come for food.)* Even though he had little money, he purchased bells, jesses/leash leather, swivels, etc., from the Texas Micheros catalog. His falconry bag was an army surplus shoulder pouch. A heavy, stout glove bought from the welding supplier at Keups rounded out his meager equipment. He made a ring perch and block perch in Industrial arts class and bought a metal whistle.

His first hawk trap was built using a design given to him by Bump. He bought the wood, wire and other materials and with Grandpa Leo's help, built the trap. It was a large, awkward contraption. Since he was not old enough to drive a car, he talked Dad into transporting it to the woods. Brother Tom and I helped. The four of us carried it to a clearing nearby. He placed two pigeons into the live bait section of the trap, and we walked the half mile back to our car. On the way out Mike spotted a Cooper's Hawk perched in a tall tree, and he assured everyone he'd have a hawk by nightfall. School and work the following day dragged on, all he could think about was removing a hawk from the trap and begin training. After work, he hopped on his motorcycle and made haste to his trap, but much to his surprise, it was empty. After giving the bait pigeons food and water, he headed home very disappointed. Over the next few weeks, he continued to set the trap in various locations in the same area, bribing Tom and me to assist him dragging the heavy trap to different spots. Finally, with the fall migration over, he admitted defeat with this trap at least.

Maybe it was good that his first trapping attempt had failed because he didn't even possess a falconry permit. Mike discovered there were many traps used to acquire raptors, but being his impatient self, he scraped together the $30.00 to purchase a Red-tailed Hawk from the bird/animal ranch in Florida. After a long wait and much reflection, he canceled the order and decided to trap his own bird, in the manner of a dedicated falconer. He had the plans for an ancient style of trap called the "BAL-CHATRI" noose cage.

The BAL-CHATRI was about a foot long. It had a wooden bottom featuring a small door for live bait and had a rounded wire top. The top and sides of the trap were covered with 100 or more fish line nooses or snares. The bait, usually a mouse or small bird was placed in the trap. The next step was to drive the country roads searching for a perched hawk. If the hawk could be seen by the human eye, the hawk could easily see the bait. The trap was tossed out onto the shoulder of the road opposite the hawk, and if the hawk was keen it usually flew to the trap and became ensnared

by the nooses attempting to secure the bait. Mike spent countless hours tying the numerous little fish line snares to the top of the trap. By the time summer arrived, he had all the falconry equipment needed, a new trap, and a renewed attitude.

Once his version of the noose cage was complete, he baited it with a live sparrow. About a mile and a half from home, he had been keeping tabs on a male Sparrowhawk and knew his habits and preferred hunting areas. An older friend with a driver's license agreed to help him attempt to catch the hawk. Upon arrival, the Sparrowhawk was not perched along the road on the telephone pole as he'd hoped, so they parked some distance away and set the cage trap in a small clearing, then opted to await the Sparrowhawk's return in a cornfield across the road. It was a hot, humid day, made much more uncomfortable lying in the dead, unmoving air of the cornfield. He laid in the dirt two hours before the Sparrowhawk finally arrived but showed a definite lack of enthusiasm only attempting a few halfhearted swoops at the sparrow before sailing off to parts unknown. It never occurred to him that the hot summer sun beating down on that poor bait bird could harm it, but upon inspection of the trap he was amazed to find the sparrow lying dead in the trap.

For his next attempt at trapping, he placed a live but crowded pigeon into the trap along with a tuna tin of water. His Sparrowhawk appeared several times near the trap but seemed to ignore it completely. By the end of the day, he was covered with a mixture of sweat and dirt from spending the day prostrate in the hot, dirty field. Disgusted, tired, and hungry he tossed the trap along with many hours of tedious watching and planning in Dad's garage and stayed focused on obtaining a baby Great Horned Owl instead.

That late winter Sonny drove Mike to check on a Red-tailed Hawk nest to see if it was used by the Great Horned Owls. The pair were present and seen by him almost every time he hiked in the ravine system, as he'd flush one or both birds most times he was there. He kept searching for their nest well into spring thaw, and the sound of rushing waters in Roberts Creek from the melted snow was a pleasant, soothing sound as he tried in vain to locate the owl's nursery.

One rainy day, he stopped to tie the lace on his boot and as he sat back against the hillside, his hand settled on a cool, mushy substance. Turning around he found himself in a patch of yellow colored mushrooms resembling a sponge clustered around a dead elm tree. He remembered Grandpa Leo telling him stories of his dad taking him out in the spring woods to pick morel mushrooms. When Great-Grandfather relocated here from Wisconsin, he introduced the area residents to these delicious mushrooms. Before then, neither the Indians nor settlers knew of the good eating these fungi would provide. He quickly picked the patch of the strange looking mushrooms and put them in his raincoat. He slung them over his shoulder Santa Claus style and started the hike home. A phone call to Grandpa Leo had him at the house in minutes. He told Mike these were morel mushrooms, about 10 pounds of them, worth their weight in gold. That evening we all feasted on this delicacy. Between mouthfuls, Grandpa Leo proclaimed that he and Mike would be back out in the woods tomorrow to search for more. With the Great Horned Owl nest on the back burner, the next day found them back in Pine Grove searching for more morels. They found them everywhere! It was difficult carrying them out of the woods, every bag hauled out was bursting with this mouthwatering delicacy. And, so started another one of Mike's hobbies; the springtime quest for morel mushrooms.

Since Grandpa Leo's influence got Mike into picking morel mushrooms, each spring he always received the first batch of morels. Grandpa Leo had always told us, "Morels are where you find them" and damn if he wasn't right. By the time Mike was getting into this hobby, Minnesota was in the midst of the Dutch elm disease epidemic. Morels grow around dead or dying elms, but once the bark falls off the tree, they disappear. With huge elms everywhere in the woods, he hit the jackpot and was only limited by the time he could spare and how many pounds of morels he could carry. But he also found them in many other places; in sandy creek beds, amongst patches of

prickly ash, along roadside ditches, under cedar trees, in meadows, etc. The fruiting requirements are known only to the morels themselves, but hot humid weather, a damp spring with lots of rain is best for finding many morels. He gave away a lot of the mushrooms he found to his coworkers. He also presented a couple of lectures at the library about the morel and had written and sold an article on this subject to 'Fins and Feathers' magazine.'

Because he supplied Grandpa Leo with so many meals of morels, he dubbed Mike "The Mushroom King." The local newspaper ran a story about morels and interviewed him along with some old timers considered experts due to the numbers of these mushrooms they found each season. One thing everyone wanted to know was where your favorite spots were, but no mushroom hunter we knew would ever reveal their secret locations and neither did Mike. He developed specialized methods in searching for this delicacy. He always wore camouflage head to toe, and usually had Lena drop him off in the woods so no one would see his

Morel mushrooms

car parked where he was picking. Often, he'd be filling a sack with fresh morels and be interrupted by other pickers carrying on a conversation, moving much too fast to spot anything. It was easy to simply drop to the ground near some cover and watch them stroll right by him and the patch he was working on.

In 1969 Mike applied for a falconry permit. Falconry was not regulated by the Federal Government, and it was easy to get into. You needed only to write to the assistant director of Game and Fish. Because Peregrine Falcons were endangered, they were excluded, but a permit for a Red-tailed Hawk or Sparrowhawk was guaranteed. (*Great Horned Owls were an unprotected species.*) And, shortly after applying, that's what he received, a permit for one Red-tailed Hawk and one Sparrowhawk. Now, all he needed was a hawk.

Turak

Mike plants his right knee on the slanted hillside and positions the other parallel to the ground while holding out his hands towards me in an acrobatic pose. It's a pose we are all familiar with because as young children, Grandpa Leo taught us how to do simple acrobats. While executing one of them, he would position himself as Mike had just done where we could easily get up onto his shoulders using his knee as a step. Once we had our two feet resting solidly on each side of his neck, he would stand straight up, let go of our hands, grab a hold of our ankles, stand tall and we would both pose with outstretched hands. Not that difficult of a feat, but to strangers, it looked awesome because Grandpa Leo stands five feet four inches tall and at the time was in his seventies.

Grandpa Leo and Theresa in front of Sonny's built trailer

I place my left hiking boot onto Mike's left knee, grab hold of his outstretched hands, step up onto his shoulders and then steady myself against the bark of the huge elm tree as he boosts me upward to within twelve inches of the first thick offshoot. "OK Mike, that's good, just hold still." With a slight bend in my knees, I leap off his shoulders, grab hold of the top of the branch, throw my legs up over and roll around above it. The next two thick branches are easily within my reach and I conquer those, but as I stand to look to the fourth, Mike's first hand report must wait for another day. The branch is at a minimum three feet above my outstretched hands and the tree trunk is still too thick to get my arms and legs around in a bear hug. Damn, I wish I would have brought a climbing rope along, but unfortunately, I didn't get to look this tree over ahead of time. Besides, Mike literally picked me up off the street on my way home from school. I had no idea this would be the day I would make the legendary climb.

Mike's nervous, pacing back and forth at the base of the tree as he always does when I climb for him. He doesn't dare watch me ascend because of his own fear of heights and just the sight of me scaling any tree over 10 feet tall, gives him the shakes! More importantly, if I fall, he knows that his ass is the one that's on the line. Lena stands 15 feet away from him, but unlike Mike, keeps her eyes glued to my every move offering words of caution and encouragement as I methodically work my way

skyward. This tree is so massive that he didn't have the nerve to bring along his camera to capture the dangerous climb on film, fearing he must keep his telephoto lens focused on me for too long. I thought that Little John had taught me everything that I would need to know about climbing trees, but he never taught me what to do, should I find myself in this precarious situation. I yell down below, "Mike…. I need a rope! There's no way in hell I'm gonna get to the birds without one."

Example of nesting tree - Notice the person near the bottom of the tree pointing to the nest

While waiting for a response, I try to pick up on what they are saying to each other 25 feet below, before Mike yells up in a frustrating groan, "Yea man, I'll get you a rope, hang tight." Then turning to Lena, "Come on Lena, let's head back to town." He doesn't' go twenty yards before glancing back at me and yells, "Dale you gonna be OK up there?" "Don't worry about me," I said leaning against the trunk and then watching them snake their way out of the vast ravine system. It doesn't take but a minute or two for the reality to set in. A cold spring wind is sweeping through the Jessenland hillside and through the thin material of my jean jacket. I'm alone deep in the woods far from the Red-tailed Hawklets above with their ticked off screaming mother circling 50 feet above the treetops, keeping a close watch on her babies and on me. I figure that Mike and Lena will be gone for about an hour because the drive from Belle Plaine and walk to the nest took damn-near a half hour, give or take a few. So, thirty minutes to Grandpa Leo's, a quick hello, I need a rope about this long and this thick, a hurried thank you and then thirty minutes back to the nest, should just about do it.

Mike's been closely monitoring this Red-tailed Hawk nest since last fall. He knows there are baby killers above because he found their broken eggshells at the base of the tree yesterday. He's eager to get a firsthand report from me on how many hawklets have successfully hatched. Usually, he has at least two active nests he keeps close tabs on. If something happens to one, he can then turn his attention to the other. He also tries to pick a tree that's climbable, which is nearly impossible. Red-tailed Hawks build their nest in the tallest trees in the woods and this one is no different. It appears to be over ninety feet tall

located one-third of the way down the hillside of a 200-foot steep angled ravine. The huge stick nest is built upon a narrow branch that juts 15 feet out and up over the deeper part of the hillside making the total height well over 100 feet, if I fall. But I never think about falling, just the pay off at the end, which is usually a carton of cigarettes or a 12 pack of beer. Besides, I'm looking forward to seeing the bird grow into adulthood and Mike train it to hunt rabbits and squirrels later this fall. This will be his second Red-tailed Hawk in as many years. His first, "Turak" was a month and a half old when his friend Jim snatched her from a nest last spring a little more than a mile from this second would-be predator...

The tale began late in March 1971, when Mike saw an adult Red-tailed Hawk fly off a nest in a tall tree not far from where we observed the courting pair of Red-tails on our first live trapping attempt. The next day he drove to the spot, hiked up the hillside and rapped on the tree with his walking stick and to his amazement, the female flew off the nest while crying out with a high-pitched scream! Finally, after much searching, he found himself an active Red-tailed Hawk nest. He raced home with the news! Mike kept a close eye on "his new-found treasure" while calculating when the babies would be old enough to survive without their parents. Twice a week he hiked up to the nest and tapped the tree and each time the female would scream in protest and circle high overhead. Sometimes the male would join her, both voicing their displeasure at his disturbance. The days passed slowly for Mike, but this gave him time to prepare everything for his first large hunting bird. As April ended, a rare spring snow covered the ground, causing anxious moments. Would the baby birds survive this snow and cold snap?

On May 3rd, Mike and two friends drove to the nest. One guy Jerry was employed by the telephone company and was used to climbing and therefore, not afraid of heights. He had actually volunteered to go up the tall tree with only a rope, pillowcase, and nylon line (to lower the baby,) as he started up the tree. Both adult hawks soared and screamed overhead but did not attack. Anticipation ran high as Jerry neared the nest, he shouted, "Hey, there are three baby hawks up here, what do you want me to do?" Mike hollered back up, "Put the two biggest ones in the sack and lower them down." In short order the pillowcase reached the ground and not far behind it, Jerry. "Man, what a view from up there, you can see for miles." Busy examining the downy covered Red-tails, Jerry's remark fell upon deaf ears. Needless to say, Mike was on cloud number ninety-nine! The two baby hawks were about the size of a cantaloupe, hog fat and seemingly healthy. It didn't take them long to leave the hillside and once in the car, Mike waited long enough to make certain the female returned to the remaining hawklet. Mike's other buddy that day, "Young Buck" had also received a falconry permit, so he took ownership of the other chick. Back home both babies were placed in a large cardboard box on an old blanket covered with paper towels, a heat lamp was placed on the side of the box along with a thermometer to monitor the temperature. Mike decided on the name for his Red-tailed Hawk long ago while he sat glued to the television set at the old house.

The name "Turak" was derived from the second movie ever to appear on TV's "Movie of the Week" titled "Harpy." It was a story about a rich architect in California who lived 40 miles from the city. He was an avid outdoorsman who took a young American Indian teen in after the kid had one too many scrapes with the law. The American Indian, John, carried a nine-inch switchblade knife in his back jeans pocket. John trapped a Prairie Falcon one day and trained it in the manner of the falconer and this interested Mr. Peter Kloone, the architect. Soon they built a hawk house

and had a Peregrine Falcon, a Cooper's Hawk, a Sparrowhawk, and a Great Horned Owl. But Peter's pride and joy was his great pet, a South American Harpy Eagle which is the largest eagle in the world. He named his prize TURAK. He and John were training it to hunt wolves. They were supposedly the first ever to train and hunt with a Harpy Eagle. Peter's ex-wife showed up and caused much trouble between the architect and his secretary; also his fiancée. As the situation became more intense there is a lot of drama and a surprise ending. The movie was perfect for Mike because of the falconry and the switchblade. He loved the movie so much he named his first Red-tailed Hawk Turak...

Mike was more than ready to take on the challenge of actually raising and successfully training the large hawk after his years of research on the ancient practice now rarely in use. After he had the birds in his tenure, the real work started. Just supplying enough meat to satisfy the two young hawks was a full-time job. He knew that he would need a steady supply of wild meat to feed them, so they would grow stalwart and healthy. He came up with some clever ways to satisfy his birds' appetites and everybody pitched in. With his urging, some of his fellow outdoorsmen organized pigeon hunting expeditions at several farms in the area which not only provided target practice for duck hunting later in the fall but also provided Mike a steady diet of the right protein he was after. All but one shooter would wait outside the barn, as the other ran up into the hayloft to scare the pigeons out into the battle zone where they were lucky to survive the ten to fifteen-second shelling. It was outstanding target practice because the pigeons came out the open door at the end of the barn flying fast and zigzagging in all directions. If you can hit a pigeon, you can hit just about any flying bird. But that was not the only source of protein he used for the growing Red-tailed Hawks.

Tom, a few friends and I drove our bikes with empty buckets to the local cemeteries a few times a week which supplied plenty of gophers milling about the fresh soft soil. When we spotted a gopher, we would chase it down a hole and then look for possible exits where one might slip out the backside and if located, plug it or guard it. One of us would then run and fill the buckets with water and pour them down the hole after covering it with a fishnet and wait. When the gophers came up to the top and tried to run, Tom would dispatch it with a mallet type club he made in industrial arts class. While he was making the walnut club, he bragged to the teacher about his gopher club and what it would be used for. The teacher gave him an F on the project, but Tom didn't care. He was proud of his gopher club and bragged to our friends of its many kills! Every one of us wished we had the club that Tom had made. As cruel as killing the gophers were, Tom's mallet proved instant and a somewhat humane weapon.

I would also travel by myself to Townsend's barn and had easy pickings with many baby birds from the numerous nests built into the rafters. Soon the family freezer held a good supply of food, much to the dismay of Mom. Although Mike marked the meat as hawk food, she didn't like it in the same freezer where we kept the food for the family.

The two baby hawks thrived on the wild food we provided. It is important to include fur, feathers, and bone along with the meat. The undigested remains were spat up or "cast" by the birds daily. Once the pellet of fur, feathers, and bone, was ejected, the birds were at once ravenous. Mike and Young Buck blew a whistle at each feeding session so the hawks would associate the sound with food. It wasn't long before dark feathers burst from the sheaths and covered a good part of the down. At six weeks, the hawks had grown considerably and were almost feathered. Mike put Turak in his hawk shed. Young Buck, however merely placed his bird on a perch inside a large cardboard box in his father's garage until permanent quarters could be arranged.

A couple days later Young Buck phoned Mike and told him his hawk, though tethered to the perch had flown up on the sides of the box knocking down a jar of paint thinner off a nearby shelf. The chemical had spilled on the young Red-tailed Hawk and now it was dead. That was the end of

Young Bucks interest in having his own bird, but he came over daily to watch Mike begin the training process and continued to help fashion falconry "furniture" hoods, jesses, perches, etc. He also was a big help in supplying food for Turak. Young Buck hung out and he would always finish the visit by talking to Theresa if she was around.

While Mike worked with his hunting birds in the backyard, Young Buck or one of his or our friends would sit on the top step of the cement wall abutting the house watching the large bird fly to his fist as if they were watching a tennis match, but they weren't the only ones who took notice. By this time, many of the town's people had seen him with the hawk perched on his fist and word eventually reached the ear of the editor/photographer and reporter of "The Belle Plaine Herald." As far as Mike knew, he was the only falconer the town ever had. He was one of the first 50 people in Minnesota to be issued a falconry permit by the

Mike with Turak flying to his fist in the back yard

Department of Natural Resources. So, he agreed to be interviewed. The story complete with photographs ran on page one October 7, 1971. Shortly after that, the high school held a lyceum program featuring a falconer who brought along several hawks and a Bald Eagle.

His guidance counselor got him out of class so he could visit with the man before and after his presentation. It was the high point of Mike's year! To top it off, he was contacted by Belle Plaine's high school superintendent's wife where she arranged for him to visit several schools in neighboring towns. At every school attended, he gave presentations and answered the student's questions just as the man from the lyceum program did. To put it mildly, Mike's hat size grew from all the recognition he was receiving.

That fall, Mike tried his hand at hunting with Turak and she took a few gophers, made several valiant attempts at grey squirrels, rabbits, and even gave chase to some flushed pheasants. He was glad that his and our friends had gotten a good supply of meat for her. The numerous frozen birds, gophers and pigeons took the pressure off him having to hunt for her food during the fast approaching winter. He thought for a first-year bird she was doing well, however, she started to chase the neighbor's pets and even a few of their children. No doubt she was attempting to perfect her hunting skills. This was a worry, but not enough for him to give up his bird so he was normally careful where he flew her, usually taking her far out of town and away from people. Mike learned a lot about that first large hawk. For a yearling hunter, the training process had gone better than he expected. By the time she reached maturity, the female had grown large, larger than most, she went through a "lot" of meat, but more importantly, she had no fear of man and became rancorously mean. Turak's fearlessness eventually turned to aggression and then to the pursuit of her human companions, who helped supply her with a steady supply of meat.

Tom, the Spiekerman brothers and I were hanging out in our stockade while Mike had his hawk out for her daily exercise routine. The brothers practically lived at our house where we spent a lot of our lazy summer days camped out in the stockade smoking cigarettes and dreaming up new and exciting things to do. Even though Tomato was a year older than Tom, they were good friends and Chip had been a classmate and a best friend since Crow School, so we often hung out

as a foursome. Tomato was originally given his nickname because when his family moved into their new house, the neighborhood boys pummeled him with tomatoes. Tom liked the name Tomato because it matched his bulky red hair and he also called him the 'Master Mind' because Tomato was always deep in thought and always had a solution for anybody's proposed problem. Chip was three inches shorter than his brother and a little heavier; took a liking to his dad's donuts more than his brother. Chip kept his blonde hair, 'highlighted with a reddish tint,' almost as long as mine, hated school almost as much as me, and we were both always in some sort of trouble in and out of school. He was also a good follower and never shook his head no if I asked him to participate in anything dangerous or out of boundaries of the law. Whether stealing from the downtown stores, gathering meat for Mike's hawks or making wine in the basement of Townsend's barn, he'd eagerly join in just to go along for the ride. Even though their dad owned the bakery in town, and they lived in a nice new house in a development on the far west end, that didn't keep either of the two from being as rebellious as Tom and me.

Turak

They were both a lot of fun to hang around. As I said, we were always seeking excitement, but the novice hunter Turak was searching for a little excitement as well and in her instinctive mind, we were nothing more than moving targets to practice her hunting skills on.

She was sitting on a fence post across the gravel road on the other side of the pasture near our secret Robin Hood fort, ready to launch on anything living that moved. Every one of us knew that the hawk was getting dangerous because of its recent attacks on dogs, cats and a few children in the neighborhood. "Take a look out the window Chip and see if she's still sittin' there," Tom said as he threw down an ace of spades and a King of Hearts ending the last game of twenty-one poker with Tomato. Chip took a deep drag off his Old Gold, cocked back his jaw and choked out a perfect thick smoke ring that shot across the fort's room and then glanced out the open tin window. "Yep, she's just sitting there." Tom went out onto the balcony and yelled to Mike, who was fidgeting with a piece of padded leather on his newly welded steel frame perch, "Hey Mike, can you put Turak away because we're about to head on out of here?" Mike stood up, held his gloved hand high and blew the feeding whistle repeatedly, but Turak just sat there not interested, and apparently not hungry. "The hell with it, you guys ready to make a run for the house?" Tom finally said. We all answered, "Sure let's go." So one after the other we shot down the ten-foot ladder made from two by fours.

The first one down to the pasture grass was Tom and unfortunately for Tomato, he was the last. Before his feet hit the ground, the hunting bird had regained her appetite, was already airborne and headed directly for us screaming as if to announce, "Your asses are mine." We all ran for our lives as the 56-inch-wide wings, intimidating open beak, and loud shrill screams closed in on us real fast. Mike stood between us and the approaching glider holding his gloved hand high, fresh meat resting on the leather, repeatedly blowing on the whistle clenched between his teeth, but watched Turak pass on by him and close

Turak flying in low for the attack

the gap on the three lead runners reaching for the safety of the house. Tom fumbled with the back-door handle for a half second, but quickly recovered his grip, swung it open, and the three of us rolled on the floor just as she crashed into the screen door with her large pointed talons piercing eight holes into the thinly lined steel. The crazed hawk hung there for a second and hissed at us through our damaged shield displaying displeasure at her near miss. Because Tomato was last, he didn't make it inside the house and realizing his dire situation, turned and ran head over heels in the opposite direction. Turak lunged away from us leaving her eight claw holes embedded in the screen and within seconds hit Tomato directly between his shoulder blades knocking him to the ground. He laid on his stomach, covered his head with his hands, and screamed like a little girl while the huge bird's sharp talons dug into his back. It walked from his shoulders to his buttocks with its feathers ruffled, wings halfway spread and proclaimed her triumphal catch in a loud and eerie high-pitched scream; almost as loud as Tomato's. Mike ran to the rescue, grabbed Turak by her jesses, lifted her off a shaken up young man whose face was as red as the crest of his head, and stood there laughing. "That was cool, you alright man?" Then we all gathered at the screen door

admiring her handy work and wondered how long it would take Mom or Dad to spot the identifiable holes embedded in the screen forever. We came right out and told them about it rather than have them discover the holes on their own, and they were okay with it. They even let us keep the claw marks as testimony to friends and relatives proudly pointing to the holes as we told the story of Turak the fearless hunter of man.

As winter engulfed the landscape, with two feet of snow on the ground and five feet deep drifts in the backyard, it became harder and harder for Mike to give Turak the full attention she required. Although Mom's freezer still

Mike hacking Turak back into the wild

held a good supply of meat, he was more interested in training his new little falcon which he had

trapped with the BAL-CHATRI noose cage while the leaves still held onto their fall color. The little falcon didn't eat near as much as the huge hawk and wasn't chasing neighborhood kids, so he tried to 'hack' *(teach the hawk to hunt and fend for itself)* Turak back into the wild woodland from where she came.

He put a plastic cable tie with colored pony beads on her leg and released her back into the wild in December near Stoppleman's creek next to the Blakeley road. Each day he returned with food, blew the whistle and she would come to his fist to eat. To his surprise, a few weeks later she was with an adult male and after he had given her the gopher meat, she returned to the male and shared it with him. Her returns to his fist became less and less as she hunted more and more on her own. Mike was feeling good about his ability to hack his gorgeous specimen back into nature. On one of his daily trips to check on her progress, he saw the wild male, but no sign of his beloved female. Although he kept searching, he never saw her again. It wasn't until long after that he discovered the fate of his trophy sized Red-tailed Hawk.

By chance, he was visiting our Uncle Dave at his house in Blakeley. Dave's neighbor was there visiting and nonchalantly told Mike that his grandson shot her off a telephone pole so he could mount her. She was a massive four-pound bird, endowed with beautiful black markings streaked on her belly and on the underside of her wings. She was also a proud bird, no doubt standing at attention before her executioner fired his weapon. Her deadly fate was met because she had no fear of her would be an assassin and had never seen the likes of a 12-gauge shotgun, allowing him to walk to the bottom of the pole, aim and pull the trigger. Mike's worst fear was that Turak would not hunt without his aid and die a slow death from starvation, never imagining her short life would come via 12-gauge shotgun pellets. He never got over the shocking news that day, and neither did the rest of the family…

Mike holding his prize Red-tailed Hawk

The Shot Heard Round the World

From my temporary perch up in the elm tree, I finally glimpse Mike and Lena in the distance weaving their way back through the valley toward the nesting tree. Obstacles of fallen trees, hanging grape vines, patches of sharp thistle and deep gorges carved into the valley's hillside make the travel cumbersome. Mike normally moves through the ravine faster than Tarzan the ape-man. He's eager to give me the rope, but Lena delays their arrival.

As they approach, he yells up to me, "I got a rope Dale, got it from Grandpa. Yea, he had an extra piece in the shed. He said I could borrow it. Here you go." He took careful aim and threw the rope a perfect 25 feet up towards me. "Catch." I snatch it, smile and examine the thick woven together twine ideal for gripping. "OK, here goes nothin," I say as I throw one end of the rope up over the branch, spit in my hands, grab both pieces together and squeezing them tightly, head up fist over fist. I momentarily pinch the two pieces of rope hard with my right hand as I let go with my left and grab hold of the top of the thick offshoot. Now that my left hand is firmly in place, I let go of the rope with my right, reach up and grab hold of the top on the other side. Then I simply throw my left leg up over the top and pull my body around and above.

Leaving the rope at my feet, I start up limb by limb, bear hugging where there are no branches to grab on to and make it up to the offshoot holding the nest, in less than ten minutes. This is where the climb gets a little tricky and I might add, a wee bit scary. Facing the nest, I effortlessly shimmy my way outward and upward closer to the open sky where the mother is still circling and screaming above. When I reach the no turning back point, I swallow hard, place my feet in the corners of two smaller branches while squeezing my knees tightly around the main shaft, and awkwardly rise while bending slightly backward to avoid hitting the outside edge of the fitted sticks blocking my way. Carefully and ever so gently, I rest my hands on the top of the loose bundle, stretch my neck up and over the top and take a peek at what very few people have the privilege to see. There, in a down-lined bowl-shaped indent are two little baby Red-tailed Hawks snuggle together keeping warm accompanied by a half-eaten red squirrel laying near the edge of the nest. "Be careful Dale," Mike practically begs me as he can see the knotty position that I'm in, high above the slanting ravine floor. Now it's Lena who dares not to look, and she turns around and stares at the hillside.

Spread before me is the vastness of the Minnesota River valley and from my unique vantage point, 'quoting Jerry, the lineman' "I can see for miles." Even though the landscape still

holds onto some of the dull grays and browns from the dead of winter, the sight is overwhelmingly beautiful. Standing proudly to the east is the silver steel graded Blakeley bridge recently reopened after the departed waters of the spring flood. In the foreground is Jessenland's church steeple barely visible above the valley tree line. The entire reach of dead river bottoms gives me a panoramic view of black empty crop fields, patches of woodland and the winding Minnesota River lazily making its way toward the mighty Mississippi in St. Paul.

I yell down to Mike, "There are two babies and a half-eaten squirrel." "Grab the biggest one Dale!" he yells back and, "Please be careful!" I rise as high as I can without compromising the grip of my feet and legs, stretching my body and limbs to the extreme and snatch the bigger baby of the two. I glance over my shoulder towards the mother's cries and breathe a sigh of relief as she soars at her present altitude making no threatening dive at 'me' the intruder grabbing one of her newborns. The handcuff size bird's huge and mysterious deep-set eyes are barely open, and it looks practically naked covered with only short white fuzz. I settle back down below the nest to get into a better position, so I can hold the bird out for Mike and shield myself from the circling mother above. And as I do, I again hear Mike and Lena talking amongst themselves below the canopy of trees before Mike shouts up to me, "Dale, I want you to take the bird now. That tree is just too dangerous to climb, and I don't want you going up there again. That's why we brought the butt pack along, just in case." "OK, Mike, whatever you say. She's coming down!"

I tuck the tiny hawklet between my legs, reach into my butt pack, pull out a thin nylon rope wrapped neatly around a wooden stick, along with a foot-long white cloth bag, stuff the tiny bird inside, tie the rope around the top and slowly snake it through the branches of the tree a foot at a time. Although far, far above the steep hillside, I can see the look of anticipation along with the anxiety on Mikes and Lena's faces as the cloth sack inches closer and closer to them. "Take your time and be careful coming down Dale," he says as he nervously fidgets with the strings tied around the top of the cloth bag. He pulls the tiny white fuzzball out of the bag, inspects his newborn prize and wonders to himself if he can keep it alive at its young age. Throwing the rope down and jumping safely to the ground I say, "Hey Mike, what will you name it?" "Haven't made my mind up yet, but I think I'll name her Turak again, Turak II."

I like the name Turak because it sounds like a name from an ancient time. Thoughts of Hercules and David and Goliath appear from the profundity of my mind. I can easily imagine a dark-skinned, straggly, long-haired warrior proudly sitting atop a white stallion dressed in animal skin with his arm extended and a hooded falcon hungry for a kill, waiting patiently on his fist.

"Dale, I'll get you a carton of Marlboros or a twelve pack of beer whichever you want. I wasn't expecting to get the bird today, but not to worry, you earned it man." He playfully slaps me on the back of my head, tucks the bird under his coat, and we start towards the road. We're all feeling good and I think to myself, this will be a great summer!

We no sooner close the doors and start the engine of the old Corvair, when "Dad" comes barreling up to us in his car, slams on the brakes, blocking our exit and the entire roadway. He jumps out, heads for the driver's side and says, "What in the hell do you think you're doing having Dale climb that tree? You had your grandfather worried to death. Dale could have fallen and killed himself." "It's OK Dad, we got the bird and there's no harm done, look." Mike holds up the fuzzy little critter

Turak; hairy little fuzz ball

to show him, but crazy-eyed Sonny wasn't interested. "And why didn't you ask me for the day off instead of Fred?" With that Mike says, "You don't sign my paychecks, man!" That's when Sonny gets pissed off and kicks in the side of the driver's door leaving a noticeable dent. Mike quickly throws the car in reverse, maneuvers it around him and heads for town.

Dad and Grandpa Leo are right, sending a thirteen-year-old kid up a ninety-foot tree, out over a steep ravine could have ended up deadly. But that doesn't seem to be Dad's only concern. He wants his children to reflect who he is, an upstanding citizen, with a solid reputation in the community, but most important, his strong work ethic. Because of those characteristics, he misses no work, even times when ill, he's always on the job, and he thinks that Mike should have been there, too.

After the baby was a couple weeks old, Mike added fur/feathers to the meat and crushed bird and gopher mouse bones for casting. Around age four weeks, feathers burst through the sheaths, now he had to feed the hawklet as much as it could hold. If they lack their required daily intake, the blood in the feather sheaths is absorbed as nutrition and horizontal lines or scars appear in the feather itself. These are called FRET marks and weaken the feather which can cause breakage. At six weeks the hawk is fully feathered and able to make short flights. Besides

raising and training all the baby killing machines, Mike was insistent on trapping these type birds, as "sort" of a sport.

He feels that building the traps himself and securing his bait is all part of the tradition of a dedicated falconer. He recently constructed another noose cage trap, more advanced than his earlier attempt. These traps are very time consuming, making and affixing the many snares is tedious and trying on the nerves. Besides the new trap, he has raised a bunch of dark domesticated mice for live bait. Without lively bait of the right kind, the trap, no matter how close it's placed near the hawk is useless. He believes that dark mice will show up best during any season, especially in the winter. Now that he finally has his driver's license, he can't wait to field test the new traps/bait. As Mike and I load up dad's 1966 Corvair with his trapping gear we assure each other the first hawk we see is in the bag.

Trapping different flying predators is not only a challenge but one of the ultimate falconry experiences. Mike has earned his stripes as a sergeant, coming up through the ranks growing wiser with each ensuing battle. He not only captures these majestic birds of prey, but he learns a little from each one of them along the way. The birds are never harmed and always taken care of in pristine conditions while giving them lots of attention and a lot of respect. He knows of their power and of their grace, he admires them, gives them the deference they deserve, and shows a great deal of love toward the species. I assist him on many live trappings experiencing the feverish anticipation, the thrill of hunting the hunter and relishing in the sight of the magnificent hooded bird sitting atop Mike's gloved fist. Going on these live trappings is much better than going squirrel, rabbit or deer hunting because catching them is only half the game. The other half is handling the fierce creatures once snared on top of the "BAL-CHATRI" noose cage!

Dodging a long sharp beak which has the power to split bird bones in half, eluding eight sharp talons with enough strength in each to carry a rabbit while trying to free and outfit the bird takes patience and precision. Handling the vicious killers has become second nature to Mike and he knows exactly the routine and procedures to follow in order to do it successfully. I may be able to ascend a 100-foot tree to get a baby, but Mike has it all over me while handling these attacking nightmares. I assist him as best I can, but he is the expert and directs me during the frantic five minutes after capture. He enjoys the sport so much he always puts aside enough cash for the material to build the trap, food for the mice, and the gas to fill up the tank.

While he pumps in two hard-earned dollars worth of gas at Skelly's Gas Station, I wait in the Corvair with the "BAL-CHATRI" noose cage sitting in my lap watching the black mouse nosing its way from one end of the cage to the other searching for a way out. "That's right little fellow, move just like that when I drop

your butt off the side of some roadway." We travel out of town towards Blakeley along the river bottoms where, as always, our destination is the Jessenland road. We like this stretch of road because there isn't a lot of traffic and it holds lots of birds of prey sitting on the hillside overlooking the river bottoms. If the hawks are not perched in a tree along the hillside, they are sometimes sitting on top of the telephone poles lining the roadway.

Today, we have two BAL-CHATRI noose cage traps. One is a larger trap painted flat white to blend with the remaining patches of snow, and a smaller version is painted flat grey to match the shoulder of the road. Both traps hold lively black mice. And, for the first time, we brought along a pigeon "vest," which is a leather coat or jacket of sorts that fits on the live pigeon with slits to accommodate the wings, so flight is possible. The entire surface of the vest is covered in fish line snares just like the BAL-CHATRI. Mike plans to use the vest for any Red-tailed Hawks or even a Cooper's Hawk if we are lucky enough to see one. When driving the backroads, the pigeon is tossed out the opposite side of the car window as the perched hawk is passed. A dragline attached to the vest slows the pigeon's flight down and it soon drops to the ground. To a hungry hawk, it appears as if the pigeon has been struck by the vehicle, and it swoops down to take advantage of an easy meal. One man watches the hawk/pigeon as the other turns the vehicle around down the road. It's important to be certain the hawk has begun feeding because in the process its talons become entangled in the nooses. Then, and only then, is the hawk approached. The weight of the pigeon and the dragline prevent the hawk from getting away. We captured the pigeon last night using Little John's method with a flashlight and a fish net in Townsend's barn.

As we arrive at the hunting grounds, he immediately spots an immature Red-tailed Hawk less than 100 yards away perched overlooking an open field. Mike slowly drives by the hawk and just at the right moment says, "Now" and I toss the pigeon out the window. We both see it hit the ground like a stone. He drives further down the road and turns around to park. When the field glasses eye the pigeon, he says, "What the hell? Why is the stupid thing just sitting there?' I wonder if it broke its neck when it hit the ground?" The Red-tailed Hawk is still there as we drive up to inspect our limp pigeon. As soon as the car nears, the hawk launches off the tree and heads for the river bottoms. Upon inspection, nothing is wrong with the stupid pigeon. To this day we can't understand why it didn't fly when tossed out of the car window. The vest fit fine and no snares had tangled the pigeon's wings. Mike retires our uncooperative pigeon on the spot and drives off in search of new trapping opportunities. After two hours of unsuccessfully scouring the Jessenland roads, we stop into Uncle Dave's and Aunt Arlene's store in Blakeley.

Their property takes up almost half of the block at the corner of Main Street totaling three buildings; residence/store, old bank building, and Dave's newly constructed body shop. They converted the old bank building into an art studio where Dave paints scenic pictures which they display throughout the store above all the groceries.

We love visiting our Aunt Arlene and Uncle Dave, not only because they always give us something for free at the downstairs store, but they are always interested in how things are going for us and the rest of the family in Belle Plaine.

Dave and Arlene are known by 100 percent of the local residents to be about the coolest people to walk the planet. When they moved from Belle Plaine to Blakeley, most everyone in

David, Arlene, Glo, and Sonny

the small town treated them as if they were rock stars. Which they are! Both Dave and Arlene were very attractive looking circus performers, she a pretty, lean brunette and he, a built-like-a-brick-shit-house sandy blonde. They had both grown up on the circus and each were seasoned performers who had thrilled audiences from Minnesota to as far as Texas. Dave is also admired for being a navy veteran who served as an aircraft mechanic in California. Most important, Dave is the second son to the circus legend himself, Grandpa Leo!

They brought the little town of less than two hundred something new and exciting to look forward to, especially the local kids. When Grandpa Leo and Uncle Dave would go out on the road during the fair season, they would always bring along two local young boys from Blakeley to be circus flunkies. Both Leon and Lloyd are very popular around Belle Plaine and their popularity, along with ours, skyrocketed after that first year out on the road. There was nobody more jealous of their good fortune than me. And to spice things up in that little town, Dave always puts on a yearly huge Fourth of July party where anything goes. There is always a band playing and keg beer on hand for all. Any age, it does not matter. A twelve-year-old can carry a plastic keg cup with them all around the huge gathering. He teams up with his local friend and boxing partner, Spit Martin and they put on a party like no other anywhere! There are firecracker fights along with guns shot right out in the open. As a sharpshooter on the circus, Uncle Dave has no inhibitions as he pulls out his handgun right out in the open and takes a shot at

one of his favorite targets. The greatest thing about Blakeley is there are no police patrols, so it is pretty much lawless...

After a free ice cream push up and soda pop, we are off to another area. Mike spots a pair of Red-tails riding the thermals several hundred feet above the road. The hawks are involved in a courting ritual where the male gains altitude by ringing up above the female. Suddenly he closes his wings and drops out of the sky, the larger female waits until he is almost upon her before she rolls on her back to meet him with outstretched talons. We pull off the road to watch the show through field glasses for a while before driving on. Though we valiantly try, we can find no opportunity to use the noose cages. Dejected and almost out of gas, we head home. Like fishing, not all outings succeed, and the same thing goes for capturing natural born killers.

With several trapping attempts now under his belt and after adjusting the BAL-CHATRI, Mike is confident that he can capture any predator bird at will. The following weekend, we pass Dave and Arlene's store, cross the Blakeley Bridge, take a left on the Jessenland road and sure enough, not over two miles past the Jessenland church, a yearling Red-tailed Hawk sits on the top of a wooden telephone pole. While looking out a set of binoculars and steering the wheel with his knees, Mike coolly tells me, "Get ready Dale. See him up on the left? I'm going to slow the car down and when I tell you, open the door and throw the trap off the shoulder of the road." As we approach the yearling, he drops the binoculars on the seat, slows the car and just as he passes the bird tells me calmly, "Now." I opened the door, throw out the trap. It lands in perfect position off the road sitting upright. Then, I hold the door closed until we are a half mile down the road.

Mike turns the car around, parks on the shoulder and then brings his binoculars up to his eyes, but before they reach them, he can see that the hawk has begun its swoops to the trap in pursuit of our bait. Within seconds the Red-tailed Hawk is caught in the noose snares and then drags the cage out into the open plowed field. Mike throws the car in drive, speeds to the hawk, parks the car and we both run to the trap while he puts on his heavy leather welding gloves. We have to work quickly before the nylon snares cut into the hawk's legs. The hawk lays on its back in a defensive position, feathers ruffled, wings half spread and hisses like a demon. Mike reaches into his falconry bag and places a leather hood

Trapping hawks with the BAL-CHATRI

over the hawk's head which immediately calms the crazed bird down. The hood confuses the bird making it impossible to see anything and is now relaxed enough to take care of other business. After freeing its leg from two of the snares, he then fits them with jesses, attaches the swivel, and a long leather leash. As soon as we arrive back home, several photographs are taken of Turak and the wild Red-tailed Hawk, Mike holding one and Lena holding the other. After the photos are captured on film, Mike set it free. Now that he is a successful trapper of hawks, he does so often, and it isn't always by throwing the BAL-CHATRI out the car door.

Turak II is weathering on her ring perch in the backyard while Mike is cutting up several gophers Tom and I captured at the cemetery. The sun is shining brightly and the mild temperature feels great after the long winter and cold spring. Mike glances up to find his Red-tailed Hawk peering intently at something across the yard near one of the tree lines along a field behind our property. Captive hawks are great spotters of migrating raptors. Often Mike observes one of his captive birds just staring into the clouds. When he glasses the sky, there is always some hawk or eagle riding the thermals. Even without the binoculars, he can see that his hawk is watching a pair of Kestrels hovering above the meadow about 300 yards away. As it is well into summer, he knows they are hunting and not involved in courtship behavior. He waits until they drift off and quickly checks the snares on his noose cage trap.

After a few adjustments, he places two of his dark domestic mice along with a couple pieces of dry dog food in the BAL-CHATRI, grabs a folding stool, runs across the yard and into the meadow. He finds a spot on the edge of the field and places the trap on the stool to get it off the ground, so he can watch it closely from our house. Sitting at the kitchen table he begins his vigil. Maybe an hour later, one Kestrel appears and perches in a tree near the trap. Bobbing its head and flicking its tail it eyes the two mice below, then makes a quick stoop (*dive*) at the bait, before it sails to a tree closer to the trap. Almost as soon as it lands in the tree, it stoops again, this time landing on the trap and dancing around trying to get at the mice. He holds his binoculars right on the hawk waiting for it to become caught in the nooses. When the tiny falcon tries to raise one of its feet towards its head, it can't, and Mike knows it's caught. He races out the door and across the backyard. If the hawk is not securely snared, he doesn't want to lose it. On approach, he can see his worries are unfounded as the bright yellow feet on the big female Kestrel are tangled in several fish line nooses.

As Mike untangles the feet of his newly caught Sparrowhawk, he marvels at her beauty. His first Kestrel was a passage or first-year bird and did not have the rich, bright colors of a mature falcon. This is the first time he's seen an adult bird up close, and the difference between her and Kee 1 are striking. She has bright yellow feet with a cere *(the waxy yellow skin at the base of the beak in which the nostrils are located.)* that matches her rich plumage

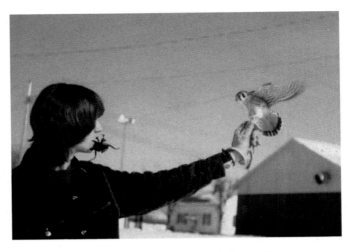

**Mike and Kee; Uncle Dave's body shop
in the background**

of orange-rust shades above and cream below. The mustache is very dark and pronounced and the area around her eyes is also bright yellow. He has never seen such a beautiful bird! After freeing her from the snares, he places her in a small nylon stocking with the toe area cut out to keep her immobile. Trap and stool in the other hand, and it's back home to begin the manning session.

Mike's new Kestrel advances quickly through the training process, and it soon becomes his favorite hawk. Seems like he spends more time with her than his Red-tailed Hawk. Though tiny, as a true falcon, she is the closest thing to a Peregrine he can possess. More than anything, he dreams of owning and flying a Peregrine Falcon, but due to the rarity of this Cadillac of falconry, he may as well wish for a Bald Eagle, another bird beyond his reach. The eagle too is on the endangered species list-brought to the brink of extinction from the pesticide DDT. Mike wrote to The Department of The Interior requesting a permit to keep a Bald Eagle but was turned down flat. So, he has to settle for the common Red-tailed Hawk and American Kestrel. Still, he is a practicing falconer and reminds himself this had only been a dream a few short years ago.

He always looks forward to the weekend. A couple days off school plus only having to work at the Chevy dealership Saturday mornings gives him a day and a half to fly his birds. Off work, Saturday at noon he showers, changes clothes and grabs his hawking gear, but feeling guilty about neglecting Turak, he flies her first. She is particularly "keen" and performs perfectly, flying to the fist and the lure without a hitch. Sometimes she's stubborn and sits in a tree or on the roof of our house ignoring his attempts to call her down until she gets good and ready. When finished feeding, he puts her out to weather in the yard. Then, he takes Kee from the hawk house and walks across the yard to the meadow where he'd caught her a few months back. It's another

windy day, but she is doing so well that he dismisses waiting until the gusts die down and prepares to fly her anyway. At the last moment, he decides it will probably be better to fly her on the creance line first to see how she reacts to the windy conditions. After all, he almost lost his first Kestrel on a day just like today. With the swivel and leash still attached to her jesses, he set her on a fence post before taking the creance out of his hawking pouch. As he reaches for her leash to attach the long line, a strong gust of wind catches her open wings and she is off and up in an instant, swivel, and leash dangling from her jesses. He can't believe it, he has done it again! A moment of complacency is all it took, now she, like his first Kestrel is facing a slow death should the leash get tangled in the trees. Ringing higher and higher in the air she drifts with the wind across HWY 169 and beyond any chance of rescue.

The only thing Mike can do is follow her in flight. Perhaps she will descend and perch on a fence post where he can get his hands on the leash. Running as fast as he can, he keeps her in sight as she drifts further and further out of town across the prairie and crop fields. After chasing the speck in the sky, he watches her land in the top of a tall tree in a dairy farmer's pasture. By the time he reaches the hawk, he can see her leash is tangled in a tree branch. He racks his brain trying to come up with something, any plan to rescue her. The only thing that comes to his mind is to call Sonny and me to get there pronto. Maybe the three of us together can figure out some plan. He runs to the nearby farmhouse and sees the farmer coming out of an outbuilding. The farmer looks at him in a strange way as Mike explains his problem. When he asks the farmer if he can use his phone, the guy cocks his head sideways and asks him, "What are you doing, keeping a "chicken hawk" as a pet?" After getting Sonny on the phone and explaining the situation, Sonny tells Mike to get back to the hawk, "I'll be there in ten minutes."

To Mike, it must have seemed like an eternity but soon we approach in the family car. He is surprised to see Sonny walking across the pasture carrying his .22 rifle; what in the world does he have in mind? After looking the situation over, he tells Mike he will shoot the branch that the leash is caught in. We have seen Sonny use the old Marlin .22 effectively squirrel hunting, taking most squirrels my brothers and I treed right through the head. He once shot a quarter through the middle at 25 paces behind the city dump. That feat, which simply amazed us, was done without a scope, only a peep sight. We know he can shoot but hitting a pencil sized branch blowing in the wind in a treetop seems impossible. We just stand back shaking our heads. Sonny's first shot misses, as does the second. Mike's telling me it'll never happen when Sonny's third shot rings true and Kee, the leash, and broken branch slowly drift to the ground at the base of the tree! After she's on Mike's fist, none the worse for the

ordeal, we examine the branch actually smaller in diameter than a pencil. This is the most amazing feat of marksmanship we've ever seen. Sonny has saved the day and the memory of that magnificent shot he made is something we'll never forget. For us, it is The Shot Heard Round the World!

Found and Lost

Now that the worst part of 'the hill' nightmare is over, my trips to the bowling alley have increased, and I'm once again hanging out down here any time I can sneak in. I've gained back enough trust from both Mark and Greg that they dare be seen with the "NARC" of Belle Plaine. Although they are the same two troubled teens who helped contribute to my demise in the first place, and tease me relentlessly, I miss the excitement of the downtown nightlife scoring, drinking alcohol, and smoking cigarettes care-freely down in the bowling alley. I've also arrived back on the scene ready and willing to participate in just about everything forbidden by dear old Sonny to further prove my worth to my rebel friends. But, they both know that Sonny is as strict as pipe iron and the mere fact that I'm trying to regain their friendship, behind his menacing back, has won me over more than anything. Although Mark still throws out the occasional, "Leo Albrecht put it in the paper..." headline, he does it as a running joke because it always receives a chuckle from the boys. Besides, if I followed Sonny's rules to the tape-line as a good Catholic teenager should, I would have never seen the girl that makes up her eyes like 'Grace Slick' of the band, "Jefferson Airplane."...

The sound of her shoes skipping down the basement stairs draw my eyes away from the bowling balls slamming into pins, as I lock onto a very cute, young, teenage girl. My first thought is, "Wow, I hope she's coming to see me!" This stranger is about the prettiest little thing that I've seen around this town in a long, long time, and I momentarily wonder, where she came from? Even though she is traveling down those stairs at a fast pace, I see her take each step in what seems like slow motion. She is dressed as though headed for a wedding dance or a local ballroom. Her form-fitting, blue dress does not cover her adorable little figure, which exposes the curves of an emerging young woman. Nor can the black nylons, which ride high on her thighs, conceal her shapely legs. But the first thing that catches my attention is her curly, dark brown hair, naturally highlighted with a reddish tint, flowing loosely an inch or two below her shoulders. Although she tilts her head slightly downward watching the steps, I get a peek of her big brown eyes coated with a liberal dose of black eyeliner and mascara. Her dark features along with her high rounded cheekbones resemble those of a pretty Indian Maiden. From her distant profile, I can barely make out the silhouette of her upper lip as it comes to a slight outward point at the crest, tucked below a delicate, rounded nose. One thing is certain, I haven't seen enough of her. I want to get a closer look! But when she reaches the basement floor, instead of heading my way and

into my life, she quickly turns and walks into the connecting bar room.

With thousands of scenarios playing out in my head, I curiously keep an eye toward the direction of the other room hoping to get another glimpse of the mysterious girl gracing my hang out. But, before I enact any of the scenarios, those shoes heard only minutes earlier, are now skipping back up the stairs. I quickly turn around, but all I can see is the back of her blue dress, black nylons and her wild, curly hair bouncing with each step, and then she's gone!

I find it hard to believe when I say to Mark, "Wow! Who was that?" while still staring at the top of the bowling alley steps. He responds with an angry and cocky smirk, "Don't get any ideas about 'Bobbie Jo' Albright because she's going out with my brother Donny." I was never any good at math, but I can figure this simple equation out in a hurry. Mark is my age, Bobbie Jo probably the same age as my little sister Mary, thirteen and Donny is about nineteen! Oh my God! Not only is Donny six years older than Bobbie Jo, but he is one of the biggest losers in town and constantly in trouble with the law. It just makes little sense. I wonder if Mark is telling me the truth because I sure as hell don't believe it. Bobbie Jo has shown herself for a reason this memorable evening and someday, I'll discover why. Unfortunately, that someday takes three months.

While sitting bored with Chip in our regular booth smoking cigarettes and shooting the shit, I keep a wary eye on the entrance to the bowling alley bar room. Tonight might be the night that Bobbie Jo will come waltzing in here along with her three sisters acting as if they own the place and when she does I'll be here to get a better look at her. But with the hour hand touching nine and still no sign of her, chances of her showing up this late are slim to none. Another night of watching and waiting for Bobbie Jo to make her appearance has gone by the wayside. Frustrated, I take my eye off the entrance, but keep it on the clock because I have to be home in time to meet Sonny's strictly enforced 10:30 curfew. With an hour and fifteen minutes to kill I head for the foosball table, so I can work on my forward push, kick and slap shot.

Somewhere out of the heavens, a lone figure of a teen girl strolls cautiously into the bar room and starts timidly heading toward the bar. I can't believe it! She is the girl I have been searching for and dreaming about for months! Better still, Bobbie Jo is alone and only a few yards away! A little chill runs up and down my spine as I stand mystified watching her make her way guardedly towards the bartender. I've pictured thousands of different scenarios of what our first meeting would be like, but no scenario provides me with this easy opportunity to make a first captivating impression. She passes right on by me, like I'm invisible, with an expression of worry etched across her brow as

she approaches the bar and then nervously waits for the owner to take her order. Not only have my many prayers finally been answered, but poured onto me a thousand fold because I didn't get to see her up close the first time, but the good Lord has given me a chance to do so now.

I walk right up next to her without regard just as she is sheepishly ordering two packs of cigarettes. That explains her nervous footsteps to the bar, but did I just hear her order 'two' packs of cigarettes? She notices me leaning on the bar next to her, but stays focused on the owner bringing two packs of Marlboro reds, probably wondering, if he will ask her age. This thirteen-year-old farm girl smokes, and she smokes the same cigarettes as I do. What can I say to her? Maybe something smart-ass that will draw any response. And then a 'brilliant' thought pops into my head and out of my mouth. "What are you, a chain smoker?" a cocky tone with a slight grin thrown in behind it for effect. My timing is off because she's busy handing two dollar bills to the owner, swooping up the cigarettes and quickly slipping them into her coat pocket. Turning to my voice, she looks at me as if pleasantly surprised and then looks deeper into my eyes, "No, I only get to town once a week, so I buy my cigarettes when I can," speaking as if I'm her first cousin. I like the sound of her voice! Then she turns and uneasily scans the bar room to see if she might recognize some relative or adult who may have seen her buying the cigarettes and tell her mom.

Even though my elbow 'strategically placed' on the top of the bar helps hold the ton of weight bearing down on my knees, I keep my cool 'Outsiders' image intact while wondering what I might say next, or should I just stand here staring at her? Those big brown eyes, high rounded cheekbones, cute little puffy lips all magnified in front of me by the power of ten. From this night forward, I will never forget her face again! I study her closer like I had studied Grace Slick's wild look that day in our bedroom while turning the pages of the Woodstock Festival book which Mike had crowned on the top rack of his bookshelf. Bobbie Jo is again wearing the heavy dose of eyeliner and black mascara mirroring Grace Slick, but it looks as though she applied it rather hurriedly. Her wild hair is a little tamer as if she quickly ran a brush through it once, or maybe twice. That form-fitting blue dress that lay etched in my mind and the one I was expecting to see her wearing is now replaced with blue jeans and a grey winter coat making her appear more like an everyday farm girl. That is, an everyday farm girl with a foxy-foxy look about her.

I wonder if she might be slightly interested in me? I want to find out! "Do you want to play a game of foosball?" "Sure, why not," she says as she stuffs the change into the pocket of her blue jeans. Hmm… During the game I keep my eyes glued on her instead of the ball, studying her every move, watching as she

spins the handles instead of flicking them with her wrist, and giggling every time the foot of the player connects with the ball shooting it across the soccer field floor.

When the game ends, she strolls slowly twenty feet to the jukebox with a glancing eye cocked toward me ten feet behind, stops and then pretends to look through the songs; again peeking at me out the corner of her left eye. I slip up beside her and we go through the list of songs picking out our favorite. She rests her finger just below 'Carly Simon's' "Anticipation." I point to 'Led Zeppelin's' "Stairway to Heaven." Grandpa Leo always tells me to, "Strike while the iron is hot," and I always trust good old Grandpa Leo's wisdom. I daringly lean in below her, look up directly into her gorgeous eyes and whisper toward her ear over the music blaring out of the jukebox, "Let's go," while motioning with my head towards the stairs five feet to our rear. To my delightful surprise, she answers with a downward nod, "OK" and we are off, heading up those lovely stairs and out onto the downtown streets leaving my friend Chip behind guessing. I am in Hoddy-Boddy Land! Bobbie Jo is walking right next to me. Just she and I alone, almost touching! I never thought this far ahead, never thought that after meeting her, we'd be walking almost hand in hand together. Grandpa Leo's words of wisdom are again, right on the money and this time they pay off in huge dividends.

"Where are we going," she asks? I have no clue, "Just for a walk" I beam and show her my best smile while 'accidentally' brushing up against her shoulder. I should steer her to the quiet street that goes by St. Peter and Paul Church less than a block away, but we instead cross over it walking along the main drag toward the four corner center of town. We hadn't gone an entire city block, and she leaves me standing on the sidewalk. She peeks into the small window centered in the solid wooden door of the Red Door Bar. "Wait out here for me, I have to go inside for a minute." I discover why. As she opens the door, I see Donny sitting in a booth near the back with some friends sipping on a glass of draft beer. I feel a little uneasy standing here just outside the bar with Bobbie Jo inside checking in with her much older and bigger boyfriend, but she's back in a flash. She pokes her head halfway out of the red door and meekly apologizes, "I need to go back inside, I'm sorry. Maybe I'll see you again sometime?" Then she hesitates for a moment before tucking her head back inside and closing the door.

While walking back to the bowling alley, I replayed our short time together repeatedly in my mind. Then I realize that it's true, she is still seeing nineteen-year-old, Donny. I heard he was going out with some other girl from Blakeley around the same age as Bobbie Jo. Oh well, at least I saw her face up closer than I thought I ever would. I know what her voice sounds like, and I also know that Donny is only a few months away from marine Boot Camp! So, there is still a shred of hope I could go out with

her someday. If nothing else, I have something more to dream about tonight and beyond.

Back at the Bowling Alley, Chip and I are again sitting in the booth discussing my encounter with Bobbie Jo twenty minutes earlier. All the sudden, I sense a shadow nearing and then stopping right beside me. I turn to look and can not believe that it's Bobbie Jo staring directly at me from less than two feet away with both hands stuffed into her coat pockets. She says not a word; not even a hello? I do a double take. I try to remain cool and collective, knowing just a few minutes before, she had left me hanging out to dry like a pair of Uncle Gary's jeans on Grandma Angela's clothesline. "Hey, you want to go riding around with me and my sister Billie Jo?" She shyly asks. I'm surprised! I don't know what happened at the Red Door Bar nor do I care, but I can only guess she was bored to tears sitting in a booth with a bunch of older drunks uneasily taking sips off a beer behind the bartender's back. Most likely, she excused herself to look for the cute blue-eyed-blonde who's just a little closer to her age and who had boldly walked up to her at the bar just moments earlier. My mind raced, hell yes, I want more than anything to go driving around with Bobbie Jo, but I can't just leave Chip sitting here all alone, "Do you mind if Chip tags along with us?" She replies, "Sure, why not?"

Out in front of the bowling alley sits a green Chevrolet Impala with the engine still running. Sitting behind the steering wheel patiently waiting is her older sister Billie Jo. She's eager to meet her little sister's newly found fascination. Being the gentleman, I was taught to be, I open the bowling alley door for Bobbie Jo. She runs to the front car door, quickly opens it, merrily slides over on top of the bench seat right up next to Billie Jo leaving the front passenger door open, "Climb in and sit up front" patting her right hand once on the top of the stiff fabric. I ease in beside her and close the door as Chip hops in the back. I can't believe that I'm really touching her after all these months of searching. Not only that, but I'm sitting right next to this wild little farmer and to think that she might actually like me at that. Poor Chip sits alone in the back seat quietly watching the show unfold in the front.

As we leave the bright lights of the downtown and those first anxious moments behind us, we enter into the darker part of the main drag, the mood in the front seat mellows along with the change in lighting. And then as if programmed, Roberta Flack's lovely voice joins the soft keys of the piano playing out of the front center speaker, "The first time ever I saw your face..." Bobbie Jo's silhouette barely visible against the glow of the dashboard lights. She hasn't a clue that I've been in love with her for months. At this very moment, I'm placing that soft image of her face to the words of the song forever in my mind.

After pulling about a half dozen traditional Belle Plaine "U" turns, I still can't believe that I'm in the same car, now leaning comfortably against Bobbie Jo. I have a hard time keeping my eyes off her without making it appear too obvious. I'm savoring every ounce of this evening's good fortune observing her shyness, yet her cockiness as well. She's a little rough around the edges like the girls found living on the "Greasers" side of town. Bobbie Jo seems a tad bit uneasy or rather fidgety sitting so close, then again, maybe she is a little nervous driving around with me while the guy she is supposed to be with sits drunk and loud-mouthed in the Red Door Bar. She appears nervous in a hyper sort of way to where it seems as though she needs to catch a fresh breath of air every so often. She just can't seem to sit still, the way she shifts about on the bench seat.

It doesn't take long for me to figure out that she's a little bashful and somewhat immature, but like me, not afraid to take chances! She's already taken two this night: *first* by accepting my invitation to the great outdoors and *second*, by boldly approaching me after her rendezvous with Donny at the Red Door Bar. She seems so innocent, but yet so untamed. Her wild look masks her uneasy persona well, and I can tell I want to see more of this girl!

Man did I hate it when it came time to embarrassingly pronounce, "I have to be home in fifteen minutes to make my 10:30 curfew." "Wow, 10:30, why so early, can't you see if you can stay out longer?" Bobbie Jo coos before shooting me a subtle glance. "There is no way in hell that I would even think to ask my parents, heck they're in bed now waiting for my knock on their bedroom door." The girls thought 10:30 was harsh since they didn't even have a curfew. They could stay out all night long if they wanted to. I wonder what they will do after they drop me off. Bobbie Jo immediately turns around, asks and then tells Chip, "Where do you live? We'll drop you off first." Oh, so little Bobbie Jo is now purposely guiding the ship into unventured waters. Talk about a bold move, and although I like her train of thought, this young, 'experienced' farm girl has me just a tad bit anxious as the old circus lot draws nearer. When we round the final turn onto Raven Street, time quietly slows down, and then it stands deafly still.

Nearing the driveway I say, "There is my house on the right Billie Jo. Just pull up along the curb. Thanks for the ride." Turning toward Bobbie Jo and again following Grandpa Leo's teachings to the letter, I place my left hand gently around the back of her neck and rest my right hand on her left shoulder. The heck with a goodnight hug as I bring my lips close to hers while watching her eyes drift shut. Her lips await my arrival. I'm pushing it, but I can't let this moment pass without touching her lips to mine. At the same time, I want to leave her with a lasting impression of me. Billie Jo sits there good-naturedly

staring at the wheel. I can only imagine what she is thinking as she watches her little sister out of the corner of her eye, gently receiving soft, excitable kisses from a soft-faced, long-blonde-haired boy who lives in a freshly built ranch house on the edge of town.

All that practice kissing girls up in the stockade might just as well have been thrown out the tin window. This first real kiss with my mystery girl feels so perfect, so natural, and so much more passionate! I can tell that the little farm girl has done some kissing as well because she returns mine better than the girls that I've kissed. I have roughly a minute and a half to go before knocking on Sonny's bedroom door, and I use up every last second savoring our first kiss which I know, will last me a lifetime. Roberta Flack's earlier words continued playing out in my mind as the last seconds tick quickly by, "The first time ever I kissed your mouth..." Then I slowly pull away, pause six inches from my kiss and drink in one last look at her dreamy disposition, "Goodnight... Thanks again for the ride." I open the car door, look back at her once more before closing it and float toward the house without looking back again.

Bobbie Jo

While walking those final steps to the garage door, I hope and pray that I can kiss her again someday. Then I realize, I didn't think to ask her when I would see her again as I never thought that far ahead. I never thought I would kiss Bobbie Jo so lovely on our first night together. Realizing my big mistake, I turn around to go back to ask her, but by then their car is halfway to Meridian Street. Now my search for her must start all over again! I wonder how long it will take to find her this time.

I want to tell the world or at least one of my three brothers or two sisters about my new found little fox, but unfortunately, the house is quiet and dark, so I go through the painstaking chore of checking in with Mom and Dad and then head downstairs to my empty bedroom. I take in one last whiff of her perfume still clinging to my shirt and throw it in the closet. I don't plan on washing it until her scent is no longer there.

Lighting up the Town

"Guess who I kissed Friday night?" I turn and whisper out the side of my mouth to Burney sitting behind me in political science class. Before he has time to think about who it might be, I answer my question with a wide smirk, "Bobbie Jo." His dark brown eyebrows rise to touch the sides of his frizzy center-parted bangs as his cheeks turn two shades darker red. "No way," the air drains from his large

Burney and Dale resting on the Jessenland hillside

chest and his shoulders drop as if he'd just been kicked in the stomach by a thoroughbred horse. "Yea, no shit, it was a French kiss, and it was long, too!" After class, I tell him all about how that kiss came to be and what it felt like. Burney has a thing for Bobbie Jo, having almost said as much while answering my questions about her over the previous few weeks. I also know that the one thing he has always wanted to do but never has is to kiss Bobbie Jo the way I kissed her a few days earlier. As I tell him the story about how the night unfolded, his mind wanders and I can almost tell from the twinkle in his green Irish eyes, that he's envisioning himself on the receiving end of those cute puffy lips. When I end this dreamlike evening's story, I describe to Burney our first kiss and Bobbie Jo's spellbound expression as I calmly say good night and exit the car. I tell him I remember floating into the house, without looking back. He mumbles just above a whisper, "That baby soft skin..." while glaring somewhere on the other side of Hoddy-Boddy Land.

Burney lives out in the country on the family farm, but he isn't what you call the traditional farm boy. He need not tend to cows or work in the fields like the O'Hanion twins who live one farm down the gravel road that sits alongside CR 19. Even though he is old enough to work the farm, his dad is already retired and renting out his land to other farmers around the area. Sometimes to Green Giant headquartered in Bobbie Jo's town of Le Sueur. His much older siblings all live in or around Belle Plaine. Some of which are already raising their growing families. The six-foot one inch, two-hundred-pound, hometown football defensive lineman

is constantly on the move traveling to neighboring farms or visiting friends or family. However, he spends most of his time hanging around the streets of Belle Plaine and usually camps out at one of his older brothers' or sisters' homes instead of his farm out in the country with his two aged parents.

My new best friend is the complete opposite of Mark's rebellious character. Burney has a squeaky clean athletic dispose about him. My parents think he's the greatest friend I've ever had, and Glo often invites him to stay for dinner. Neither of my parents like Mark or Chip, but they like Burney. It didn't take him long to lay on the charm and win them over outright. However, I know the darker side of Burney and that is the side that attracts me to him. He displays a different personality in front of coaches, teachers, and adults than he does around his friends. Behind the scenes, Burney loves to party and does so often. He also loves his marijuana as much as me. We often skip class and get stoned (Always off his stash!) Besides knowing where to get his hands on some good weed, he knows everyone, including my 'mystery girl.' He is the only person I know of who knows where Bobbie Jo lives. His parent's farm is only a few miles from hers and he's been there on at least two separate occasions. One time, he even laid down on the couch with her while watching TV in their living room. Until her mother, Elaina saw them and told them to knock it off! Even though I haven't asked him yet, I'm hoping that he will be the one to show me exactly where her farm is located and possibly deliver me right to her front doorstep.

I've only come across Bobbie Jo a couple of times this past winter and all were by chance meetings. At 14, I still rely on my boots to get me around, so my travel is somewhat limited. She lives ten miles 'somewhere' on the other side of the rainbow. She attends Le Sueur High School; tack on another five miles. We may as well be on opposite sides of the world. I'd love nothing more than to call her on the phone, but I don't have her number, and even if I did, I can't afford to make the expensive long distance call. Our only chance of getting together rests with her three older sisters who cruise into town unannounced a few times a month. Every time the girls pile into the old green Chevrolet heading to Belle Plaine, Bobbie Jo looks for me. Instead of waiting for her return to the bowling alley, I spend more time on the downtown streets watching for the girl's car.

Meanwhile, my climbing for or assisting Mike has become even more intense. I would say that his desire to capture and train birds of prey has grown into more than a little bit of an obsession. Now that it's nesting season, he has two Great Horned Owl nests mapped out along with several Red-tailed Hawk nests. He even has located a pair of American Kestrels residing along the Jessenland road but is still searching for their elusive nesting tree. He and Lena are fortunate to find and rent a beautiful old farmhouse only a few miles out of town which features a barn and several outbuildings. One of which he turns into a large (mews) or hawk house. It's spacious enough to accommodate a Kestrel, a Red-tailed Hawk, besides his most sought after Great Horned Owl. Mike sends me up every tree imaginable to satisfy his quest

Dale posing with baby crows

to fill his new hawk house, most of which are the highest and most difficult in the woods. We also have our goal set on finding a crow's nest and possibly snagging one or two of those. Interestingly enough, our fascination with crows stems from none other than our beloved Grandpa Leo who stated that he had a pet crow as a boy. This bird was part of his sideshow in his first circus back in 1899.

Grandpa Leo also tells us these birds are interesting and inquisitive pets, all are great mimics, and that some even talk. Naturally, we have to have one! So, Mike goes out in search of one and soon locates a nest in Pine Grove not over two football fields away from "The Wooden Fence." Eager to check the contents of the nest, Mike comes back to town, grabs me and tells me to bring along my climbing gear. As we approach the tree, the mother flies off the nest which is a good sign she is tending to something up there. Unfortunately, I find no hatchlings but find eggs. No matter, I lower a few eggs to Mike who places them in an incubator borrowed from one of his teachers at school. The eggs hatch with no problems, but despite keeping the hatchlings warm and providing them with plenty of food, they're found dead two mornings later.

Not to be deterred, Mike and I go out searching for another nest, which we soon find in the same grove of cedars as the first. This time we let the mother care for her young while keeping a close watch on the progress of their growth with binoculars from down below. When feathered and hopping around the edges of the sticks, we make our move. I climb up the forty-foot tree and lower three babies in a sack down to Mike waiting patiently on the ground capturing photos of the climb. After taking a few more photos of the crows on my arms, I climb back up the tree returning one, so the mother won't come home to an empty nest. We kept one crow for ourselves and gave the other one to Young Buck.

We feed the baby crows dry dog food run through a hand grinder to which we add insects, night crawlers, some hamburger, raw eggs, and a vitamin supplement. Mike bent a small spoon to simulate the beak of a mother bird and uses this to get the gooey mixture into the open mouths of our babies. The chicks eat a lot and grow rapidly. They now look like adults, but still act like hungry children by extending their stretched necks, flapping their wings and crying out to us at feeding time. They are even winging their way around the yard and feeding on our outstretched fists, just as the hawks.

Grandpa Leo is correct because crows are very inquisitive and curious birds showing great interest in anything shiny. Our bird collects bottle caps, aluminum foil, gum wrappers, pocket change, and stashes it in the gutter on the roof of our house. Just for our entertainment, we throw rolled up tin foil into the air as the crow is flying overhead. Almost always, without fail, the bird catches it in his beak and then flies to the gutter placing his latest prize alongside the rest of his contraband. Since

Crow holding a piece of tinfoil in his beak before hiding his contraband in the gutter

the crows are allowed free reign, we often see them out and about the town. One of their favorite perches is on the Rexall Drug Store sign in the center of the downtown area. Our family receives an occasional phone call from people scared out of their wits because the crow attempts to land on their shoulder as they do us when it comes feeding time. It seems like everyone in town knows who brought these large menacing black birds into our quaint little town. Mike is known for being the bird man of Belle Plaine.

Our crow's ten minutes of fame comes one day in mid-July at the expense of an old lady who arrives for her visit with the

dentist across Willow Street next to our house. Tom, a few buddies and I are just hanging out in our yard with the crow flying around loose as usual but sticking close to us. He normally doesn't stray too far from our property unless something is happening in and around our neighborhood. If so, he flies over to satisfy his curiosity. Unfortunately for her, this day the little old lady's appointment with the dentist sparks his curiosity. She gets out of her car, puts her cane to the ground and begins her slow and unsteady march to the front doorsteps. The crow flies over to the tree above the car, then nonchalantly drops onto her shoulder, announces his arrival with a caw and she about poops herself. She throws the cane at least two dozen feet, screams as loud as the noon whistle, takes off running full speed for the entrance, and leaps inside the door. Despite our uncontrollable laughter, Sonny doesn't think it's funny after receiving a phone call from a very annoyed dentist. But when he questions us about it, we blame the incident on Young Buck's crow who already has a bad reputation for getting into much trouble.

Many of the local residents think that a single crow causes havoc and mischief around town when in reality, it is actually two, each displaying opposite personalities. Our crow is like Dr. Jekyll who stays close to our property and loves to hang out with family. Young Buck's crow is more like Mr. Hyde who spends most of his days flying around town bothering the general population. Sometimes Mr. Hyde wings his way down to our neck of the woods, grabs Dr. Jekyll, and takes him on a robbing spree. At any rate, the combination of stockade and horse pasture now complete with a pet crow winging its way around the old circus lots is more than we could have ever hoped for our ever growing Animal Kingdom.

Most everyone around town is talking about the Albrecht's latest in wild pets plucked from the woodland and now residing alongside the rest of the town folks. Our friends think Dr. Jekyll is about the coolest pet we've had and because he is such a unique character, we all make him the mascot for our tin fortress sitting atop railroad ties. We even leave a stockade window open for him when we aren't around, so he has a place to go if it rains.

In a somewhat unpretentious way, dear old Sonny's plans to provide his boys with nothing more than an innocent playhouse has backfired on him because the stockade is the teenage hangout, we use for everything but innocent child play. Because of the stockade, Tom and I are the envy of just about every young teenager in town, most of whom have slept overnight here on one or more occasion. We practically live here in the summer spending most of our time just goofing around with the neighborhood boys, sometimes kissing girls, smoking cigarettes or climbing up on the roof to look at and admire our nice big yard and pastureland for Sheba. The view from the roof is so good, we can see every car and truck traveling in the distance on HWY 169, besides viewing

Townsend's entire farm sitting kiddy corner across the hillside meadow.

It's been a busy spring and summer collecting all kinds of birds for Mike, but Tom and I have kept busy collecting a variety of stolen goods from downtown stores. To truly enjoy our fortress in the sky, we need to fill it with things that neither of us can afford, so we simply revert to our Robin Hood days. That is, steal from the rich and give to 'us' poor, and we didn't go it alone.

Tom and I taught all our thievery skills to the Spiekerman brothers. We have become good at our craft. It doesn't take us long to collect the variety of loot locked up securely inside an old green trunk given to us by good old Grandpa Leo. Our four foot long, two feet deep and three feet high treasure chest is the lone piece of furniture sitting against the tin fortress wall. Perhaps we mimic our crow the way he hides his stolen shiny objects inside the gutter of the house. Our trunk holds much plunder such as BB's, lighter fluid, cigarette lighters, cigarettes, matches, .22 caliber shells, wine tipped swisher sweets cigars, and a prized wind-up alarm clock with the red price tag of $20.00 still stuck to the top.

We head uptown two at a time, lift what we can and then come back to the stockade with lots of treasures bragging all the way. We have a saying we derived from a 7 UP commercial running on television where at the end a guy says, "The smell of success is never too sweet," and then laughs in a deep, deep voice. When Wile E. and I approach the stockade after one successful mission, Tom is waiting on the balcony and calls out from above, "How did the lift go?" I glance up and respond, "The smell of success is never too sweet!" He laughs his ass off. When we arrive inside our fortress, I plop down the new $20.00 alarm clock, a master padlock and two packs of Old Gold cigarettes.

Despite living under Sonny's strict set of rules and "sort" of going steady with Bobbie Jo, my rebellious defiance intensifies as I continue to stay one step ahead of dear old Dad and the long arm of the law. On a few rare occasions, Sonny visits the stockade, but thankfully never asks us to unlock the trunk so he can see what we have locked up inside. I cringed during one of his unexpected visits when his eyes fixated on the shiny new master paddle lock mounted to the top center of the trunks lid, but he never said a word. Either he respects our privacy or he is afraid to discover what the trunk holds; more than likely, it is the later of the two.

We started off stealing just for the thrill of it besides picking up a few things necessary for hunting or to supply our newfound smoking habits. But over time, we have become hooked on the illegal sport like a drug and carefully plan what we will steal ahead of time. Our next plan involves lighter fluid, beer, and a night sleeping out in the stockade.

The large black bird lands with a thud on the stockade's open window announcing his arrival with a loud cawing of, "Crow, Crow, Crow." He crouches low while turning his head left to right, up and down, before jumping onto the patched carpeted floor where Tom and I are sitting. We are hanging out with none other than the Spiekerman brothers. "Hey crow, you want to play?" I say as I grab a box of large stick matches from out of our green trunk and set it down next to him on the floor. Laughing, "Hey guys watch this shit man!" The crow immediately walks over to the two inch by a six-inch rigid cardboard box, steps up on the top and begins wildly pecking away at the small crack at the top of the very end. Once his beak makes its way inside, he slides the box open wide enough to pull out one of the stick matches. Then he drops it onto the carpet, holds it down with both feet

Crow wearing a pair of jesses

and nips away at the white-tipped sulfur end. As soon as the match ignites, he instinctively jumps two steps backward while blowing out the fire with his right wing. We all laugh each time the crow goes through his lighting and blowing out stick matches routine. After six black tipped matches lay scattered on the floor and my cigarette about finished, I say, "Here crow, have a smoke." I hold the filter end of my smoking cigarette towards him. He doesn't hesitate but a second or two grabs it with his beak and out the window he flies. No doubt he's heading to one of his favorite hangouts somewhere around the neighborhood. I can only imagine what the person on the street thinks as they look up and see a crow flying on by smoking a cigarette.

That afternoon we mirror our crow and collect select items to be used for later tonight, when the little town will be sleeping. Our first destination is the store on the southwest corner of Main and Meridian Street. There, we empty their shelf of seven cans of lighter fluid. We first secure the lighter fluid inside our green trunk and then traverse back and forth through the culvert tucked under HWY 169 stealing over a half of a case of beer and two packs of cigarettes from the gas station across the highway. The gas station is a perfect target because it's less than 300 yards from our launching platform.

By eleven o'clock, the beer is gone, the cigarettes are half smoked, the house is dark, and the time comes to engage in a little old-fashioned small town fun. It doesn't take us long to figure out what to do with empty beer bottles and tons of lighter fluid. With several cans of lighter fluid sticking out of the

back pockets of our blue jeans and a Molotov cocktail in hand, we slip down the stockade ladder and make our way to the alleyway a block away directly behind the football coach's house. "Light it," I whisper holding the explosive bottle in my outstretched hand. Tom lights the dampened cloth and I throw it out into the middle of the alley. When it hits, it explodes into a large ball of flames lighting up the block like a Christmas tree. None of us are expecting to be so exposed and visible without the cover of the previous darkness so we take off running, and don't stop until we reach the end of the block. We lay in the shadows watching and wondering how long it will take for that darn fire to burn itself out when Tom mutters, "Hey, I think we better go put that out, I don't want to leave here with that thing still burning." Regrettably, we all agree.

Little do we know our well-built football coach is waiting for us hidden behind a set of bushes in his yard? As we approach the flames, he jumps out and grabs Chip in one arm and Tomato in the other. "What are your names?" he demands while squeezing them nice and tight around their midsection! They strain to answer, "Chip Spiekerman, Craig Spiekerman," barely able to get their names out because he is squeezing them so tightly. As Tom and I witness the capture of our arson friends, we scramble and hide behind trees about fifteen feet away, then watch the drama unfold before our disbelieving eyes. "I know there are two more of you out there, where are you?" he loudly demands. "You better come out where I can see you and tell me who you are or I'm calling the police!" We nod to each other, begrudgingly show ourselves and announce our names. We feel sure that we are busted but good this time and that we will soon face the wrath of Sonny. "What are you kids doing?" the coach demands as he continues to hold Chip and Tomato in a tight bear hug. Tomato, the mastermind, and I might add pure genius, comes up with this line. "We were sleeping out heading over to visit friends when we came across the fire. We decided to put it out before it got out of control." Amazingly the coach buys the story, thanks us, and lets us go. "Head home now boys, I don't want to see you around here again." Yes, sir coach! We all sincerely answer.

Instead of heading home as the coach had ordered and as we all agreed, we take a left on Willow Street and head for the downtown area with several cans of lighter fluid still stuffed in the back pockets of our jeans. We stop near our old house to regroup and re-plan our next move. "That was close. Now what do we do? The night is still young!" Tom's answer comes in actions rather than words as he commences to pour lighter fluid across the tarred road. The rest of us join in the fun until the street is a soaking explosion itching for some heat. Tom lights a match and throws it on top of the streaming liquid which immediately causes a vibrant flame to shoot up and across the roadway. "Cool, come on let's go light some more stuff up!" We then sneak through

our old yard ending up in the familiar confines of our childhood
alleyway. About every third house, we fill upside down trash can
lids full of the remaining cans of lighter fluid torching them
off as we go. By the time our arsonists' play is complete, the
once dead and darkened alleyway is lit up with patches of fire
and smoke.

Euell the Great

When are we going to Bobbie Jo's farm?" I ask Burney while staring beyond his bobber floating motionless in the center of the sandpit watering hole; for what seems like forever. My long sought after visit to her farm has taken several weeks to set up and lots of hounding. Little do I know his escort service comes with strings attached. I thought we might visit the O'Hanion brother's farm tucked next to CR 19, hang out there for a while and then head on over to Bobbie Jo's afterward, but when Burney skips O'Hanion's and instead grabs his fishing pole, I know I'm in for a long wait. He can tell I am restless, so he makes a futile attempt to ease my anxiety, "We don't want to get there too early because the girls are still working out in the barn. Besides, we're going to stop by Borine's farm before heading over there to kill some more time. Relax Albright, we'll get there." So, I lay back looking up at the clouds dreaming of Bobbie Jo going about her daily chores inside the barn and wondering what her reaction will be like when she sees me ride up her driveway on the back of his 50CC motorcycle. The thought of that cute little farm girl pushing calves into their mother's udder only a few cornfields to the west, makes my anticipation grow even more. Burney finally packs up his fishing pole. We spend about a half hour visiting Borine's, (a name which fit her personality to a tee,) and before too long, he is pointing to Lloyd's farm about a half mile off in the distance.

As we turn onto the narrow gravel driveway heading toward the farmyard, I can't help but laugh as I see four girls scrambling from every exit of the crooked barn and running full speed for the house. A pack of barking dogs of all shapes, colors, and sizes run to greet us then follow alongside the motorcycle to the farmyard. They encircle us and continue barking up a storm along with two chained up bellowing coonhounds while we wait for Bobbie Jo to make her debut. A few minutes later, she steps shyly out the side door barefoot and timidly approaches us wearing a short, tight, blue, shirt, and fitted

Lloyd's farm on right side of tree line behind cornfield

jeans commanding the dogs by name to quiet down, including Snowflake; a long-haired white dog dragging her left rear limp leg. Bobbie Jo is also wearing an embarrassing smile because we had seen her running from the barn dressed in her farm wear, and we are standing among farm buildings badly in need of a paint brush.

There she stands in the raw, a petite and wild farm girl trapped beautifully inside her natural setting. Her true self exposed to me amongst the strong pig odor blowing about by the open winds and buildings that appear as if years of Minnesota's freezing temperatures and driving summer rains have overtaken the white paint. A second-hand tractor towing a weathered hay wagon parks ahead of a flat tire car anchored where it died there years before. Standing behind the old car is a detached car garage which is void its own car but replaced with odds and ends stacked halfway to the rafters. A couple of dozen chickens scatter and peck about the yard and it seems as if cats are in or around every building. The house is as Billie Jo had described it while driving around the streets of Belle Plaine: a white, two-story cedar sided farmhouse standing between cornfields on the left and farm buildings to the right. Lloyd's thirty cows are all inside the barn giving up the last round of milk for the day. Another fifty to sixty pigs rummage inside a muddy yard enclosed via old weathered boards; not all standing.

She stands directly across from me inside the edge of a mud puddle looking at me or down at the puddle while responding to questions posed from Burney. She only glances in his direction occasionally. I too look down at the mud puddle, but I am consumed with her dainty feet squeezing the mud between her toes. "Did we surprise you Bobbie Jo?" I look up and tease. "Yea, I never expected you guys in a hundred years. What brings you out here anyway?" She blushes speaking in a lower than normal tone. "I came to see you and wanted to see where you lived, and I can't believe I'm standing here. When are you coming into Belle Plaine again?" I throw her my best smile. "I'm not sure, maybe next Friday or Saturday night, I hope."

I want to step into her mud puddle and kiss her right here in front of Burney, the dogs or any of her three sisters peering out the window but can't get up the nerve to do so. Just as she is loosening up and feeling more comfortable inside her surroundings, Elaina carrying two metal buckets of pig feed yells, "Bobbie Jo, you need to get back to work." She apologizes and looks deep into my eyes, half smiles and says, "Thanks for coming out. I hope to see you this weekend," before swishing her feet through the water, turning around and heading back to the side door. I watch her until the door closes behind her and then hop on the back end of the running motorcycle and say, "Let's roll!"

The dogs again run and bark alongside us all the way to the end of that long driveway and another quarter mile down the gravel road. I keep my eyes fixed on the farm hoping to get one more glimpse of her heading back to the barn until the buildings disappear beneath the tops of the cornfield. All the while I'm thinking about those cute little toes playing in the mud puddle. I ride back to Burney's with mixed feelings... It was great seeing her and discovering where she lived, but I'm disappointed that the long-awaited trip to her farm only lasted for a few precious moments…

After almost a year of searching for each other, we finally exchanged phone numbers and addresses towards the end of the summer of 1974. Although we hardly ever make the expensive 40 cents minimum long distance phone call, we use a ten cent stamp and a letter stuffed into an envelope to communicate and plan for a weekend night. My homework suffers because the letters always take priority. I spend hours polishing them and the envelopes off with all sorts of different crazy decorative artworks. I keep her abreast of all the exciting things going on around the old circus lots: who is coming, going or whoever is hanging out in the family room down the hallway giving me crap while I try to write. Missed homework assignments, bad midterms, detention and skipping school at least once or twice a week top the list. I mailed this one off just the other day...

Yesterday, me and Burney skipped the last two hours of school. He drove, and we got stoned as usual ending up right in front of your high school. I wanted to go inside to look for you in the halls or peek through the classroom windows, but Burney was against the idea saying, "We'd probably get picked up or something." I also wanted to stick around until school got out to maybe surprise you at your bus, but that was an hour away so we hung out at the mall for a little while and pigged out on the way back at Dairy Queen. You asked me how it was going, now that I'm not grounded. This is the dullest night this week. Monday I got the highest I've ever been. Last night, I went drinking with Tomato, Chip, and Tom. Today, I got detention for getting kicked out of class. The principal left for an hour and a half to run some errands, and we had the run of the place. Races down the halls, then cocking off to the teachers, girls and the janitor too. And now, I'm writing a letter to you with a beer in my hand, wishing I could use the phone.

Our town has its fair share of colorful characters always doing something out of the ordinary or giving me something interesting to write to her…

Reese Cup and Smite were driving around town dragging a couple cobs of corn. The cop pulled them over and asked, "What in the hell are you doing with that corn dragging on the back of your car?" Whereas Smite answered, "We were trying to catch a pig, and it looks like we did." Or the time John Stier finally

*climbed up the water tower in the wee hours of the morning with
Lee Blume ten feet behind. Unfortunately, a local cop drove up
and parked a half a block away and sat there for forty-five
minutes. When they saw the cop's headlights approaching, they
froze halfway up the steel rungs and waited patiently for him to
leave. Two minutes into their wait, a can of paint fell out of
John's pocket and bounced off Lee's forehead before falling to
the ground. Lee held onto the steel rungs even though an open
gash bled from his forehead. Nonetheless, when the cop finally
drove off, they continue their mission to the top painting "1974"
in large print across the large tower's front.*

This year, I started working for The Garage, a second time
joining both Mike and Tom who started here through the School
Work for Credit Program. I began working here at age 12 starting
at 25 cents an hour, but when a state inspector paid The Garage a
visit and discovered that I was underage and on the payroll, Fred
was forced to let me go. The state also required The Garage to
compensate me for the difference between what they were paying me
and the minimum wage for all those hours. Sonny called me into
his bedroom a few weeks later and showed me the check written for
over $800.00. He told me that Fred was a good man for hiring me.
He said that I should sign the check and hand it back over to The
Garage. I had never seen that much money before, but as they say,
easy come easy go. I reluctantly did as he had requested.
Swallowing hard, I signed the back of the large check.

I love working at The Garage because it is nice getting away
from school in the afternoons, and it also gives me some extra
spending money. I spend a lot of the money on presents for Bobbie
Jo like jewelry, and a green silk shirt she wore for her school
picture. Besides the money and the time away from school, I also
like working here because it is a blast.

Stepping into The Garage is like stepping into a three-ring
circus with Sonny Albright directing his three boys, his brother
Gary, and the rest of the crew. I often wonder how the owners
Fred and Paul put up with the likes of Mike, Tom and me, all
working here along with our Uncle Gary infamous for operating his
meticulously maintained lube rack. Fred handles the maintenance
and parts end of the business whereas Paul handles the sales end.
Perhaps each of their position's fit their personalities well
because Fred seems always the worry wart and all business while,
cool Paul dresses sharply, wears a million dollar smile,
constantly chews gum, and takes everything in stride. Paul is
smooth, for example when his wife walked in his office one day
while he was sneaking a cigarette, he quickly set it in the
ashtray facing opposite of him and told her that a customer had
just stepped out. Yes, Fred is the quiet one and Paul, the
outgoing brother, but both always try to make customers happy. A
slew of characters works here as well! Besides the behind the
scenes fun, Keups has quite a reputation for being fair and

honest with its customers and dam good at what they do. Many customers drive all the way from Minneapolis to have their car serviced.

Bump still lives across the alley from The Garage. I often see him about his property or standing in the large garage doors visiting with the mechanics. Mike knows that I want a Screech Owl for myself and tells me to talk to Bump as he had years earlier. "I think Bump has a Screech Owl living in one of his birdhouses," he teases. I get up the nerve and knock on the back door of the house and nervously wait to see if the door opens. Having a little owl for my very own would put me on par with Mike the real falconer. When Bump answers the door with a cold stare I say, "I'm Mike's younger brother and he told me that you might have Screech Owls living on your property." He laughed at me and closed the door leaving me embarrassed and disappointed. Bump gave Mike plans to build his first hawk trap, but he won't give me the time of day. The heck with Bump and his stupid humongous trap. On our time off from The Garage, we use the "BAL-CHATRI" noose cage while searching for and trapping wild hawks.

Most of our experience is with the more common species of hawks and owls, not that we are only interested in them. The sight of any bird of prey anytime is a thrilling and a sought-after experience. Every time we spot a rare Bald Eagle in passing, it's a big deal. When Grandpa Leo was a boy back in the early 1900s, Bald Eagles commonly nested in the area. They constructed their nests near bodies of water. Mike's research of old local newspapers and a book on Belle Plaine history written by our great uncle Harold revealed many references to eagles as a common species here until the late 1950s, before DDT made its way into the bird's bodies.

Mike is very interested in obtaining either a Sharp-shinned or Coopers Hawk to train but always finds the nests in the fall after the young have fledged and left for the migration. Barred Owls are residents here and seen by us occasionally, though hearing their calls is a more frequent occurrence. Short-eared Owls are seen sometimes during pheasant hunting in sloughs and marshy habitats, as is the Harrier or (*Marsh Hawk*.) We never see any Long-eared Owls although they are listed as being residents. In the spring great (*kettles*) or flocks of soaring broad-winged hawks fill the skies, but not every year.

My great grandfather who once owned the corner hotel saloon had a large cage in the back of his business which housed a young Bald Eagle and a Great Horned Owl. Even though the eagle is much bigger than the owl, Grandpa Leo said the eagle feared the owl and perched as far away as it could. Great Horned Owls are called 'the flying tiger of the air' for a reason. They have driven Bald Eagles away and out of their nests, so they can then claim the nest for their own egg laying. Other than Great Horned and

Screech Owls, the only other owl that Mike has any experience with is the very secretive and tiny Saw-whet Owl.

Smaller than the Screech Owl, its discovery is usually an accident unless one regularly seeks its presence by checking out groves of dense conifers in the snows of winter looking for roosting sites. This owl will use the same roost several days in succession, and it is easy to see the pile of regurgitated pellets on the white ground. It was during a bow hunting trek with Young Buck in a woodlot south of town during this thrilling year of 1974 that Mike came upon a Saw-whet. Investigating a disturbance caused by a mob of songbirds harassing something in a tangle of grape vines brought him face to face with this tiny owl. The little thing sat patiently enduring the frantic dive-bombing of the Chickadees. The Saw-whet Owl's instincts are to sit tightly frozen until the last moment before flying off, unlike the buck deer that remains frozen even if a hunter steps over it. This is really a survival mechanism. At any rate, the Saw-whet can actually be grabbed and caught by a quick hand. Mike caught the only two Saw-whets he ever saw. Both captures were within four miles from town and the first was an exciting experience.

Bow hunting in the heart of the Minnesota wild, Mike's attention is drawn to a mob of Chickadees dive-bombing at something tucked inside a thicket not more than 15 yards away. His eyes zero in on a little Saw-whet Owl tolerantly ignoring the parade of attacks from the angry little birds. Finally, the Chickadees disperse and it is just Mike and the owl. Perhaps it is his camouflaged clothing that allows him to approach the spectacle so closely. Slowly, ever so slowly his hand moves towards the beautiful elf-like owl. He actually touches it before it leaves the perch and flies a short distance and lands in another tree. The same thing occurs several times, Mike almost gets his hand around the bird only to have it fly off at the last second. He fears that in another 30 minutes, it will be dark and the Saw-whet will disappear into the night. Finally, when it seems like his last chance, Mike carefully takes off his cap and holds it in his left hand as he attempts to get his right hand around the owl. Just as he is about to make the grab, he flings his cap into the air. This catches the owl's attention and that is all it takes to wrap his fingers around the tiny bundle of feathers. The Saw-whet is his. Naturally, it snaps its beak, bites his fingers and pierces his hand with its needle-sharp talons, but it makes no difference because he won't let go. Retrieving his bow and cap Mike carries the struggling dwarf owl to his car and makes the four-mile drive to town.

Mike enlists Young Buck to hang a camouflaged jacket on the wall in the corner of their storage room, along with a dead oak tree branch and some fresh cedar branches arranged to perfection in front of the jacket. the next step is to place the Saw-whet on the oak stub. Even up close it looks like the bird is perched out in the woods; a natural setting. The tiny owl cooperates and Young Buck exposes several rolls of black and white and color film. The photos turn out perfect, as good or better than anything seen in a book or magazine. After the

Saw-whet Owl

photos are developed and printed the little owl is driven back out to the same woodlot and released.

With fall migration upon us, Mike turns his attention towards one of his favorite hobbies, searching for and trapping the ferocious hunting birds. And so the trapping games continue with both family and friends throughout the winter months until the mercury slowly rises and the birds that migrated the fall before return to their stick nests resting near the tops of the tallest trees in the woods. The first birds to claim their sticks in the sky are the mighty Great Horned Owls.

Mike is shocked to discover that a friend from nearby Shakopee, MN who had once kept a Kestrel tells him of a woodlot near his place is home to a pair of Great Horned Owls. His friend had listened to a pair of these owls calling back and forth during courtship on the deer stand in November and December. A characteristic of Great Horned Owls is their much earlier need to nest than other birds of prey. Females have been observed brooding a clutch of eggs with an inch or more of snow on their backs in late February, a month or more earlier than Red-tailed Hawks. There is a good reason these owls start their family so early. It is because baby horned owls are slow to mature, needing a longer care period by the adults. By the time the woods and fields are full of young rabbits, squirrels and other prey species, these adolescent owls are ready to hunt and have all these vulnerable baby animals out and about to practice on.

At any rate, I accompany Mike and his friend on a cold, damp, March day to the woodlot. This woodlot is fairly open and on the small side, perhaps five acres at most. Between the three of us, finding a nest should be easy, we think. Despite searching

from end to end, not a single old Red-tailed Hawk or crow's nest can be located, which doesn't make sense as we flushed both adult owls during our search. After a disappointing three-hour search, Mike notices a drey, (*a leaf nest homemade by grey and fox squirrels.*) Glassing it with binoculars, he spies several bits of "down" amongst the outer edge of the drey, and determines this has to be it! The tree is by far the largest in the woods, spanning over 100 foot tall and the drey resting, as usual, is way up there near the very top. With no hesitation I make my way up, a foot at a time, hand over hand, bear hugging, applying every trick Little John taught me years before. Once I make my way to the top and peek inside, I inform them there are two tiny down covered owlets tucked inside the drey. One chick lowered in a sack and safely inside Mike's coat for warmth we make our way to the car. As we walk, Mike and his buddy slap me on my back thanking me repeatedly for my help. Not that big of a deal, but Mike's friend is very impressed. This long-haired, skinny little kid has done what neither of them has the skill or nerve to try.

He places the newly hatched owl, which he figures to be less than a week old, in a soft nest inside a cardboard box with a heat lamp for warmth. Despite a nutritious diet and plenty of warmth, the owl fails to thrive and dies within a week. Heartbroken and desperate for the mighty Great Horned, he grabs his binoculars and spotting scope to check out several old Red-tails nests he knows of outside of town. One cold, windy day looking through the 25 power scope, he sees what appears to be a large cat with ears blowing in the wind atop a Red-tailed Hawk nest in the middle of a large woodlot only two miles from the old circus lots. After years of searching, he has finally found an active Great Horned Owl nest on his own!

Elated at having found the Great Horned Owl's nest, Mike drives back to the old circus lots, grabs me, practically throws me in his car, and he drives me out to see if the tree is climbable. As usual, the Red-tails that used the nest the year before have built it at the top of the tallest tree in the woods, but I assure him that for a carton of Marlboro cigarettes I should be able to make the climb, without too much of a problem. We wait a few days, and then he calculates that the baby owls are of the right age, still blue-eyed and therefore not yet imprinted on the mother owl. If Mike's timing is off and the baby owl's eyes have turned yellow, it will be untamable, and he will be out of luck until the next year.

With our gear assembled, we make the hike across a large plowed field to the nest. Though the tree is challenging, I methodically make my way up to the large stick nest. The mother owl perches in a nearby tree and then makes a couple half-hearted swoops close to my head so Mike gets out his harmonica and plays

some blues hoping to distract the angry mother owl. Lucky for me, it works!

Dale holding up the baby Great Horned Owl for Mike

Once at the nest, I hold up one of the three babies so Mike can see its size, but all he yells is, "What color are its eyes?" I take a quick look and yell back, "BLUE!" Then I proceed to put one in the sack and lower it down to Mike. From the very start of nest raiding, we always leave at least one baby hawk or owl in the nest to make certain the nesting season is successful for the adult pair, ensuring they will return to nest in the same area in succeeding years. Once the owlet is secure inside its new accommodations and maturing nicely, Mike begins what seems like endless feedings of large quantities of wild meat. He thought his earlier baby Red-tailed Hawks had huge appetites, but his new owl seems to have a tapeworm. He names his "BLUE EYED" owl 'Euell' after Euell Gibbons the famous woodsman. Between Tom, Young Buck, Mike, and I, we provide meals for the insatiably hungry owl, and it grows strong and healthy as the weeks pass on by.

Now that Mike finally has his long-awaited tame Great Horned Owl residing comfortably in his new hawk house, he sets his sights on a Red-tailed Hawk nest in the Bush Woods not far from his newly rented farm. For the novice, the nesting tree looks like a difficult one to climb. It begins with a five-foot-wide semi hollow base which extends 30 feet straight up before splitting into a wide 45-degree angle Y. The nest is in the uppermost branches on the left side another 40 feet up and out before splitting into the final smaller Y. At the very end holds the five-foot diameter stick nest. Because the tree is so easy for me to climb, Mike and I make several trips out to the Bush Woods so we can get a firsthand check on the progress of the babies. For weeks, he is like a mother hen brooding over that nest worrying about raccoons or something getting at the eggs and then the babies. However, as the warmer weather comes, so do the swarming bees; thousands of them.

On the scheduled day to finally take the bird, we discover the hollow base of the tree has been taken over by thousands of honeybees. We abandon the climb until we can come up with a way to get around and above the bees. Any obstacle we come across is normally solved and equipment in hand within a few hours. But

this sticky situation requires us to turn to help from someone with a lifetime worth of experience. Naturally, we seek Grandpa Leo who advises us to use protective clothing instead of trying to get rid of the bees. Soon, Grandpa Leo and Mike have me outfitted with a heavy pair of white coveralls complete with gloves and screen taped over my face onto the side of the white hood. They also tape my ankles and wrists with duct tape preventing bees from getting inside my clothing. We head back to the Bush Woods to claim his prize.

Dale holding baby Red-tailed Hawk

The outfit works like a charm. Once I reach the first Y where the bees no longer pose a threat, I then remove the protective screen/gloves and throw them down to Mike who is, as always, capturing photos of the climb. Although the tree is fairly easy, Mike sees me fall a hundred times in his mind and worries until my feet are planted back firmly on solid ground. He takes several photos including one of me at the nest with the female soaring not too far above me in the background.

I lower the sack down to Mike. He unties the sack to inspect the baby and notices that both of its ears are full of tiny white worms which appear to be maggots. I jump the final 15 feet past the busy bee's nest and roll away from the hive as soon as my feet hit the ground. He tells me that the worms are a common occurrence in downy hawks and not to worry. Once home, he applies a solution of a few drops of mineral oil in each ear causing the worms to vacate the orifice. As the young hawk grows, it doesn't seem as if the worms caused any damage to its hearing. Despite having to overcome the obstacle of swarming bees, this is the most enjoyable and interesting Red-tailed Hawk nest experience out of them all because I got to observe the birds progress from eggs into big fat little monsters.

Living at the hobby farm is definitely the heyday of Mike's falconry experience. It has been a busy climbing spring starting with two Great Horned Owl nests, the Red-tailed Hawk nest and now I'm getting ready to climb a Sparrowhawk nest which Mike found when he saw a female disappear into a woodpecker hole in a 60-foot dead snag by MacGuire's hill. The area around the farmhouse is ideal featuring country-meadows, fields and small groves of trees. It is the perfect place to train the birds to fly to his fist, chase lures and eventually hunt wild game. Though the Sparrowhawks fly gracefully to the lure, they catch nothing except the odd sparrow or starling he lets loose for them. It

doesn't matter because he loves the species for their beauty in flight and their colorful plumage.

Euell isn't much of a hunter either, he'll much rather laze around the yard, perched in the weeping willow or on the house and wait for the feeding call. With the third Red-tailed baby it's a different story, she is not the screamer, ill-tempered hawk as his first Red-tailed Hawk and seems to have a knack as a game hawk. Rabbits, squirrels, and gophers are all successfully taken by her. She even makes a valiant attempt at a few pheasants that Mike flushes around the slough across the road from the farm. Her favorite method of hunting is from a high vantage point. Mike casts her off the fist and beats the brush for the game as she follows him from perch to perch. Once the animal or bird is flushed, she drops off the treetop, wings closed and makes her attack. The hawk's success rate is one out of every 10-12 tries.

Mike's new Great Horned Owl is friendly compared to the wild Screech Owls he's kept earlier. Euell seems to enjoy getting his (or her) ears scratched, and Mike spends many long hours attending to his new 'friend.' The owl is actually affectionate, more like a loving dog than a 'flying tiger of the air.' Compared to the Red-tailed Hawk he is raising, the owl is maturing much slower. Many young horned owls are called, "branchers" because they leave the nest before they can fly often jumping from branch to branch begging the adults for food. Some babies even spend a week on the ground near the nest giving their shrill calls for food. Mike's Red-tailed Hawks are fully feathered and flying at seven weeks, but not so with Euell. Mike and I walk Euell out into his pasture and toss it up into the air to exercise its wings.

Dale teaching Euell to fly

Now that late summer is here so are Euell's feathers and it is now flying around the property. Each day at feeding time Mike hears Euell's food call from a big weeping willow in the yard. He calls the owl to his fist, feeds it and puts Euell in the hawk house before dark.

One afternoon Mike received a call from a neighbor asking him to drive over to, "Get that damned owl off his porch." Seems Euell ventured a mile down the road and tried begging the farmer's wife for lunch! The poor woman was frightened to death, but they knew who to call as most neighbors had seen Mike with

both hawks and owls on his fist walking along the gravel road by his rented farm.

Since his owl flies quite a distance from his place, he attaches special snap-on jesses on its legs with its name and address written on them with a permanent marker. Sometimes he gets a phone call to come and collect his owl. Euell causes no problems other than frightening folks who find it perched on their decks or on a fence post.

Other than Euell's wanderings, the biggest problem he faces is having enough food for all his birds. There isn't enough time in the day to collect the pigeons, and gophers required to feed the Red-tailed Hawk, Great Horned Owl, and now two Sparrowhawks. Mike decides to raise his own mice to save on hunting time and help replenish the food supply. He has a basement full of wire

An immature Euell and the Bush woods Red-tailed Hawk

topped aquariums and cages with an assortment of small animals-mostly rats, mice, and gerbils. And there is a kid living on a farm one-half mile away who raises white rabbits which he sells for meat. He purchases them once a month to vary the menu of his birds.

Working and trying to devote enough time to falconry, plus pursuing his love of bow hunting eventually burns him out, and he decides to give the sport a rest. Another factor that plays into his exit from the pastime he so deeply loves is the increasingly strict regulations placed upon falconers. The days of simply writing in for and receiving a permit are long gone. Now, it's necessary to apprentice under a master falconer, pass written and oral exams, and deal with onsite inspections by either a State or Federal official.

The two Kestrels are released back into the wild right from the farmyard and old Euell, still frightening people when he shows up in their yards, is donated to The Duluth, MN Zoo. Sadly, he eventually releases his Red-tailed Hawk as well.

Now that Mike has conquered his role as a falconer, he's on to the next character. With his raptors gone, and no need for the hobby farm and mews house, he moves back into a temporary apartment near downtown Belle Plaine.

Mike holding a young Euell the Great

Tarzan's Fall

One by one each one of us graduates high school and begins leaving the nest. I have to admit that my last year at Belle Plaine High School is a lot of fun because, for the first time in all my school years, I try. I have to try because if I fail just one class, I won't receive my diploma. Even though Burney and I skip class on a tri-weekly basis, we never get caught! Thanks to Theresa who forges Mom's writing and signature, so I can hand it to the receptionist the next morning. She comes up with very realistic and clever excuses, I can't even tell the difference between Theresa's signature and Glo's, therefore, the notes are never questioned. Most importantly, I don't want to be labeled a high school dropout or look bad in the eyes of Bobbie Jo as I did during the spring of my junior year.

I remember the day well... Chip and I got caught stealing in the Target store at Bloomington, MN, while we were supposed to be in school. Our small town thievery skills didn't work out so well for us in the big city. Besides the shame it caused, I was grounded for a month. Poor Bobbie Jo cried her eyes out when I called to tell her the sad news. All she kept saying between sobs was, "A MONTH!" For her, being stuck on the farm for thirty days was like being locked up in solitary confinement. I shortened my prison term though by intentionally bugging the shit out of Glo. She got so tired of it, she talked Sonny into letting me go free midway into my sentence. After that, I quit doing some of the stupid things that could ground or jail me.

As they say, all good things end, and although I love my Sheba, I put her out to pasture to live out her remaining years. I can't afford both Bobbie Jo and her. True to character, Sonny finds a pony farm that will take her where she can munch on tall prairie grass all day and run alongside the rest of the herd as she did the first time, I laid eyes on her. He takes Sheba to her new home while I'm not around (probably on purpose) and I never see her again. I occasionally ask him exactly where he dropped her off so I can go check on her, but he always gives me general directions and I never find the place. After she's gone, we remove the barbed wire and all the fence posts. The only thing we didn't remove, is the entrance to the corral affixed center to our open prairie.

The once vibrant stockade sits idle most of the time, but still stands proudly anchored on the right side of the old circus lots. It has served successfully as our launching platform in the sky for the good part of our innocent years, but as we each obtain our drivers' licenses, so do our horizon's. If only those four tin walls could talk, they would giggle endless tales of mischievous youthfulness and proclaim Grandpa Leo's never-ending love of the circus. The stockade will remain as one of the

fondest memories of our youth. Our fortress still overlooks the sapling fence that Sonny built protecting the sacred burial grounds of the circus animals and Thursday and Friday. Their spirits remain undisturbed keeping the old circus lot's magical powers alive and well. I'm sure Sheba misses their company! Unlike Sonny, who doesn't miss his two most troublesome teens living on their own.

Now that Mike and I are out fending for ourselves, Dad has mellowed quite a bit. I can't say that I blame him because both of us are the ones that kept him up at night for years. Now that we're gone, he has the right to kick back and enjoy his rejuvenated life. Sonny is slowly regaining a real sense of freedom and escapes to the Castle on The Lake whenever he can get away. He's even reignited his old smoking habit and we often enjoy one together while out on wrecker runs.

Mike finally has settled down as well buying a new house at the opposite end of town near the Minnesota River. He doesn't work at The Garage anymore and both Tom and I miss his company, especially his spats with Uncle Gary. He got a job at the local plastics plant working his way up to third shift foreman. Working nights and sleeping during the day leaves no time to devote to falconry. Although he has no hunting birds, he spends any time he can in the woods either bow hunting or searching for morel mushrooms. Some of his fondest memories as a boy were when he played Tarzan the Ape Man in the Seven Ponds ravine, but trying to relive those childhood memories as an adult was not a wise decision and it proved to be deadly.

Last fall while stopping to catch his breath exploring the Jessenland hillside, he cuts a thick grapevine hanging from the canopy of trees above to wet his lips. When he was done sucking drops of water from the severed end, he let the vine go, watched it swing naturally ten feet toward the creek bed below as a faint smile formed on the corners of his mouth. He realized that the vine was in the perfect spot to swing out over the gorge. His eyes followed the vine upward through the treetops judging the thickness, and then he tugged and pulled on it with his hands testing its strength before jumping on and putting his full weight onto it. He concluded that the vine was more than safe and despite his fear of heights gave the vine a whirl! Vine swinging is probably a carryover from our fantasy years playing Tarzan in Hoddy-Body Land; silly for our age, but still fun just the same. Mike backed up away from the vine, took a three-step run, jumped, and held on for dear life as the vine took him way out over the steep ravine and back to where he started giving him the thrill of a lifetime. Ever since then he shares his newfound exciting past time with anyone that is willing to make the two hour round trip hike.

Throughout the rest of the fall, he brings several of us along with him so we can experience the wonderful rush for ourselves. Burney and I accompany him on one fun-filled afternoon while exploring the Jessenland hills eventually making our way toward Mike's natural ride. When we reach the cove of vines, Mike pulls out a large knife from the sheath hanging on the left side of his belt loop and with a few chops, he cuts through the two-inch diameter vine, "Dale, hold the end of it a couple of inches from your mouth. I want to get a close-up shot of the drops falling in." After taking a few photos, we press on over fifty yards to the vine ride. "Have at 'er Dale," Mike says grabbing the vine and walking it up the hillside until the bottom of it is almost touching the ground. I run, grab onto the vine and begin my swing way out

Dale showing off on the vine ride

over the valley floor yelling, "Alright boys, this is how it's done!" I swing my feet up above my head turning upside down and perform a perfectly executed backflip landing squarely on my feet despite the uneven hillside. "Awesome man, I got a photo of you hanging upside down with your red headband falling three feet below your head. I hope it turns out." Next up is Burney, but he hesitates, "Hey Mike, aren't you worried that over time, with everyone swinging on this thing, that it'll break?" "No, because the vine is part of at least twenty smaller offshoots that are tangled through several branches spreading the weight evenly over all of them." It makes sense, so Burney tries it as well and when his big body, dressed in army greens lands heavily back on the solid ground he says, "Whew that's a lot of fun, but scary as hell. You guys can have at 'er. Once is enough for me." When I ride the vine the second time, instead of hamming it up, I look upward following the weighted branches pulling evenly over the canopy of trees above as Mike described to Burney. The only thing that would make the entire out of body experience any better would be a cool pool of water at the end of the swing. Instead, the landing pad is a rock hard surface that will cripple or kill us, if we fall.

Now that the small game season is underway, Mike and his good friend Jim do a little squirrel hunting and deer scouting along the ravine system forged deep into the Jessenland hillside. This is beyond the area where he acquired his first two baby Red-tailed Hawks. Spotting the squirrels in the trees is challenging because it's only the second week of September, and the leaves on the trees have not yet fallen. They eventually make their way to

a steep hillside which holds a treasure trove of grape vines interwoven throughout the tops of the numerous large trees that scatter along the 60-degree slope. His vine ride has been patiently waiting for his return since the fall prior...

Mike nears his vine and says to Jim, "I'm going to take just one swing and then we'll head over to the other side of the ravine to continue scouting for deer." "Go for it man." The husky built, long-haired, frizzy blonde grabs the vine, walks it up to the bottom of the hillside and holds it out as if he's holding out a gift. Mike doesn't realize that the unusually dry summer has dried up the vines causing them to become as brittle as dried up kindle wood. He takes a three-step run, jumps, grabs the vine away from Jim and launches himself yodeling like Tarzan the ape-man, "awe awe aye awwwwe, awe awe aye awwwwe" ensuring this single swing will be his best one ever. But, as he nears the very end taking him way out over the bottom of the ravine and his full weight pulls on the brittle vines, they snap, crackle and pop like Rice Krispies in a bowl of milk. Each snap and crackle jolt him down a foot or two until the final pop drops him like a rock the remaining 35 feet below. A thousand thoughts run through Mike's head, but the ones that stick are rapid-fire still frames of Jim Morrison of the "Doors" jumping off a cliff while tripping on acid. But as the raspy baritone singer accelerates faster towards the shallow shoreline, he sees an uneven hard valley floor coming at him fast and the Morrison look-alike braces for impact.

Mike swinging on his vine

Now it doesn't take but an instant to drop that distance and when he hit, he hit hard! There are a thousand thoughts going through Jim's mind, too as he watches the mind-boggling plummet unfold. He cringes when he hears the snaps of the vines and then what sounds like a pistol shot as Mike's legs buckle underneath him. The severed vine falling on and all around him. Mike is laying there still in a heap, not a sound of pain escaping his breath. Jim immediately runs down to him, sees that his right leg and foot is in a very unnatural position. His mind races through several scenarios of what he can do and ruling out things he cannot do. He thinks to himself, "This is bad, really bad, and out in the middle of nowhere." Mike stirs and blurts out, "My leg and back are broken, I think I'm gonna die!" Jim's eyes are bugged out as he tries to make him as comfortable as possible. Jim's mind is reeling. This buddy, this friend lies helplessly

with a busted up leg and a compressed backbone. "Don't worry Mike your gonna be OK." He props up Mike's head on top of his rolled up jacket and because he is incoherent, grabs his .22 caliber rifle fearing Mike might attempt to use it on himself while he's on his way to get help. Then Jim runs leaping over fallen logs and foliage on his way to the nearest farm yelling once or maybe twice, "Don't worry Mike, I'll be back!" Mike hears the echoes bouncing off the hillside until they fade away into nothingness. He's busted up, hurts a number ten of ten, he is alone, and he's possibly dying back deep in his beloved Minnesota woods.

Mike drifts in and out of consciousness and in what seems like an instant but is actually an hour, Jim is back to check on him to see if he's still alive. "Mike, how you doing buddy? Help is on the way, I have to go back and meet the ambulance crew at the farm so I can guide them back here. We'll get you outta here. Hang tuff, man!" Then he's off again hurdling fallen logs and brush as he runs. As Mike waits, shock sets in! His foot and ankle flop around uncontrollably. He drifts into and out of the state of consciousness a second, third, and fourth time.

Eventually, two emergency medical people following fifty yards behind Jim arrive huffing and puffing but do not stop to rest. One of them takes his vital signs and the other pulls out a pair of snips from his medical bag and places the edge of the blade on Mike's right hiking boot. Mike's living through hell and he clearly isn't thinking straight, but he sees the scissors flash toward his boot, "Those boots are brand new, you're not cutting nothin" he rambled throwing his head back from another severe shot of pain shooting up from his lower back and right leg. Instead, they uncrumpled his leg the best they could, applied a blow-up splint and installed a neck brace before lifting him off the ground and placing him onto the stretcher.

They begin the burdensome walk back toward the farm taking turns carrying the heavy stretcher over the uneven landscape for they know that time is of the essence. At every dip in the valley floor or slip of the foot, Mike grimaces, moans, and grits his teeth. Luckily Jim knows the landscape well and directs them to a nearby deer trail which takes them right to the farmer's yard. Mike slips into unconsciousness again. He comes around inside the ambulance. The ride to the hospital isn't what you'd call a picnic either as every bump in the road causes severe pain, and he sobs all the way to the emergency room.

Jim and the ambulance crew have accomplished their part of the lifesaving effort, and now it's up to the hospital to save his life. We have all swung on that thrilling vine a time or two and no doubt Mike would have given it a leap had he been alone that day, but lucky for him, he had Jim with him who is one of the best outdoorsmen around. Because Jim had reacted so calmly and quickly, Mike is still clinging on to his life...

By the time he arrives in intensive care, the pain is literally unbearable. Mike yells to the doctor, "Stop examining me until you give me something for this pain!!!" With a nod to the nurse, the doctor says, "OK give him 6 milligrams of morphine." As the morphine slowly works its way through his system and he's able to think semi-straight again, he hears the doctor on the phone talking to the orthopedic surgeon and is not surprised to learn just how busted up he is. The doctor reports his long list of injuries as if giving out baseball stats after the game: "His right leg is broken in eleven places, shattered from the force of the fall, he has two compression fractures of vertebrae in his lower back, a hairline fracture in his neck as well and his right ankle and knee are pretty much mutilated. The impact of hitting the solid ground from that height, the young man is lucky to be alive."

Three hard taps on the door bring Glo face to face with the local policeman, "Hello Mrs. Albrecht, I'm afraid I have some bad news to tell you. Your son Mike took a bad fall back in the Jessenland hills, and he's over at Waconia Hospital in the intensive care unit." Glo immediately phoned Sonny at work who flew back to the house to pick her up. We all were waiting along with Glo. When Sonny came to a screeching halt, we all climbed into the car and took off speeding for the hospital.

At first, the head nurse said that no one could see Mike because he was in intensive care and barely clinging to life. But, Glo insisted, "Listen, I am his mother and this is his father. We have a right to see our son, and we want to see him as soon as we can!" She was forceful but diplomatic. The nurse let out a large gasp and softened, "Come with me." She led us to his room where Mike lay with a needle in his arm, a tube running up through his nose and hooked up to a vitals machine. Then he semi-woke up when Glo and Sonny both called out his name. He rambled about what happened back in the woods. I couldn't believe what I was watching. This invincible brother I had idolized was at this very moment fighting for his life. This was real and no longer one of his many performances. I said nothing. It was as if I were watching everything unfold from the corner of the ceiling above everybody in the room. I listened to the doctor softly explaining to Sonny and Glo the prognosis, and I couldn't believe what I was hearing. "He has a 50/50 percent chance of surviving a trauma of this severity. Unfortunately, we won't know until sometime early tomorrow morning or the next day. A femur shattered this badly can cause fat emboli, whereas the bone marrow fat can escape into the bloodstream. Typically, fat embolism occurs suddenly 12-36 hours after an injury. Signs and symptoms of fat embolus include central nervous system dysfunction that may progress to coma or even death. Our surgeon can attempt to straighten his leg, but there isn't much we can do about the fat emboli other than to let nature run its course."

Luckily, Mike has his young age going for him whereas a middle-aged man would have succumbed to the trauma. He survives those first anxious days and then begins the long healing process. The first couple of weeks he's in a fog due to the continual injections of heavy duty painkillers. The doctors tell him he might lose his leg, or that he won't be able to walk again. At a minimum, his leg will end up an inch or two shorter than the other; serious stuff.

His life this last year has been all about body and leg and walking casts, crutches, and canes. But, Mike is stubborn and relentless in his efforts to strengthen his leg. He even put plastic garbage bags over his casts so he can hike through the winter snow. It's slow going and very painful, but he continues to perform this style of physical therapy. He limps around OK although he wears a boot with an inch and a half thicker heal than the other.

Being cooped up in the house all the time is boring for a natural woodsman. Besides his walks through the snow, every once in a great while, he talks a few of his friends into driving him out along the Jessenland road. There, he throws out the "BAL-CHATRI" noose cage to try to snag a raptor. But the injury and the continuing complications are enough to end his days as a falconer. It's a shame that he'll never fly a majestic bird again. His love of the birds of prey has never diminished and he still spends time limping around his old haunts seeking hawks and owls to observe and try to photograph.

It's so surreal... Friends I haven't been around for months organize a side yard football game just for the old-time sake. After an exciting game, our roughhousing and lighthearted conversation change abruptly. Somewhere out of left field, everybody talks about going into the military. My old Crow School friend, Joe and best friend, Burney announce that they are going into the army. Both Spiekerman brothers proudly announce, "We're going into the navy!" and brother Tom says he's joining them in the buddy program. I'm shell-shocked. I have been thinking about my future while attending vocational school for auto/truck mechanics and the prospects are not all that inspiring. I don't want to get stuck working at The Garage where a mechanic moves up a notch once someone retires at 70 or older. The other thing I face is working at some gas station somewhere around the Minneapolis area. Now that we have outlived the adventures of our tiny town, the realization of adulthood and the bombardment of responsibilities that come with that title weigh heavily on our minds. Instantly the decision comes easy. "No Way... "If you guys are joining the navy, so am I."

After the boys depart, I gather up my nerve and give Bobbie Jo a phone call to tell her my plans. I remember the call I made to her when I got caught stealing and was grounded for a month! I'm not quite sure how she'll take me being away for months on

end, but she doesn't hesitate, "If you go in the navy, you have to marry me first and take me with you." So, unfortunately, I never had the chance to propose to my first and only love but made up for it by purchasing an expensive $800.00 engagement ring that also served as my wedding ring gift to my future bride. It consists of three rings totaling 42 diamonds, 1¼ total carats that fit together in a curved fashion. Now, I wish I would have kept that $800.00 check I signed back over to The Garage years earlier, so I could pay for it. While shopping for the ring, I even surprised Theresa when I fixated on the mass of diamonds. So, I sell my motorcycle and the toolbox/tools gathered while working at The Garage to Lee Blume, my old neighborhood friend and coworker at The Garage. I know that once I leave for the navy, I will need neither.

Sonny's more than giddy at the prospect of two of his boys following in his footsteps and experiencing the adventures of the navy. He even helps us get ready for our departure and gives Bobbie Jo and me advice on how to avoid an aircraft carrier where if assigned, I will hardly ever see her. He tells me to apply for a land-based aircraft saying, "Dale, if you ever want to see your new wife, apply for a VR or VP aircraft squadron because they don't go on carriers that are out to sea all the time." He schools Bobbie Jo and me about all the pros and cons of living as a married couple in the navy as he had done while stationed out in Hawaii with Glo. Ironically, I select the same rate that Sonny had back in the 1950s; aircraft engine mechanic.

Our father-son relationship returns to the type we enjoyed when I was a child looking out the upstairs window of The Old House watching the fire raging two blocks away. Dad is out there front and center rescuing people and putting out fires. When I stop to think about it, Dad has been putting out fires literally and figuratively his whole life. My fearless, selfless hero never backs down from what is right for any good cause or anyone who needs a hand.

Childhood friend John Stier marries my little sister Mary in August 1977, just two months after she graduates high school. Bobbie Jo and I marry a few months later in December. It's only fitting my best man, Lee hand me the wedding ring he paid for. I leave for Great Lakes, IL Naval Recruit Naval Center two months later. After I finish boot camp, Bobbie Jo joins me for Technical Training School in Millington, TN. Then, another new and amazing adventure begins!

Afterword

After I graduated Navy Technical Training School, I applied for a VP or a VR squadron in the northeastern part of the country. I accepted orders to VP23 Naval Air Station, Brunswick, ME. These are land-based aircraft that deploy to overseas locations for six months at a time. Being away from my new wife was tough but not nearly as bad as deploying on an aircraft carrier at a moments notice. Sonny's advice proved crucial and paved the way for a very successful 26-year naval career.

As our new naval adventure continued, I often drifted back to vivid memories of Grandpa Leo's guiding hand and Dad's integrity and wisdom that helped shape my adulthood. As I shared tales of Tarzan swinging on vines in the Seven Ponds ravine, Little John policing Sherwood Forest, Turak, the Red-tailed Hawk attacking his food providers, Dr. Jekyll, the crow lighting matches and smoking cigarettes, or our explorations beyond The Wooden Fence, people from all walks of life were not only dazzled and amazed but wanted to hear more.

This book got its start by writing a few short stories. I shared these memories with family, friends, and classmates. As the stories piled up one after the other, I tied them together and soon, had enough material to put together a book. Mike always wanted to write a book on falconry titled, 'The Wooden Fence.' The falconry chapters in this book are my very favorites because most of what is written came from Mike's recollections. Hopefully, I transcribed his words as he intended.

Many times I still wonder about friends who have left me and what might have become of them. My thoughts trail back to those uncomplicated times in my youth when the life that seemed so hard, was in all reality, so simple and so, so perfect. I am grateful to have had so many amazing experiences with kids who needed a friend and a family that loved me as much as I loved them.

Made in the USA
Columbia, SC
05 August 2021

17.50
Art/Design

The MIT Press
Massachusetts Institute of Technology
Cambridge, Massachusetts 02142

**The Modern Dutch Poster /
The First Fifty Years**

Edited by Stephen S. Prokopoff
Text by Marcel Franciscono

Ann Tyler Design

The 102 magnificently reproduced full-color posters in this book illustrate a little-known and individual body of graphic art, ranging from the richly decorative to the purely abstract, informed by art nouveau and symbolism, de Stijl and art deco, and expressing above all the vital connection between commerce and art.

The book accompanies the first exhibition devoted exclusively to the modern Dutch poster, and Marcel Franciscono's text provides a detailed and fascinating history of these neglected works. He considers the posters chronologically within the history of the modern movement, pointing out artists and works of special distinction – including some of the major figures of art nouveau (Jan Toorop, Johan Thorn Prikker, R. N. Roland Holst), some of the artists associated with the de Stijl (Bart van der Leck and Piet Zwart), and Jan Sluyters, whose work is among the few fauve posters anywhere. Building on the relationship between text and image, Franciscono traces the changing styles of the posters and the qualities that distinguish them from those of other countries.

Each poster is illustrated in color and fully documented, including, when known, the facts of the poster's commission, execution, and printing. The texts of the posters are printed in translation, and a special section provides brief biographies of the designers.

Stephen Prokopoff is Director of the Krannert Art Museum at the University of Illinois. Marcel Franciscono is associate professor of Art History at the University of Illinois at Urbana-Champaign. Distributed by The MIT Press.

PROMP
0-262-66061-X